MW01285326

# Alien Citizens

How does international context influence state policies toward religious minorities? Using parliamentary proceedings, court decisions, newspaper archives, and interviews, this book is the first systematic study that employs international context in the study of state policies toward religion, and that compares Turkey and France with regard to religious minorities. Comparing state policies toward Christians in Turkey and toward Muslims in France, this book argues that policy change toward minorities becomes possible when strong domestic actors find a suitable international context that can help them execute their policy agendas. Turkish Islamists used the context of Turkey's bid to join the European Union to transform Turkish politics in the 2000s, initiating a reformist moment in state treatment of Christians. The far right in France utilized the rise of Islamophobia in Europe to adopt restrictive policies toward Muslims. Ramazan Kılınç argues that the presence of an international context that can favor particular groups over others shifts the domestic balance of power, and makes some policies more likely to be implemented than others.

Ramazan Kılınç is Associate Professor of Political Science and Director of the Islamic Studies Program at the University of Nebraska at Omaha. He has published articles in multiple journals including *Comparative Politics, Political Science Quarterly, Politics and Religion, Turkish Studies*, and *Studies in Conflict and Terrorism*. He is co-author of *Generating Generosity in Catholicism and Islam: Beliefs, Institutions, and Public Goods Provision* (Cambridge, 2018) and the editor of *Siyasa: A Forum on Islamic and Middle Eastern Politics*.

# Cambridge Studies in Social Theory, Religion, and Politics

*Editors*

David E. Campbell, University of Notre Dame
Anna M. Grzymala-Busse, Stanford University
Kenneth D. Wald, University of Florida
Richard L. Wood, University of New Mexico

*Founding Editor*

David C. Leege, University of Notre Dame

In societies around the world, dynamic changes are occurring at the intersection of religion and politics. In some settings, these changes are driven by internal shifts within religions; in others, by shifting political structures, by institutional contexts, or by war or other upheavals. Cambridge Studies in Social Theory, Religion, and Politics publishes books that seek to understand and explain these changes to a wide audience, drawing on insight from social theory and original empirical analysis. We welcome work built on strong theoretical framing, careful research design, and rigorous methods using any social scientific method(s) appropriate to the study. The series examines the relationship of religion and politics broadly understood, including directly political behavior, action in civil society and in the mediating institutions that undergird politics, and the ways religion shapes the cultural dynamics underlying political and civil society.

Gary J. Adler Jr., *Empathy Beyond US Borders: The Challenges of Transnational Civic Engagement*
Mikhail A. Alexseev and Sufian N. Zhemukhov, *Mass Religious Ritual and Intergroup Tolerance: The Muslim Pilgrims' Paradox*
Luke Bretherton, *Resurrecting Democracy: Faith, Citizenship, and the Politics of a Common Life*
David E. Campbell, John C. Green, and J. Quin Monson, *Seeking the Promised Land: Mormons and American Politics*
Ryan L. Claassen, *Godless Democrats and Pious Republicans? Party Activists, Party Capture, and the "God Gap"*
Darren W. Davis and Donald Pope-Davis, *Perseverance in the Parish? Religious Attitudes from a Black Catholic Perspective*
Paul A. Djupe and Christopher P. Gilbert, *The Political Influence of Churches*
Joel S. Fetzer and J. Christopher Soper, *Muslims and the State in Britain, France, and Germany*
François Foret, *Religion and Politics in the European Union: The Secular Canopy*
Jonathan Fox, *A World Survey of Religion and the State*
Jonathan Fox, *Political Secularism, Religion, and the State: A Time Series Analysis of Worldwide Data*
Anthony Gill, *The Political Origins of Religious Liberty*
Brian J. Grim and Roger Finke, *The Price of Freedom Denied: Religious Persecution and Conflict in the 21st Century*
Kees van Kersbergen and Philip Manow, editors, *Religion, Class Coalitions, and Welfare States*
Mirjam Kunkler, John Madeley, and Shylashri Shankar, editors, *A Secular Age Beyond the West: Religion, Law and the State in Asia, the Middle East and North Africa*

Karrie J. Koesel, *Religion and Authoritarianism: Cooperation, Conflict, and the Consequences*

Ahmet T. Kuru, *Secularism and State Policies toward Religion: The United States, France, and Turkey*

Andrew R. Lewis, *The Rights Turn in Conservative Christian Politics: How Abortion Transformed the Culture Wars*

Damon Maryl, *Secular Conversions: Political Institutions and Religious Education in the United States and Australia, 1800–2000*

Jeremy Menchik, *Islam and Democracy in Indonesia: Tolerance without Liberalism*

Pippa Norris and Ronald Inglehart, *Sacred and Secular: Religion and Politics Worldwide*

Amy Reynolds, *Free Trade and Faithful Globalization: Saving the Market*

Sadia Saeed, *Politics of Desecularization: Law and the Minority Question in Pakistan*

Amy Erica Smith, *Religion and Brazilian Democracy: Mobilizing the People of God*

David T. Smith, *Religious Persecution and Political Order in the United States*

Peter Stamatov, *The Origins of Global Humanitarianism: Religion, Empires, and Advocacy*

Kenneth D. Wald, *The Foundations of American Jewish Liberalism*

# Alien Citizens

## The State and Religious Minorities in Turkey and France

**RAMAZAN KILINÇ**

*University of Nebraska*

CAMBRIDGE
UNIVERSITY PRESS

# CAMBRIDGE
## UNIVERSITY PRESS

University Printing House, Cambridge CB2 8BS, United Kingdom

One Liberty Plaza, 20th Floor, New York, NY 10006, USA

477 Williamstown Road, Port Melbourne, VIC 3207, Australia

314-321, 3rd Floor, Plot 3, Splendor Forum, Jasola District Centre, New Delhi - 110025, India

103 Penang Road, #05-06/07, Visioncrest Commercial, Singapore 238467

Cambridge University Press is part of the University of Cambridge.

It furthers the University's mission by disseminating knowledge in the pursuit of education, learning and research at the highest international levels of excellence.

www.cambridge.org
Information on this title: www.cambridge.org/9781108701785
DOI: 10.1017/9781108692649

First published 2020
First paperback edition 2022

A catalogue record for this publication is available from the British Library

ISBN 978-1-108-47694-2 Hardback
ISBN 978-1-108-70178-5 Paperback

*To my parents Münevver and Hüseyin Kılınç*

# Contents

List of Figures                                                          *page* x
List of Tables                                                                 xi
Acknowledgments                                                               xii
List of Abbreviations                                                         xiv

INTRODUCTION                                                                     1
1   Rethinking State Policies toward Religious Minorities                        3

PART I   HISTORICAL INSTITUTIONS                                                37
2   Secularism and Christians in Turkey                                         39
3   Secularism and Muslims in France                                           61

PART II   INTERNATIONAL CONTEXT                                                 85
4   The European Union and Christians in Turkey                                87
5   Islamophobia and Muslims in France                                        107

PART III   DOMESTIC ACTORS AND POLICY CHANGE                                  129
6   Kemalists, Conservatives, and Christians in Turkey                        131
7   Radical Right, Liberals, and Muslims in France                            153

CONCLUSION                                                                     181
8   Testing the Argument Beyond the Scope of the Study                        183
9   Conclusion                                                                 206

Bibliography                                                                   219
Index                                                                          247

# Figures

6.1 The flow of arguments: the state and Christians in Turkey    *page* 133
7.1 The flow of arguments: the state and Muslims in France    155

# Tables

1.1 Policy influence of international context and domestic power
    configuration                                                    26
1.2 Indicators of international pressure and global discourses        31
2.1 Reforms improving the status of Christian minorities             58

# Acknowledgments

This book started as a dissertation at Arizona State University, but it ended up a completely different project. I would like to express my deepest gratitude to Carolyn M. Warner, my mentor not only during the graduate school years but also afterwards. I am thankful for her constant support, patience, and encouragement. I have always felt the comfort of knowing that her unconditional support was with me. Other members of my dissertation committee, Miriam F. Elman, Miki C. Kittilson, and George M. Thomas, provided me with invaluable support during my years as a graduate student. Colin Elman helped me to grasp qualitative research methods.

I am indebted to the Graduate College and the School of Politics and Global Studies at Arizona State University and to the University Committee on Research and Creative Activity at the University of Nebraska at Omaha for providing me with funding to complete my field research. I would like to thank Hamit Bozarslan in Paris and Louis Pelatre in Istanbul for their help in making connections during my fieldwork in France and Turkey. I owe special thanks to scholars, politicians, religious leaders, and community members in Paris and Istanbul for taking the time to participate in interviews. Their openness and assistance facilitated the project. Mohammad Ayoob has been a great mentor and friend since we met during my postdoctoral fellowship at Michigan State University. I was lucky to have the friendship of such a great mind during the preparation of this study. I am indebted to Randall Adkins, Jody Neathery-Castro, David Boocker, and my colleagues in the Political Science department for providing me with opportunities at University of Nebraska at Omaha to complete the book. My graduate assistants Robbi Kannas, Glen Billesbach, Media Ajir, and Aidana Jenishbek Kyzy provided me with valuable research assistance at different stages of the project.

I thank Sara Doskow of Cambridge University Press for her great editorship during the review and production processes of the book. I am indebted to three anonymous reviewers who guided me with their helpful comments and feedback. Kenneth D. Wald and the other series editors of Cambridge Studies in Social Theory, Religion, and Politics provided me further comments, which helped me improve the study. Some portions of the book are drawn, in revised form, from my article "International Pressure, Domestic Politics and Dynamics of Religious Freedom: Evidence from Turkey," *Comparative Politics*, 46/2 (2014): 127–145. I thank City University of New York for giving me the permission to use the article, and I thank the anonymous journal reviewers and the journal editors for their helpful comments on it.

This book could not have been possible without the support of my loved ones. I want to thank my parents, Münevver and Hüseyin Kılınç, for their endless love and support throughout my life. This book is dedicated to them. I am thankful to my beloved wife Halide Görgün Kılınç. Her endless support, love, and belief in me guided me through all the trials and tribulations of writing this book. Last but not least, I am obliged to my children Ahmed Etka, Münevver, and Mehmet Selim for infinitely enriching my life.

# Abbreviations

| | |
|---|---|
| AKP | Adalet ve Kalkınma Partisi (Justice and Development Party) |
| CHP | Cumhuriyet Halk Partisi (Republican People's Party) |
| ECHR | European Court of Human Rights |
| EEC | European Economic Community |
| EU | European Union |
| FN | Front National (National Front) |
| GDF | General Directorate of Foundations (Vakıflar Genel Müdürlüğü) |
| HRW | Human Rights Watch |
| MHP | Milliyetçi Hareket Partisi (Nationalist Action Party) |
| NATO | North Atlantic Treaty Organization |
| UN | United Nations |
| USCIRF | United States Commission on International Religious Freedom |

# INTRODUCTION

# I

# Rethinking State Policies toward Religious Minorities

On May 21, 1903, as a gesture of goodwill, the Ottoman sultan Abdulhamid II joined the Greek Orthodox patriarch Joachim III to celebrate the grand opening of the Büyükada Greek Orphanage, which housed Greek orphans of both the late Ottoman Empire and modern Turkey until 1964. When Turkey developed tensions with Greece over Cyprus in 1964, the state's General Directorate of Foundations (GDF, Vakıflar Genel Müdürlüğü) closed down the historic 20,000-square-meter wooden orphanage, which is located on an island in the Sea of Marmara that was popular with tourists. The GDF did not repair the building after that and left it to dereliction. In the 1990s, the Greek Orthodox patriarchate started a legal process against the Turkish state to register the ownership of the property under its name. The Turkish state denied the claim and argued that the GDF had the right to seize the property because it had not fulfilled its original function for more than ten years. When the Council of State, the supreme administrative court in Turkey, dismissed the patriarchate's claim in 2003, the case was carried to the European Court of Human Rights (ECHR). In 2010, the ECHR ruled in favor of the Greek Orthodox patriarchate and transferred the ownership of the property to the patriarchate.[1]

In October 1989, Leila and Fatima Achaboun and their cousin Samira Saidani were expelled from Gabriel-Havez high school in Creil, a suburb of Paris, for wearing headscarves on the school premises. The school principal, Eugène Chenière, claimed that he expelled the girls to implement the constitutional principle of secularism. Their expulsion drew extensive media attention, but very few supported the girls' dismissal from school.[2] The students returned to the school after the Council of State, the highest administrative court in France, decreed that the principal had overstepped his authority. In its decision, the council stated that the school could dismiss the girls only if they disrupted order at the school. To the court, wearing a headscarf in itself was not incompatible with the principle of secularism.[3] This ruling would set the

---

[1] Yorgo Kırbaki, "AİHM: Rum Yetimhanesi Patrikhane'ye Verilsin," *Hürriyet*, June 16, 2010.

[2] *Libération*, "Le Port du voile heurte la laïcité du collège de Creil," October 4, 1989.

[3] Avis du Conseil d'État No. 346.893, November 27, 1989.

precedent for headscarf cases for the next fifteen years until the passage of a new law in 2004, which banned the wearing of ostentatious religious symbols at public schools.

The story of the Büyükada Greek Orphanage is just one of many cases in which the Turkish government discriminated against the Christian minority. This case illustrates the traumatic consequences of Turkey's nation-building process for minorities. The official Turkish national discourse, based on a vision of a homogeneous society defined by secularism and nationalism, made life difficult for minorities. In France, the story of the three Muslim girls at Gabriel-Havez high school is one of many cases in which the French courts protected Muslims' religious freedoms when their rights had been violated. Despite its unfriendly stance on religion compared to other European countries, French secularism provided religious minorities with religious freedom, including students' manifestation of religious symbols at schools.

However, by the early 2000s, state policies toward religious minorities were taking a different trajectory in both Turkey and France. Between 2000 and 2010, Turkey implemented new reforms that expanded the rights of religious minorities while France passed new laws that restricted religious freedoms for Muslims. The international context played a significant role in these policy changes in both countries. While Turkey was implementing new laws under the pressure of its European Union (EU) membership bid, France was enacting new restrictions within the context of rising Islamophobia in Europe in the wake of the terrorist attacks of September 11, 2001. These developments raise a significant question: How does the international context influence state policies toward religious minorities? To answer the question, I examine shifting state policies toward the Christian minority in Turkey and the Muslim minority in France between 2000 and 2010.

Scholars have explained state policies toward religious minorities by referring to several factors, including modernization processes that undermined the power of the majority religion, historical legacies shaped over extended periods of time, competition over ideology, and strategic interaction among religious and political actors. Although these approaches provide valuable insights to explain the Turkish and French cases, they cannot account for the importance of the international context, which played a crucial role in the passing of new regulations in both countries. I argue that given structured relationships among sets of domestic groups competing over different policies, the presence of an international context that can favor particular groups over others shifts the domestic balance of power, making some policies more likely to be implemented than others. The adoption of new policies depends on the presence of strong domestic actors who would benefit from the international context and support the reforms due to either their material interests or their normative commitments. The international environment structures domestic politics through actors that mediate between external factors and domestic policies.

Reforms in Turkey became possible because of the emergence of strong domestic actors who would benefit from the reforms required to join the EU. For Islamic actors with relatively large social bases, the repressive political environment dominated by the military in the late 1990s left no option but to devise strategies through which they could enhance political space at the expense of the authoritarian bureaucracy. They utilized Turkey's relations with the EU and supported the implementation of reforms to decrease the power of the military in Turkish politics. The government instituted religious rights for Christians as part of its democratizing agenda to bring Turkey closer to the EU. Liberal groups, social democrats, and some Islamic groups contributed to this outcome by justifying pluralism through their civil society activism. In short, international norms on religious freedoms diffused into the Turkish political system only after strong domestic actors facilitated their adoption, either instrumentally or normatively.

Similarly, the restrictive policies toward Muslims in France were an outcome of the interaction of international context and domestic politics. The proponents of restrictive policies in France utilized the rise of Islamophobia in the wake of the September 11 terrorist attacks in 2001. Due to the rise of anti-Muslim sentiments globally, the proponents of the headscarf ban were able to portray the wearing of headscarves as a symbol of antirepublicanism and antisecularism in France. By doing so, they could more easily engender strong popular support for their policy agendas. The rise of the far right in France led centrist parties to embrace anti-Muslim rhetoric. As a result, a social coalition emerged to pass the headscarf ban in the French parliament.

In the rest of this chapter, I first present the research puzzle that I address in this book, with a brief background on Christians in Turkey and Muslims in France. I then review previous explanations of state policies toward religious minorities, identifying their strengths and weaknesses. Next, I provide my own explanation, which combines international contexts and domestic politics. I introduce strategic and normative mechanisms that connect international contexts to domestic politics. Finally, I discuss the methods of analysis through which I demonstrate this argument. I explain the case selection, basic concepts, variables, and their measurements. I present the methodologies of comparative case studies and process-tracing with the justifications of why I chose them for my analysis.

## THE PUZZLE: CHRISTIANS IN TURKEY AND MUSLIMS IN FRANCE

### Christians in Turkey

The Christian presence in Turkey dates to the early era of Christianity. Anatolia was home to numerous apostles and saints in the Christian tradition. Under the Ottoman Empire, Christians, along with other religious minorities, were organized according to the *millet* system, whereby they were protected by the

Sultan in return for their loyalty to the empire. Under the *millet* system, religious minorities had freedom of belief, implemented ecclesiastical law in civil matters such as marriage and inheritance, and ran autonomous courts for deciding judicial issues among their own members. Christians, though, were required to pay a special tax to the state for these protections (Barkey and Gavrilis 2016, 25).

With the increase of influence of foreign powers over the Ottoman Empire in its later centuries, the *millet* system was reformed. The first blow against the *millet* system was the increasing role of foreign powers in the protection of Christian minorities in the Ottoman Empire. With treaties known as "capitulations," the Ottoman Empire granted privileges to European countries and their nationals in economic, religious, and commercial areas. The first capitulation treaty was concluded with France in 1535. This was followed by other treaties signed with Britain (1583), Austria (1615), Russia (1711), Spain (1782), and other European countries (De Groot 2003). While capitulations started with mutual consent in the earlier years, "major European powers increasingly used coercion to secure rights for Christians" (Krasner 1999, 77). As the empire got weaker, foreign powers used minority issues to exert influence over the Ottomans and in their diplomatic relations with the Ottoman Empire. In 1774, the Ottoman Empire granted substantial rights to its Orthodox subjects and made the Tsar of Russia the protector of the Orthodox Christians in the Ottoman lands (Türkmen and Öktem 2013, 465). The Russian ambassador became the legal representative of Christians in the Ottoman Empire (Krasner 1999, 86).

The modernization reforms that the Ottoman sultans implemented in the nineteenth century, especially the Tanzimat Edict of 1839 and the Islahat Edict of 1856, brought equality among the subjects of the Ottoman Empire. These reforms, which made non-Muslims equal to Muslims, replaced the *millet* system of the traditional era. The Treaty of Berlin of 1878 provided religious minorities with international guarantees of equality in social life, access to public service, freedom to worship, freedom to travel, and freedoms to exercise ecclesiastical authority (Türkmen and Öktem 2013, 465).

When the Ottoman Empire collapsed and the Republic of Turkey was established in 1923, the new elite recognized the rights of religious minorities in the Treaty of Lausanne. Turkey recognized Greeks, Armenians, and Jews as official minorities and gave them civil and educational rights. However, at times of political crises, the minorities were discriminated against. For example, in November 1942, the state implemented a capital tax for two years and taxed non-Muslim minorities with high rates. Some minorities were not able to pay the taxes and were deported to eastern Turkey for forced labor (Bishku 2017, 41). Similarly, when Turkey underwent a political crisis with Greece over the island of Cyprus in the 1960s and 1970s, Turkey put pressure on Greek minorities, forcing many to migrate to Greece (Toktas 2005: 410).

Today, Christians constitute less than 1 percent of the Turkish population. No accurate statistics on Christians have been recently produced by the Turkish state. According to the estimates of the United States Department of State's 2016 international religious freedom report, the largest Christian minority in Turkey is Armenian Orthodox Christians with a population of 90,000, of which 30,000 are illegal immigrants from Armenia. Catholics constitute the second-largest minority with a population of 25,000, including a large number of immigrants from the Philippines and from African countries. Syriac Orthodox Christians constitute the third-largest Christian group with a population of 20,000. Due to recent immigration from Russia, there are about 15,000 Russian Orthodox Christians in Turkey. The report also estimated that Turkey has 5,000 Jehovah's Witnesses, 7,000 members of various Protestant denominations, 3,000 Chaldean Christians, and up to 2,000 Greek Orthodox Christians. In addition, there are small numbers of Bulgarian Orthodox, Nestorian, Georgian Orthodox, Ukrainian Orthodox, Syriac Catholic, Armenian Catholic, Anglican, Maronite Christians, and Mormons.[4] In 2012, the Turkish state reported that there were 349 active Christian churches in Turkey.[5] Christian minorities in Turkey encountered problems in republican Turkey such as state seizure of their property, restrictions in religious education, limitations on the opening of houses of worship, and the lack of legal personality. The extent of discrimination increased at times when Turkey had political crises with Greece and Cyprus (Yannas 2007, 58).

Between 2000 and 2010 the Turkish parliament passed laws enhancing the liberties of religious minorities in areas such as property rights, religious education, and the construction of houses of worship. The parliament passed laws to return the properties that the state had expropriated from non-Muslim foundations over several decades; laws that increased opportunities for non-Muslims by legalizing education, broadcasting, and publication in their mother tongues; and laws that made it easier for non-Muslim minorities to open houses of worship.

Although these recent reforms stopped far short of addressing all the issues concerning Christian minorities in Turkey, their passage is still puzzling to many observers in the context of previous trends. First, for decades, the Turkish state had discriminated against Christian minorities in religious, economic, and educational domains. In the early years of the republic, Turkey and Greece undertook large-scale population exchanges to homogenize their respective societies (Aktar 1996, 10–12; Gökaçtı 2004). In the late 1960s, while Turkey disputed with Greece over Cyprus, the Turkish state expropriated properties owned by non-Muslim community foundations and closed down

---

[4] US Department of State, "International Religious Freedom Report 2016: Turkey," 2016, available at www.state.gov/documents/organization/269120.pdf (last accessed on April 8, 2018).
[5] Meriç Tafolar, "Bozdağ: Türkiye'de 349 Kilise Var," *Milliyet*, October 1, 2012.

the Theological School of Halki in Heybeliada (Macar and Gökaçtı 2006, 8–9). Both the people at large and the elite in Turkey had negative perceptions about Christian minorities because of the narrative that portrayed them as a threat to national unity. Yet this legacy did not prevent the Turkish parliament from passing the laws that enhanced the liberties of religious minorities.

Second, Christians comprise less than 1 percent of the Turkish population and have never exerted substantial influence in Turkish politics. For many years, there was not a single Christian deputy in the Turkish parliament; indeed, there was no Christian representative in the parliament when the reforms on Christian minorities were passed between 2000 and 2010. Because of their small population, Christians in Turkey do not have powerful interest groups or lobbying power. Given the light weight of Christians in Turkish political life, the passing of reforms that increased freedoms for religious minorities was a significant achievement.

Furthermore, most of the reforms were passed under the rule of the Justice and Development Party (AKP, Adalet ve Kalkınma Partisi), a political party with an Islamist background. Although the AKP was critical of the secularist legacies of the Turkish state, it subscribed to the nationalist narratives of the Turkish establishment. There are diverse opinions about the status of non-Muslim minorities in Islam, but Islamists in many countries took an aggressive stance against Christians. Few would have expected that the AKP would be strongly supportive of reforms that would enhance liberties for non-Muslim minorities.

Finally, even though Turkey had maintained a long-lasting relationship with European institutions since the 1950s, it was only in the 2000s that the EU played a significant role in the passing of these reforms. European pressure on Turkey had not produced any change before the 2000s. Turkey's membership in other Western institutions such as NATO or the European Council did not make a difference in Turkey's established policies toward religious minorities until the 2000s.

## Muslims in France

The Muslim population reached a significant number in France after the French colonization of North Africa in the nineteenth and twentieth centuries. There had been sporadic Muslim conquests in southern France immediately after Arabs took control of France in the mid-eighth century, but Muslim groups residing in the southern territories of France were expelled in the late tenth century (Wenner 1980, 71). In 1543–1544, Ottomans, as part of their alliance with France, kept control of Nice and made Toulon a naval base (Soucek 2004, 260). Some of the Muslims expelled from Spain between 1609 and 1614 entered and stayed in France (Jonsson 2007, 196). The real encounter of Muslims with the French state starts with the colonization of the Muslim lands by France in the nineteenth century. The direct colonization of Algeria, West Africa, and

Equatorial Africa made millions of Muslims *de facto* French citizens. France's protectorate relationship in places such as Morocco and Tunisia and its mandate relationship in places such as Syria and Lebanon deepened the French state's relationship with Muslims (Hale 2008). During the colonial period, the French state established entities to rule over Muslims. Yet most of these Muslims stayed in their own territories and did not constitute the basis of the Muslim population in contemporary France.

Most of the Muslims now in France are descendants of those who moved to the mainland in the twentieth century, first as soldiers who fought for France during the First World War and then as workers after the Second World War. To commemorate the service of Muslims who served in the French army, the state opened the Paris Mosque in 1926 and the Avicenne Hospital in 1935 (Bayoumi 2000, 268). In the interwar period, the North Africans residing in French colonies were allowed to move to France basically to help meet the demand for labor. The state allowed more immigrants to move to France to help reconstruction after the infrastructural collapse of France during the Second World War. Industrial areas such as Paris, Marseille, Lyon, Lille, and Alsace received thousands of Muslim immigrants from former French colonies such as Algeria, Morocco, and Tunisia (Hansen 2003, 26–27). Although France stopped receiving new workers after the 1970s, the Muslim population substantially increased after the passage of legislation in 1976 that allowed family reunifications for immigrant workers.

Because it is illegal to ask about religious affiliation in the French census, official statistical information on the Muslim population of France does not exist. The United States Department of State's international religious freedom report estimates that about 8 percent of the French population is Muslim.[6] The French Ministry of the Interior similarly estimates that 8–10 percent of the French population is Muslim.[7] The largest Muslim immigrant community in France is of Algerian descent, with a population of about 1.5–2 million. Those of Moroccan descent constitute the second-largest group, with a population of about 1–1.5 million. The two next-largest groups are of Tunisian descent with about 700 thousand and of Turkish descent with about 500 thousand.[8] Although they have faced social and economic marginalization, Muslims did not until recently face much discrimination regarding religious freedoms.

Between 2003 and 2010, the French state implemented new policies toward the Muslim minority. The state helped Muslim associations organize around a Muslim federation in 2003 and supported the building of large mosques in urban centers

[6] US Department of State, "France 2016: International Religious Freedom Report," 2016, available at www.state.gov/documents/organization/269058.pdf (last accessed on April 8, 2018).
[7] Michael Cosgrove, "How does France Count its Muslim Population?," *Le Figaro*, April 7, 2011.
[8] Michèle Tribalat, "L'Islam reste une menace," *Le Monde*, October 13, 2011.

(Laurence 2012, 133–197). Yet the state restricted Muslims' manifestation of religious symbols in public spaces, banning the wearing of headscarves in public schools in 2004 and the wearing of veils that cover the full face in the streets in 2010. The establishment of a Muslim federation and the building of large mosques increased the state's monitoring of Muslim organizations, and the ban on religious symbols increased state control over Muslim individuals.

Considering the political atmosphere in France in the early 2000s, the headscarf ban was expected; however, it is puzzling how France came to the point of banning headscarves in public schools. First, the number of headscarf-wearing girls in public schools was very low compared to the total number of students in France. The number of students wearing a headscarf was not more than 2,000 before the controversy erupted.[9] Before the law was passed, problematic cases numbered around 150.[10] Research conducted by the French daily *Le Monde* just before the passage of the law shows that "91 percent of all teachers in France had never even encountered a student in a headscarf at their current school" (quoted in Bowen 2006, 121). It is astonishing that this tiny number of female students became the center of public attention in France and led the parliament to ban headscarves.

Second, although the French state has a more restrictive approach toward religion compared with other European nations, it had until this point never banned the students' wearing of religious symbols in classrooms. The state had put restrictions on teachers in the classroom, but not on students. Furthermore, referring to the French constitution and international human rights agreements, France's highest administrative court, the Council of State (Conseil d'état), had upheld the right of girls to wear headscarves in school provided there was no disruption of public order in all of its decisions since 1989. The courts tolerated the wearing of the headscarf on the ground that the female students had the right to express their religious convictions in school. Given that established historical institutions were against the banning of headscarves in France, what motivated French policymakers to pass the law in parliament is an intriguing question.

Third, although there was no international pressure on France not to pass the law, the ban was to reflect negatively on France's global image. Many countries including the United States, Germany, and the United Kingdom criticized the law because it would limit freedom of religion and expression.[11] Human rights organizations also criticized French legislators for bringing the headscarf bill to

---

[9] Xavier Ternisien, "Il n'y a que 150 cas conflictuels, selon la médiatrice de l'éducation nationale," *Le Monde*, May 10, 2003.

[10] Haut Conseil à l'intégration 2000.

[11] For example, as a response to the headscarf bill, John V. Hanford, the Bush administration's top-ranking official on issues of religious freedom, stated that "A fundamental principle of religious freedom that we work for in many countries of the world, including on this very issue of head scarves, is that all persons should be able to practice their religion and their beliefs peacefully, without government interference, as long as they are doing so without provocation and

the parliament. Given the response of other countries to the law after its passage in the parliament, it is puzzling why French policymakers risked the image of their country to get rid of a small number of headscarf-wearing students in public schools.

## The puzzle: Turkey and France

Although French policies toward religious minorities remain generally more progressive than Turkish policies, policy shifts in opposite directions in the 2000s are puzzling. Between 2000 and 2010, Turkey implemented relatively more liberal policies toward Christians while France implemented relatively more restrictive policies toward Muslims. Given the Turkish legacy of hostility to religious minorities, the limited political weight of Christians in domestic politics, the rule of an Islamist political party, and the restrained role of the EU in previous periods, why did Turkish legislators pass laws enhancing religious liberties for Christians in the 2000s? Similarly, why did the French parliament ban the wearing of headscarves in public schools even though it was not strategically beneficial to France, was incompatible with French historical legacies and legal interpretations, and was detrimental to France's international credibility? This study focuses on these two questions and explains the variation in Turkish and French state policies toward religious minorities. In answering these questions, the study brings up the relevancy of international contexts in the formation of state policies toward religious minorities.

EXPLAINING STATE POLICY ON RELIGIOUS FREEDOMS:
MODERNIZATION, HISTORICAL INSTITUTIONALISM, IDEOLOGY,
AND RATIONAL CHOICE

Scholars have offered diverse explanations to account for state policies toward religious minorities. Modernization theorists refer to macro-level social transformations that undermined majority religions and opened more space for minorities. Historical institutionalists look at the formation of state–religion relations within specific historical conditions over an extended period of time and explain the freedoms of religious minorities based on the room provided by historically established regimes. Scholars focusing on ideology examine ideological competition in a given country to account for religious freedoms with the expectation that dominant ideologies with pluralist norms allow more freedoms. Rational choice theorists look at the strategic interaction between political and religious actors and reach conclusions based on the balance between the two. These theories have provided helpful explanations for

intimidation of others in society." Christopher Marquis, "U.S. Chides France on Effort to Bar Religious Garb in Schools," *New York Times*, December 19, 2003.

religious freedoms. However, a coherent perspective is needed to address the influence of the international context in domestic policymaking.

Developing a coherent theory of religious freedom requires accounting for both international and domestic contexts. Those who explain a change in religious freedoms by referencing international factors analyze the international context within which a country functions. However, in explaining the influence exerted by international factors, one needs to take domestic political mechanisms into account. In an attempt to develop a theory of religious freedoms, I offer a model that takes seriously the interaction between international context and domestic politics. Such an approach draws insights from historical institutionalist, ideological, and strategic perspectives, and suggests a contextualized yet coherent theory of religious freedoms.

## Modernization and Religious Freedoms

Modernization theorists associate the rise of religious liberty with the change of macro-social structures that led to the secularization of the political field. To these scholars, industrialization and urbanization transformed social structures in a way that allowed the expansion of liberties for religious minorities. The differentiation between the roles of the state and religion stripped religion of its conventional functions, weakened the position of majority religions, and paved the way for religious pluralism and more freedom for religious minorities (Berger 1969; Durham 1997). René Rémond (1999, 125–152), for example, relates the expansion of freedoms for religious minorities in European countries to macro-level secularizing social transformations in Europe during the eighteenth and nineteenth centuries. Mary Douglas (1982) discusses how modernity opened the path of religious pluralism. Peter Berger (1969) relates pluralism to modernization, which he dates back to the Protestant Reformation. To him, modernization set forth new ideas including secularism and expanded religious freedoms.

This strand of scholarship would offer little to explain the changing policies toward religious minorities in Turkey and France. First, historically, the radical secularization process opened up space for religious minorities in France, but it increased their repression in Turkey. In line with the premise of modernization theory, the contestations between the church and the state in France had marginalized the majority religion, Catholicism, by the late nineteenth century and expanded freedoms for religious minorities. As the Catholic Church lost its dominance and political authority, opportunities for other religious minorities increased. The French state recognized Protestants and Jews as proper citizens of the republic and granted religious freedoms to non-Catholics in the early nineteenth century. As secularism became part of the French political system in the late nineteenth century, the Catholic Church lost its privileges in education, and compulsory secular public education became the norm. In short, modernization and secularization processes created more favorable policies for religious minorities in France.

In contrast to France, the Turkish state repressed Christian minorities at a time when the state was making its most revolutionary break from its past and undergoing a radical secularization process in the 1920s and 1930s. In the early republican period, Turkey went through a comprehensive secularization process. The secular reforms decreased the social status of Islam and the political power of the Islamic establishment, i.e. Islamic scholars; however, the decreased status of Islam did not necessarily create greater room for non-Muslim minorities in the Turkish context. Armenian and Greek minorities were gradually excluded from being part of the nation (Aktar 1996). In the 1930s, to decrease the number of Christians, Turkey engaged in large-scale population exchanges with Greece: Turks in Greece migrated to Turkey while Greeks in Turkey migrated to Greece.

Second, increased industrialization after the Second World War period did not necessarily create a more permissive environment in state policies toward religious minorities in either Turkey or France. Turkey saw rapid industrialization in the 1950s and 1980s, but this did not bring improvements in the status of Christian minorities. In the 1950s, Turkey even increased its pressure on Greek Christians during its political conflict with Greece over Cyprus. In 1955, the businesses and properties of Turkey's Greek citizens were attacked by nationalist mobs, and there is significant evidence that the police did not take measures to stop these attacks (Güven 2006). Similarly, the status of non-Muslim minorities did not change when Turkey enjoyed considerable economic growth in the 1980s. Turkey passed several liberal economic and political reforms and integrated into global markets; however, these years passed without any real progress in freedoms for religious minorities.

Similarly, France saw huge restructuring and industrialization in the postwar period, particularly in the 1950s and 1960s, but this progress did not necessarily bring more rights for religious minorities. Furthermore, the 1959 Debré Law, which allowed the state to sponsor educational institutions established by religious groups, mostly favored Catholicism, the majority religion in the country. Even though the law did not single out Catholicism as the beneficiary of the new regulation, it increased the role of Catholicism by opening the path for thousands of Catholic schools to be sponsored by the state.

Finally, secularization cannot explain the recent policy changes toward religious minorities in Turkey and France. In Turkey, the government implemented several reforms of policy on religious minorities in the 2000s, but the secularization process did not decrease the influence of the majority religion. Turkey experienced rapid economic growth; however, this growth did not decrease the impact of the Muslim majority on politics. On the contrary, growth and development in Turkey was accompanied by an increasingly assertive public religiosity. The AKP normalized the public manifestation of religious symbols, increased the number of public employees with religious sensibilities, and legitimized the rise of conservative and religious discourses in public. Conservative Muslim populations in Turkey constituted the major social base of the political party that passed these laws. Contrary to the premise of secularization theory, religious freedoms for Christian minorities came at a time when politically active Muslims had more access to power structures. In short, the reforms of policy on religious minorities were not the result of the decreasing influence of the majority religion.

In France, the government passed laws in the 2000s that constrained the freedoms of Muslims, but these restrictions were hardly outcome of a desecularization process. The anti-Muslim laws were not a reflection of an increasing Catholic influence; they were mostly the result of an increase in the impact of the far right, which championed an anti-immigrant discourse. The Catholic Church did not support the laws that limited religious liberties for Muslims. Most of the laws were implemented under a right-wing majority parliament, but these reforms received strong support from socialists as well. Within an increasingly anti-immigrant and nationalistic political environment, the center parties developed a new discourse in order to appeal to the voters.

With the assumption that industrialization and secularization will make religions obsolete, modernization theory has a teleological view of history and blinds itself to increasing religious activism and its political consequences (Bruce 1992; Norris and Inglehart 2004; Wilson 1982). Furthermore, the view that modernization undermines the status of the majority religion and opens a path toward freedoms for religious minorities does not always hold true. In both France and Turkey, modernization did not necessarily lead to religious freedoms for the minorities. Instead of predicting the outcome only from the point of view of macro-social structures, one should focus attention on the micro-processes underlying certain political and historical contexts.

## Historical Institutions and Religious Freedoms

Certain scholars explain freedom for religious minorities with reference to historical institutions that establish state–religion relations. Considering institutions as the legacies of concrete historical processes (Thelen 1999), these scholars see different state policies as reflections of institutional structures. For example, Stephen Monsma and Christopher Soper (1997), who compare church–state relations in five pluralist democracies, argue that different historical trajectories created different patterns of church–state relations: "strict separation" in the United States, "principled pluralism" in the Netherlands, "pragmatic pluralism" in Australia, "partial establishment" in England, and "partnership and autonomy" in Germany. Similarly, Jocelyn Cesari (2004, 65) uses a typology based on unique historical experiences to depict the models of state accommodation of Muslims in Western Europe. To her, in countries such as Austria, Belgium, Italy, Spain, and Germany, the state legally recognizes all religions and has allowed Islamic institutions to develop. In countries such as the United Kingdom, Denmark, and Greece, there are varying degrees of recognition for minorities but the existence of an established religion sometimes creates problems. Finally, in France, the dominance of anticlerical secularism largely limits the state's capacity to accommodate Muslims. Other scholars examine historical nation-state philosophies of each nation to explain state policies toward immigrants (Brubaker 1992; Favell 1998; Joppke 1999; Kastoryano 2002) or toward religions (Jelen 2005, 2010; Jelen and Wilcox 2002; Tamadonfar and Jelen 2013b).

Historical institutionalism focuses on the processes that sustain institutions over long periods of time through the arguments of path dependence and increasing returns (Collier and Collier 1991; Krasner 1988; Mahoney 2000; North 1990; Pierson 2000). Policy changes are possible if they are in line with the historically established regimes of state–religion relations. The limits of change, then, are drawn at the critical junctures when the institutions are formed in the first place. In line with this logic, Joel Fetzer and Christopher Soper (2005), in their study on state accommodation of Muslims' religious practices in Britain, France, and Germany, contend that "the development of public policy on Muslim religious rights is mediated in significant ways by the different patterns of church-state institutions within each of these countries" (Fetzer and Soper 2005, 7). For Fetzer and Soper, these institutional differences have been shaped in the course of history as each of these countries had unique historical experiences. This is why the same external condition, the increasing number of Muslim immigrants in Europe, created different policy responses in Britain, France, and Germany.

Radical transformations that depart from historical practices are less likely to occur at stable times. Radical changes are possible only at the time of turning points in which extraordinary conditions make sudden bends in the path of history. Ann Swidler (1986, 278–282) draws a distinction between "settled" and "unsettled" times, according to which political and social transformations occur during "unsettled" times and become consolidated during "settled" times. Recognizing the strength of historical state–religion institutions, Matthias Koenig (2007) demonstrates how supra-state Europeanizing processes have pushed the boundaries of institutional change by setting shared standards for the recognition of minorities. Yet he acknowledges that Europeanization gives "new legitimacy to historical institutional arrangements by reframing them as expressions of national identities" (Koenig 2007, 913).

The historical institutionalist approach would expect that recent policy changes in Turkey and France were implemented within the borders drawn by the historical institutions of state–religion relations. Alternatively, these scholars would expect that Turkey and France experienced external shocks that allowed them to change their historically established institutions so as to make recent changes possible. However, recent policies in Turkey and France deviated significantly from historically established regimes without there having been any critical juncture that would have led to an institutional change.

Turkey's recent state policies toward Christian minorities cannot be explained by the country's historical pattern of state–religion relations. The Turkish state had systematically discriminated against Christian minorities throughout its modern history, particularly at times when Turkey had political conflict with Greece. Given the exclusionary policies that the state had historically implemented, recent policy changes that granted the Christian minorities rights such as property rights and the right to build places of worship may be considered revolutionary. Even though Turkey did not experience a significant turning point during the time of these reforms, policy changes that contradicted historical legacies still became possible. One could argue that Turkey's relationship with the EU was the external shock that led to institutional change in state–religion relations and eventually produced a reformist moment in the treatment of Christian minorities. This argument, however, misses the point that Turkey had already had a strong relationship with Europe for a long period without revising its policies toward Christians. Furthermore, the new policies did not follow any large-scale institutional changes in state–religion relations; Turkey largely kept its institutional setting intact, but granted rights for Christian minorities notwithstanding.

In France, the state approach toward religion is more restrictive compared to the approaches of other Western countries; however, the French state had traditionally granted religious minorities the right to freedoms. Until the recent laws that restricted the wearing of headscarves in public schools and of the burqa – the veil that covers the full body except the eyes – in public places, Muslims did not have serious difficulty in manifesting their religious symbols in schools and public places. The French laws on secularism banned the state from supporting religion but guaranteed religious freedoms. The higher administrative court, the Council of State, overturned almost all of the cases in which Muslim girls were dismissed from schools for wearing a headscarf. The court considered the wearing of the headscarf to be a matter of religious freedom. Yet the parliament passed laws that would limit Muslims' manifestation of religious symbols in public spaces. These recent ventures outside the borders of France's established historical institutions did not come after a significant turning point that would have led to the change of the state–religion regime in France. One could consider the anti-Muslim political discourse that came after the 9/11 terrorist attacks to be an external shock. However, France had had similar experiences in the past, especially during the Algerian Civil War in the 1990s, but these did not result in significant policy changes toward Muslims at that time. Furthermore, as was the case in Turkey, recent policy changes were not an outcome of a large-scale broad institutional shift in state–religion relations.

Although historical institutionalist arguments are persuasive in "articulating the mechanisms of reproduction behind particular institutions" (Thelen 2003, 211), they provide insufficient tools for understanding incremental policy changes. Many cases of institutional change do not conform to this model, which limits the explanation of such change only to "periods of extreme openness" (Thelen 2004, 30). Some cases exhibit changes through periodic political realignment and renegotiation. Smaller-scale changes occurring in "settled" times can cumulatively generate significant institutional transformations over time (Thelen 2004, 292; Katznelson 1998). In other cases, states can increase their role in minority integration not necessarily because of historical institutional arrangements but for contextual reasons (Laurence 2012). In both Turkey and France, strong institutional structures did not prevent policy changes that deviated from the status quo. One needs to examine the role of ideology and actor strategies, and their interaction between domestic and international contexts, to fully account for the new reforms in Turkey and recent limitations on religious minorities in France.

## Ideology and Religious Freedoms

Another group of scholars explains religious freedoms for minorities based on ideological battles among different groups. To them, ideologies rather than interests mobilize people against or in support of religious freedoms. In places where restrictive and authoritarian ideologies dominate, religious freedoms are less likely; in places where liberal and pluralist ideologies dominate, religious freedoms are more likely (Kuru 2007a; 2009). The domination of one or other ideology depends on the struggles among the actors involved. For example, Russia under Vladimir Putin shifted toward more authoritarianism and nationalism, developing a new concept, "spiritual security," to constrain Protestant missionaries. Any challenge to the influence of the Russian Orthodox Church, an important national identity marker, was considered a national security threat (Payne 2010).[12] Christian Smith (2003) explains the disestablishment of religion and the dominance of secular values in the US public sphere with reference to the battles among the elite in the nation's founding period. To him, the secular elite prevailed in political contestations, established the separation of state and religion, and set up the hegemony of a secular public discourse. Ahmet T. Kuru (2009) explains the different trajectories of state–religion relations in the United States, France and Turkey with reference to the ideological struggles that these countries went through in their founding periods. Ani

---

[12] In the Polish and Iranian context, Mehran Tamadonfar and Ted G. Jelen (2013a) show that religion, when it is a constituent element of national identity, can play a role in regime transformation.

Sarkissian, Jonathan Fox, and Yasemin Akbaba (2011) show that states repress some religious minorities more than others in Muslim-majority countries on an ideological basis. In this case, ideology toward groups with certain identities becomes an important factor in explaining why some groups face greater repression than others.

The ideological explanation is important in shifting the attention to the role of ideas along with the processes through which these ideas turn into action, instead of focusing only on social structures or historical legacies. The scholars in this genre take seriously the role of ideas in the creation of political action. They are interested in actors' mobilization of ideas rather than their material interests. Although this explanation is similar to the rational choice approach (discussed in the next section) in its focus on the process of interaction among actors, it differs from that perspective by identifying ideological commitments, not material interests, as the basic motive behind strategic interaction.

The ideological explanation sheds light on the recent policy changes in Turkey and France. Ideology can explain both why Christians in Turkey were marginalized in the first place and why their status improved in the 2000s. Kemalism (the Turkish republic's founding ideology), with its "assertive secularism" (Kuru 2009) and nationalism, led the state to marginalize religious minorities. The Kemalist vision of creating a homogeneous nation alienated religious and ethnic minorities (Brockett 2011; Çınar 2005; Dressler 2015; Özyürek 2006). Kemalism used secularism to control religious groups, and restricted the institutionalization of religion not only for non-Muslims but also for Muslims (Yavuz 2003, 59–80). Nationalism created a hostile political discourse against non-Muslims, portraying them as agents of the foreigners (Aktar 1996; Gökaçtı 2004; Macar 2003). This discourse fed hostile social attitudes toward religious minorities.[13] The reforms improving the status of Christian minorities came at a time when the founding ideology of the Turkish state started to weaken. Between 2000 and 2010, a social coalition of Islamists, liberals, and minorities undermined the Kemalist establishment and decreased its influence in bureaucracy and politics. Assertive secularism and nationalism gave way to passive secularism and relative pluralism in the 2000s (Kuru 2009). This relatively more liberal ideological environment led to the passing of reforms in favor of Christian minorities.

Similarly, ideology helps explain why French politicians implemented policies that restricted Muslims in the 2000s (Kuru 2008). Despite France having a strong secular political culture, it had conventionally allowed the expression of religious beliefs in the public sphere. Religious groups operated autonomously from the state and enjoyed religious freedoms in public places. However, the laws that restricted Muslims' manifestation of religious symbols came at a time of increasing Islamophobia in Europe in

---

[13] Author's interview with Elçin Macar, Istanbul, Turkey, June 27, 2012.

the wake of the September 11 terrorist attacks. Supporters of restrictive policies utilized the new ideological atmosphere to implement their policy agendas. Anti-immigrant organizations fueled the fear of "the Islamist threat." The proponents of restrictive regulations also used this political environment to gain the support of the broader public. The broad-based popular support for the banning of Muslim religious symbols led the French deputies to take a hostile stance against Muslims and to pass restrictive bills. In short, an anti-Muslim, anti-immigrant right-wing ideology replaced the relatively pluralist ideology, and the results constrained Muslims in their religious liberties.

The ideological explanation provides insights to account for Turkish and French cases, but it is of limited use in explaining the emergence of the ideological environments that let certain discourses dominate over others. For Turkey, the emergence of a more permissive ideological environment between 2000 and 2010 needs to be addressed. An explanation should refer to domestic and international factors that challenged the dominance of Kemalism and yielded a more pluralist understanding and a movement toward diversity. Furthermore, the explanation should also demonstrate how proponents of reforms utilized the new environment to pursue their policy agendas. Given that Turkey lost its pluralist environment after 2012, one needs to account for the conditions that led to the short life-span of the pluralist era. A careful analysis should consider not only the influence of the EU on Turkish policymakers but also how domestic actors in Turkey utilized EU pressure to push for their policy agendas.

The dominance of Islamophobia and anti-immigrant discourse in France played a significant role in the passing of laws that restricted Muslims, but a complete explanation of the limitation of religious freedoms should assess how those who aimed to restrict Islamic symbols in schools and public sphere made their case. In other words, the explanation should evaluate how the actors utilized global and Europe-wide fears about Muslims in pushing their policy agendas. In making such an assessment, one needs a two-level analysis that requires going beyond the ideological explanation. First, one needs to show the efforts of domestic actors to "nationalize" Islamophobia and carry the discourse through their civil society activism. Second, one needs to demonstrate how the proponents of the ban accessed the political decision makers and persuaded them to take steps to ban Muslim religious symbols in schools and public places. This brings us to a careful analysis of actor strategies, which I now turn to.

## Rational Choice and Religious Freedoms

Scholars of rational choice theory focus on strategic interaction among political and religious actors to explain policy decisions on religious freedoms. They stress the importance of choices that state and church actors make rationally in explaining state policies (Finke and Stark 1992; Stark and Iannaccone 1994). They contend that political actors are motivated to stay in power, while religious actors are motivated to have a greater influence over society. The effects on religious freedoms are the outcomes of different combinations of actor strategies. Majority religions use their influence over their countries' governments to restrict the impact of minority religions, ultimately resulting in less religious liberty. Governments are less likely to increase religious liberties when there are threatening and relatively powerful religious minorities in the country but are more likely to increase liberties when there are non-threatening and weaker religious minorities (Gill 2008, 26–59; Gill and Keshavarzian 1999).

For example, Anthony Gill explains the expansion of religious freedoms in Latin America after the 1990s by referring to the interests of the political and religious leaders (Gill 2008). He argues that political leaders expand the scope of religious freedoms when doing so increases their ability to stay in power or enhances the economic well-being of the countries that they rule. Rejecting the suggestion of a direct relationship between secularization and religious liberties, Gill focuses on the motives and interests of politicians and religious leaders (Gill 2008, 26–59). Shifting attention from macro-level social transformations to micro-level individual motivations, Gill prioritizes processes over structures. Ani Sarkissian (2015) examines the nonviolent repression of the civil and political rights of religious groups in authoritarian settings with reference to the interaction of the level of political competition and the structure of religious divisions in society. In another study, Sarkissian (2012) shows how the rulers in authoritarian and semi-authoritarian regimes in Muslim-majority states utilize policies toward religion to limit political competition and prevent democratic transition.

Rational choice theory can provide partial explanations for the recent policy changes in Turkey and France. From the logic of the theory, one would expect that Muslim religious leaders in Turkey contributed to the marginalization of Christians for many years in order to decrease the influence of Christianity over society, while political actors enhanced religious freedoms for Christian minorities when doing so served to their interests: i.e. when it helped them stay in power. This argument can be supported only partially. It is difficult to explain the initial marginalization of Christians from a strategic point of view. Christian minorities were very small, and giving them more rights would hardly have threatened the government. In contrast, when Turkey was threatened by the Soviet Union during the Cold War period, Turkey could have expanded reforms in favor of Christians in order to enhance its relations with the Western powers. Instead, relying on a strong nationalist-secularist ideology, the state restricted the freedoms of Christian minorities.

The change of the status of Christians in the 2000s can provide empirical evidence for rational choice theory. Political actors, especially the AKP, supported Turkey's EU membership, and they implemented civil and political liberties, including the rights of Christians, because they needed to consolidate their position vis-à-vis the authoritarian elite (Dağı 2006). The AKP considered democratic reforms necessary to restrain the bureaucratic military elite so as to open up space for politics. The social base of the AKP also supported these policies because democratic reforms would serve their interests, which had been heavily undermined by the military in the late 1990s (Cizre and Çınar 2003).

From a rational choice perspective, one could explain France's restrictive policies toward Muslims by taking into account the interests of political and religious actors. Accordingly, the politicians would have implemented these policies to gain ground in elections and to enhance their public support. The Catholic Church would have benefited from the restrictive policies toward Muslims as such policies would undermine Islam's increasing influence in France. Rational choice theory is persuasive in explaining the position of political actors but weaker in explaining the motivations of the Catholic Church. By passing the restrictive laws, political actors took advantage of an environment of increasing Islamophobia. After the far right gained political influence in the early 2000s, center-right and even center-left parties embarked upon a less immigration-friendly discourse so as not to leave the ground to the radical right. These parties found political capital in endorsing anti-Muslim policies in parliament. By doing so, center right politicians competed for the nationalist vote that was being lost to the far-right political parties. Similarly, the center left competed for the support of secularist voters, who were concerned about "the Islamist threat." However, the Catholic Church did not actually support the restrictive policies toward Muslims. The church saw the state's banning of religious symbols as an attack against religious freedoms regardless of which religious group the target was.

Although rational choice theory illuminates the motivations behind domestic political support for policies regarding religious minorities, it does not account for the context that made these policies possible. The interplay of international and domestic forces prepared the groundwork for strategic interaction on religious minority rights in Turkey and France in the 2000s. The moves of the AKP cannot be understood without taking into account the international pressures exerted by the EU, as well as the domestic "norm entrepreneurs" who persuaded the AKP leaders and supporters to become more receptive to reform. Similarly, the support of the political parties for more restrictive policies toward Muslims in France cannot be explained without reference to increasing Islamophobia in Europe after 2001, and the strong campaign of strict secularists who utilized this international environment to push for more restrictive policies.

## Summary: Theoretical Contributions to the Explanation of State Policy on Religious Freedoms

Ultimately, modernization theory added little to explain the Turkish and French cases. Neither religious freedoms nor limitations were an inevitable result of modernization. Explanations referring to historical institutionalism, ideology, and rational choice theory have contributed to our understanding of recent policies on religious freedoms for Christians in Turkey and Muslims in France; however, none of these approaches alone can fully explain the political outcomes. Historical institutionalists explain the general framework of state–religion relations, but they cannot account for the recent gradual changes that departed from historical patterns. Explanations based on ideology are blind to the material interests and environmental contexts that change the dominant ideological positions. Rational choice theory, which focuses on the strategic interaction between political and religious leaders, ignores the role that ideologies play in political moves. Explaining policy on religious freedoms in Turkish and French contexts require a careful analysis of the interaction of international contexts and domestic politics (Kılınç 2014a). To explain the expansion of religious liberties in Turkey and limitations of freedoms in France, we need an analytical framework that integrates the international context so as to examine the interaction of ideology and interests.

## INTERNATIONAL CONTEXT, DOMESTIC POLITICS, AND RELIGIOUS FREEDOMS

Although religion is a global phenomenon, previous studies have not systematically analyzed the interaction of international context and domestic politics in explaining state policies toward religion. In an era when state–religion relations are vulnerable to worldwide developments and local contestations over sacred and secular, we need an analytical framework within the study of religion and politics that enables us to analyze the interactions of global, local, and historical processes. Scholars of international relations have developed our understanding of international factors' impact on domestic structures since the publication of Peter Gourevitch's (1978) well-known article, "The Second Image Reversed," which brought up the necessity of taking international politics seriously in analyzing domestic politics. Scholars have identified the mechanisms through which the international context structures domestic political outcomes. Scholars in the fields of state development, democratization, and domestic institutional formation have produced works that combined the two areas. However, scholars studying the interactions of religion and politics have tended to ignore the influence of international politics on domestic institutional change.[14] The literature on religion and politics can borrow from other fields to cross-fertilize the theories

---

[14] There have been studies that examine the role of religion in international relations (Fox and Sandler 2004; Hurd 2009; Petito and Hatzopoulos 2003; Philpott 2000; Sandal and Fox 2013; Thomas 2005; Toft et al. 2011), but studies that focus on the interaction between international context and domestic politics remain limited.

of international politics and domestic institutional development. This study is a modest attempt in this direction.

I specifically argue that to produce reform, the international context must be mediated through domestic actors who are motivated by material interests or normative commitments. The policy changes toward religious minorities in Turkey and France became possible only when domestic actors utilized the opportunities provided by the international context in pushing their policy agendas. In developing my argument, I draw on previous studies that combined international and domestic variables. I develop a systematic model that helps analyze the interaction between the international context and domestic politics as it relates to state policies toward religious minorities. By bringing the relevance of the international environment to the study of religion and politics, I offer an explanation of religious freedoms that can be part of a dialogue among scholars of international relations and comparative state–religion relations. I identify two mechanisms through which the international context influences domestic policymaking: strategic interaction and normative commitment.

In strategic interaction in this context, domestic actors take advantage of international pressure to increase their power positions in the domestic realm. They seek to maximize their own interests by exploiting international pressure in order to change the domestic power configuration so that it favors them. Dominant international norms can be a game-changer for domestic politics if actors appropriate those norms to empower their own policy positions. In terms of state policies toward religion, the international context can empower religious groups or political leaders in pushing new changes or keeping existing institutions. By empowering certain actors over others, international dynamics can shift the balance of power among actors and produce policy changes.

The strategic logic of how international dynamics influence domestic policy change has been employed by several scholars. In the literature on the origins of states, scholars explain the emergence of domestic political institutions with reference to the international security environment. To them, external security pressures strongly influence the development of political, bureaucratic, and administrative institutions. State-makers reacted to international security environments strategically and crafted institutions so as to mobilize resources effectively for engaging in geopolitical competition (Desch 1999; Downing 1992; Ertman 1997; Herbst 2000; Skocpol 1979; Tilly 1992; Tilly and Ardant 1975). In the field of democratic transitions, some scholars see external factors as pressures and background reasons for movement toward democratization (Pridham 1991; Whitehead 1996). Laurence Whitehead (1996, 3–25), for example, argues that "democratization through convergence" occurs when a non-democratic country joins a preexisting democratic community of states. To Whitehead (1996, 24), in these cases, domestic actors align their strategies based on international factors.

Several scholars have looked at how international institutions can structure the interests and strategies of state and bureaucratic actors. Scholars of European politics, in examining the impact of EU regulations on domestic political institutions, have studied the strategic impact of external factors on domestic politics (Burley and Mattli 1993; Checkel 1999; Cowles et al. 2001; Hooghe and Marks 2001; Risse-Kappen et al. 1999, 2001; Schimmelfennig 2002; Schimmelfennig and Sedelmeier 2005). Milada Anna Vachudová (2005), for example, demonstrates the role of the EU in pushing liberal democracy in Eastern and Central European countries. Examining six countries, Vachudová answers the question "How does membership of an international organization transform state strategies and preferences?" (Vachudová 2005, 7). Building her analysis on a strategic logic, Vachudová argues that the EU shifted the domestic balance of power toward pro-EU actors because the "attraction of EU membership" and the "deliberate conditionality exercised in the EU's pre-accession process" gave them a strategic advantage in domestic political contestations (Vachudová 2005, 63). Similarly, Liliana Andonova (2004), in examining the impact of the EU on environmental regulations in candidate and member countries, argues that EU integration has had a positive impact on environmental policies in Bulgaria, the Czech Republic, and Poland through incentives stemming from regulations on export-competitive industries.

While strategic logic focuses on the shifting balance of power among actors, the mechanism of normative commitment may be used to explain how the international context can advantage or disadvantage certain groups by increasing the popularity of particular norms globally or regionally. International norms are internalized through the logic of appropriateness (March and Olsen 1989). That is, domestic actors internalize international norms because they believe that it is legitimate to do so (Finnemore and Sikkink 1998). The norms do not necessarily enhance the domestic actors' formal means–ends efficiency (Hall and Taylor 1996, 947). Similar organizational practices diffuse across the world through "the impact of world-institutional development on nation states" (Meyer et al. 1997, 148). Domestic change, in the normative conception, occurs when it enhances the social legitimacy of an organization or its participants (Boli and Thomas 1999; Meyer and Scott 1992; Powell and DiMaggio 1991; Scott and Meyer 1994; Thomas 1987, 1989, 2004). Transnational organizations, national civil society organizations, and public intellectuals are influential in promoting norms (Frank and Meyer 2002; Gurowitz 1999). A key factor for reformists is to produce popular legitimacy for the norm they wish to see adopted, and the international context can play a significant role in spreading ideas. The change of ideas on a specific policy issue through time also increases the likelihood of institutional change.

Scholars who have systematically studied the domestic impact of international norms (Cortell and Davis 2000; Finnemore and Sikkink 1998; Keck and Sikkink 1998; Risse 2000; Schmidt 2004) have taken domestic actors into consideration and shown how international context provided them with strong ideas in their domestic contestations. To these scholars, norms provide language and grammar for domestic actors in making their case (Kratochwill 1989; Onuf 1989). Scholars have identified several factors in examining the influence of international norms on domestic settings: the congruence between norms and domestic political culture (Checkel 1999), the "domestic legitimacy" of international norms (Cortell and Davis 1993), the compatibility between the "organizational culture" of institutions and international norms (Legro 1997), and whether or not the nature of state–society relations allows room for international factors to function (Risse-Kappen 1995). In terms of state policies toward religion, domestic actors can appropriate globally popular ideas and spread them in domestic politics to propagate their policy preferences. Religious or political actors can justify their positions with reference to the global popularity of their arguments.

Scholars such as Gary Goertz (1994), Doug McAdam, Sidney Tarrow, and Charles Tilly (2001) have shown how these two mechanisms function together in producing state behaviors or social outcomes. Goertz (1994) shows how system structure, normative environment, and history constitute the context of state actions in international politics by examining the cases of oil nationalization, decolonization, USSR–East European relations, and enduring military rivalries. In the social movement context McAdam, Tarrow, and Tilly (2001) argue that the success or failure of social movements depends on political opportunity structures. Social actors exploit the existence of certain political opportunities to reach their goals.

In this book, I have drawn on studies that employed both strategic and normative mechanisms to reach a synthetic theory. The strategic and normative mechanisms provide a coherent analytical framework that combines insights from the study of historical institutionalism, ideology, and rational choice theory. As scholars of political opportunity structure argue, the international context creates new opportunities for domestic actors to pursue their policy agendas. Simply put, I argue that policy change toward religious minorities becomes possible when strong domestic actors find a suitable international context that can help them execute their domestic policy agendas using strategic and/or normative mechanisms.

The existence of high international pressure or dominant global discourses supportive of a particular policy can influence domestic policy outcome; however, international pressure cannot exert a change unless there are strong domestic actors supportive of the policy. Where there is a lack of both high international pressure and strong domestic actors supportive of a policy, the status quo is preserved, and a policy change is unlikely. When there is no high international pressure but there are strong domestic actors, a domestic coalition around reform needs to emerge in order for a policy change to take place. In the existence of high international pressure and strong domestic actors supportive

TABLE 1.1 *Policy influence of international context and domestic power configuration*

|  |  | Is there high international pressure or a dominant global discourse supportive of a particular policy change? | |
| --- | --- | --- | --- |
|  |  | Yes | No |
| Are there strong domestic actors supportive of a particular policy change? | Yes | Policy change | Policy change requires a domestic coalition around reform |
|  | No | Policy change requires a domestic coalition around reform | No policy change |

of change, the policy shift is more likely; however, the relevant mechanism of change (either strategic interaction or normative commitment) depends on whether there is a convergence between domestic historical institutions and the policies supported by the international context. When there is high international pressure for a policy but no strong domestic actors supportive of the policy, the change is less likely since international pressure is unable to create reform without domestic supporters; however, the convergence between domestic historical institutions and the policies supported by the international context can still influence the possibility of the emergence of a coalition around reform in the long run (see Table 1.1).

The international context, by restructuring domestic politics via strategic and normative mechanisms, pushes states to change their policies toward religious minorities (Müftüler Baç 2005; Naxidou 2012; Toktaş and Aras 2009). When international pressure and strong domestic actors favoring policy change exist together, the convergence between domestic historical institutions and the policies supported by the international context becomes important in predicting the micro-causal mechanisms that produce policy change. When there is high convergence between the international context and domestic institutions, strategic interaction is a more likely mechanism for policy change. When the convergence between the international context and domestic institutions is low, normative commitment becomes a necessary mechanism for change, because in the lack of convergence, justification of policy change is needed to persuade actors. When high international pressure exists for a particular policy but there are no strong domestic actors supportive of the policy, a convergence between domestic historical institutions and the policies supported by the international context can predict change in the long run. If the convergence is low under this condition, policy change is unlikely. If the convergence is high, the policy change requires a coalition of domestic actors supportive of the policy shift.

Turkey and France were under the influence of external conditions at the time of their policy changes toward religious minorities. Turkey's process of negotiation for membership in the EU constituted the international context for reform of policies toward Christian minorities, while the rise of Islamophobia in Europe helped frame policy changes toward the Muslim minority in France. In both cases, the international context empowered certain actors over others and provided ideas that would result in the prioritizing of particular policies over others.

Turkey's relations with the EU played a significant role in pushing reforms in the treatment of Christian minorities. Turkey had been under the surveillance of several international organizations, but the EU's impact was most significant for the expansion of religious freedoms for Christians. Turkish membership negotiations with the EU gave the European Commission the necessary mechanisms to influence Turkish policies. International pressure during the EU candidacy period is highly effective because EU sanctions, which include termination of candidacy status, can be severe for candidate countries. The EU influenced the implementation of reforms in Turkey, especially after 1999. In this period, there was a lot of EU activity in this area, sustained over a long period, and pursued in an organized way. In short, international pressure on Turkey was intensive, persistent, and systematic. The EU shaped Turkey's domestic politics through relevant domestic actors who pushed democratization further via strategic and normative mechanisms.

The reforms in Turkey became possible because strong domestic actors, who would benefit from the reforms required to join the EU, emerged. Domestic political actors within Turkey's repressive state utilized the international environment to gain ground against the authoritarian bureaucracy. Between 2002 and 2010, Islamic actors used Turkey's EU membership bid as an opportunity to liberalize the Turkish political system so as to strengthen their position against the authoritarian establishment. EU pressure led to the reform of religious minority rights when the AKP utilized that pressure to advance its own political interests. Due to EU pressure for reform, the AKP was able to minimize the role of the military and other bureaucratic organs in politics and enhance its maneuvering room. EU reforms also included improvements in the status of religious rights for Christians, so the AKP's liberalizing policies contributed to the elevation of the status of religious minorities. Because there was low convergence between Turkey's domestic institutions and the reforms demanded by international bodies, the government needed the help of norm entrepreneurs. Norm entrepreneurs such as liberals, social democrats, and some Islamic groups organized activities and produced discourses that would justify pluralism in which Christians found a safer space. The spread of liberal ideas through EU pressure contributed to the work of the norm entrepreneurs. The activism of norm entrepreneurs persuaded the conservative social base of the AKP to take a stand with the reformers. The AKP built a broad coalition with liberals, social democrats, and minorities. This coalition provided the social basis for the reforms in favor of religious minorities. Domestic actors with relatively strong social bases facilitated the adoption of international norms on religious liberty, in either instrumental or normative ways.

The global rise of Islamophobia in the wake of the September 11 attacks provided the international context of policymaking in France. The responses of European societies to rising violent extremism across the globe created a social base for xenophobia and prepared the groundwork for the rise of radical right groups in the European context. All across Europe, there was an intensive change of attitudes toward Muslims. The Islamophobic environment persisted for a long time and anti-Muslim actors made a systematic effort to spread their ideas. In short, there was an intensive, persistent, and systematic effort to keep Islamphobia as a factor in public debates in Europe. As Islamophobia grew stronger, the radical right gradually rose in the domestic politics of European countries including France. Public debates on French Muslims evolved within an international environment that provided a discriminatory vocabulary to the debate on Muslims and empowered those who took an anti-Muslim position.

Although the historical-legal institutions governing the public manifestation of religious symbols in France allowed the wearing of religious headscarves in public schools, the strength of the Islamophobic environment helped the proponents of the headscarf ban push for their policy preferences. In France, strict secularists and the radical right utilized the anti-Islamic global environment that emerged after September 11, 2001, to restrict the public manifestation of Muslim religious symbols. These groups used global Islamophobia to portray Muslims as a threat to French values of secularism and republicanism. By referring to the principles of republicanism and secularism in framing their policy preferences, these actors utilized French constitutional principles to justify policies that were against the principles of historical domestic institutions of state–religion relations. Doing so garnered them the support of conservatives and socialists, who had supported religious minorities in the past. Mainstream groups such as conservatives and socialists shifted to a more restrictive approach toward minorities in a climate of increasing anti-immigrant public discourse in France. Although there were liberal groups who supported Muslims' rights on the basis of a normative stance, their impact was largely eliminated by the dominance of anti-Islamic and anti-immigrant discourse in domestic politics. Islamophobia, by strengthening the far right and weakening the liberals, made the passing of anti-Muslim laws easier.

## DATA AND METHODS

My argument dictates a three-step research method. First, I measure my dependent variable: change in state policies toward religious minorities. Second, I measure my explanatory variables: domestic historical institutions, the international context, and strategies of domestic actors in framing their policy agendas. Finally, I demonstrate empirically the strategic interaction and normative commitment mechanisms through which the international context influenced policymaking within the domestic environment in which political and civil society actors interact.

The dependent variable, "change in state policies toward religious minorities," represents the change in a course of action toward religious minority groups adopted and pursued by a government. The term "religious minority" is controversial in both Turkey and France. "Religious minority" in this study is defined as a group of people who subscribe to a religion different from the majority religion in a particular country. The crux of the debate is the controversy over which groups to include in or exclude from the category of religious minorities, because not every belief system is recognized as a religion by every state. In France, the state does not recognize sects such as Jehovah's Witnesses as a religious group, while in Turkey there is not a consensus on whether Alevis would be included as a religious minority or a sub-group within the majority religion of Islam.[15] This study avoids those debates and focuses on two religious groups on whose minority status there is no disagreement: Christians in Turkey and Muslims in France.

To measure policy change, I look at the changes in domestic law (judicial codes, laws, and constitutions) in my case countries from the 1980s to the 2000s. I examine changes in the implementation of laws through analysis of court decisions and public discussions as reflected in print sources such as newspaper articles and official meeting proceedings. In Turkey, the state lifted the long-lived ban over the acquisition and disposal of real estate by religious minority foundations, made possible the opening of language and educational institutions in minority mother tongues, and made the opening of the places of worship easier, even though practical difficulties still continued. The Turkish state continued its ban on the training of minority religion clergy in Turkey and its non-recognition of legal personality for religious communities. In France, the state banned the wearing of religious symbols at public schools, banned the wearing of the burqa in public spaces, and created hurdles in issuing contracts for Muslim schools. On the other hand, the French state worked with Muslims on the issue of Muslims' corporate representation and in the opening of new mosques.

In measuring policy change, one needs to take historically established state–religion relations into account so as to detect deviations from established norms and rules. To measure departure from conventional policies, one first needs to identify what those policies are. Identifying the nature of historical institutions is a two-step process in my study. First, I construct a historical narrative by relying on monographs dedicated to the development of state–religion relations in France and Turkey. Building on a key historical institutionalist insight,

---

[15] The status of sects in France is briefly covered in Chapter 8.

I explore how certain legal and bureaucratic structures in each issue that I examine were replicated over time and had been locked into legal codes and bureaucratic practices since the 1980s. Second, I carry out a content analysis of major print media in the case countries to identify the dominant public discourses within each case country. Then I construct a typology of historical institutions with respect to state–religion relations for each issue. After identifying the nature of historically established institutions influencing state–religion relations, I analyze recent changes on state policies toward religious minorities as prescribed above.

A key variable in this study is international context, and I focus on its impact on domestic policy change. For the purposes of this study, I define international factors either as regulatory mechanisms that apply cross-nationally and are beyond the control of policymakers in individual countries (Freiden and Rogowski 1996, 25) or discourses that go beyond borders and legitimize certain policies over others. International factors can have a strong or weak influence over states based on institutional congruence. Only high international pressure or dominant global discourses can create a viable policy change, because they are effective in changing the balance of power in favor of those who have an interest in the consequences of the pressure. International pressure and dominant global discourses are measured through three indicators: intensity, persistency, and a systematic approach or effect. If international pressure or global discourses involve a lot of activity at one time, they are "intensive"; if they have continued to exist for a long time, they are "persistent"; and if they have operated in an organized way, they are "systematic." If international pressure or global discourses lack any one of these attributes, they are considered "low" (see Table 1.2). The data I have used to measure the indicators of international pressure or global discourses comes from the reports of governmental (mostly EU and United Nations) and nongovernmental organizations (such as Human Rights Watch and Amnesty International). I examine these reports, the criticisms made against the countries, and the consequences of those criticisms to measure the extent of international pressure or global discourses.

Based on these indicators, Turkey was under the strict monitoring of the EU between 2000 and 2010, although there were also other international bodies that induced Turkey to pass reforms on the treatment of Christian minorities. Turkey has been under intensive, persistent, and systematic international pressure with regard to its policies toward Christian minorities. Based on EU conditionality, Turkey amended its constitution and passed laws to ameliorate the religious freedom of Christian minorities. The EU monitored Turkey through its progress reports, and Turkey implemented the reforms in seeking full membership to the EU. Although international bodies other than the EU also put pressure on Turkey, their impact remained low since the pressure was not intensive, persistent, and systematic.

TABLE 1.2 *Indicators of international pressure and global discourses*

| | Intensity | Persistency | Systematization |
|---|---|---|---|
| The influence of international pressure or global discourse is high | A lot of activities at a time are imposed by external factors | External factors have continued to exist for a long time | External factors operate in an organized way |
| The influence of international pressure or global discourse is low | Frequency of external activities is low | External factors are not sustained for a long time | External factors operate in an ad hoc way |

In contrast to Turkey, France was not under strict pressure from an international institution. It is an EU member, but the EU did not exert any pressure on France on the issue of religious minorities. However, the global rise of Islamophobia provided the international context of domestic policy change in France. The discourse on the rise of "Islamic fundamentalism" in Europe was strong enough to structure the power of the domestic actors in France in both strategic and normative ways. The influence of the discourse was intensive, persistent, and systematic in terms of influencing the state's relations with the Muslim minority. Increasing concerns about "Islamic militancy" dominated French public discourse and fed anti-Muslim sentiments. Islamophobia, combined with the nationalist backlash against globalization and against the increasing power of the EU, contributed to the rise of the far right. Although Islamophobia existed before the 2000s, its degree was not high enough to structure domestic change. After the September 11 attacks, Islamophobia became intensive, persistent, and systematic.

This study shows that the international context matters to domestic policymaking. However, what makes the external context relevant is its uses by domestic actors in shaping domestic public debates. I look at the strategic and normative moves of domestic actors in making use of the international context to produce an environment in which their policy agendas prevail. I trace the public debates on each issue by especially looking at the positions of state officials, religious leaders, and civil society representatives. I look at official documents to trace the state's position in these public debates. I first identify the policy agenda of the actors.

In line with John K. Kingdon (1995, 3), I define a policy agenda as "the list of subjects or problems to which governmental officials, and people outside of government closely associated with those officials, are paying some serious attention at any given time." Accordingly, it is important to analyze the agenda-setting process of the actors. In analyzing this process, I trace how actors frame problems and propose solutions to them. Defining a problem is an "active manipulation of images of conditions by competing political actors" (Stone

1989, 293). By defining a problem in their own frames, the actors implicitly privilege certain types of solutions over others (Cobb and Elder 1983; Stone 1989). In other words, defining a new problem can eventually change policy by promoting certain policy solutions as more acceptable than others (Jeon and Haider-Markel 2001, 216). For these reasons, the identification of the policy agendas of each relevant actor in France and Turkey gains priority. I demonstrate how these actors used the international context in framing problems related to state policies toward religious minorities and offering their solutions to these problems. To do so, I analyze the policy agendas of each relevant actor in both Turkey and France as well as the processes through which the actors converted their agendas into real policy outcomes.

I chose France and Turkey as my case countries for both substantive and methodological reasons. Substantively, Turkey and France have been secular democracies of Europe in which the issues of politics and religion have shaped the public debates in the recent decades or so. Secularism in both countries is an important national identifier, not just a legal separation. The trajectory of political Islam in Turkey in recent decades has also brought to the fore the debate about the proper role of religion in a secular democracy. Political Islam in Turkey had a reformist moment between 2002 and 2010 but gained a more authoritarian stride after that. In France, the increase of Muslim populations and the demands made on them by the French state resurfaced the issue of state–religion relations. These changes mean that an analysis that takes international and domestic contexts into account is valuable. From a methodological point of view, Turkey and France are both similar enough and different enough to suit a comparative political analysis. In both countries, the state's approach toward religion is shaped by the historical evolution of the principle of secularism. However, Turkish secularism is much more restrictive than the French approach. The Turkish state offers only limited legal guarantees for religious groups to operate independently from the state.

I chose the policy issues relevant to Christians in Turkey and Muslims in France based on their politicization in public debate. The major policy issues that Christian minorities have faced in Turkish politics were the acquisition and disposal of real estate by community foundations of Christian minorities, restrictions on religious education and on the opening of places of worship, and the lack of a legal personality for religious institutions. The main issues that the Muslim minority confronted in France were the establishment of an umbrella organization for French Muslims, the issue of permits for mosques, the opening of Muslim schools that have a contractual relationship with the state, and the regulation of the manifestation of Muslim religious symbols in public spaces. For the French case, I particularly provide broad discussion on the passing of the headscarf law, which was at the forefront of French public and parliamentary discussions between 2002 and 2004. The fact that the headscarf issue was extensively and intensively debated over a long time provides me with empirical material to test the argument of the book.

I use the comparative case study as my data analysis method, because it fits best with my research objectives. Single-case studies are good for exploring causal mechanism in greater detail; however, their conclusions cannot travel across cases. Large-sample quantitative studies are suited to deducing generalizable causal claims; however, they offer limited opportunities for exploring causal mechanisms among the relevant variables (Fox 2008). A comparative case study, on the other hand, allows me to test my argument and alternative theories without sacrificing empirical richness. Comparative case studies are "much stronger at identifying the scope conditions of theories and assessing arguments about causal necessity or sufficiency in particular cases" (George and Bennett 2005, 25). Assessing the causal mechanisms in each of my case and examining whether similar or different mechanisms are at work in other cases, I specify the necessary and sufficient conditions of political outcomes. Detailed analysis of my cases and structured comparisons of each case with the other provide me with the context of relevant causal mechanisms. In using a comparative method, I pay close attention to problems of causal complexity, particularly the effects of multiple interactions. Although the findings of comparative case studies do not have universal validity and are relatively weak in estimating the causal weight of variables across a range of cases, the comparative method is good for fulfilling the theoretical objective of this study: to develop a middle-range theory that is empirically rich and theoretically subtle.

In addition, I employ the technique of process-tracing in my within-case analysis. Process-tracing strengthens my causal inference in that it demonstrates "whether the intervening variables between a hypothesized cause and observed effect move as predicted" (George and Bennett 2005, 207). Process-tracing, by exploring the chain of events, helps me demonstrate whether my causal argument is consistent with what actually happened in each case. I focus on the sequence of events that led to legislative changes in certain issue areas. By uncovering the causal mechanisms between independent and dependent variables, process-tracing controls for the possibility of equifinality, namely the fact that different causal processes can lead to similar outcomes of a given dependent variable.

The data in this study is drawn from legal documents of international institutions (the UN and the EU) on religious freedom, reports of governmental and nongovernmental organizations on religious liberty, judicial codes, laws, court decisions, and print media sources. I obtained much of the data through my fieldwork in France and Turkey. My fieldwork included collecting data from parliamentary proceedings in both Turkey and France, court decisions, newspaper archives, and interviews with government officials, politicians, and community leaders during my frequent visits to Istanbul and Paris between 2007 and 2015.

## THE PLAN OF THE BOOK

In this chapter, I have laid out the research question of the book, the literature that can help answer this question, the argument of the book, and the data and methods through which this argument is developed. Modernization theory explains secularization processes well, but secularization has not always come with the outcome of religious freedoms for minorities. Historical institutionalists draw the limits of change by identifying historical legacies that shape the state–religion institutions, but they do not account sufficiently for gradual policy changes. Scholars who explain religious freedoms in reference to ideology develop a process-oriented perspective by focusing on various groups' struggles to shape the dominant ideological framework that would eventually shape religious freedoms, but they underplay the role of the material interests of religious and political actors. Rational choice theorists take interest-based motivations seriously and develop a process-oriented perspective in line with the scholars of ideological explanation. Yet they overlook the normative commitments of religious and political actors in explaining political outcomes. To address these issues, I have outlined a theoretical framework that integrates the international context into explanations of policymaking on religious freedoms. I identified two micro-level mechanisms of strategic interaction and normative commitment through which the international context structures domestic politics. The integrated framework that I have developed employs the insights of historical institutionalism, ideological explanation, and rational choice theory. In developing this argument, I use comparative case studies and process-tracing to systematically compare French and Turkish cases and to show the causal mechanisms between suggested variables and religious freedoms. The rest of the book is organized as follows.

In Chapters 2 and 3, I show the long-term historical formation of state policies toward religious minorities in Turkey and France respectively. In these chapters, I also outline recent policy changes toward religious minorities, Christians in Turkey and Muslims in France. In explaining the formation of state–religion regimes in Turkey and France, I look at how ideological battles between various actors during certain historical epochs in each country gave birth to particular regimes of state–religion relations, and how states approached religious minorities within these historically established regimes. Both Turkey and France established secularism as a constitutional principle and championed a secular identity that excluded religion from the public sphere. They however, followed different policies toward religion: the secular Turkish state regulated religion highly, while the French state marginalized it without direct intervention in the religious field.

In Chapters 4 and 5, I analyze the international contexts within which Turkish and French states operated during the periods in question. To demonstrate the influence of the international environment on state policies, I document the international context in which recent policy changes toward religious minorities in Turkey and France were implemented. In Chapter 4, I look at the significant influence that Turkey's EU membership bid had on Turkish state policies toward the Christian minority. The Turkish public and politicians paid considerable attention to the European Commission's progress reports on Turkey, resolutions passed in the European parliament about Turkey, and official statements of European leaders on Christians in Turkey. These reports, resolutions, and statements influenced domestic policy discourses in Turkey as domestic actors used them to advance their positions. In Chapter 5, I examine the international context within which the French parliament passed restrictive laws regarding Muslims' public manifestation of religious symbols. I review the rise of Islamophobia globally and in Europe and look at how it framed the debate about Muslims in the French public sphere.

In Chapters 6 and 7, I examine how domestic actors utilize the strategic opportunities and normative repertoires provided by the international context in executing their policy agendas in the political field. In Chapter 6, I demonstrate how conservatives, who had been heavily dominated and controlled by the secular elite, used Turkey's EU membership bid as an opportunity to constrain bureaucratic authoritarian institutions, including the military, and liberalized the Turkish political system between 2002 and 2010. The chapter shows how conservatives built a broad social coalition with liberals, social democrats, and minorities, using Europeanization as an instrument. This coalition, which included the Christian minority, facilitated the passing of reforms for the benefit of religious minorities. In Chapter 7, I focus on how the radical right and strict secularists in France utilized rising Islamophobia in Europe to restrict the public manifestation of Islamic religious symbols. By using an anti-Islamic discourse, these actors portrayed Islamic activism and Islamic religious symbols as a threat to French secularism and republicanism, and they built a broad coalition, which included conservatives and socialists, to ban Muslim religious symbols in the public sphere.

The last two chapters test the argument beyond the cases discussed in the book and summarize the findings and implications of the study. In Chapter 8, I test the argument of the book in contexts beyond the scope of the study. I first look at the trajectory of the status of Christians in Turkey and Muslims in France after 2010. Second, I examine state policies toward the Jewish minority in Turkey and sects in France. Finally, I discuss how the argument raised in the book can be helpful in understanding state policies toward religious minorities in places other than France and Turkey. In Chapter 9, I summarize the major theoretical contributions and empirical findings of the book. I restate the causal mechanisms through which Turkish and French states changed their policies toward Christian and Muslim minorities respectively. Finally, I discuss how the analysis of the interaction between the international context and domestic actors can contribute to scholarship on the study of religion and politics in general, and religious freedoms in particular.

PART I

HISTORICAL INSTITUTIONS

## 2

# Secularism and Christians in Turkey

On March 7, 2009, Andrew Higgins of the *Wall Street Journal* wrote a story on a Christian monastery's battle against the Turkish state over a land dispute. The Mor Gabriel Monastery was founded in 397 and is one of the world's oldest functioning monasteries. It is located in the town of Midyat in southeast Turkey. Syriac Orthodox Christians view it as "second Jerusalem." Because of a new land-surveying program, the state claimed more than half of the land owned by the monastery. Bishop Timotheus Samuel Aktaş fortified his defense of the monastery by hiring two lawyers and mobilizing support from foreign diplomats, clergy, politicians, and the Syriac diaspora in Europe. The European Union (EU) took the issue seriously and sent representatives to the court hearings.[1]

The case of the Mor Gabriel Monastery arose at a time when the Turkish government was passing several reforms to ameliorate the status of Christians in Turkey. Although the monastery won its legal fight in the end, it was at the time a matter of course that Christians in Turkey had difficulties registering their properties, using their own mother tongues, opening houses of worship, and engaging with the state authorities. Turkish secularism, along with nationalism, shaped the state's policies toward the Christian minority in Turkey. Turkish secularism did not leave space for religious communities to grow independently from the state. Instead, exclusionary secularism, combined with the bitter legacies of the late Ottoman period in the state's relations with non-Muslim minorities, led to discriminatory policies toward minority religions. This chapter provides a historical and political context for the Turkish state's treatment of the Christian minority.

In the first part of this chapter, I offer an analysis of the historical development of state–religion relations in Turkey, which was shaped in the 1920s and 1930s during the early republican period. The founders of the republican regime, who subscribed to a nationalist ideology, implemented secularization reforms. In an effort to establish a nation-state in the ashes of a multiethnic and multireligious empire, the Turkish revolutionaries

---

[1] Andrew Higgins, "Defending the Faith: Battle over a Christian Monastery Tests Turkey's Tolerance of Minorities," *Wall Street Journal*, March 7, 2009.

implemented a top-down modernization program that aimed to keep religion within the purview of the state. When challenged, the state protected the idea of secularism through military interventions in 1960, 1971, 1980, and 1997. Only in the 2000s did political Islamists in Turkey shatter the idea of secularism as it was defined in the early republican period and form a more conservative public sphere. In the second part of the chapter, I document the Turkish state's policies toward Christians with a more detailed discussion of the reforms that the government of the Justice and Development Party (AKP, Adalet ve Kalkınma Partisi) implemented in the 2000s. Although the republican state had systematically violated the rights of the Christian minority in Turkey, this approach changed in the 2000s. The state implemented new laws ameliorating the status of religious minorities, especially in the areas of property rights, religious education, and the opening of places of worship. A number of significant problems still remain at the time of writing, and the likelihood of addressing those issues is low given the authoritarian path that the AKP took after 2012; however, considering the long history of discrimination, the reforms between 2000 and 2010 were revolutionary.

## SECULARISM IN TURKEY: A HISTORICAL OVERVIEW

State–religion relations in the Ottoman Empire had a two-tiered system. The state organized its relations with the Muslim majority through the office of the şeyhülislam,[2] while it conducted relations with non-Muslim minorities by giving them limited autonomy. The leaders of those religious minorities were the main interlocutors with the Ottoman sultan. This system was known as the *millet* ("nation") system, with each *millet* defined by religious affiliation, and it gave relative autonomy to non-Muslim minorities (Braude and Lewis 1982). The *millet* system recognized non-Muslims as minorities while considering Muslims to be the "core nation" (*millet-i hakime*) of the Ottoman Empire. The Ottoman Empire allowed religious minorities to implement their own legal systems in their social lives, mostly through civil law. In other words, "privileges and obligations were distributed not on the basis of political membership to the Ottoman state, but on the particularistic basis of peoples' communal membership" (İçduygu and Soner 2006, 450).

The office of the şeyhülislam was an important post in the Ottoman bureaucracy. The Ottoman sultan was regarded as the leader of the country in both political and religious terms, and the şeyhülislam was the sultan's representative in running religious affairs (Erdem 2008, 201). The authority of the office of the şeyhülislam increased over time, and the şeyhülislam became one of the leading bureaucrats of the empire. In the nineteenth century, the office's jurisdiction included religious services,

---

[2] The şeyhülislam was the head of the *ulema* ("learned"), the scholars of Islamic jurisprudence.

religious counseling, justice affairs, and educational services within the empire. In the words of Gazi Erdem (2008, 202), "This means that the functions and duties of the Ministry of Justice, Ministry of Education, the General Directorate of Foundations, and the Presidency of Religious Affairs of modern Turkey were carried out and implemented by the Office of the Şeyhülislam." It was the şeyhülislam who would make the final judgment on whether or not the Sultan's use of power was in line with the observance of *shari'a* (Islamic law) (Sakallıoğlu 1996, 233). However, the şeyhülislam was not independent in his decisions as were church organizations in Western Europe at the time. He was responsible to the sultan, and the Ottoman sultans dismissed many şeyhülislams when they did not agree with their legal advice (Erdem 2008, 203; cf Kara 2004). In the history of the office, 80 out of 130 şeyhülislams were dismissed by sultans and some others were forced to resign from duty (Erdem 2008, 206).

The şeyhülislam's role gradually diminished during the Tanzimat reforms, which played a major role in the secularization of Ottoman political institutions.[3] These reforms created "far-reaching liberalization that had profound cultural and social effects" (Yavuz 2003, 41). The reforms set up a duality between Ottoman state bodies, especially between the scholars of Islam (*ulama*) within the empire and the other bureaucrats (Berkes 1964, 155–248). The Tanzimat reforms deprived the şeyhülislam of much of his power. New secular courts were established even though the *shari'a* courts still continued to exist. This duality was also visible in education: madrasas were administered by the office of the şeyhülislam, but new secular schools were opened to educate civil and military bureaucrats. New secular judicial regulations were instituted (Berkes 1964, 160–200).[4]

With the transfer of power from the Sultan to the Committee of Union and Progress (1908–1918), the secularization of the Ottoman system reached its zenith.[5] The new government established new ministries in 1916; those ministries included the Ministry of Justice, responsible for all of the courts, and the Ministry of Education, overseeing all of the madrasas, schools, and other educational institutions (Erdem 2008, 205). From then on, the office of the şeyhülislam would be responsible for only religious affairs.

When a new government was established under the Turkish National Assembly in 1920, the functions that the şeyhülislam had fulfilled in the

---

[3] For historical accounts of modernizing Ottoman reforms, see Lewis 1968; Ahmad 1993; Zürcher 1993.

[4] For an extensive study of the place of Islam in politics in the late Ottoman period, see Karpat 2001.

[5] For more studies of the ideas of the Committee of Union and Progress, see Mardin 2000 [1962]; Hanioğlu 1995.

Ottoman Empire were transferred to the Ministry of Religious Affairs and Foundations. This ministry had more authority than the şeyhülislam of the Ottoman Empire, ranking as the second most important government office after that of Prime Minister (Erdem 2008, 206).

In March 1924, six months after the proclamation of the republic, the caliphate was promulgated. The Directorate of Religious Affairs replaced the Ministry of Religious Affairs and Foundations on the grounds that religion and politics needed to be separated (Gözaydın 2009, 59). With this change, the directorate would fulfill only religious functions and would not have any duty related to other issues such as education. Its role was to "administer the Islamic affairs of faith, rituals, moral principles, and to enlighten the society about religion and govern the places of worship" (Yavuz 2003, 49).[6] Although the aim in creating this office was to separate religion from state affairs, this change gave the state the opportunity to control religion. The directorate was attached to the undersecretary of the prime ministry. Religious institutions in Turkey came under the strict control of the state, and the state used them to consolidate the new national identity (Sakallıoğlu 1996, 234). The republic's founders used religion as "another force to glue the nation together," instead of purging it completely from state affairs (Turam 2007, 41).

Several secularizing reforms followed the establishment of the Directorate of Religious Affairs. On the same day that the directorate was opened, the madrasas were closed down. In 1925, the state banned all Sufi orders, their lodges (*tekke*), and their religious sanctuaries (*türbe*). This initiative was revolutionary in that it aimed to destroy the traditional form of Islam that had mobilized people for centuries (Ocak 1999, 109).[7] Between 1925 and 1928, traditional religious garments for men were banned and men were forced to wear European-style hats; Arabic script was replaced with Latin script; the Swiss civil code, German commercial law, and the Italian criminal code replaced Islamic law; and the Western calendar replaced the Islamic calendar. More importantly, Article 2 of the 1924 constitution, which designated Islam as the state religion, was annulled. Turkey completed its secularizing reforms in 1937 by inserting the principle of secularism into the constitution (Berkes 1964, 461–506).[8]

These reforms constitute an important moment in the evolution of Turkey's state–religion relations; developments in the following years did not change the main framework. Characteristics of this relationship can be summarized as follows. First, the founding fathers of the Turkish republic placed religion under the strict control of the state to facilitate the consolidation of the nation-

---

[6] For comprehensive studies of the Directorate of Religious Affairs, see Kara 2004; Gözaydın 2009.

[7] This law did not destroy the Sufi orders; it only caused them to go underground. Sufi orders became public again when the political atmosphere softened in Turkey in subsequent decades (Özdalga 1998, 26).

[8] For a critical account of secularist policies under one-party rule, see Başgil 2003 [1942].

state. As Hakan Yavuz (2003, 46) states, "in order to protect its founding ideology, the Kemalist elite opportunistically employed Islam for the realization of a modern secular Turkey."[9] In putting religion under the strict control of the state and installing the principle of secularism, the state eradicated religion from the public sphere. The state perceived any attempt that brought religion into the public sphere as a threat to the Turkish secular system.

Second, the leaders wanted to banish religion from the public realm and confine it to the private lives of the people. The leaders aimed to push religious practices into the private realm and disestablish social and political institutions influenced by Islam (Toprak 1981, 40). Even "Islamic activities in the private realm, unless confined to the individual, gradually came to be seen as subversive" (Turam 2007, 42).

Finally, the principle of secularism became instrumental in creating new republican elites and in controlling the social and political realm (Göle 1997, 49). Secularism became the major source of legitimacy for almost any Turkish political movement from the left to the right, even those with radically different aims (Dressler 2015, 87–89; Keyman 2007, 220–223; Özyürek 2006, 14). Secularism, in the minds of the new elites, was not only a legal provision but also an important worldview that shaped culture and lifestyle in Turkey (Ocak 1999, 104). This approach made secularism an instrumental tool in controlling Turkish society. In subsequent years, state elites used secularism as "an instrument of othering and criminalizing opposition" (Yavuz 2003, 247). For example, the military justified its interventions in the democratic system in 1960, 1971, 1980, and 1997 by arguing that they were reconstructing civilian politics to ensure the continuity of the secular nature of the regime (Cizre and Çınar 2003, 312).[10]

The state softened its policies toward religious groups to a certain extent after Turkey shifted to a multi-party democracy. In 1950, the Democratic Party, which claimed to represent the provincial populations against the secularist establishment, came to power. Until it was overthrown by a military coup in 1960, the Democratic Party implemented a relatively tolerant attitude toward religious groups, which "soothed the discontent of alienated religious masses" (Turam 2007, 44). One month after coming to power, the party annulled the law that required the call for prayer (*ezan*) to be read in Turkish (Özdalga 1998, 34). It introduced religious radio broadcasts, permitted voluntary religious courses in primary schools, and opened several prayer-leader and preacher schools (*imam-hatip liseleri*) (Sakallıoğlu 1996, 237).[11]

---

[9] Along the same lines, Berna Turam (2007, 41) writes that "Starting from this early Republican period, Turkish history has been an experiment in *integrating* Islam into the secular institutional milieu rather than totally abolishing it or merely separating from it" (cf Davison 2003, 341).

[10] For an extensive review of state–Islam relations in Turkey, see Cizre 1999.

[11] It should also be mentioned that prayer-leader and preacher schools and the Faculty of Divinity at Ankara University were first opened in the last years of the one-party regime under the Republican People's Party.

The Justice Party (Adalet Partisi), the center-right party established by the followers of the Democratic Party, dominated the period between the 1960 military intervention and the 1980 coup. The party used Islam as a powerful weapon against communism, which was on the rise in the 1970s in Turkey (Sakallıoğlu 1996, 240). The Justice Party supported religion by building new prayer-leader and preacher schools. The number of such schools increased from 26 to 219 between 1965 and 1977 (Sakallıoğlu 1996, 239).

The first Islamic-oriented political party was also founded in this period. The National Order Party (Milli Nizam Partisi) was established in 1970 under the leadership of Necmettin Erbakan with a distinctly nationalist-religious tone. The Constitutional Court closed down the party in 1971 on the grounds that it was exploiting religion for political purposes. Erbakan and his followers established a new party, the National Salvation Party (Milli Selamet Partisi), in 1972. The party received almost 10 percent of the votes in the 1973 and 1977 elections and played an important role by participating in coalition governments throughout the 1970s. The military regime that came to power after the 1980 coup closed down the party, along with others, in 1981 (Dağı 2005, 24–26).

The 1980 military coup was an important turning point for state–religion relations in Turkey. The military government that ruled the country between 1980 and 1983 supported religion as a way to balance the "communist threat." The 1982 constitution prepared by the military regime instituted compulsory religious classes in primary and secondary schools.[12] The state expanded religious services and used the Directorate of Religious Affairs for the "promotion of national solidarity and integration" (Karakas 2007, ii).

After the military regime, the Motherland Party (Anavatan Partisi), under the leadership of Turgut Özal, came to power in the 1983 parliamentary election. Özal's neoliberal policies radically transformed Turkey by opening its economic and political spheres to the world. Özal's policies "definitely contributed to the expansion of the public sphere in multiple directions" (Turam 2007, 49). In this period, the monopoly of the secular establishment was broken to some extent. The government "tolerated Islamic elements in the political-public realm that had until that point been under the monopoly of secular standards and criteria" (Sakallıoğlu 1996, 244). These policies increased the political strength of Islamic groups in the post-1983 era even though they still did not have full access to power.

Islamic political parties became very influential in this era, especially after Özal's death in 1991. Necmeddin Erbakan's followers founded a new party, the Welfare Party (Refah Partisi), in 1983, when the military government resumed democratic elections. The party's share of the vote in elections gradually increased in the course of the 1980s and 1990s. The party gained the support

---

[12] For a study of the place of secularism and religious liberty in the 1982 constitution, see Erdoğan 2005.

of the urban poor through its election campaigns emphasizing social welfare programs. The party ranked first in the 1995 elections, receiving 21.1 percent of the popular vote. After the failure of a coalition government formed by center-right parties, the Welfare Party formed a government in coalition with the center-right True Path Party (Doğru Yol Partisi) in 1996. Necmettin Erbakan became the prime minister in the new government. The Islamists' rise to power as a coalition partner drew the attention of the secularist bureaucracy, particularly the military, which strictly monitored the government.

While in power, the Welfare Party could not stop the increasing polarization of the country. The military, along with the civilian component of the secular establishment, launched a campaign against the Welfare Party by arguing that the coalition government was a threat to the secular nature of the republic. This campaign against the government gained the support of mainstream business people and media networks, challenged by the rise of a new bourgeoisie supported by the policies of the Welfare Party (Yavuz 2003, 240). These pressures reached their high point on February 28, 1997, when the National Security Council forced the government to enact a set of laws and regulations aimed at clamping down on Islamic movements. After the declaration of the February 28 decisions, pressure from the military and its civil supporters forced the Welfare Party to resign in June 1997. Meanwhile, the public prosecutor sued the party in the Constitutional Court on the basis that it had become a focal point for antisecular activities. The court closed down the party in January 1998 (Kılınç 2014b). After the party was disbanded, the Welfare Party deputies joined the Virtue Party (Fazilet Partisi), which was established before the Constitutional Court's decision to replace the Welfare Party in case of a possible closure.

As a result of the military-led campaign which forced the Welfare Party from power, the social and economic bases of Islamic-oriented social and political groups were weakened (Dağı 2005, 27). The military expanded its control over different areas, from education to politics, from the judiciary to business (Yavuz 2003, 246). The initiators of this process reconstructed the political and economic structure of the country to reestablish the ideological power of "assertive secularism" (Kuru 2009). Several restrictions on Islamic groups came into force immediately after the 28 February decisions. Hundreds of female university students had to drop out their schools because of strict dress regulations that banned the wearing of headscarves on campuses. Firms that had been established by pious people were discriminated against by the state.

After the 1997 military intervention, Islamists moderated their political vision and embraced democratization reforms in the following decade. The Virtue Party developed a democratic discourse, giving up its nationalist/religious discourse and making democracy and human rights an important part of its program. In its election campaign in 1999, the Virtue Party supported Turkey's bid for European Union (EU) membership and promised its electorate to improve human rights in Turkey. The party received 15 percent of the votes in the 1999 elections. The decrease in the party's share of votes (from 21.1 percent to 15 percent) facilitated intra-party opposition. The younger reformist wing, led by Recep Tayyip Erdoğan, criticized the senior traditionalists by isolating the party from larger populations (Kılınç 2014b, 303–310).

These diverging viewpoints created two political parties after the abolishing of the Virtue Party by the Constitutional Court in 2001. The reformist wing established the Justice and Development Party (AKP, Adalet ve Kalkınma Partisi) while the traditionalist wing formed the Felicity Party (Saadet Partisi). The AKP renounced its Islamic credentials and courted the center-right electorate by identifying its political identity as conservative democracy. The Felicity Party claimed to follow the vision and mission of the Welfare Party tradition. The AKP won the 2002 parliamentary elections with a majority and formed a single-party government.[13]

In its early years in power, the AKP denounced Islamism and pursued a democratic political strategy (Driessen 2014, 201). In an effort to pursue democratic policies, the AKP, with the backing of liberals, minorities, and other Islamic groups, supported Turkey's bid for membership of the EU. It was this democratic coalition that weakened the military and strengthened Turkish democracy in the 2000s. The AKP and its allies passed reforms related to the status of Christian minorities in Turkey, as discussed in the next section of this chapter. The AKP continued to further the EU reform packages that its predecessor governments had started to implement in 1999, after Turkey became a candidate country to the EU. However, once the AKP had weakened the military's role in politics, it turned to authoritarianism in the 2010s in an effort to control the political system.

## STATE POLICIES TOWARD CHRISTIANS

The legal status of Christian minorities in Turkey was established by the 1923 Treaty of Lausanne, the founding treaty of the Turkish republic. In this treaty, Turkey recognized non-Muslims as legal minorities and denied other ethnic and linguistic groups the status of minority; it guaranteed equal treatment to Christian minorities as well as Jews. Although the Treaty of Lausanne identified minorities in Turkey as "non-Muslims," the Turkish state pursued a selective approach in implementing the provisions of the treaty. The state identified three groups as minorities: Armenian Orthodox Christians, Greek Orthodox Christians, and Jews. Other groups were not granted the status of minority. Minority status is important in Turkey because it grants certain privileges to recognized groups. Christian minorities that did not have this status, such as the Syriac community, had difficulties in keeping their religious

---

[13] The party continued winning elections and forming single-party governments from that point until the time of writing in 2018.

identities alive. The lack of status prevented them opening new places of worship and using their languages in publications.[14] According to the Treaty of Lausanne, the "recognized" Christian minorities would be free to open their own schools in their own languages (which was banned for all other groups), to profess their own religions freely, and "to establish and operate whatever charitable, religious, social, and educational institutions they wished" (Shaw and Shaw 1976, 367).

The rights of the non-Muslim minorities guaranteed by the Treaty of Lausanne have systematically been violated by the state. In this section I review the problems that Christian minorities confronted and the reforms that aimed to solve these problems between 2000 and 2010. The major problems that Christian minorities faced can be grouped under four headings (Kılınç 2014a): (1) acquisition and disposal of real estate owned by the community foundations[15] of Christian minorities; (2) restrictions on religious education, especially in training of the clergy; (3) the opening of places of worship; and (4) the lack of a legal personality for religious institutions.

### Acquisition and Disposal of Real Estate by Community Foundations

For a long time, community foundations in Turkey lacked the right to purchase real estate and dispose of it. They could not even register the real estate that already belonged *de facto* to them. This issue came to the fore especially after 1974, when Turkey had political problems with Greece over Cyprus.

Since the Ottoman era, Christians in Turkey had operated foundations to finance their religious and charitable services. These foundations were generally established by decrees of the Ottoman sultans and did not have founding charters. The foundations gained legal personality through a law passed in 1912 by the Ottoman parliament and were then able to register their properties under their legal personality. However, the modern Turkish state did not pass any law regarding community foundations until 1935. According to the Law on Foundations passed on June 5, 1935 (Law No. 2762),[16] community foundations had to declare their properties to the state organ of the General Directorate of Foundations (GDF, Vakıflar Genel Müdürlüğü).[17] The community foundations declared their properties in 1936 without knowing that this would create several problems forty years

---

[14] Author's interview with Zeki Basatemir, President of the Istanbul Syriac Foundation, Istanbul, Turkey, June 22, 2012.

[15] "Community foundations," in legal terms, refers to the foundations owned by non-Muslim minorities in Turkey.

[16] "2762 Sayılı Vakıflar Kanunu," Law No. 2762, June 5, 1935, available at www.vgm.gov.tr /001_Menu/02_Mevzuat/01_Kanun/2762.cfm (last accessed on June 16, 2016).

[17] The General Directorate of Foundations is the state organ that deals with issues related to community foundations.

later (Reyna and Şen 1994, 82).[18] The foundations also declared other properties that they acquired after 1936 to the city administrations, and these properties were registered in the name of the community foundations by the written statements of the city administrations (Reyna and Şen 1994, 87).

In late 1960s, the Turkish state began to use its Greek minority population as a bargaining tool in its relations with Greece. The dispute over Cyprus between Turkey and Greece led the Turkish state to implement policies discomforting to the Christian minorities. In the late 1960s the GDF asked the community foundations to submit their founding charters (*vakıfname*). Because most of the community foundations had been established by decrees of the Ottoman sultans, they did not have charters and thus they failed to submit charters to the GDF. The GDF then issued a ruling according to which the declarations submitted by the community foundations in 1936 would be considered to be the charters of the foundations. This was the first step toward the state's seizure of the community foundations' properties. The community foundations objected to this decision, but their objections made no difference (Oran 2004, 83–86).

As the next step, the GDF expropriated real estate acquired by the community foundations after 1936 on the ground that these foundations could not acquire property because they had not stated their intention to acquire property in their 1936 "charters." In fact, given that these were just declarations of properties owned by the community foundations at the time, there were no means by which they could have been expected to state an intention to acquire new properties. The properties expropriated by the GDF were returned to their previous owners or the previous owners' beneficiaries without any cost. In the cases where there were no inheritors, they were transferred to the state treasury (Oran 2007). These expropriations created legal disputes between the GDF and the community foundations.

In the first legal dispute, the Balıklı Greek Hospital sued the treasury in 1971 on the grounds that its property (acquired after 1936) was transferred to the treasury without any legal grounds. The local court found the expropriation legal. The Balıklı Greek Hospital appealed the court decision, and in May 1974 the Court of Appeals upheld the decision of the local court.[19] The highest office within the Court of Appeals also upheld the decision in June 1975.[20] From then on, other community foundations lost their properties on the grounds that they had not stated in their "charters" that they would acquire or dispose of real estate. The Council of State gave similar verdicts in several cases which were brought to its agenda by community foundations.[21] This situation continued until August 2002, when the parliament passed a new law that would allow community foundations to acquire and dispose of real estate.

---

[18] The declaration made by community foundations is generally known as the "1936 Declaration."
[19] "Hukuk Genel Kurulu," No. 1974/505, May 8, 1974.
[20] "Yargıtay 1. Hukuk Dairesi," No. 3648–6595, June 24, 1975.
[21] For example, see "Danıştay 12. Daire," No. 1976/1508, June 21, 1976. See Oran 2004, 86.

After Turkey gained EU candidacy status in 1999, the Turkish parliament instituted several reforms to ameliorate human rights issues in Turkey. The status of Christian minorities in Turkey was not an exception. The Turkish parliament passed four major laws regarding the issue of property rights for community foundations. The first three of these laws amended the 1935 law (No. 2762) under the framework of "European Union Harmonization Laws," so the impact of Turkey's EU candidacy on the passing of these laws is obvious. The final law, which replaces the previous Law on Foundations (No. 2762), came after frequent pressure from EU officials.

The first amendment to the Law on Foundations came on August 3, 2002 (Law No. 4771) with a legislative package that amended several legal regulations in Turkey to meet the criteria for EU membership.[22] This amendment stated that community foundations were allowed to acquire or dispose of property in order to meet their religious, charitable, social welfare, educational, health, and cultural needs. The amendment also allowed the foundations to register properties under their names that were clearly substantiated by tax records, rental agreements, and other documentation and that were used by these foundations in whatever way they saw fit to meet their religious, charitable, social welfare, educational, health, and cultural needs.[23] This amendment prevented the GDF from seizing community foundations' properties on the grounds that they had not indicated in their charters that they planned to acquire new properties. The law enabled community foundations to acquire or dispose of real estate. It also gave them the opportunity to register the properties that had been used by them.

This law did not resolve the injustices that had been imposed by the state since the 1974 decision of the Court of Appeals. The approval of the Council of Ministers was required for community foundations to acquire or dispose of real estate. This was not something required of other foundations, and it would lengthen the process for community foundations because the Council of Ministers would be unlikely to issue approvals quickly due to its busy schedule. Furthermore, although the law allowed the community foundations to acquire or dispose of property, it did not give their confiscated properties back to them. The state expropriated a number of properties from the community foundations after 1974, but the law did not mention them. The law gave the community foundations the opportunity to register the properties that were in their use (i.e., those not confiscated by the state and not registered under the community foundations).

Having considered the drawbacks of the law, the government proposed a new amendment to the Law on Foundations on January 2, 2003, along with several

---

[22] Ersin Kalkan, "Azınlık vakıflarında kaybedilmiş eşeği bulmanın sevinci," *Hürriyet*, August 10, 2002.
[23] "Çeşitli Kanunlarda Değişiklik Yapılmasına İlişkin Kanun," Law No. 4771, August 3, 2002, available at the website of the Turkish parliament: www.tbmm.gov.tr/kanunlar/k4771.html (last accessed on June 18, 2017). This law is also known as the Third European Union Harmonization Law. The translation here was made by Otmar Oehring (2004, 11).

other changes.[24] This package, generally known as the Fourth European Union Harmonization Law, shifted the authority to approve whether community foundations could acquire or dispose of property from the Council of Ministers to the GDF. The government passed an additional amendment on July 15, 2003, because several community foundations had been unable to finish filing their claims within the time frame specified in the previous law passed in August 2002. The July 2003 law, which came as part of the Sixth European Union Harmonization Law, extended the submission period for non-Muslim foundations to eighteen months, starting on the day that the amendment came into force.

Although these amendments eased the registration process for community foundations, there were still problems with the law. The amendments did not remove unequal treatment of non-Muslim minorities. Even though the GDF would approve the applications of the foundations to acquire new properties, it would first solicit the recommendations of related ministries and public agencies. The state agencies alluded to were the Ministry of Foreign Affairs and the security and intelligence agencies. This showed the lawmakers' perception of non-Muslim Turkish citizens as "foreign" and "suspect" (Oran 2007, 53).

Although somewhat limited in content, these legal amendments not only improved circumstances for the non-Muslim minorities, but also gradually changed the state's approach toward minorities. For example, the Higher Council for Minorities, which was established in 1962 in secret and had met in secret since then, whose membership was also secret and whose decisions were binding, was said to have been dissolved in February 2004.[25] Along the same lines, in 2005, the Council of State made a decision in favor of a community foundation (Büyükada Rum Erkek ve Kız Yetimhanesi Vakfı) in a property dispute with the GDF. The court decided that the GDF did not have the authority to expropriate the properties of community foundations if the properties had been in use by the foundation.[26]

These legal amendments gave community foundations the right to acquire or dispose of real estate, and to register their unregistered properties that were in use; however, these laws did not give the properties expropriated by the state back to the non-Muslim community foundations. This omission was frequently criticized by international organizations and agencies and by non-Muslim groups in Turkey. To address this problem, the government proposed a new bill in late 2006. Instead of making new amendments, this bill would repeal the previous Law on Foundations (Law No. 2762) and would enact a new law.

Considering the Turkish state's practice with regard to foundations over the republican era, this new bill was revolutionary. The bill would lift all restrictions on acquiring and disposing of property. Community foundations would not need the approval of the GDF to acquire and dispose of property. The foundations would be free to establish companies to boost their income. Most importantly,

---

[24] *Radikal*, "Cemaate iyi haber," January 25, 2003.
[25] Şükrü Küçükşahin, "Sessiz Azınlık Devrimi," *Hürriyet*, February 23, 2004.
[26] *Zaman*, "Danıştay: Azınlık vakıflarına el konulamaz," July 30, 2005.

the GDF would then give all the properties expropriated after 1974 back to the community foundations. Non-Muslim community foundations would have a representative in the fifteen-member assembly of the GDF. Community foundations would be free to cooperate with foundations in foreign countries, both in their activities and for financial matters. This opened up the opportunity for community foundations to accept financial contributions from abroad. The law would also allow foreigners to establish foundations in Turkey. This point was especially important for the Protestant minority in Turkey because many of them did not have Turkish citizenship.

The parliament passed the bill on foundations in November 2006,[27] but President Ahmet Necdet Sezer vetoed the bill on the grounds that it was against the Treaty of Lausanne.[28] The government did not bring this bill to the parliament's agenda until the end of Sezer's presidency. Abdullah Gül, one of the sponsors of the Law on Foundations, became president in August 2007, after which the government again brought the Law on Foundations to the parliament's agenda. The new bill underwent very minor revisions, but the main components of the previous bill was kept. The parliament passed the bill on February 20, 2008 (Law No. 5737), [29] and the president approved it on February 26, 2008.[30]

The law seemed to have resolved several of the issues related to community foundations; but there were still problems. The most important unresolved issue concerned the expropriated properties transferred to third parties by the GDF. Although the community foundations would get back the properties confiscated by the state, the law did not allow the returning of properties that had been transferred to third parties through sale or for any other reason. There were also problems in the bureaucratic implementation of the law. To facilitate its implementation by local bureaucrats, the prime minister's office issued a circular in May 2010. In a historic move in August 2011, the cabinet issued a decree by which the state was required to pay compensation to community foundations for properties transferred to third parties.[31] These laws brought significant improvements for the Christian minority on the issue of property rights.

### Religious Education

There have been two issues at stake regarding the rights of Christian minority in Turkey to religious education: (1) the use of minority languages in education, press, and radio and television broadcasts and (2) the training of clergy. The state had not allowed the use of local languages other than Turkish in publications,

---

[27] *Hürriyet*, "Yabancılar Türkiye'de vakıf kurabilecek," November 3, 2006.

[28] *Hürriyet*, "Sezer Vakıflar Yasasını veto etti," November 29, 2006.

[29] *Radikal*, "Vakıflar Yasası'na TBMM'den ikinci onay," February 21, 2008; "Vakıflar Kanunu," Law No. 5737, February 20, 2008, available at the website of the Turkish parliament: www .tbmm.gov.tr/kanunlar/k5737.html (last accessed on June 18, 2017).

[30] *Radikal*, "Cemaat vakıflarının mal edinmesini sağlayan yasaya onay," February 27, 2008.

[31] Mine Tuduk, "Azınlıklara Çifte Bayram," *Radikal*, August 29, 2011.

educational institutions, radio and television broadcasts, political meetings, etc. (i.e. in the areas outside private life) until the early 2000s. The only groups that were exempt from this policy were the minorities that are "recognized" as a "minority" under the Treaty of Lausanne: Armenians, Greeks, and Jews. These minorities had their own schools and publishing houses, and they used their own languages in educational and publishing activities.[32] Other Christian minorities that are not recognized by the state within the meaning of the Treaty of Lausanne were not allowed to have their own schools or publishing houses. For example, two monasteries in Southeastern Turkey (Mor Gabriel Monastery and Deyr-ül Zaferan Monastery) reported that they could not teach their children in their mother tongues (Surit and Turoyo) or teach their clergy in their liturgical language, Suroyo (Oehring 2004, 25).

With regard to the training of clergy, the situation is much more complicated. According to Article 24 of the Turkish constitution, religious education cannot be offered outside state control.[33] In other words, religious groups, regardless of whether they are Muslims or not, cannot open educational institutions to teach religion; religious education is under the monopoly of the state. Although the recognized minorities should have been exempted from this rule according to the provisions of the Treaty of Lausanne, the state did not allow the minorities to open higher educational institutions to train their own clergy.[34]

The reforms undertaken by the Turkish government in the first decade of this century improved conditions for minorities on the issue of the use of different languages other than Turkish, but improvements on the issue of the training of clergy remained very limited. Between 2002 and 2005, the Turkish parliament, in order to grant minorities the rights to use their own languages, amended the Law on the Press (Law No. 5680);[35] the Law on Foreign Language Education and Teaching (Law No. 2923);[36] and the Law on the Establishment and Broadcasting of Radio Stations and Television Channels (Law No. 3984).[37]

---

[32] Ironically, these groups were not allowed to open radio and television stations in their own languages until very recently, because such provision was not included in the Treaty of Lausanne. When the treaty was signed in 1923, radio and television facilities were not widely, if at all, known. The Turkish state interpreted the treaty very narrowly so as not to give this right to the recognized minorities as well.

[33] Constitution of the Republic of Turkey, available at www.tbmm.gov.tr/Anayasa.htm (last accessed on June 18, 2017).

[34] However it should be noted that Greek Orthodox and Armenian Orthodox Christians had their own schools until 1971, when a Constitutional Court decision made this practice impossible. The details will come later in the chapter.

[35] The law is available at the website of the Directorate General of Press and Information: www .byegm.gov.tr/basinmevzuati/kanunlar.htm (last accessed on June 5, 2015).

[36] The law is available at the website of the Ministry of National Education: http://mevzuat .meb.gov.tr/html/136.html (last accessed on June 18, 2017).

[37] The law is available at the website of the Higher Council of Radio and Television: www .rtuk.gov.tr/sayfalar/IcerikGoster.aspx?icerik_id=45bb098-100d-409d-b448-cba6831399a4 (last accessed on June 5, 2015).

The parliament amended the Law on the Press on March 26, 2002, under the Second European Union Harmonization Law to lift any restrictions on publishing in languages other than Turkish.[38] By this law, the previously unrecognized religious minorities gained the right to publish books, newspapers, and other publications in their own languages. This law made possible the use of liturgical languages in religious affairs. This change was preserved when the parliament repealed the Law on the Press and introduced a new version (Law No. 5187) on June 9, 2004.[39]

The parliament amended the Law on Foreign Language Education and Teaching twice to allow minorities to teach their own languages in private courses and educational institutions. The amended law allowed the establishment of courses for local languages in existing educational institutions. The first amendment came under the Third European Union Harmonization Law on August 3, 2002.[40] This amendment changed the title of the law to include languages spoken in Turkey: "The Law on Foreign Language Education and Teaching, and the Learning of the Different Languages and Dialects of Turkish Citizens." The law also allowed the establishment of language courses to teach the languages and dialects used in Turkey. Parliament made a second amendment to this law in its Seventh European Union Harmonization Law on July 30, 2003.[41] This law made minor changes to clearly state that Turkish was the official language.[42] The law amended relevant articles of the constitution to ease the implementation of the law on language instruction.

Although these amendments in the Law on Foreign Language Education and Teaching improved the situation for minorities, they could not solve the problems completely. The law specified several qualifications necessary to become a teacher of a minority language.[43] Teachers were required to hold Turkish citizenship, to have had an education related to teaching the language

---

[38] "Çeşitli Kanunlarda Değişiklik Yapılmasına İlişkin Kanun," Law No. 4748, March 26, 2002, available at the website of the Turkish parliament: www.tbmm.gov.tr/kanunlar/k4748.html (last accessed on June 18, 2017).

[39] "Basın Kanunu," Law No. 5187, June 9, 2004, available at www.tbmm.gov.tr/kanunlar/k5187 .html (last accessed on June 18, 2017).

[40] "Çeşitli Kanunlarda Değişiklik Yapılmasına İlişkin Kanun," Law No. 4771, August 3, 2002; available at the website of the Turkish parliament: www.tbmm.gov.tr/kanunlar/k4771.html (last accessed on June 18, 2017).

[41] "Çeşitli Kanunlarda Değişiklik Yapılmasına İlişkin Kanun," Law No. 4963, July 30, 2003; available at the website of the Turkish parliament: www.tbmm.gov.tr/kanunlar/k4963.html (last accessed on June 18, 2017).

[42] Actually, the amendment goes further than saying that Turkish is the official language. It states: "No languages other than Turkish can be taught to Turkish citizens in schools as their mother tongue." By this statement, the law assumes that Turkish is the mother tongue for all Turkish citizens.

[43] "Türk Vatandaşlarının Günlük Yaşamlarında Geleneksel Olarak Kullandıkalrı Farklı Dil ve Lehçelerin Öğrenilmesi Hakkında Yönetmelik," published in Official Gazette on December 5, 2003, No. 25307, available at the website of the Ministry of National Education: http://mevzuat .meb.gov.tr/html/25307_0.html (last accessed on June 18, 2017).

in question, and to have had at least a university degree. It was difficult for minorities to find teachers that meet all the requirements.

The final set of legal regulations was passed in the Law on the Establishment and Broadcasting of Radio Stations and Television Channels to allow broadcasting in different languages and dialects traditionally used by Turkish citizens. The amendment that came under the Third European Union Harmonization Law stated that "there may be broadcasts in different languages and dialects used by Turkish citizens in their daily lives."[44] A second amendment passed on July 15, 2003, allowed state and public radio and television channels, as well as private ones, to broadcast in different languages and dialects used by Turkish citizens.[45]

Another issue related to the educational rights of the Christian minorities is the training of clergy. The Armenian and Greek minorities in Turkey had their own seminaries until the 1970s, but their seminaries were closed down in 1970 and 1971 respectively due to a Constitutional Court decision which nationalized all private institutions of higher education.[46] Although this problem influenced all religious minority groups living in Turkey, the status of the Theological School of Halki became well known because of the international lobbying activities of the Greek Orthodox Patriarch of Istanbul.[47] The recent reforms did not make any improvement on the issue of the training of the clergy. The Theological School of Halki's status has been widely discussed by the government but no solution has yet been reached.

This school was opened in 1844 to train the Orthodox clergy and continued to do so after the establishment of the Turkish republic until its closure in 1971. Between 1950 and 1964, the school was allowed to enroll international students. The Orthodox Patriarchate in Istanbul has lobbied since 1971 to reopen the school. Since the reform process regarding the Christian minorities started, Patriarch Bartholomew has met several state officials including then Foreign Minister Abdullah Gül[48] and Minister of National Education Hüseyin Çelik[49] to discuss the reopening of the school. He also solicited international

---

[44] "Çeşitli Kanunlarda Değişiklik Yapılmasına İlişkin Kanun," Law No. 4771, August 3, 2002, available at the website of the Turkish parliament: www.tbmm.gov.tr/kanunlar/k4771.html (last accessed on June 18, 2017).

[45] "Çeşitli Kanunlarda Değişiklik Yapılmasına İlişkin Kanun," Law No. 4928, July 15, 2003, available at the website of the Turkish parliament: www.tbmm.gov.tr/kanunlar/k4928.html (last accessed on June 18, 2017).

[46] *Hürriyet*, "Özel Yüksek Okullar Kapatılacak," January 13, 1971.

[47] The name of this school has been translated into different English forms. Some other translations are Halki Seminary, the Heybeliada School of Theology, Halki Theological School, and Heybeliada Theological Seminary. I chose Theological School of Halki since it preferred by the school's website: www.ec-patr.org/mones/chalki/english.htm (last accessed on June 18, 2017). The Turkish original is Heybeliada Ruhban Okulu.

[48] İbrahim Asalıoğlu, "Bartholomeos, ruhban okulu için resmi müracaatını yaptı," *Zaman*, October 31, 2003.

[49] Kaan İpekçioğlu, "Ruhban Okuluna Vize," *Yeni Şafak*, August 9, 2003.

support for the opening of the seminary. He met with the presidents of the United States and of the EU.

Between 2002 and 2008 the government came up with a number of proposals, but reconciliation between the government and the Patriarchate could not be reached. The government wanted to allow the school to reopen provided that it would be under state supervision. In one proposal, it would be tied to Istanbul University, a public university; in the other, it would serve as a vocational school under the auspices of the Ministry of National Education.[50] The Patriarchate wanted the school to be under its own control independent of the state, because state control might curtail the Orthodox Church's ability to control the school curriculum (Yannas 2007, 67). The state opposed this solution because it would open the door for other religious groups, including Muslims, to open their own independent religious schools. The Patriarchate and the state have disagreed over whether the school would recruit foreign students and teachers. The Patriarchate has been very insistent on this issue because the school would have difficulty recruiting students and teachers from Turkey: there are only around 3,000 followers of Greek Orthodoxy in Turkey. The state has been against the recruitment of foreign students and teachers because that would consolidate the Patriarchate's status as the leader of world Orthodox churches. While the Patriarchate claims to be the Ecumenical Patriarchate, the state recognizes it only as the office for the Greek Orthodox citizens of Turkey (Macar 2003, 55), as discussed later in this chapter.

The Ministry of Foreign Affairs sought to reach a solution on the issue of the Theological School of Halki between 2005 and 2010, on the basis that this would strengthen Turkey's hand in its negotiations with the EU. In 2008 the Minister of Foreign Affairs, Ali Babacan, announced new proposals under which the Ministry of National Education and the Council of Higher Education would work to reopen the school.[51] However, other state organs and nationalist groups in Turkey opposed the reopening of the school because they saw it as detrimental to the national interests of Turkey.[52] Their hesitation came from their suspicions that the school might play a role in boosting the national interests of Greece.[53]

## Opening of Places of Worship

Christian minorities in Turkey faced legal limitations on the opening of places of worship until June 2003. This was not a problem for the congregations of the

---

[50] Dilek Güngör, "Ruhban için kavga," *Radikal*, June 20, 2004; Hilal Köylü, "Ruhban Okuluna formül bulundu," *Radikal*, June 24, 2004.
[51] Gündem, "AKP'nin Ruhban Okulu aşkı," *Ortadoğu*, January 27, 2008.
[52] Ismet Berkan, "İki Kilise Öyküsü," *Radikal*, November 29, 2004; Sedat Ergin, "Milli Güvenlik Siyaset Belgesi Değiştiriliyor," *Hürriyet*, November 24, 2004.
[53] Yusuf Gedikli, "Heybeliada Ruhban Okulu açılmalı mı?" *Ufuk Ötesi*, August 23–29, 2002.

Armenian and Greek Orthodox Churches because their existing places of worship were enough to meet their religious needs. However, Syriacs living in Istanbul and Protestants who had recently migrated to Turkey needed new places of worship. This had been a particular problem for expatriate communities living in Turkey.[54] Turkish laws assumed that all places of worship in Turkey would necessarily be mosques and did not have regulations for the opening of churches.

Until 2003, Turkish legal statutes never referrerred to "churches" in their regulations regarding construction and city planning. The government addressed this issue through an amendment made in the Law on Construction (Law No. 3194) on July 15, 2003. Accordingly, several articles of the law were rephrased to address the need for places of worship for people of different religious traditions.[55] Before the amendment, the Law on Construction referrerred only to mosques; the amendment replaced the word "mosque" with the phrase "place of worship" to include all religious groups living in Turkey. Religious communities were granted the right to open places of worship with the permission of local administrators. This law also gave churches *de jure* the same status as mosques. This allowed churches to use public resources as mosques did, so churches were able to use water and electricity free of charge (Goltz 2006, 176). On the basis of this amendment, the Council of State overruled on June 21, 2005, a decision of a local administrative court in Ankara that would prevent churches from the right to use water and energy for free.[56]

The enactment of a law was not enough to allow Christian minorities to open churches without difficulties. The implementation of the law created some problems. In the regulations enacted to implement the law, the state decided that a church needed a certain number of followers in the area in order to operate. This has been a problem for several religious groups whose members' homes are dispersed among different areas. Another problem stemmed from the fact that the Turkish state did not recognize religion-based organizations. Churches in Turkey (as well as other religious organizations) do not have legal personality. The lack of legal personality created the problem of who could apply to open a church. The most successful way had been to establish cultural associations, as did Muslims who wanted to open mosques. Alevis established cultural associations to open their own worship houses, *cemevis*. Churches were averse to this idea, though, because this arrangement would narrow their control over their own places of worship.[57]

---

[54] Hugh Pope, "Rahibin kilise çilesi," *Radikal*, November 29, 2004.
[55] "Çeşitli Kanunlarda Değişiklik Yapılmasına İlişkin Kanun," Law No. 4928, July 15, 2003, available at the website of the Turkish parliament: www.tbmm.gov.tr/kanunlar/k4928.html (last accessed on June 18, 2017).
[56] *Radikal*, "Kiliseler için bedava su yolu açılıyor," June 22, 2005.
[57] Adnan Keskin and Tarık Işık, "Kilise açabilirsiniz demek dile kolay," *Radikal*, May 26, 2004.

## The Lack of Legal Personality

One of the key problems with regard to the Christian minority that did not improve in the reform process was that the Turkish state does not grant legal personality to religious organizations. The Armenian and Greek Orthodox Patriarchates, and the other Christian Churches in Turkey, do not operate legally.[58] After the proclamation of the republic, the state repealed the legal status of all religious organizations.[59] The state nationalized Islam through the Directorate of Religious Affairs,[60] and left others unrepresented. Religious groups, including the Christian minorities, have organized around culturally- and socially based foundations and associations.

The lack of legal personality creates several problems. Churches cannot engage in legal transactions, nor can they solicit their rights in the courts when their rights are violated. For example, when the Theological School of Halki was closed down in 1971, the Greek Patriarchate applied to the Council of State to overrule the decision. The application was turned down on the ground that the Patriarchate did not have the right to file a suit since it did not have legal personality.[61]

Christian Churches in Turkey have met with Turkish officials and the representatives of international organizations in attempts to resolve the question of legal personality (Oehring 2004, 47–50). While international organizations have imposed pressure on Turkey for a resolution of the problem, the Turkish state sees the practice of not recognizing religious organizations legally as a constitutional requirement of the principle of secularism. The state is concerned that Muslim communities will derive for themselves rights to form autonomous institutions if the state gives legal personality to non-Muslim religious organizations (Goltz 2006, 179).

Another issue related to the lack of legal personality is the dispute between the Turkish state and the Greek Orthodox Patriarchate over the title of the Patriarch. The Turkish authorities do not allow the Patriarch to use the term "Ecumenical" in his title, recognizing him only as the head of Turkey's Greek Orthodox community. The Patriarchate, on the other hand, claims that "Ecumenical Patriarch" is the historical title of the Istanbul Patriarch among Orthodox Christians. The Turkish state does not want to recognize the title "ecumenical" because it considers the title to be in conflict with the sovereignty of the Turkish state. To the state, the title allows the Patriarch to have

---

[58] Orhan Kemal Cengiz, "Temel sorun: Tüzel kişilik," *Radikal*, May 27, 2004.

[59] This is valid also for Muslims and other religious groups. The only church that has some sort of legal personality is the Catholic Church; however, it is not regarded as a "Church," but as a diplomatic representative of the "Vatican State." In terms of a religious organization, the Catholic Church also lacks legal personality in Turkey.

[60] This is also criticized by several Muslim groups on the grounds that the state has the monopoly over the interpretation and practice of Islam in Turkey.

[61] Elçin Macar, "Çözüm gibi bir çözüm şart," *Radikal*, July 13, 2004.

a territorial claim over Turkey as being the head of the world's Orthodox Christians.

Table 2.1 summarizes the reforms undertaken to improve the status of Christians in Turkey.

CONCLUSION

Turkish institutions dealing with state–religion relations were shaped during the early republican period. The secularists in Turkey gained the upper hand because of the authoritarian one-party rule that they built. The one-party state imposed its secularizing reforms between 1924 and 1937, purging Islam from the public sphere. In the following years, the state maintained the secular nature of the republic and restrained religious actors in their activities. In doing so,

TABLE 2.1 *Reforms improving the status of Christian minorities*

| Subject | Law No. | Date Passed | Improvements |
|---|---|---|---|
| Acquisition and disposal of real estate by community foundations | 4771 | August 3, 2002 | Non-Muslim community foundations had the right to acquire and dispose of property with the approval of the Council of Ministers. |
| | | | Such foundations had the right to register the unregistered properties in their names. |
| | 4778 | January 2, 2003 | The authority to approve the acquisition or disposal of real estate by community foundations was shifted to the General Directorate of Foundations. |
| | 4928 | July 15, 2003 | The deadline for community foundations to file a claim to register their registered properties was extended. |
| | 5737 | February 20, 2008 | The new Law on Foundations allowed community foundations to get back their expropriated properties. |
| | | | Foreigners had the right to establish foundations. |
| | | | Community foundations had the right to start businesses and to have cooperation with foreign foundations. |
| Religious education | 4748 | March 26, 2002 | Restrictions on the use of different languages in the press were lifted. |

(*continued*)

TABLE 2.1 (*continued*)

| Subject | Law No. | Date Passed | Improvements |
|---|---|---|---|
| | 4771 | August 3, 2002 | Restrictions on the launching of courses to teach local languages were lifted. Restrictions on broadcasting in different languages were removed. |
| | 4928 | July 15, 2003 | State and private radio stations and television channels were allowed to broadcast in different languages. |
| | 4963 | July 30, 2003 | The teaching of different languages became easier. |
| | 5187 | June 9, 2004 | The new Press Law did not include any restrictions on the use of languages spoken by Turkish citizens. |
| Opening of places of worship | 4928 | July 15, 2003 | The Law on Construction was amended to make the opening of churches easier. |
| Legal personality | N/A | N/A | No improvement. |

instead of separating religion from politics, the state took religion under its control via the bureaucratic organ of the Directorate of Religious Affairs. This control supported Sunni Islam, in that the state pays the salaries of the imams in the mosques. The control bias led the Turkish state not to recognize "religious" organizations as legal entities. The rise of political Islam in the late 1990s and early 2000s challenged the conventional meaning of secularism and led to the rise of conservative politics in Turkey. However, state control of religion, which was initially established by the Kemalists, gave new opportunities for the Islamists to forge their own understanding of religion in public.

Christian minorities in Turkey have generally been regarded as "local foreigners with Turkish citizenship" (Çetin 2000, 81). This perception has manifested itself both in the state's approach toward such minorities and in social prejudices about them. Even the Courts of Appeal in Turkey in 1974 upheld the decision to expropriate the properties of the Christian community foundations on the ground that "foreigners" did not have the right to acquire property in Turkey.[62] As Goltz writes, "hampered by the prevailing implicit, and sometimes explicit, mistrust of these 'local foreigners,' the reforms concerning the non-Muslim communities have consisted so far of piecemeal

---

[62] "Hukuk Genel Kurulu," No. 1974/505, May 8, 1974.

changing in existing laws or regulations with limited positive effects on communities' lives" (Goltz 2006, 175). Christian minorities have confronted several difficulties in getting their newly granted rights recognized, because the state bureaucracy responsible for the implementation of the laws made the procedures complicated.[63]

Two domestic institutional structures, formed throughout the history of the Turkish republic, determined the hostile relationship with the Christian minorities: Turkish practices of nation-state building and Turkish secularism. First, the Turkish experience of nation-state building rested on the ideal of building a homogeneous society. The founding fathers of the republic of Turkey established a nation-state in the ashes of the multi-ethnic and multi-religious Ottoman Empire. The founding leaders invested their energy in creating a homogeneous nation simply in order to consolidate the newly established Turkish nation (Lewis 1968, 15). Second, the Turkish state resisted the demands of religious groups due to the constitutional principle of secularism. Turkish secularism limited the manifestation of religion in the public sphere (Kuru 2009). The Turkish version of secularism is exclusivist, not allowing religion to develop its own organizations independently of the state (Berkes 1964; Davison 1998; Navaro-Yashin 2002; Özyürek 2006). This led the state to limit religious organizations.

However, the government was able to pass new reforms in the first decade of the 2000s. Considering Turkey's historically established discriminatory stance against Christian minorities, the reforms passed between 2000 and 2010 were revolutionary. Christians still faced problems in the implementation of these reforms on the ground, as can be seen in the example of Mor Gabriel Monastery included in the beginning of the chapter,[64] but they regarded the recent developments as very promising.[65] To Rinaldo Marmara, a prominent historian of Christianity in Turkey, "despite the existence of several lingering issues, the recent reforms were extraordinary given the painful historical legacies."[66] The Christians saw their situation to be much better than it had been twenty years before. How did this transformation occur? This change was an outcome of international and domestic factors that interacted in the early 2000s. In Chapter 4, I document how the international community put considerable pressure on Turkey to pass laws reforming the state's relationship with Christian minorities. In Chapter 6, I document how domestic actors exploited international pressure to execute their policy agendas and brought on the passing of reforms in the state's treatment of Christian minorities.

---

[63] Adnan Keskin and Tarık Işık, "Kilise açabilirsiniz demek dile kolay," *Radikal*, May 26, 2004.
[64] Andrew Higgins, "Defending the Faith: Battle over a Christian Monastery Tests Turkey's Tolerance of Minorities," *Wall Street Journal*, March 7, 2009.
[65] Author's interviews with Christian community leaders in summer 2010 and summer 2012.
[66] Author's interview with Rinaldo Marmara, Istanbul, Turkey, June 4, 2010.

# 3

# Secularism and Muslims in France

On September 24, 2003, two high school students, sisters Lila (18) and Alma (16), received a letter from their school in the northern Paris suburb of Aubervilliers telling them that they were forbidden to enter the school because they covered their heads with "ostentatious" scarves. The administration claimed that the students had violated the dress code because their headscarves disrupted educational activities. Lila and Alma, Muslim daughters of atheist parents, had begun wearing headscarves a year before the school's decision to exclude them. The girls' father, Laurent Lévy, fiercely opposed the dismissal decision and accused those who defended the girls' exclusion of being "ayatollahs of secularism preaching a new doctrine of intolerance."[1] To what extent did the principle of secularism play a role in the school administrators' decision to exclude the sisters from school?

Secularism ("laïcité") is a constituting principle of the French nation-state, and it still plays a significant role in the making of policy on religious minorities in France. A deeper historical analysis shows that secularism is not simply a legal principle but is an important national identifier for French citizens. Secularism has constituted the center ground of public debates and controversies around the presence of Muslims in France and of state policies toward Muslims. For this reason, any analysis of state policies toward Muslims that does not sufficiently address the issue of secularism cannot be complete.

The first part of this chapter provides a historical context for the study through a brief analysis of the development of state–religion relations in France. The Catholic Church gradually lost its influence over state and society after the French Revolution, and secularism was institutionalized in the Third French Republic (1870–1940) as an outcome of a series of struggles between the Catholic Church and republicans. The long-lasting fight between the republicans and the Catholics left an imprint not only on French legal documents but also on the cultural imagination of French society. This

---

[1] Hugh Schofield, "Jewish Dad Backs Headscarf Daughters," *BBC News*, October 1, 2016, available at http://news.bbc.co.uk/2/hi/europe/3149588.stm (last accessed on May 22, 2018).

historical background explains why secularism is considered a founding principle by the majority of French people.

As the Muslim population increased from the 1960s, secularism became the general framework for the shaping of France's state policies toward religious minorities. However, it would be misleading to say that French policies toward Muslims stayed within the borders delineated by French secularism as it has been distilled through the nation's history. Contextual developments led French policymakers to redraw the lines in regulating state–Muslim relations. This was especially the case after 2001, when European publics became concerned about the so-called "Islamist threat." French lawmakers and policymakers revised the laws and regulations about the representation of Muslims in civil society and toward the state, the construction of mosques, support for Muslim schools, and the manifestation of Muslim religious symbols in the public sphere. The second part of this chapter provides a brief summary of the changing of French state policies toward Muslims in these issue areas. I particularly examine the headscarf controversy and the processes that led to the laws that banned its wearing in public schools. Because the headscarf issue dominated public debate in France in the 2000s, it provides a great deal of material to demonstrate the argument of this book.

## SECULARISM IN FRANCE: A HISTORICAL OVERVIEW

Secularism is considered one of the founding principles of the French state. Secularism in France emerged through decades of struggle between the Catholic Church and republicans, particularly between 1870 and 1905. Prior to the French Revolution, the Catholic Church and the state had had a close partnership. In the wake of the revolution, religion gradually lost its influence on politics and society. During the Third Republic, the Catholic Church was radically weakened and its privileges in education were removed. By the early twentieth century, republicans had won out over their Catholic rivals and established secularism as a strong pillar of the French legal system. Although there have been ups and downs in subsequent decades, secularism has become an unquestionable principle in the French political system. The rise in the population of Muslim immigrants in France in recent decades has brought the old question of state–religion relations back to the fore of French public discourse.

Until the French Revolution, the Catholic Church and the French state had a cooperative relationship. The state accepted Catholicism as the state religion. Referring to the close relationship between church and state, many called the French state "the eldest daughter of the Church" (Larkin 1974, 29). In return, the church supported the French king by legitimizing his power and recognized the king as the supreme authority in temporal affairs. This was due to the church's relatively independent position toward the pope in its national affairs, though it was not completely separated from the pope as was

Anglicanism in Britain.[2] The relative independence of the French church contributed to its amicable relations with the state.

The friendly relations between the Catholic Church and the state had a negative impact on non-Catholic minorities. Non-Catholics were not considered proper citizens of the country for most of its pre-revolutionary period. Protestants enjoyed religious freedoms for only a limited time: the Edict of Nantes, issued by Henry IV of France in 1598, guaranteed religious freedoms for Protestants, but Louis XIV revoked the edict in 1685 with the Edict of Fontainebleau, putting French Protestants in a vulnerable position (Rémond 1999, 20–45).

Relations between state and church changed radically after the French Revolution, which dissociated "faith and citizenship" and opened "a new chapter in the history of relations between religion and society" (Rémond 1999, 37). In the early years after the revolution, the Catholic Church did not take a hostile position against the state. Some leaders within the Catholic Church even supported revolutionary republican ideals. For example, Abbé Grégoire, a leading figure in the French church, was among the revolution's ardent supporters. A prominent republican of the time, he strongly advocated the abolition of the monarchy (Ravitch 1967). As the revolutionaries increased authoritarian measures to implement their political ideals, relations between pro-revolutionary forces and the church deteriorated. Gradually, the revolutionary groups came to consider the clericalism of the church as a challenge to their political authority. The new leaders perceived the Catholic Church as a threat to the sovereignty of the republican state. They aimed to weaken religion in political and public life by banishing it to the private realm. The anticlerical movement expanded and gained supporters, especially among leftist republicans. This anticlericalism was a response to the church's claim to political domination over the country, but it was not necessarily antireligious. Rather, the anticlericals believed that religion should be kept in the private sphere (Baubérot and Milot 2011, 99–104).

The new revolutionary state gradually increased its power vis-à-vis the Catholic Church and removed its privileges. In the last decade of the eighteenth century, the state recognized Protestants and Jews as proper citizens of the republic. In 1790, the revolutionaries passed a law to cut the French church's ties with the Vatican. After a series of conflicts, Napoleon Bonaparte and Pope Pius VII signed a concordat in 1801 that structured the relationship between the French state and Rome. The pope gave up his claims to former church properties that had been expropriated by the state. Additionally, Rome would no longer appoint Catholic bishops and priests in France; and French clergy were required to swear allegiance to the French state. In return, Napoleon accepted Catholicism as the religion of "the majority of the French

---

[2] For a discussion of various perspectives on the relationship between the Vatican and the French church, see Warner 2000, 56–59.

people" (not the religion of France). The state was to pay the salaries of the priests, and the French church would be loyal to Rome only in doctrinal matters (Judge 2004, 3). Three years later, the 1804 civil code granted religious freedoms to non-Catholics. This development constituted a milestone in the decline of the public dominance of the French Catholic Church (Rémond 1999, 48).

In the early years of the revolution, the anticlerical movement did not directly target religion; rather, it aimed to decrease the institutional authority of the church (Baubérot and Milot 2011, 266–269). This situation gradually changed in the second half of the nineteenth century as the positivist ideas of the Enlightenment spread among republican politicians. The anticlericals of the late nineteenth century perceived religion as "an outdated explanation of the world that offered only a backwards orientation, irrelevant to the context of modern democracies" (Baubérot 2003, 459–460). Jean-Jacques Rousseau, whose ideas influenced many French republicans at the time, proposed that a republican public order should replace religion. For Rousseau, the republic was responsible for producing social and moral virtues, which had traditionally been the responsibility of the church (Modood and Kastoryano 2006, 165). Jean Baubérot (2003, 460) identifies this worldview as "secular religion." Claude Nicolet (1995) describes the republic as "an Enlightenment Church" that used religious metaphors in establishing its moral rules. To counter the republican surge and reinstate its social and political position, the Catholic church allied with the monarchists. In the new political context, the Catholics and monarchists fought against anticlericals and republicans. It was this divide that shaped the political contestations in the Third Republic, established after France's defeat in the Franco-Prussian War of 1870.

The Third Republican period, which Emile Poulat (1987) portrays as the "war of two Frances," is significant for the institutionalization of state–religion relations in France. The republican politicians won consecutive elections over the monarchists in the first four decades of the Third Republic. These electoral victories gave the republicans the opportunity to shape the French political system and consolidate the primacy of the republic over the church and monarchy (Kalyvas 1996, 114–166). As Maurice Larkin (2003, 206–207) writes, "by 1879, government was safely in the hands of committed republicans; and the way was clear for a program of *laïcité* [secularism]."[3]

Contestations between the republicans and the monarchists first appeared in the area of education. The new Enlightenment intellectuals of France increased their criticism of the church's involvement in education. They argued that the church must distance itself from education because its teachings were outdated. The republicans saw education as a means to the flowering of "a new

---

[3] Some scholars prefer to keep the French word for secularism, "laïcité," in English writings to reflect the peculiarities of French secularism. In this study, I translate it as "secularism" and qualify the characteristics of French secularism when necessary.

democratic social mobility and to the formation of free, tolerant and socially active citizens" (Chadwick 1997, 49). Beginning in the 1870s, republican politicians worked for a free and compulsory public education, which, for them, would develop the "citizens" of the French republic. The interior minister Léon Gambetta, for example, suggested as early as 1871 that the monopoly of the church over the delivery of mass education should be eliminated. For him, a state monopoly over education was necessary to inculcate a republican identity and morality in future generations (Chadwick 1997, 49). As Kay Chadwick (1997, 49) writes, "the Third Republic's aim was not only the cessation of church involvement in state education, but also the creation, formalization, and dissemination of a left-dominated republican ideal intended to counter Catholic influence and to provide a new unifying social and political focus for France's citizens."

These ideas would be implemented in 1882, when Jules Ferry, who is considered the founding father of the modern "republican school" (*l'école républicaine*), became the minister of education. Ferry thought of school as the agent of assimilation of children by the republic. Schoolchildren were to be instilled with a common republican political identity regardless of what their backgrounds were. Ferry instituted a series of laws that secularized public education. The laws made primary education free, secular, and compulsory. Later, in 1886, priests were banned from becoming teachers in public schools (McManners 1972, 45–54).

The republicans defeated the monarchists in all elections between 1876 and 1906 (Kalyvas 1996, 147). These electoral defeats of the Catholics were due in part to their weak organization (Warner 2000, 59). As Carolyn Warner writes, "precisely at the time when the French church was under anticlerical attack, it had no organization that could speak for it as a whole." This weakness, for Warner, was due to the interference of the Vatican, which had opted for a decentralized French church to ensure that the bishops and priests could not coordinate against Rome (Warner 2000, 60). Stathis Kalyvas explains the failure of Catholic politicians by their miscalculation (1996, 131–141). The church's calculus was based on the assumption that the monarchy would be reinstalled and the republic would collapse. Therefore, the church's ancillary organizations failed to mobilize their supporters. For others, the overall secularization of French society was an important factor in the failure of Catholic ancillary organizations (e.g. Weber 1976).

After the republicans had established their power and secured the institutionalization of their policy agendas, they softened their stance and agreed to limit religion only in the public sphere; they abandoned their antireligion stance in policymaking. In 1905, republicans and Catholics reached a compromise and the parliament passed a law on the separation of church and state. According to this law, the state would neither recognize nor subsidize any religion. The state would be neutral in religious matters. Church buildings built before the law was passed would become public property, and the state would maintain these buildings. At the same time, the state would guarantee religious belief and expression, provided that religious manifestations were confined to the private domain and did not intervene in public life or state affairs (Guerlac 1908).

To Baubérot (2003), the 1905 law was an outcome of republican moderation. The republicans were satisfied by the reforms they had passed during their long tenure in government, concluding that the republic was stable enough and the monarchy could no longer be restored. They departed from their antireligious stance and opened the way for religious freedoms. For example, Ferdinand Buisson, a leading figure among the republicans, supported religious freedoms and pointed out the weakness of their previous policies: "What is left of the Catholic Church? A single role, one that cannot be reasonably taken away from her: religion, religion alone. For even morality, joined for so long to religion, has been separated from her. Our laws, our regulations, even our schools no longer know anything but *laïque* morality" (quoted in Fetzer and Soper 2005, 72).

Ferry also defined his struggle as anticlerical, not antireligious: "My struggle is the anticlerical struggle, but the antireligious struggle? Never! Never!" (quoted in Fetzer and Soper 2005, 72). However, the republicans were not unified on the law. After this compromise, argues Baubérot (2003, 461–462), the strict republicans separated from the mainstream republicans and allied themselves with the socialists, who had an antireligious stance. This alliance would become the representative of "assertive secularism" in the years to come (Kuru 2009).

On the other side, the Catholics had been tired of their struggles with the republicans and had become convinced that it would be difficult to reinstate the monarchy. Like the republicans, the Catholics were divided on their views about the 1905 law. Some Catholic organizations considered rallying against the law; however, the Vatican did not approve this course of action (Warner 2000, 63). Although the Catholic church garnered some power between 1905 and 1940, it was unable to change the conditions set by the 1905 separation law. Addressing the importance of what happened in the Third Republic for the emergence of the 1905 separation law, Baubérot and Milot (2011, 279) state that "the history of French secularism cannot be understood without accounting for the transition between the periods of 1899–1904 and 1905–1908." To them, the ideological context of the era and its transformation from anticlericalism to separation marked the shape of French secularism in later decades (Baubérot and Milot 2011, 279).

Secularism came under threat when Germany invaded France during the Second World War. In June 1940, Germany occupied France, and the Vichy regime under General Philippe Pétain was established in the unoccupied area of southern France. This German-controlled regime had a very close relationship with the Catholic Church. The Catholics welcomed the Vichy regime because they saw it as "a final vindication of all the struggles of

Catholics during the lifetime of the Third Republic" (Ravitch 1990, 127) and a new opportunity for the reconstruction of Christian morality in France (Warner 2000, 69). General Pétain revoked laws to create more capacity for the Catholic Church. However, the Church "limited its possibilities for action after the war" because of its collaboration with the German invaders (Warner 2000, 71).[4] After the Vichy regime ended, the Church was stigmatized for its collaboration with the regime and lost its legitimacy (Warner 2000, 70–71).

When the Fourth Republic was established in 1944, the church had to accept the inclusion of the principle of secularism in the constitution (Byrnes 2005, 215). Secularism became a constitutional principle in the 1946 constitution, which mentioned secularism in its preamble as one of the defining characteristics of the republic. The principle of secularism was also included in the constitution after the establishment of the Fifth Republic: "France is an indivisible, secular, democratic, and social Republic. It ensures equality to all of its citizens before the law without distinction of origin, race, and religion. It respects all beliefs."[5]

The first serious postwar contestation over the relationship between state and religion occurred in the 1950s on the issue of subsidizing religious private schools. When the minister of education Michel Debré[6] proposed a new bill that would make state funding available to religious schools, the left vehemently opposed the bill. To the leftists, this law would be a violation of the 1905 law that forbade state funding of religions. Despite the leftist opposition, the Debré Law was enacted in December 1959. The law instituted a contract system between the state and religious schools. The state would pay the teachers' salaries and some of the schools' expenses; in return, the schools would meet the educational standards that the state imposed on them. They would not discriminate against students based on their ethnic or religious affiliations, and they would follow the curriculum that the ministry of education would prepare (Larkin 2003, 221).

The socialists criticized this law in their election campaigns in the years to come. When the socialist government of François Mitterand was formed in 1981, it attempted to cut state funding to religious schools, but many demonstrations organized by Catholic activists forced the government to withdraw its proposal (Chadwick 1997, 54).

French secularism, which had been structured by the decades-old contestations between the Catholic Church and republicans, entered a new era in 1981 when the Mitterand government allowed foreigners to establish associations. The new regulation came at a time when the number of Muslim

---

[4] For a review of political contestations during the Vichy regime, see Hoffmann 1963, 34–58.
[5] Article 1 of the French Constitution, available at www.conseil-constitutionnel.fr/conseil-constitutionnel/root/bank_mm/constitution/constitution.pdf (last accessed on November 5, 2018).
[6] Michel Debré was also the head of the government (prime minister) at the time.

immigrants was increasing in France due to immigrant workers' family reunifications. In the years to follow, secularism became one of the most important issues in the state's relationship with Muslims. The issue has gained particular public recognition through the debates over wearing of headscarves in public schools during the late 1980s. Other issues such as the accommodation of Muslim organizations, the opening of mosques and religious schools, and state support for Muslim schools also became major battlefields for French secularism (Laurence and Vaïsse 2006). The challenge of Islam led French policymakers to return to public debates around secularism similar to those preceding the 1905 law of separation (Baubérot and Milot 2011, 280–306). The next section of this chapter surveys French state policies toward Muslims and the role of secularism in the shaping of these policies.

## STATE POLICIES TOWARD MUSLIMS

The integration of Muslims into broader French society has been on the agenda of French governments since the 1980s. State policies toward Muslims have transformed from being relatively neutral to more regulatory over time. In the 2000s, the French state became motivated to control Muslims through restrictive state policies. State regulation of Muslims' political, social, and religious life gradually increased from the start of the twenty-first century.

In this section, I evaluate four issues that reflect the transformation of the French state's position toward Muslims. First, the French state led the establishment of an umbrella organization for French Muslims in 2003. Muslims had previously never had an organization that would represent them in dealings with the state. Motivated to have more control over Muslims, the state encouraged Muslims to establish a federation and played an active role in elections and appointments to its leadership roles. Second, throughout the 2000s and 2010s, the central government became more involved in the debates on the issuing of permits for the opening of large mosques. Muslims had difficulties in getting permits to open new mosques. Local politicians played a significant role in the controversies around mosques by creating obstacles to their construction. In recent years, the central government and local administrators have intervened in these debates in favor of opening big mosques in order to have more surveillance over Muslims.

Third, the French state maintained a firm stance against the opening of Muslim schools that have a contractual relationship with the state to make state funding available for Muslim schools, based on the 1959 Debré Law. To set up such a contractual relationship is still difficult for Muslims. Finally, the French state increased its regulation of the manifestation of Muslim religious symbols in public spaces. In 2004, the state limited the display of religious symbols in schools with a law that banned wearing headscarves in public schools. In 2010, the state passed another law to ban the wearing of veils covering the full face even on the streets.

I briefly review these issues and the change of state policies over time. Then, I provide a fuller discussion on the passing of the headscarf law, which was debated extensively by the French public and the parliament. That the issue was intensively debated over a long period has offered me extant discursive and attitudinal empirical material to demonstrate the argument of the book, i.e. the impact of the international context on domestic actor strategies in pushing their policy agendas.

## Muslims' Representation in France

Starting in the late 1990s, the French state supported the idea of establishing a representative council for French Muslims. The diverse Muslim groups in France had established their own organizations, but they lacked a unified representative council or federation. The state did not have an interlocutor in its dealings with Muslims. An increasing number of statesmen and politicians were concerned with the lack of a unified Muslim body in the late 1990s and early 2000s. To address this issue, the state played a leading role in establishing a representative council for Islamic organizations.

Other minority religions historically had councils that represented them with regard to the French state,[7] but – in contrast with its role in the formation of a Muslim representative council – the state had heretofore played little or no role in the establishment of such organizations. In 1999, interior minister Jean-Pierre Chevènement took the initiative in establishing a representative council of Islamic organizations. He met representatives of various Islamic groups but he could not reach a consensus with these groups about creating an umbrella organization. His successor, Nicolas Sarkozy, put further efforts into creating a representative Muslim council. After several meetings with Muslim leaders, Sarkozy was able to reach a deal among Muslim organizations in 2003 and led the establishment of the French Council of the Muslim Religion (Conseil français du culte musulman).

According to the deal, major Muslim federations in France took leadership positions in the council. Four Muslim federations played significant roles in the formation of the French Council of the Muslim Religion. Of these organizations, Great Mosque of Paris, which receives support from the Algerian government, represents most of the Algerian Muslims living in France. This organization has historically had good relations with the French state (Fernando 2005, 13). Another organization constituting the council was the Union of Islamic Organizations of France, known by many as the French branch of the Muslim Brotherhood (Laurence and Vaisse 2006, 98–133). The National Federation of Muslims of France, which mostly represents Moroccan Muslims and is supported by the Moroccan state, also joined the council

---

[7] Two examples are the Fédération protestante de France (Protestant Federation of France) and the Jewish Consistoire central de France (Central Consistory of France).

(Dumont 2008, 793). Finally, the Coordinating Committee of Turkish Muslims of France, which represents Turkish Muslims and gets support from the Turkish state, cooperated in the formation of a federation for French Muslims.

According to the agreement between the state and the Muslim organizations, each mosque in France had an electoral weight based on the square footage of their prayer spaces. Based on their space, mosques nominated grand electors to elect two-thirds of the council's administrative committee. The Ministry of the Interior would appoint the remaining one-third of the committee. Two ministerial advisors would attend council meetings.[8] Sarkozy aimed to create a French Islam by having control over Muslims through influencing the formation of the French Council of the Muslim Religion and developing corporatist relations with the council (Laurence and Vaisse 2006, 135–162). The bureaucrats from the Ministry of the Interior and the state-vetted members would have a weight in shaping the demands made by Muslims of the state. The state's involvement in the creation of the French Council of the Muslim Religion marginalized those Muslim groups that were not affiliated with any of the four constituting organizations.

## Building of Mosques

Aside from a few examples such as the Paris Mosque, the French state had historically done little to help in the building of places of worship for Muslims (Bowen 2009a, 29). In the 2000s, though, the state's policies toward the construction of mosques changed. The state became supportive of the construction of larger mosques, and the central government took initiative in the construction of mosques, whereas local governments had been more involved in the past.

The demand for mosques increased substantially from the 1970s, when the Muslim population in France increased due to the reunification of immigrant workers' families. There are many prayer rooms, but the number of well-equipped mosques is very limited in proportion to the large Muslim population in France. By 2005, there were about twenty mosques in all of France that could accommodate more than 1,000 attendees (Laurence and Vaisse 2006, 83).

Throughout the 1980s and 1990s, local governments had dealt with the issue of mosque construction. Although in some cities, such as Lyon, the city administrators supported mosque projects, many mayors, especially from the far-right National Front (FN, Front national), resisted issuing permits for the construction of new mosques. A telling example is the controversy around the construction of the Grande Mosquée de Marseille. There are about 250,000 Muslims living in Marseille and there had been several proposals to build a big

---

[8] Author's interview with Bernard Godard, Ministry of Interior Affairs, Paris, France, July 25, 2007.

mosque in the city since 1839. The city council accepted a proposal to build a mosque in 2006 and the project started in 2010. In October 2011, the administrative court in Marseille announced that it would stop the project.[9] The court of appeals revoked the decision of the administrative court.[10] Because of a lack of funding, the city terminated the contract of the project in November 2016. The administrative court approved the city's decision.[11]

Even though there is still a debate about whether or not city governments should support the building of mosques, the trend in recent years has been toward more state support for mosques. Those politicians and statesmen who support mosque construction argue that big mosques would facilitate the integration of Muslims into French society because they would replace smaller, non-controlled, and underground mosques.[12] The construction of big mosques makes Muslims more "traceable." Reflecting this motivation, then minister of the interior Nicolas Sarkozy once stated that the French people should not fear minarets, but they should fear garages and basements.[13] On the other hand, city governments that create obstacles to the issuing of permits for mosque construction defend the idea that the widespread visibility of mosques symbolically challenges French cultural values and secularism.

## Contracts for Islamic Schools

Although the French state encouraged the establishment of the French Council of the Muslim Religion and supported the construction of mosques in cities, it made it difficult for Islamic schools to set up contractual relationships with the state. In France, religious schools are eligible to get state funding based on the 1959 Debré Law. According to this law, the state meets about 80–85 percent of these schools' expenses; in return, the religious schools are expected to implement a state-approved curriculum and to accept students from any background without discrimination.

Although several Muslim organizations made applications for such contractual status, by December 2014, only the Lycée Averroès (Averroès High School) in the northern French city of Lille was funded by the

[9] Maime de la Baume, "France: Court Cancels Permit for Grand Mosque of Marseille," *New York Times*, October 27, 2011.

[10] Agence France-Presse, "French Court Agrees Permit for Marseille Mega-mosque," *Hurriyet Daily News*, June 19, 2012.

[11] Imane Youssfi, "Mosquée de Marseille: La Justice résilie définitivement le bail," *Saphir News*, January 24, 2017, available at www.saphirnews.com/Mosquee-de-Marseille-la-justice-resilie-definitivement-le-bail_a23400.html (last accessed on November 8, 2018).

[12] Christian Fraser, "Marseille's Muslims Eye Long-Awaited Mosque," *BBC News*, July 6, 2010, available at www.bbc.co.uk/news/10508069 (last accessed on June 20, 2017).

[13] Nicolas Sarkozy, "Les Musulmans ne doivent pas avoir plus de droits. Veillons à ce qu'ils n'en aient pas moins," *Le Monde*, October 26, 2004.

state.[14] The French authorities explain the lower level of support for Muslim schools by the schools' failure to meet the eligibility requirements for state funding. By the time a school applies for a contractual relationship, it must have already been functioning for five years. The academic credentials and quality of the teachers must be satisfactory. The school must have a relatively large number of students and the school facilities must meet certain standards (Fetzer and Soper 2005, 85).

Many Islamic schools do not meet these criteria. However, the French state did not enter contractual relationships even with those schools that did meet the criteria. It may seem surprising that the French state, which pursued a policy of extending its control over Muslims in other issue areas, did not grant contract status to Muslim schools, as such status would have forced them to develop a curriculum in line with the state's priorities. Since most private schools are supported by the state in France, it is not easy to keep up with the costs of a private school that does not have state support. Parents are less willing to pay high tuition for a private school when others are available for a more reasonable price. This makes the contract system the most common way of running private schools. In the absence of a state contract, Muslims are less likely to open their own schools. Considering this, the lack of state support for Muslim schools leads Muslim parents to send their children to state schools or private schools run by Catholics. Some French Muslims are also against the opening of Islamic schools on the grounds that such schools could lead to more segregation from broader French society and increase the ghettoization of the Muslim minority (Fetzer and Soper 2005, 86).

## Manifestation of Religious Symbols in Public Places

Since the early 1990s, the manifestation of religious symbols in public places has been a significant issue between the French state and Muslims. In the 2000s, the French state passed laws to restrict the manifestation of religious symbols in the public sphere. The two major issues in this regard are the debate around the wearing of headscarves in public schools and the controversy over the wearing of the burqa (a garment that covers the whole body except the eyes) in public places by Muslim women.

The debate over the wearing of headscarves by female Muslim students in public schools dominated the French public discourse between 1989 and 2003. This issue stirred a debate on the meaning of secularism and Muslims' presence in the French public sphere. Although there were cases in which school administrators expelled girls for wearing headscarves between 1989 and

---

[14] France 24, "France's First Private Muslim School Tops Ranks," March 29, 2013, available at www.france24.com/en/20130329-france-first-private-muslim-school-tops-ranks-averroes (last accessed on April 4, 2019).

2003, most of these expulsions were overturned by the Council of State (Conseil d'État), the highest administrative court in France, on the ground that the expulsions were against religious freedoms. However, in 2004, the French state passed a law that banned the wearing of "ostentatious" religious symbols in schools. A detailed analysis of the headscarf controversy is presented later in this chapter.

From 2009 to 2010, the controversy around the manifestation of religious symbols in public shifted to another issue: the wearing of the burqa by Muslim women on the streets. In 2009, President Nicolas Sarkozy formed a commission to evaluate whether and to what extent the burqa should be banned in France. In January 2010, the commission produced a report, the Guérin Report.[15] It recommended banning of the burqa in public places to protect French secularism. In line with the conclusions of the report, in 2010 the French Assembly and the Senate passed a law that banned the burqa in public places. The constitutional court approved the ban in October 2010, and the ban went into effect in April 2011.[16] Without mentioning the burqa, the law bans the wearing of full-face veils in all public places such as public transportation, markets, streets, etc. According to the law, a woman wearing a face-covering veil caught by a law enforcement officer is subject to a fine of 150 euros or a mandatory French citizenship course. Anyone who forces a woman to wear such a garment would be subject to a fine of 30,000 euros or a year of imprisonment; if the woman so forced is a minor, the punishment is doubled (Heider 2012, 3).

It is estimated that the number of people who were affected by the laws on headscarves and burqas was only about 4,000 out of France's five to six million Muslim population. To many scholars, the French state passed these laws for more symbolic than practical reasons with the aim of sending a message to Muslims that emphasizes the principle of secularism (Heider 2012, 3). In increasing its regulatory stance toward Muslims, the French state aimed to shape the behavior of French Muslims to be more aligned with French values and ideals, even if this stance required putting limitations on religious freedoms.

## THE HEADSCARF CONTROVERSY IN FRANCE

The French public dealt with the headscarf controversy between 1989 and 2004. Initially, most French intellectuals and parties of the center right and center left defended the right of girls to wear the headscarf in schools. However,

---

[15] The report can be accessed on the French parliament's website: Assemblée Nationale, "Au nom de la Mission d'information sur la pratique du port du voile intégral sur le territoire national," January 10, 2010, available at www.assemblee-nationale.fr/13/pdf/rap-info/i2262.pdf (last accessed on November 8, 2018).

[16] Steven Erlanger, "France Enforces Ban on Full-Face Veils in Public," *New York Times*, April 12, 2011.

in the years just before the passing of the law in 2004, the positions of these actors shifted. The French public gradually changed its position, and support for a ban on headscarves increased. Those who took a strong position against the banning of the headscarf when it was first debated in 1989 became supporters of the ban in the early 2000s.

The wearing of headscarves in public schools first became an issue in October 1989 when a principal in Creil, Eugène Chenière, dismissed three schoolgirls from a junior high school on the grounds that they were wearing headscarves. In this school, about half of the students were children of Arab immigrants. To justify the dismissals, Chenière claimed that he was enforcing the constitutional principle of secularism in the school.[17] This incident, which drew extensive press coverage, initiated a debate on the meaning of secularism and whether or not the wearing of headscarves in public schools violated it. Representatives of Muslim, Christian, and Jewish organizations, many socialists, and several politicians from the center right opposed the expulsions of girls wearing headscarves in public schools. Far-right politicians, most feminists, and several secularist intellectuals opposed the practice of wearing headscarves in public schools (Bowen 2006, 84).

Lionel Jospin, the minister of education at the time, argued that wearing religious symbols should not, in itself, be grounds for expelling a student, and referred the headscarf question to the Council of State, the highest administrative court in France (Idriss 2005, 272). Although Jospin wanted to put an end to the debate, the Council of State ruling of November 1989 was ambiguous. The Council of State interpreted the principle of secularism, the constitution, and France's international obligations in such a way as to leave more room for religious freedoms. The council stated that the French legal system allowed students to exercise their freedom of religion in schools although it put some constraints on the teachers in the name of state neutrality. The council also stated that students should respect pluralism and others' freedom in exercising their own freedoms and manifesting their religious beliefs in schools. Based on these interpretations, the Council established the following jurisprudence, which framed the legal issues around headscarves until 2004:

The wearing of signs by students through which they wish to express their membership in a religion is not by itself incompatible with the principle of secularism. But this liberty does not permit students to display symbols of religious membership that, by their nature, by the conditions under which they are individually or collectively worn, or by their ostentatious or protesting character disturb the order or normal functioning of public services.[18]

In short, the Council of State allowed the wearing of headscarves as long as students who wore headscarves did not disrupt public order in the schools.

---

[17] *Libération*, "Le Port du voile heurte la laïcité du collège de Creil," October 4, 1989.
[18] Avis du Conseil d'État No. 346.893, November 27, 1989.

According to some analysts, the court's decision reflected a delicate balance between the principles of liberty and neutrality in implementing French secularism (Judge 2004, 10). By allowing the students to wear headscarves, the Council of State fulfilled the liberty premise of the 1905 law on secularism, and by disallowing public officials, school teachers in this case, it fulfilled the state neutrality premise of French secularism.[19]

Based on the ruling of the Council of State, Jospin issued a circular that left it up to school authorities to decide whether or not headscarves were admissible.[20] School principals would decide on a case-by-case basis whether or not girls wearing headscarves undermined public order. The Council of State held its position throughout the early 1990s. It did not approve any expulsion of headscarf-wearing girls if they were not violating public order. For example, in one of its later rulings in 1991, the Council stated that

To force a Muslim woman to take off her headscarf which expresses her religious conscience and her free choice, is to be considered as the severest kind of oppression of women which is contrary to the French values calling for respect for the dignity of women and their religious, human, and personal freedom (Shadid and van Koningsveld 2005, 40).

The Council of State rulings did not satisfy teachers, who wanted to be on solid ground in dealing with students wearing headscarves; however, public attention on the headscarf issue gradually decreased until mid-1993.

The debate around the headscarf intensified again in 1993 around the expulsion of four girls from a high school in Nantua, a small city northeast of Lyon (McGoldrick 2006, 72). This controversy was followed by nationwide teachers' strikes protesting the appearance of headscarves in schools. The tension increased to its highest point when Eugène Chenière, the main actor in the 1989 affair, became a deputy representing the department of the Oise for the conservative Rally for the Republic party (Rassemblement pour la République). He prepared a bill that would ban all "ostentatious" religious symbols in the schools (Scott 2005, 107).

In September 1994 the minister of education, François Bayrou, confronted with these public responses, issued a circular to prohibit the wearing of ostentatious religious symbols in public schools.[21] In the circular, he stated: "It is not possible to accept the presence and multiplication of ostentatious signs in

---

[19] During my interviews in France in summer 2007, French state officials (Bernard Godard), journalists (Alan Gresh), academics (Riva Kastoryano, Patrick Weil, Catherine de Wenden, Nilüfer Göle, Olivier Abel), and activists (Haydar Demiryürek) brought this point to my attention. For the 1905 law see www.legifrance.gouv.fr/texteconsolide/MCEBW.htm (last accessed on October 6, 2007).

[20] *Journal Officiel*, "Laïcité, port de signes religieux par les élèves et caractère obligatoire des enseignements," December 15, 1989, 15777.

[21] *Le Monde*, "La Circulaire de François Bayrou à propos du port du foulard islamique," September 21, 1994.

schools whose signification involves the separation of certain students from the rules of common life of the school."[22] Although the Bayrou circular seemed not to be in conflict with the Council of State's decisions for the reason that "ostentatious" was defined as "harming the public order," it actually was: Bayrou defined the headscarf as an example of an ostentatious religious symbol, while he did not identify Christian crucifixes or Jewish skullcaps as ostentatious. Bayrou and his conservative government related their decision to integration and immigration issues, arguing that the Muslim schoolgirls had to accept French ideals of republicanism and secularism and to stop "the infiltration of religious fundamentalisms" in the public schools (Freedman 2004, 14–15).

The Bayrou circular could not make any real change in the status quo established by the Council of State in 1989. After Bayrou's circular appeared, some of the girls who were then expelled from schools applied to the courts. Many of the courts and the Council of State overturned the expulsion decisions, reaffirming the 1989 ruling (Scott 2007, 28). The court upheld only those cases in which the students disrupted disciplinary order in the schools (McGoldrick 2006, 71; Idriss 2005, 273–275). Thus the courts deactivated the circular by developing "a clear and consistent jurisprudence on the issue: schools could expel girls if they failed to attend all their classes or if their case led to protests, but not merely for wearing scarves" (Bowen 2006, 92).

The controversy around the headscarf seemed to disappear toward the end of 1990s. In 2000, a French governmental body, the High Council on Integration, reported that "of the 49 disputed cases arriving at the Council of State between 1992 and 1999, 41 led to a reversal of the decision of the school officials against the girls" (Haut Conseil a l'Intégration 2000, 50). This report also applauded the Council of State's jurisprudence and stated that the legal perspective taken had peacefully resolved the matters related to the headscarf question at public schools. The report of the High Council especially praised the balance that the Council of State established between freedom of religion and the maintenance of order and discipline in the schools (Haut Conseil a L'Intégration 2000, 52). In 2003, Hanifa Cherifi, who was appointed by the government in 1994 as the mediator between students and teachers in the headscarf disputes, stated that "the average number of problematic cases per year had dropped from 300 to 150."[23] In short, the headscarf debate seemed to fade in the early 2000s; however, "it was only a calm before the storm" (Gunn 2004, 458).

Following the 2001 terrorist attacks on the World Trade Center, the number of headscarf incidents increased in public high schools.[24] Schoolteachers

[22] François Bayrou, "Le Texte du ministre de l'education nationale," *Le Monde*, September 21, 1994.

[23] Xavier Ternisien, "Il n'y a que 150 cas conflictuels, selon la médiatrice de l'éducation nationale," *Le Monde*, May 10, 2003.

[24] *Le Monde*, "Les Professeurs du lycée Léonard-de-Vinci ont mis fin à leur mouvement de grève," March 28, 2002.

organized strikes to put pressure on the parliament to ban the wearing of the headscarf in schools.[25] These incidents reached their peak in 2003, when the cases of new dismissals drew the media attention.[26] Parliamentarians from the center right group Union for a Popular Movement (Union pour un mouvement populaire) started to talk about a new bill that would ban the wearing of headscarves in schools. At the end of March 2003, prime minister Jean-Pierre Raffarin stated in a television interview that his government supported a headscarf ban to "reinforce the principle of secularism."[27] On April 3, Raffarin reiterated his position by indicating the necessity for the prohibition of headscarves in public schools.[28]

Public debates around the headscarf became widespread after the provocative speech of interior minister Nicolas Sarkozy at the meeting of the Union of Islamic Organizations of France (Union des organisations islamiques de France) on April 19, 2003. When talking about equality before the law, he said that all citizens must have their picture taken for identity cards with their heads uncovered; he then added "Nothing would justify that woman of the Muslim confession benefits from a different law" (Bowen 2004, 49). Three days after Sarkozy's speech, Luc Ferry, who was the minister of education at the time, announced that he was personally against the wearing of headscarves in public schools. He stated that he would propose a law banning headscarves to strengthen secularism in the public schools.[29]

From April 2003 on, the government started to speak more loudly about the passing of a law on religious symbols in the public schools. On April 29, Prime Minister Raffarin, in his reply to a deputy's parliamentary question on the banning of religious symbols in schools, said that public schools were to be cleaned of "conspicuous signs of communalism" in the name of "republican secularism." Raffarin asserted that the government would strengthen French secularism via new legislation. He stated that the school must remain "the space *par excellence* of the Republic and therefore of secularism." Raffarin said that students should leave their religious affiliations outside of the classroom and participate in the classroom as equal members of the French nation.[30]

[25] Simon Catherine, "Le Voile est un piège, qui isole et marginalize," *Le Monde*, December 17, 2001; Luc Bronner, "Les Professeurs d'un lycée de Seine-Saint-Denis en grève contre l'islamisme," *Le Monde*, March 25, 2002.

[26] For example, see Olivier Bertrand, "Un foulard déclenche une grève dans un lycée de Lyon," *Libération*, March 13, 2003.

[27] Eric Aeschimann and Emmanuel Davidenkoff, "Le Gouvernement ne hisse pas le voile," *Libération*, April 23, 2003.

[28] *Le Monde*, "Le Premier ministre contre le voile à l'école," April 5, 2003.

[29] Eric Aeschimann and Emmanuel Davidenkoff, "Le Gouvernement ne hisse pas le voile," *Libération*, April 23, 2003.

[30] Sophie Hunt, "Jean-Pierre Raffarin veut un débat sur le voile islamique," *Le Figaro*, April 30, 2004.

The right-wing Union for a Popular Movement was not alone in support of a law that would ban religious symbols in the schools. Socialists also demanded legislation about religious dress in public schools. In April 2003, the Socialist Jack Lang, who was a former minister of education, announced that he would propose a bill to prohibit symbols that show an adherence to any religion.[31] On May 17, 2003, a former Socialist prime minister, Laurent Fabius, in his address to the party congress, said that "the school is not just one among many places; it is the place where we mold our younger citizens. There are three legs: secularism, Republic, school; these are the three legs on which we stand." He also stated, "the republican school cannot become the testing ground for those who confuse politics and religion."[32]

By the summer of 2003, the government and the parliament initiated new legislation. In May 2003, a parliamentary inquiry commission, led by Jean-Louis Debré, was established in the National Assembly on the "question of wearing religious signs in schools." In July, President Jacques Chirac created a commission to deal with broader issues related to secularism. The commission, which became widely known as the Stasi Commission after the name of its chairman, Bernard Stasi, was "charged with conducting an analysis of the application of the principle of secularism in the Republic." Both the Debré and the Stasi Commissions issued their reports in December 2003.[33]

The Debré Commission recommended passing legislation to ban all religious symbols in all public schools and in private schools operating under contract with the national education system: "The reaffirmation of the principle of secularism must take the form of a legislative action explicitly to ban the visible wearing of any sign of religious or political allegiance on school property" (Debré 2003, 3). The conclusions of the Stasi report gained more public attention than the parliamentary commission's report, due mostly to the reputation of its constituting members.[34] The Stasi Commission, in its comprehensive report, made a number of suggestions to improve secularism and to facilitate the integration of immigrants in France. Among other

---

[31] Nicole Penicaut, "Laïcité et voile: Raffarin noie le poisson," *Libération*, April 30, 2003.

[32] *Le Monde*, "M. Fabius appelle les militants a défendre la laïcité contre les intégrismes et le communautarisme," May 19, 2003.

[33] Although the parliamentary commission announced its report on December 18, the Stasi Commission announced its report on December 11. The final report of the Debré commission can be accessed at www.assemblee-nat.fr/12/pdf/rapports/r1275-t1.pdf and www.assemblee-nat.fr/12/pdf/rapports/r1275-t2.pdf. The Stasi report can be accessed at http://lesrapports .ladocumentationfrancaise.fr/BRP/034000725/0000.pdf (last accessed on October 6, 2007).

[34] The members included, in addition to Bernard Stasi and the rapporteurs, Mohammed Arkoun, Jean Baubérot, Hanifa Chérifi, Jacqueline Costa-Lascoux, Régis Debray, Michel Delebarre, Nicole Guedj, Ghislaine Hudson, Gilles Kepel, Marceau Long, Nelly Olin, Henri Pena-Ruiz, Gaye Petek, Maurice Quenet, René Remond, Raymond Soubie, Alain Touraine, and Patrick Weil.

proposals, the commission recommended the banning of clothing and signs manifesting religious affiliation at public schools (Stasi 2004, 4).[35]

On December 17, 2003, based on the recommendations of the Stasi Commission, President Chirac presented a bill proscribing overt religious symbols in public schools. In his speech, he stated that "Communitarianism could not possibly be France's choice." He then praised the principle of secularism and mentioned the social and political function of secularism in keeping the French nation unified.[36] The National Assembly adopted the law on February 10, 2004, with the support of the vast majority of parliamentarians (494 voted for the law while 36 voted against it). The Senate approved it on March 3, 2004, with strong support from the senators (276 to 20 in favor of the legislation).[37]

The law amended the French Code of Education, which specifies the principles of public education in France. The law did not mention any religious symbol in particular, though many considered this law to be against the wearing of headscarves. The law states that: "In state primary and secondary schools, the wearing of signs or dress by which pupils overtly manifest a religious affiliation is prohibited. The school rules shall state that a dialogue shall precede the institution of disciplinary proceedings with the pupil."[38] Legislators also added an explanation to clarify what was to be considered as "overtly manifested" dress: conspicuous signs such as a large cross, a veil, or a skullcap would be banned while discreet signs such as medallions, small crosses, stars of David, hands of Fatima, or small Korans would be allowed. The law came into effect on March 15, 2004, when it was published in the official gazette of France. On May 18, 2004, the minister of education François Fillon presented a circular about the implementation of the law. This circular made clear that the wearing of headscarves would not be allowed in French public schools: "The prohibited signs and dress are those by which the wearer is immediately recognizable with regard to his or her religion, such as the Islamic veil, whatever its name, the kippa, or a crucifix of manifestly exaggerated dimensions."[39]

---

[35] Patrick Weil, one of the members of the Stasi Commission, expressed his disappointment that the parliamentarians ignored several recommendations that the commission made (author's personal interview with Patrick Weil, Paris, France, July 27, 2007). Other members of the commission also stated their discontent that many of their recommendations were ignored by the media and policymakers. For an example, see Philippe Bernard and Sylvie Kauffmann, "Voile: Les États d'âme de quatre 'sages' de la commission Stasi," *Le Monde*, February 3, 2004.

[36] *Le Figaro*, "Jacques Chirac a longuement condamné hier le communautarisme," December 18, 2003.

[37] Agence France-Presse, "French Senate Votes Ban on Religious Insignia in State Schools," *Agence France-Presse*, March 3, 2004.

[38] Loi no 2004-228 du 15 mars 2004. *Journal Officiel* No 65, March 17, 2004. 5190. The full text of the law can be seen at www.legifrance.gouv.fr/WAspad/UnTexteDeJorf?numjo=MENX0400001L (last accessed on November 9, 2018).

[39] Martine Laronche, "Le Conseil supérieur de l'éducation a adopté la circulaire sur le voile," *Le Monde*, May 19, 2004.

In short, support for banning the headscarf in public schools increased gradually in France. Those who defended the girls' right to wear a headscarf in the early 1990s changed their position in later years. French lawmakers defended the restrictions by arguing that they were reinforcing French secularism in the wake of increasing "Islamist threat" in Europe. The French legislators claimed that they were revamping their own national and historical characteristics in an increasingly changing Europe. However, a quick historical overview of the French state's handling of manifestations of religious symbols in public places shows that recent policies are actually deviations from historically established French institutions of secularism.

The 1905 law on the separation of church and state, the founding document of French secularism, was a compromise between the anticlericals and the church, and it guaranteed the right to manifest religious beliefs.[40] Although this law came after long-lasting struggles between the anticlerical movement and the church, the combative anticlerical movement gave birth to a progressive and pacific form of secularism (Bauberot 2003, 461–462). When republicans became confident that the church and the monarchy would never be a threat to the state, they moderated their positions. The forerunners of secularization such as Jules Ferry and Ferdinand Buisson differentiated religion from clericalism and defined the enemy as "clericalism"; and they provided the church with religious liberties. This was also the case for the Catholic Church: when it saw that it could not reinstall the monarchy and turn back the process of secularization, the Catholic Church worked to secure religious liberties. Bauberot (2003, 463) writes that there were two models of secularism on the agenda: one was combative, defended by prime minister Emile Combes, and the other liberal, supported by Aristide Briand, who would eventually also serve as a prime minister. The group that preferred a peaceful and less confrontational transition won out: the 1905 law represented the victory of the liberal model, which ensured freedom of conscience, guaranteed the freedom to exercise religion, and respected the self-organization of each religion, even if no religion was recognized or subsidized. The conflict between the church and the state vanished progressively after this law, and religion ceased to be a political problem.[41] In short, the 1905 law did not limit the manifestation of religious symbols in classrooms.

---

[40] Many scholars that I interviewed during my fieldwork in France in Summer 2007, including Alain Gresh, Patrick Weil, Bernard Godard, and Olivier Abel, agreed with this point. For example, Alain Gresh told to me that the 2004 law is a victory of strict secularists and destroyed the compromise of 1905 between religions and the state (author's interview with Alain Gresh, Paris, France, July 18, 2007). While Patrick Weil also sees the 1905 law as a compromise between the church and the state, he sees the 2004 law as a compromise as well, between the state and Muslims (author's interview with Patrick Weil, Paris, France, July 27, 2007).

[41] There was a short period under the Vichy regime during which the 1905 compromise was lifted. In this period, the state intervened in religious affairs in favor of the Catholic Church. Religious liberties for other denominations, especially for the Jewish population, were removed. However,

A historical analysis of the French policies of accommodating religious practices in schools reveals that the state had tolerated students' wearing of religious symbols in schools. Even in the early 1880s, when the conflict between republicans and the church was at its height, Jules Ferry issued a circular recommending that schoolteachers be respectful of students' beliefs and religious symbols. He advised teachers: "Ask yourself if a father, I mean a single one, listening to you in your classroom, could in good faith, refuse his assent to what you are about to say" (Roy 2007, 108). Christian schoolchildren were allowed to wear crosses in the classrooms, and Jewish schoolchildren were also allowed to wear yarmulkes in the schools (except during the Vichy regime of 1940–1944). In the later years, French Sikhs were allowed to wear turbans in public schools. Muslim girls were also allowed to wear headscarves, even after 1989 when the first affair appeared in the media. The French courts, including the highest administrative court, the Council of State, followed a similar path. In many cases, the courts decided that the wearing of a headscarf in itself was not a problem if it did not violate public order.

In sum, the historically established rule was that the French state was to provide a neutral classroom to its citizens, but not impinge on the religious freedoms of the students if they were in conformity with public order and health. The French courts took this stance throughout the 1980s and 1990s in their dealings with the issue of headscarves in public schools. However, support for the headscarf-wearing students decreased in the 2000s and the lawmakers passed a law banning headscarves in public schools in 2004 without significant social resistance to it.

CONCLUSION

French state–religion institutions were shaped during the Third Republic after republicans mobilized an anticlerical attack against the Catholic Church. The republicans gained an upper hand due to their continuous electoral successes in consecutive elections during the late 1800s and early 1900s. They were able to impose laws that restricted the power of the Catholic Church in society and politics. The success of the republicans culminated in the 1905 law on secularism, which became the foundation of the state–religion regime in France. In later periods, religious groups gained some concessions, but the secular character of the French state remained except in the period of Vichy rule during the Second World War.

French secularism is both a constitutional principle and a national identifier. The French constitution clearly states that France is a secular state. Secularism, in this sense, is a legal principle that separates religion and state. The degree of separation, however, varies across issues. The state is neutral toward religion,

this did not leave any influence on French secularism after the fall of the Vichy regime (Hoffmann 1963, 33–52).

but it supports religious schools. While supporting religious schools may seem problematic for secularism, this support is conditional upon certain requirements, including implementation of a curriculum approved by the state. Besides being a constitutional principle, French secularism is also an important national identifier. French secularism played an important role in the construction of the French nation-state during the Third Republican period, and it is regarded as an important characteristic of French republican identity. In France, education is regarded as an important realm in the implementation of the principle of secularism. The French state unified the curriculum for state schools at the height of its secular revolution during the Third Republic in order to bring up "secular" citizens. French secularism, in line with French republicanism, has a universalistic bias, meaning that it is opposed to communitarianism and multiculturalism. France champions a citizenship regime that emphasizes commonalities and does not recognize the diversity of its citizens. This outlook has played an important role in shaping the state's policies toward Muslims.

Overall, the French state has developed policies toward Muslims in line with its legacy of secularism; however, there have been deviations from the historical path in French policies toward Muslims in the 2000s. The French state implemented relatively friendly policies in the creation of a representative organization for Muslims and in the building of mosques, kept its unwillingness to support Islamic schools, and employed discriminatory policies in the issue of the manifestation of religious symbols in public places. The state's security concerns, especially after the September 11, 2001, terrorist attacks, played a significant role in the state's efforts to create a representative organization for French Muslims. In doing so, the state aimed to set up institutional mechanisms so as to have more control over Muslims. In line with its desire to have more control over Muslims, the state also helped some Muslim groups build relatively larger mosques in various cities in France. The state kept its reluctance to extend a contractual relationship to Islamic schools because this was seen a threat to better integration of Muslims into the broader French society. The strict secularist groups in France used the international context to mobilize support for the banning of headscarves in public schools and the burqa in public areas.

Although the French state has a more restrictive approach toward religions compared to its European counterparts, the wearing of religious symbols for students in classrooms had never been banned by law until 2004. The established historical institutions of secularism accommodated the wearing of headscarves in France until then. A question arises: what motivated French legislators to pass a law banning headscarves in the early 2000s? I address this question with reference to the international context and the strategic interaction between political and religious actors in France. In Chapter 5, I show how the international and European context, especially the rise of Islamophobia, influenced state policies toward Muslims. In Chapter 7, I demonstrate how domestic actors utilized this international context to mobilize support for their own policy agendas and how, because of this, they were able to achieve outcomes not in line with the historical legacies of French secularism.

PART II

INTERNATIONAL CONTEXT

# 4

## The European Union and Christians in Turkey

On April 11, 2008, the president of the European Commission, José Manuel Barroso, along with the European enlargement commissioner Olli Rehn, met ecumenical patriarch Bartholomew in Istanbul during their official visit to Turkey to discuss the progress toward Turkey's European Union (EU) membership. After the visit, Barroso praised Turkey's "decision to return property, such as school buildings, churches and orphanages, seized from Jewish and Christian foundations decades ago."[1] In their meeting, the patriarch and the EU representatives discussed the status of the historical Theological School of Halki and urged the Turkish government to facilitate the reopening of the school, which had been closed down in 1971.[2] This visit was not the first of its kind. World leaders including President Barack Obama visited the patriarch during their official visits to Turkey. The patriarch himself visited Brussels and several other European capitals to explain the grievances of the Turkish Christians. These exchanges occurred with the assumption that international pressure could change Turkey's policies toward Christians.

As exemplifed in these visits, the international community, specifically political leaders, has long put pressure on Turkey to facilitate reforms. This pressure gained special importance with Turkey's bid for EU membership. This chapter demonstrates the existence of international pressure that led to increases in religious liberties for the Christian minority in Turkey. Between 2000 and 2010, Turkey was under intensive, persistent, and systematic international pressure with regard to its policies toward Christian minorities, and this pressure produced changes in policy: Turkey amended its constitution and some relevant laws to improve the status of Christians. The most important international actor in this process, the EU, enforced several policies on the Turkish state through progress reports prepared by the European Commission. The EU demanded that Turkey improve its record in order to achieve full membership to the Union. EU pressure involved lots of activities at

---

[1] *International Herald Tribune*, "EU Chief Visits Orthodox Patriarchate in Istanbul," April 11, 2008.

[2] Ibid.

a time (intensive), continued for a long time (persistent), and operated in an organized way (systematic). The United States joined the EU in exerting pressure through its religious freedom reports and diplomacy. The United States' influence remained limited due to other strategic necessities of the Turkish–American relationship, such as the United States' need for Turkey's support in the Iraq War. The United Nations and other international nongovernmental organizations had also raised issues related to the religious freedom of the Christian minority in Turkey; however, their pressure created little or no change.

Turkey's decades-old relationship with Western institutions in general and the EU in particular created room for international pressure to structure domestic policies. In this chapter, I first provide a context for understanding Turkey's special relationship with the West, particularly with Europe. In doing so, I address how the issue of non-Muslim minorities played a role in this specific historical relationship. Second, I document the extent of EU pressure through an examination of the European Commission's progress reports on Turkey and other reports prepared by EU institutions. Given that the EU played a significant role in the passing of laws on religious minorities in Turkey, it is important to understand the transnational mechanisms through which the EU exerted pressure on Turkey, and I provide an explanation for why EU pressure mattered more than the pressure of any other international body in making a difference in Turkish domestic policies. Finally, I review the stance of non-European international institutions on Christian minorities and the mechanisms through which they put pressure on the Turkish government. I also evaluate why non-European pressure could not produce the desired outcomes in shaping Turkish state policies toward religious minorities.

## TURKEY, THE WEST, AND THE EUROPEAN UNION

Turkey's connection with the West, which dates back to the modernization efforts of the late Ottoman period, influenced the state's relationship with Christian minorities. The diffusion of Western institutions and values started in the nineteenth century and continued in the republican era. Turkey sought to become part of the Western world. From its security alliance with NATO during the Cold War years to its pursuit of EU membership in the post–Cold War period, Turkey has always been part of the Western political and economic establishment. Although Turkey's relationship with the West has had ups and downs, it has maintained strong connections with Western and European institutions. This connection has influenced the status of Christian minorities in several ways.

The Ottoman history of modernization in the nineteenth century shaped the parameters of Turkey's relations with the West. These modernization reforms aimed to integrate the Ottoman Empire into the West politically and economically. After the loss of territories in the Balkans and the Middle East, Ottoman statesmen looked for ways to regain the strength held by the empire in its classical age. Reformers implemented a modernization process that led to the adoption of Western political and economic structures. In the late nineteenth century, reformers implemented legal and educational systems similar to those of Western countries and signed agreements with Western states to incorporate the Ottoman Empire into the Western economic structure. Furthermore, the leaders established alliances with European countries, particularly Britain and France, which were used to defend the Ottoman Empire against Russia and sometimes against internal rebellions. Modernization efforts reached into the cultural realm; the late Ottoman modernizers sent hundreds of Turkish students to European countries. These intellectuals started a fierce debate on how to save the empire from collapse in the last few decades of the Ottomans (Hanioğlu 2008).

This modernization process impacted the rights of Christian minorities. From the mid-nineteenth century on, the Ottoman Empire faced strong Western pressure to grant equal rights to its non-Muslim minorities. European powers used the issue of minority rights as a pretext to intervene in Ottoman affairs (Weitz 2008, 1330). Ottoman modernization efforts, known as the Tanzimat reforms, always included propositions to improve the status of Christians on the basis of equal citizenship for all. European pressure was the major reason for the decrees that improved the status of non-Muslim minorities (Finkel 2005, 447–487). The Ottoman Empire's integration into the European state system required reforms protecting Christian minorities. Russia used the pretext of protecting the interests of Slavic populations in the Balkans in its intervention in Ottoman affairs. European powers were interested in the protection of Catholic and Orthodox Christian minorities. It is not surprising that the notion of equality among Ottoman nationals went hand in hand with other modernizing reforms such as centralization and secularization.

Turkish modernization reached its zenith after the proclamation of the republic in 1923. In the nation-building process, the new leadership departed from the Ottoman-Islamic past and sought to create a modern secular nation-state. The Turkish republic modeled its newly established polity on Western economic, political, and even cultural institutions. Three principles – secularism, nationalism, and modernization – defined the identity of the new republic. In this era, Turkey had deep-rooted cultural and civilizational motivations in its pursuance of becoming part of the Western world. Turkish modernization rested on the idea that Turkey would be part of a "modern" and "civilized" Europe in the future (Mardin 1991; 2006). Turkey developed peaceful relations with Western countries after years of war. Turkish policymakers implemented new reforms and adopted several legal codes from European countries. The founding leaders adopted the Latin alphabet and removed many Arabic and Persian words from the Turkish language. The cultural transformation went so far that the state cut support for traditional

Turkish music and established orchestras to perform Western music. The state sent students to European universities to speed up the modernization process.

In the period after the Second World War, this Western cultural transformation shifted to political and economic spheres. Turkey fell under severe threat from Soviet Russia after its expansion toward Eastern Europe in the postwar period. Turkey increased its strategic relations with the United States and European countries and gradually became part of Western political and economic institutions. Turkey was a founding member of the United Nations immediately after the Second World War. In August 1949 Turkey joined the Council of Europe, which was established to promote human rights, democracy, and economic development. In February 1952 Turkey became a member of NATO, three years after it was established. Turkish membership of NATO marked its inclusion in the Western alliance during the Cold War years. Turkey played a major role in the NATO alliance by protecting Western borders against the Soviet Union, while Western countries provided significant security guarantees to Turkey vis-à-vis the Soviet threat. In August 1962, Turkey was one of the founding members of the Organization for Economic Cooperation and Development. In June 1973, Turkey became a member of the Organization for Security and Cooperation in Europe, which was established to promote arms control, human rights, freedom of the press, and fair elections.

In 1959, Turkey applied to join the European Economic Community (EEC), which was established in 1957. In 1963, Turkey signed a treaty with the EEC that established a roadmap for Turkey to become a full member. However, developments in later years created obstacles to the roadmap being followed. In 1970, Turkey and the EEC signed a new protocol that detailed the terms of a full customs union between the two parties that would include free circulation of goods and people. The 1971 military intervention in Turkey slowed down relations and made this agreement difficult to implement. The 1980 military coup and subsequent human rights violations in Turkey further damaged relations with the EEC. Turning back to civilian rule in 1983 improved relations; however, the chances of reviving the 1963 agreement remained limited. In 1987, Turkey again applied for full membership of the EEC. In 1989, the European Commission declared Turkey's eligibility to become a member if Turkey met the political and economic criteria.

In 1993, the EEC, which was deepening its political integration, changed its name to the European Union (EU). In 1995, Turkey signed a customs union agreement with the EU. The union included industrial and processed agricultural goods. In addition to the abolishment of duties in these sectors, Turkey harmonized its tariffs and trade agreements for trade with third-party countries. The partial customs union generated hope for a full membership; however, events in the late 1990s decreased hopes on both sides. In 1997, the European Commission decided to start membership negotiations with Cyprus and raised a number of political questions about Turkey's bid for full membership in the EU. The commission required Turkey to normalize relations with Cyprus, which it does not recognize as a sovereign state. In return, the Turkish government froze its relations with the EU for the following two years.

The newly negative atmosphere was replaced by a more hopeful one in 1999, when the European Council declared Turkey to be a candidate country to the EU at the Helsinki Summit. This development opened a new era in Turkey's EU membership bid. Between 1999 and 2004, Turkey implemented a number of legislative changes to adapt its legal system to that of the EU, particularly in the areas of human rights, minority rights, and the economy. Once a country becomes a candidate country, it is expected to transform its legal system to fulfill the Copenhagen Criteria: the minimum political requirements of being part of the EU family. In 2004, the European Commission decided that Turkey fulfilled those requirements and prepared a roadmap to start accession negotiations. The commission recommended starting the negotiations in 2005, and this plan was approved by EU leaders in December 2004. Turkey and the EU officially started membership negotiations in October 2005 (Rumford 2013, 101).

There were several roadblocks in Turkey's path toward full membership. The changes of government in France and Germany stalled the process. The French president Nicolas Sarkozy and the German chancellor Angela Merkel promoted the idea of establishing a "privileged partnership" instead of offering full membership to Turkey. After Sarkozy left office, France became warmer to the idea of Turkish membership in the EU, but the increasing Islamophobia in Europe decreased popular support for Turkish membership. The financial crisis of 2008 made the membership bid even more difficult as EU countries focused on their internal problems. After Cyprus became a full member of the EU in 2004, it gained the ability to block Turkish membership. Since 2009, due to the veto power of Cyprus, the EU has blocked the opening of chapters in its negotiations with Turkey. As a result, as of December 2018, Turkey had completed only one of the thirty-five chapters that need to be adapted to EU law.[3] Fifteen chapters have been opened and negotiations over the other nineteen chapters have not yet started.

The impact of Turkey's European connection on its treatment of Christians has been limited until recently. Throughout the Cold War years, strategic priorities defined Turkey's relationship with Western institutions. Both Turkey and its Western allies saw the relationship as significant in preventing the expansion of the Soviet Union. Even though Turkey had committed to remaining a democracy and promised not to violate universal human rights, specific issues related to Christian minorities were not on the agenda in its relationship with the Western institutions. Even when the status of Turkey's Greek minority became at risk as Turkey and Greece had political problems

---

[3] See the European Commission's website at http://ec.europa.eu/enlargement/countries/detailed-country-information/turkey/index_en.htm (last accessed on December 12, 2018).

over the status of Cyprus, Turkey's Western connection did not deeply alter. However, once the Cold War ended, the priorities of the actors changed. It was after this development that the amelioration of the Christian minority's status gained new momentum.

Most reforms regarding the Christian minorities were passed between the 1999 Helsinki Summit and the start of Turkey's EU membership negotiations in 2005, although the reform process continued until 2010. Turkey aimed to meet the criteria to start membership negotiations with the EU. The decision of the EU to declare Turkey a candidate country at the Helsinki Summit in 1999 gave the Justice and Development Party (AKP, Adalet ve Kalkınma Partisi) a "legitimacy and a unique opportunity to introduce reforms for compliance with the Copenhagen criteria" (Çavdar 2006, 488). Thanks to this external pressure, the AKP would introduce many reforms after coming to power in November 2002 on the grounds that those reforms were necessary for Turkey's EU membership.

The pressure coming from the EU facilitated the reforms for Christian minorities because there was a consensus among several actors on becoming part of European institutions. It was difficult for the bureaucratic establishment to oppose reforms that would help Turkey become an EU member. The AKP, which came to power in November 2002, used this situation as an opportunity to transform the political system. The political transformation would create more room for the party to function, as it would liberalize the domestic political system.

There were economic considerations associated with Turkey's EU membership bid. EU membership would provide Turkey with greater economic opportunities. Over 70 percent of Turkey's trade volume was with EU member countries in the early 2000s. Membership of the EU would increase trade and foreign direct investment. Many Turkish people also supported membership for economic reasons because it would create new job opportunities. Membership would bring new funds to Turkey to increase the structural adaptation of its economy to that of the EU (Uğur 2006; Eder 2003; LaGro 2007; Katırcıoğlu 2007).

Because the founders of modern Turkey had sought to make the country part of Europe, the Turkish bureaucratic establishment did not raise significant opposition to the new reformist environment. There was no serious resistance to the AKP's reforms between 2002 and 2010. As Turkey improved its relations with Western institutions, the issue of minorities became part of a larger diplomatic effort between the two parties. The rights of the Christian minority gained prominence in the years after Turkey became an EU candidate country.

## EUROPEAN PRESSURE AND CHRISTIAN MINORITIES

Turkey was under intensive, persistent, and systematic European pressure with regard to its policies toward Christian minorities between 2000 and 2010. The

European Commission's annual progress reports urged Turkey to implement reforms. Further pressure came in the form of statements from EU representatives, reports prepared by the European Parliament, and diplomatic exchanges with the European Commission.

EU conditionality provided the union with opportunities to produce change in Turkish domestic politics. The EU structures domestic policies in candidate countries through annual progress reports prepared by the European Commission. These reports are usually released late every autumn before the meetings of the EU leaders at which decisions about candidate countries are made. The progress reports assess the candidate country based on the steps taken to meet the standards that are required to become a member of the EU. Because major decisions about membership are made based on the progress reports, candidate countries pay the utmost attention to the issues raised in the reports. As the reports are prepared annually, the candidate countries are expected to address the issues raised in the previous year's report.

I have analyzed fourteen progress reports on Turkey published by the European Commission between 1998 and 2011. Many reforms in policy towards Christian minorities were passed by the parliament during this time. The reports between 1999 and 2001 mention the issue in only a few sentences, but the EU gradually increased its attention to the status of Christian minorities. As Turkey improved its human rights records, details on various issues gained significance. While Turkey was implementing the conditions required by the EU, the victims of Turkey's human rights violations, including the Christian minority, became more active in order to get the attention of the EU reporters. After Turkey had adopted laws to improve the status of the Christian minority, new problems emerged in their implementation; and the European Commission addressed those issues in their reports.

The 1998 progress report stated that there were "bureaucratic restrictions" for non-Sunni religious groups, but did not specify what these restrictions were other than saying "for example, the ownership of premises and expansion of activities."[4] The report also mentioned the obligatory religious education classes in public schools which are taught from a Sunni Islamic perspective. Interestingly, the report listed only one Christian group, Assyrian Orthodox Christians. The report indicated that Assyrians were not recognized by the state, which made it difficult for them to exercise their religious liberties. The 1999 report is even less sensitive to the problems of the Christian minorities. It included only the statement, "as far as freedom of religion is concerned, there

---

[4] European Commission, "1998 Regular Report from the Commission on Turkey's Progress towards Accession," 1998, available at http://ec.europa.eu/enlargement/archives/pdf/key_documents/1998/turkey_en.pdf (last accessed on June 20, 2017).

still exists a difference of treatment between those religious minorities recognized by the Treaty of Lausanne and other religious minorities."[5]

In 2000, the progress report addressed for the first time the question of the reopening of the Theological School of Halki, which the Turkish state had closed down in 1971 and had not allowed to reopen since then. The report had a positive tone on other issues related to the Christian minority. It noted "a few signs of increased tolerance towards certain non-Muslim religious communities," and mentioned a government circular which made it possible for Christian minorities to restore their buildings and charitable institutions without seeking permission from the state.[6]

The 2001 report noted "signs of increased tolerance towards certain non-Muslim religious communities" and mentioned Turkish authorities' help with Christians' ecumenical events during the commemoration of the Christian jubilee in the city of Tarsus. On a positive note, the report mentioned a government circular that reaffirmed "the rights of Syrian Orthodox Turkish citizens, who had emigrated, to return to their villages in regions covered by the state of emergency and in adjacent provinces." The report mentioned the difficulties that the Christians had with respect to ownership of property and the issue of the lack of legal personality for churches. The 2001 report brought these two issues to the attention of the EU for the first time. As a follow-up to the previous year's report, it also addressed the issue of the Theological School of Halki.[7]

From 2002 on, the EU progress reports included detailed portrayals of the problems faced by Christian minorities. The three issues that stood out in the 2002 report were the "lack of legal personality, the issues related to the property rights, and the ban of the training of clergy in Turkey." The report discussed in detail the confiscation of the properties of community foundations. It discussed the flaws in the legal changes (Law No. 4771) that gave non-Muslims the right to acquire and dispose of property. The report mentioned how the properties of non-Muslim minorities had been confiscated in the past and the lack of regulations in the new law to return such properties to their original owners. The report listed issues that the Christian minority faced in registering their properties under their own names. The requirement to get the permission of the Council of Ministers for acquiring or disposing of property was mentioned in the report. The report criticized the "discretionary power of the Directorate

[5] European Commission, "1999 Regular Report from the Commission on Turkey's Progress towards Accession," October 13, 1999, available at http://ec.europa.eu/enlargement/archives/pdf/key_documents/1999/turkey_en.pdf (last accessed on June 20, 2017).

[6] European Commission, "2000 Regular Report from the Commission on Turkey's Progress towards Accession," November 8, 2000, available at http://ec.europa.eu/enlargement/archives/pdf/key_documents/2000/tu_en.pdf (last accessed on June 20, 2017).

[7] European Commission, "2001 Regular Report from the Commission on Turkey's Progress towards Accession," November 13, 2001, available at http://ec.europa.eu/enlargement/archives/pdf/key_documents/2001/tu_en.pdf (last accessed on June 20, 2017).

General of Foundations over religious foundations." It reviewed the problems regarding the training of clergy with a special reference to the Theological School of Halki. The report mentioned the difficulties with visa and residence permits for non-Turkish clergy. It pointed out that the Ministry of National Education required non-Muslim schools to have Turkish deputy heads. The report noted that the Syriac community was not allowed to open its own schools to teach its liturgical language to pupils. For the first time in the 2002 report, the European Commission referred to the problems that Protestant religious groups faced in Turkey. The report identified obstacles to the construction of churches and to the rental of places of worship as the two most important problems for Turkish Protestants.[8]

The 2003 report repeated the problems laid out in the 2002 report. In addition, the report gave a detailed review of the issue of property rights with regard to the legal amendments that the Turkish parliament passed in January 2003 (Law No. 4778). It discussed the improvements in property rights for religious minorities by specifically focusing on the removal of the requirement to obtain permission from the Council of Ministers to acquire or dispose of property and the extension of the deadline for community foundations to register their properties. It criticized the fact that the permission requirement had not been completely removed, but the authority to overhaul the community foundations in the acquisition and disposal of property was transferred to the General Directorate of Foundations (GDF). The report urged the Turkish government to pass legislation to return the confiscated properties of religious minorities. It mentioned the practical difficulties faced by the foundations in registering their properties and indicated that "116 foundations have made a total of 2234 applications, of which the majority were either found to be inadmissible because they were registered in the names of public institutions or private individuals (622), or were returned to the applicant for completion (910)." The report brought up the problems related to the issue of the internal management of community foundations owned by religious minorities. It reviewed how the GDF had intervened in the management of the foundations: the GDF had dismissed the trustees of foundations and had become involved in the management of those foundations' assets and accountancy. The report stated that the GDF dissolved 406 foundations between 2001 and 2003. The report detailed the problems faced by Protestant churches, especially the problems related to opening churches and hiring foreign clergy. It mentioned the 2003 amendment in the Law on Construction that made opening of places of worship easier. However, it mentioned how the lack of legal status for Protestant churches created problems for constructing places of worship and hiring clergy. Finally, the

---

[8] European Commission, "2002 Regular Report from the Commission on Turkey's Progress towards Accession," October 9, 2002, available at http://ec.europa.eu/enlargement/archives/pdf/key_documents/2002/tu_en.pdf (last accessed on June 20, 2017).

report discussed Turkey's unwillingness to grant the title "ecumenical" to the Greek Orthodox patriarch in Turkey.[9]

The 2004 progress report, in addition to reviewing the problems that Christian minorities faced, evaluated Turkey's progress on these issues in great detail manner. According to the report, religious freedom in Turkey was subject to serious limitations as compared to European standards, especially "for the absence of legal personality, education and training of ecclesiastic personnel, and full enjoyment of property rights of religious communities." The report looked at the implementation of the legal regulations that had been passed in the Turkish parliament in 2002 and 2003. The report gave the number of community foundation properties that were registered in the names of the foundations: "of the 2234 applications for registration of property in line with the January 2003 Regulation, 287 have been accepted." The report noted the GDF's requirement that all religious community foundations must seek permission from the state to participate in projects with international organizations. It criticized the GDF's involvement in the internal management of community foundations. It assessed the implementation of the laws on places of worship. It criticized the fact that local administrators had not fully implemented the law that made possible the opening of places of worship. It gave the example that the state had refused a Protestant church's longstanding application to register a place of worship. It noted that Panagia Greek Orthodox Church was not given permission to carry out repairs on its building. The report recommended that Turkey improve its record on the implementation of the laws passed by the parliament to ameliorate the status of religious minorities. The report specified unresolved issues such as the reopening of the Theological School of Halki, the ban on the training of clergy, the restrictions on the ability of non-Turkish clergy to work for certain churches such as the Syriac or Chaldean, and the restriction on the public use of the title "ecumenical" by the Greek Orthodox patriarch.[10]

The 2005 progress report covered the same problems included in the previous reports while including recent improvements in the implementation of legal regulations. The report's section on religious freedom started with the sentence, "With respect to freedom of religion only very limited progress has been made since October 2004 in terms of both legislation and practice." The report in particular gave detailed information about the progress in property

[9] European Commission, "2003 Regular Report from the Commission on Turkey's Progress towards Accession," 2003, available at http://ec.europa.eu/enlargement/archives/pdf/key_documents/2003/rr_tk_final_en.pdf (last accessed on June 20, 2017).

[10] European Commission, "2004 Regular Report from the Commission on Turkey's Progress towards Accession," October 6, 2004, available at http://ec.europa.eu/enlargement/archives/pdf/key_documents/2004/rr_tr_2004_en.pdf (last accessed on June 20, 2017).

rights, with special reference to positive judicial decisions and the number of properties registered in the names of foundations. According to the report, "of the 2285 applications for registration of property in line with the January 2003 Regulation, 341 have been accepted." The report recommended that the Turkish government pass a new law on foundations immediately, as the current law "falls short of European standards." The report noted two Council of State decisions in favor of Christians. In June 2005, the Council of State narrowed the scope of the GDF's involvement in community foundations by overturning the decision of the GDF "to assume the management of the Büyükada Greek Girls' and Boys' Orphanage Foundation in 1997 on the grounds that it no longer fulfilled its charitable services." In another decision, the Council of State issued a ruling in favor of a radio station broadcasting to promote Christianity. The report noted that the Protestant church that was mentioned in the previous year's report was able to register as a place of worship. The report ended with unresolved issues such as difficulties in the training of clergy, problems related to the reopening of the Theological School of Halki, obstacles to hiring non-Turkish clergy, and restrictions on the use of the ecumenical title for the Greek Orthodox patriarch.[11]

The 2006 progress report devoted less coverage to minority rights than the reports of the previous years. The report especially required action from the Turkish government on a few issues including the training of clergy with a focus on the Theological School of Halki, regulations that would ease the employment of foreign clergy in Turkey, the GDF's involvement in the internal management of community foundations, and the lack of legal personality of religious minorities. The report noted the Turkish governments' efforts to reach out to non-Muslim minorities to discuss their problems and possible solutions.[12]

The 2007 progress report particularly focused on attacks against Christian clergy and churches. It criticized the media's and the Turkish bureaucracy's portrayal of missionaries as a threat to the integrity of the country. It cited the killing of three Protestants in a local Protestant publishing house in Malatya, Turkey. The report noted improvements especially in the area of the approval of work permits for foreign clergy and ameliorations in the position of community foundations with regard to property issues. It mentioned the Turkish authorities' efforts to improve dialogue with representatives of minority religions. However, as an overall evaluation, the European Commission stated its dissatisfaction

---

[11] European Commission, "2005 Regular Report from the Commission on Turkey's Progress towards Accession," November 9, 2005, available at http://ec.europa.eu/enlargement/archives/pdf/key_documents/2005/package/sec_1426_final_progress_report_tr_en.pdf (last accessed on June 20, 2017).

[12] European Commission, "Turkey 2006 Progress Report," November 8, 2006, available at http://ec.europa.eu/enlargement/pdf/key_documents/2006/nov/tr_sec_1390_en.pdf (last accessed on June 20, 2017).

by indicating that "no real progress can be reported on the major difficulties encountered by [...] non-Muslim religious communities."[13]

The 2008 report focused on the new Law on Foundations passed in the parliament early in the year. The report noted the deficiencies of the law, particularly the government's failure to pay the value of the properties of the community foundations that had been transferred to third parties. The report covered attacks against missionaries, non-Muslims, and their places of worship in a number of provinces. It noted that "two Protestant churches and a Jehovah's Witnesses assembly have been unable to register their places of worship." As with the previous reports, it reminded the Turkish government of the unresolved issues related to the Christian minority.[14]

The 2009 report assessed the implementation of the 2008 Law on Foundations, acknowledging the improvements in terms of property rights for the Christian minority. It again raised the concern that the government had not paid the value of the properties transferred to third parties. The report praised the state for extending work permits for Christian clergy. It addressed the social pressure that Christians faced daily. The report ended with a reminder of the unresolved problems of the lack of legal personality for religious groups, the issues related to the reopening of the Theological School of Halki, and the Turkish government's nonrecognition of the Greek Orthodox patriarch as "ecumenical patriarch."[15]

The 2010 progress report addressed the problems that Christian minorities faced including social discrimination, obstacles to the training of clergy, issues about transfer of properties owned by community foundations, and issues related to the opening of places of worship, but the report did not detail the issues as it had in the previous years. The report noted positive developments in the status of the Christian minority. In August 2010, the Greek Orthodox patriarch Bartholomew celebrated the Divine Liturgy of the Dormition of Theotokos at the Soumela Monastery in the Black Sea province of Trabzon for the first time in nine decades. In September 2010, a religious service was held at the Armenian Holy Cross church on Akhdamar Island on Lake Van for the first time since 1915. The report noted that "the Turkish authorities granted Turkish citizenship to fourteen members of the Greek Orthodox clergy."[16]

[13] European Commission, "Turkey 2007 Progress Report," November 6, 2007, available at http://ec.europa.eu/enlargement/pdf/key_documents/2007/nov/turkey_progress_reports_en.pdf (last accessed on June 20, 2017).

[14] European Commission, "Turkey 2008 Progress Report," November 5, 2008, available at http://eur-lex.europa.eu/legal-content/EN/TXT/PDF/?uri=CELEX:52008SC2699&from=EN (last accessed on June 20, 2017).

[15] European Commission, "Turkey 2009 Progress Report," October 14, 2009, available at http://eur-lex.europa.eu/legal-content/EN/TXT/PDF/?uri=CELEX:52009SC1334&from=EN (last accessed on June 20, 2017).

[16] European Commission, "Turkey 2010 Progress Report," November 9, 2010, available at http://eur-lex.europa.eu/legal-content/EN/TXT/PDF/?uri=CELEX:52010SC1327&rid=3 (last accessed on June 20, 2017).

The 2011 report focused on new legislation enacted in August that addressed the issue of properties that had been transferred to the third parties. The European Commission praised the new legislation and noted that the government would pay the community foundations the value of their properties that had been transferred to third parties. The report also praised the second celebration of the Divine Liturgy of the Dormition of Theotokos at the Soumela Monastery in August 2011 and "the second religious service at the Armenian Holy Cross church on the Akhdamar Island in lake Van" in September 2011. Although the report acknowledged that a Protestant church was opened in the city of Van, it also stated that "non-Muslim religious communities report frequent discrimination, administrative uncertainty, and numerous obstacles to establishing or continuing to use places of worship."[17]

The fourteen progress reports that the European Commission released between 1998 and 2011 drew a roadmap for Turkish policymakers aiming to improve the status of the Christian minority. Earlier reports covered the issue very briefly; however, the reports published between 2002 and 2009 gave very detailed descriptions of the problems that Christians faced. Once the government had made progress on a particular issue, the reports provided a more detailed examination of those issue areas. In this regard, the issues around property rights and places of worship were included in some detail. Unresolved issues, such as obstacles to the training of clergy and the lack of legal personality for churches, were systematically included in the reports.

The annual progress reports were the most important medium through which the EU exerted pressure over Turkey, but there were other supplementary mechanisms that the EU employed to push the Turkish government to speed up the reform process. The European Commission, the European Council, and the European Parliament monitored the Turkish government's reform process. The Turkey–European Union Troika meetings, which were held twice a year, provided another forum for international pressure. In these meetings the Turkish foreign minister met with representatives from the European Commission, from the country that was currently in charge of the presidency of the EU, and from the country that would next take over the presidency. The status of Christian minorities was always raised in the troika meetings, with the EU representatives urging the Turkish government to implement reforms on the issues raised in the annual reports. Because these meetings were held at the highest diplomatic level, the issues they addressed imparted a high priority to the reform process.[18]

---

[17] European Commission, "Turkey 2011 Progress Report," October 12, 2011, available at http://ec .europa.eu/enlargement/pdf/key_documents/2011/package/tr_rapport_2011_en.pdf (last accessed on June 20, 2017).

[18] Hilal Köylü, "AB: Uygulama zayıf," *Radikal*, March 8, 2005; Serhan Akkan, "El Yakan Ödev," *Tercüman*, May 8, 2008; *Zaman*, "Türkiye-AB Troykası'nın gündemi, yeni açılacak fasıllar ve reformların devamı," June 4, 2007; *Sabah*, "Troyka temkinli," November 24, 2004.

The letters sent by the European Commission to Turkey prior to the release of the progress reports also pressed for reforms. In these letters, the Commission warned Turkey about possible issues to be included in the upcoming progress reports if Turkey did not take the necessary steps before the report was released. Turkey received a number of letters that requested improvements on issues affecting Christian minorities. For example, a letter in July 2005 focused only on the issue of Christian minorities with reference to the problems that had been included in the previous progress reports. The letter asked Turkey to speed up the reform process by passing the Law on Foundations to improve the status of Christian minorities. The letter stated that the 2005 progress report would include severe criticisms on this issue if Turkey did not take action.[19] The Commission also warned the Turkish state about these issues through its representatives in Turkey.[20]

The European Parliament put pressure on Turkey to improve the status of Christian minorities. The reports prepared by the parliament are secondary as compared to the Commission's annual progress reports, but they are important in the context of Turkey's efforts to influence European public opinion about Turkish membership of the EU. These reports also addressed the problems faced by Christian minorities in Turkey.[21] For example, the report approved by the European Parliament in May 2008 reviewed the status of Christian minorities in detail and asked Turkey to implement the laws passed by the parliament. The Law on Foundations was especially mentioned as an important step toward the solution of the problems of the Christian minorities, but the report noted the need for its implementation.[22] Christian Democrat parliamentarians were very vocal about minority rights in Turkey. For example, Camiel Eurlings and Hans-Gert Poettering called on Turkey to ameliorate the situation of Christian minorities; they were especially critical of Turkey's failure to progress on the opening of the Theological School of Halki.[23]

The EU's pressure on Turkey created visible policy outcomes. The Turkish government considered the EU's criticisms seriously and took steps to ameliorate some of the issues raised in the progress reports and the statements of European representatives. The Turkish state prepared a national program after each EU progress report and identified a roadmap to improve the status of Christians, especially on the issues included in the annual progress reports.

---

[19] Hilal Köylü, "AB: Din notu zayıf," *Radikal*, July 19, 2005. For other letters of this kind see Barçın Yinanç, "Olli Rehn'den Abdullah Gül'e 301. madde mektubu," *Referans*, September 1, 2006; *Sabah*, "AB: Onlar olmazsa başınız çok ağrır," April 13, 2006.

[20] Hilal Köylü, "Kretschmer: Bu, kriz değil," *Radikal*, June 12, 2006.

[21] Yaman Törüner, "Avrupa Parlamentosu bizden ne istiyor?" *Milliyet*, October 23, 2006: *Referans*, "Avrupa Parlamentosu Türkiye raporunu onayladı," May 22, 2008; *Yeni Şafak*, "AP Türkiye Raporu: Ordu demokratik gelişmeye engel," May 14, 2003.

[22] *Hürriyet*, "AP, Türkiye raporunu kabul etti," May 21, 2008.

[23] *Hürriyet*, "Eurlings: Ruhban okulu açılmalı," October 21, 2005; and *Sabah*, "Pottering: Ruhban okulu açılmazsa Avrupa'da İslam fobisi artar," October 20, 2005.

In its 2001 national program, the Turkish government promised "to take further practical measures to facilitate religious practice for non-Muslim foreign nationals residing in Turkey and practices in other areas pertaining to these persons."[24] Similarly, the 2003 national program outlined proposed improvements with regards to freedom of worship and the use of languages other than Turkish. The program hinted at legislative change that would make the opening of places of worship easier for non-Muslim minorities. It described another change that would make legal the learning of and broadcasting on ethnic and local languages and dialects.[25] Indeed, these regulations were put in place shortly after the national program was released.

In the 2008 national program, the Turkish government indicated its "full commitment to improve the effectiveness of all reforms made with regard to fundamental rights and freedoms, democracy, rule of law, human rights, protection of and respect to minorities in practice and to urgently implement the necessary complementary legal provisions." It then listed some of the improvements that would help non-Muslim minorities in their daily lives. The government promised that "the appropriate measures will be taken in order to meet the need of clergy of non-Muslim communities." The program mentioned previous improvements such as the freedoms related to the use of dialects and languages in both cultural life and broadcasting. The program noted that the "efforts on revising curriculum including removal of the expressions that may contain discrimination from the textbooks will continue."[26] In short, the Turkish government took the progress reports seriously and addressed the issues raised in the reports. The legislative debates which I will discuss in Chapter 6 demonstrates the extent to which European requests for reform shaped policymaking in Turkey.

## NON-EUROPEAN MECHANISMS OF INTERNATIONAL PRESSURE

In addition to EU pressure, Turkey was under the influence of other international bodies pushing for reforms in the treatment of Christian minorities. The United Nations Commission on Human Rights addressed the minority issues in Turkey. The United States, through its International Religious Freedom Commission and Department of State Religious Freedom Reports, put pressure on Turkey. International nongovernmental human rights groups addressed the violations of religious freedoms in Turkey. Unlike the activities of the EU, the pressure exerted by these actors was not intensive, persistent, and

---

[24] 2001 National Programme of Turkey for the Adoption of the EU Acquis, 2001, available at www.ab.gov.tr/_195_en.html (last accessed on December 12, 2018).

[25] 2003 National Programme of Turkey for the Adoption of the EU Acquis, 2003, available at www.ab.gov.tr/_196_en.html (last accessed on December 12, 2018).

[26] 2008 National Programme of Turkey for the Adoption of the EU Acquis, 2008, available at www.ab.gov.tr/42260_en.html (last accessed on December 12, 2018).

systematic. Due to the lack of a strong monitoring system, the actions of these organizations did not visibly affect domestic policy change in Turkey.

The United Nations (UN) reports on human rights issues addressed the status of Christian minorities in Turkey. The 2000 interim report of the special rapporteur of the Commission on Human Rights, which discussed the elimination of all forms of intolerance and of discrimination based on religion or belief, systematically analyzed the difficulties that Christian minorities faced in Turkey. The report identified four major problems. First, the report raised the issue of the absence of legal personality for religious minorities, reviewing the problems that stemmed from this lack of legal personality for Greek Orthodox, Armenian Orthodox, Roman Catholic, and other churches. The report covered the failure of the Turkish authorities to recognize the Greek Orthodox patriarch as "ecumenical."[27]

Second, the report brought up the problems related to the training of clergy for the Christian minorities. It especially emphasized the issues around the reopening of the Theological School of Halki and the Armenian Orthodox seminary. It noted that the Armenian patriarchate "currently has only 24 priests in Istanbul, serving 38 churches." The report stated that the Armenian patriarch had "initiated a private dialogue with the education authorities for establishment of an Armenian religious department in a state university."[28]

Third, the UN report identified major problems in the implementation of laws and regulations on the management and property rights of Christian community foundations. It noted that the Greek patriarchate had not been allowed "to transform its orphanage on Princess Island into a hotel." The GDF's expropriation of four Greek Orthodox churches in Galata was addressed in the report. The report identified problems in the implementation of the Treaty of Lausanne for the benefit of Greek Orthodox and Armenian Orthodox populations.[29]

Finally, the report reviewed the difficulties that the Christian minorities, especially Protestant groups, had faced in their missionary activities. It identified both state policies and societal stereotypes about Christian missionaries. It gave the example of a Christian convert who was detained because he was distributing bibles in Izmir province. The court considered this act to be a crime against public order.[30]

After this review, the UN report argued that nationalism underlay the problems faced by Christian minorities: "The political manipulation of nationalism [...] has made itself felt in particular, and in an intolerant and discriminatory way, against the Christian minorities."[31] The report

---

[27] Interim report of the Special Rapporteur of the Commission on Human Rights on the Elimination of All Forms of Intolerance and of Discrimination Based on Religion or Belief, August 11, 2000, available at http://docplayer.net/8007408-Elimination-of-all-forms-of-religious-intolerance.html (last accessed on June 20, 2017).

[28] Ibid.    [29] Ibid.    [30] Ibid.    [31] Ibid.

recommended that: "the [Turkish state] authorities should establish a clear principle whereby nationalism is not to be used against minority religious communities."[32]

The United States' pressure on Turkey to implement reforms came primarily through two mechanisms: the United States Commission on International Religious Freedom's work to improve religious freedoms globally, and the US State Department's reports on religious freedom. The US Commission of International Religious Freedom raised the problems of Christian minorities in its 2007 annual report. The report devoted an entire chapter to Turkey. It identified the absence of legal personality for churches as the major issue which "resulted in serious problems with regard to their right to own, maintain, and transfer property as a community and as individuals and to train religious clergy, leading in some cases to a critical decline in these communities on their historic lands."[33]

Problems related to the training of clergy were also addressed in the report. It indicated that there were 20 clergy in the Armenian Orthodox community to operate 38 churches.[34] In response to the Turkish authorities' excuse that the reopening of the Theological School of Halki might lead to the opening of Islamic private schools, the report stated that "the Halki Seminary was open and functioning from 1923 to 1971 without threatening the relationship between the state and Muslim institutions of higher learning."[35] It criticized the Turkish government for its failure to solve the problems related to the operation and property rights of the community foundations: "the rules governing the foundations of minority religious communities in Turkey have been found to be intrusive and in many cases, onerous."[36]

In its conclusion, the report recommended that the United States government put pressure on Turkey on the following issues: recognizing the legal personality of religious minorities, guaranteeing full property rights to religious minorities, permitting religious minority institutions to train religious clergy, and easing the opening of worship places for Christian minorities.[37]

The US Department of State issued eleven International Religious Freedom Reports between 2001 and 2011. Starting with the 2002 report, the State Department raised the issue of the property rights of community foundations in Turkey.[38] After 2004, the reports tracked the implementation of the reforms aimed

---

[32] Ibid.

[33] United States Commission on International Religious Freedom, "Annual Report 2007," May 1, 2007, p. 16, available at www.uscirf.gov/images/AR_2007/annualreport2007.pdf (last accessed on June 20, 2017).

[34] Ibid., p. 17.    [35] Ibid., p. 20.    [36] Ibid., p. 19.    [37] Ibid., pp. 21–24.

[38] State Department Bureau of Democracy, Human Rights, and Labor, "2002 International Religious Freedom Report," May 2002, available at www.state.gov/g/drl/rls/irf/2002/13986 .htm (last accessed on June 20, 2017).

at ameliorating the property issues of community foundations.[39] Although the State Department reports did not raise the problems of legal personality in a systematic manner, the fact that the Turkish state had not recognized the "ecumenical" status of the Greek Orthodox patriarch was addressed in the reports from 2002.[40]

There were primary issues that were emphasized in each and every report. First, the reports raised the concern that Protestant missionaries encountered bureaucratic and social obstacles in exercising their religious liberties. Given that there are many American citizens among the Protestant missionaries in Turkey, this is not surprising. The 2005 report claimed that the Turkish state had developed an official anti-missionary policy through its organs. The report alleged the presentation of state-sanctioned sermons that included negative descriptions of missionary activities. It referenced the ministry of the interior's internal rulings aimed at preventing the infiltration of missionaries.[41] It noted that the Turkish state, through its Directorate of Religious Affairs, had "initiated a public campaign against Christian missionary activity in the country." The 2006[42] and 2007[43] reports gave detailed information about the cases in which the Christian missionaries had been discriminated against. The 2006 report noted that there were 1,100 missionaries in Turkey and that "government officials asserted that missionary activity was a threat to the state and was not covered under the concept of religious freedom." The 2007 report cited an incident in which the police "arrested four street evangelists in Istanbul for missionary activity, disturbing the peace, and insulting Islam." The issue of missionaries was covered in the remaining reports with exact numbers of incidents that Protestant missionaries experienced in Turkey.

Second, the State Department reports always included the issue of the reopening of the Theological School of Halki. The 2001 report was the shortest of all the reports, but the issue of Halki was still in it.[44] The reports

[39] State Department Bureau of Democracy, Human Rights, and Labor, "2004 International Religious Freedom Report," May 2004, available at www.state.gov/g/drl/rls/irf/2004/35489 .htm (last accessed on June 20, 2017).

[40] State Department Bureau of Democracy, Human Rights, and Labor, "2003 International Religious Freedom Report," May 2003, available at www.state.gov/g/drl/rls/irf/2003/24438 .htm (last accessed on June 20, 2017).

[41] State Department Bureau of Democracy, Human Rights, and Labor, "2005 International Religious Freedom Report," May 2005, available at www.state.gov/g/drl/rls/irf/2005/51586 .htm (last accessed on June 20, 2017).

[42] State Department Bureau of Democracy, Human Rights, and Labor, "2006 International Religious Freedom Report," May 2006, available at www.state.gov/g/drl/rls/irf/2006/71413 .htm (last accessed on June 20, 2017).

[43] State Department Bureau of Democracy, Human Rights, and Labor, "2007 International Religious Freedom Report," May 2007, available at www.state.gov/g/drl/rls/irf/2007/90204 .htm (last accessed on June 20, 2017).

[44] State Department Bureau of Democracy, Human Rights, and Labor, "2001 International Religious Freedom Report," May 2001, available at www.state.gov/g/drl/rls/irf/2001/5694 .htm (last accessed on June 20, 2017).

gave detailed background on the school, its opening, its operation until 1971, and the political context that led to its closure. The reports urged the Turkish government to find a middle way to open the school under the auspices of the Greek Orthodox patriarchate.

International human rights organizations also put pressure on Turkey to improve the status of minorities. While there was some criticism of Turkey by nongovernmental human rights organizations with regard to the state's policies toward the Christian minorities, it was not systematic and continuous. Human Rights Watch, for example, did not issue reports on the religious freedoms of Christian minorities in Turkey. It addressed these problems on some occasions; but even on those occasions, it only referenced the reports prepared by other international organizations. In its 2002 report, Human Rights Watch cited the UN report that is discussed earlier in this chapter.[45] In its 2006 report, Human Rights Watch again cited the reports prepared by the EU in a few sentences.[46]

The International Helsinki Federation for Human Rights gave little attention to the problems of Christian minorities in Turkey.[47] The organization referenced the issue only on a few occasions, one of which was its 1999 annual report. The organization reviewed the problems of the Christian minorities in an unorganized way with little substance. It addressed three issues related to three different Christian groups: the nonrecognition of the Syriac Orthodox Christians as a minority, state interference in the internal management of minority foundations, and issues about the training of clergy for the Greek Orthodox Church.[48]

The capability of non-European international pressure on Turkey to create a policy change toward Christian minorities was limited. In contrast to the EU, the UN did not have strong monitoring mechanisms. The United States had some leverage over Turkey, but that leverage was not diffused enough to create change in domestic policies toward religious minorities. Military cooperation and strategic partnership in the Middle East were the priority issues for United States–Turkish relations. Nongovernmental human rights organizations did not put enough emphasis on the issue of religious freedoms and their monitoring capabilities remained limited. In short, the pressure created by non-European states and institutions did not influence policy changes.

CONCLUSION

Beginning in the late Ottoman period, Turkey adopted several institutions from European countries. The Turkish republic was founded on the idea of a modern nation-state based on secularism, nationalism, and Westernization. In the period after the Second World War, Turkey became part of several Western

---

[45] Human Rights Watch 2002.  [46] Human Rights Watch 2006.
[47] This organization ceased to exist in November 2007.
[48] International Helsinki Federation for Human Rights 1999.

institutions such as the Council of Europe, NATO, the Organization for Economic Cooperation and Development, and the Organization for Security and Cooperation in Europe. From 1963 on, Turkey aspired to be a member of the EEC and the EU. Turkey's Western orientation influenced its domestic and foreign policy. It was this special relationship that allowed the EU to put pressure on Turkey to pass relevant legislation improving the status of non-Muslim minorities.

The intensive, persistent, and systematic European pressure created opportunities to push Turkey to transform its domestic policies toward the Christian minority. Turkish policymakers implemented structural changes under the influence of EU pressure. Because becoming a member of the EU was an important stake for the Turkish state, EU pressure created a notable change in Turkish domestic institutions. The EU put systematic pressure on Turkey on the issues of property rights for Christian community foundations, particularly their right to acquire and dispose of properties without state limitations; the training of clergy; religious education; places of worship; and the lack of legal personality for religious entities. The Turkish parliament enacted laws that improved the status of Christian minorities on property rights, places of worship, and issues of religious education. The pressure coming from the UN, the United States, and international nongovernmental organizations had a limited role in pushing Turkey for reform because those actors did not have strong monitoring mechanisms.

EU pressure definitely helped the passing of the Turkish democratizing reforms; however, these reforms would not have been possible without the deliberate choices made by domestic actors who used the possibility of EU membership as leverage. The AKP government saw the EU membership bid as a powerful catalyst for domestic political reform, which would bring about the elimination of authoritarian aspects of Turkish politics that narrowed the room for maneouver of the political parties. Only the excuse of the EU membership bid could provide the government with the opportunity to decrease the role of the military in politics. With this consideration in mind, the AKP saw EU membership bid as an important opportunity to transform Turkey so as to guarantee its political future (Kotsovilis 2006; Keyman and Düzgit 2007; Öniş 2003). In Chapter 6, I examine how domestic actors exploited the international context to execute their agendas for reform.

# 5

# Islamophobia and Muslims in France

In 2003, Dounia Bouzar and Saïda Kada, two French Muslim women activists, wrote a book titled *L'Une voilée, l'autre pas* (One Veiled, the Other Not) on their views on Muslims' participation in French republican modernity (Bouzar and Kada 2003). Even though they represented two different Muslim perspectives, one wearing a headscarf and the other not, they were united in the idea that most of the Muslim women in France sought to be part of the modern republican public sphere. Kada challenged the view that the wearing of the headscarf symbolizes submission to men; rather, she argued that it symbolizes submission to God and contributes to spirituality. Both authors criticized the patriarchy and argued that there are several ways to counter it; sometimes wearing a headscarf is part of that struggle. At a time when Muslim women were being presented by the media as uniform and submissive, Bouzar and Kada attempted to demonstrate the subjectivity of Muslim women. However, their message fell on deaf ears. The French media kept presenting Muslims as a monolithic category characterized by patriarchy, bigotry, and fundamentalism. Why did the nuances of a debate on Muslims disappear, and why did the French public accept such simplistic descriptions of Islam and Muslims in the early 2000s? This chapter shows that the global rise of Islamophobia and its impact on France made it difficult for Muslim voices to be heard. In an increasingly polarizing political environment, the nuances that might have informed public debate were lost to hatred and discrimination. Anti-Muslim public actors were able to exploit this environment in pushing their Islamophobic policy agendas.

The global rise of Islamophobia and its manifestations in France helped the actors supportive of restrictive policies toward Muslims by provoking fears about the rise of "fundamentalism," which many French citizens perceived as a threat to republicanism and secularism. The increasing concern about "Islamist militancy" provided anti-Muslim actors with the opportunities to expand their social and political support base. Islamophobia, combined with the nationalist backlash against globalization and the increasing power of the EU, contributed to the rise of the far-right National Front party (FN, Front national) in France. In competition with the FN, center-right and center-left parties revised their political discourses to make them more anti-immigrant and anti-Muslim than they had been. In the early 2000s, the French public reached a consensus on decreasing the visibility of the Muslim presence, giving strong support to the headscarf ban in 2004. This chapter documents the effect of Islamophobia in creating a political environment that restricted Muslim actors and their liberal allies in France.

In this chapter, I start by documenting the rise of Islamophobia globally and in Europe. The aftershocks of European colonialism, the marginalization of Muslim immigrants in European countries, and international events that created tension between Muslims and Western countries led to the increase of Islamophobia throughout the world. European countries increased their pressure on Muslim populations, especially after the September 11 terrorist attacks. Second, I look at how Islamophobia gained ground in France and led to the rise of the far right. The far-right FN took advantage of anti-Muslim sentiments and pursued an anti-immigrant political campaign. Finally, I analyze international forces that attempted to mitigate the impact of Islamophobia by putting pressure on France to cease anti-Muslim legislative actions. Although a few international bodies criticized the state policies that undermined the status of Muslims, these voices did not change the dominant political environment in France.

## THE GLOBAL RISE OF ISLAMOPHOBIA

The Runnymede Trust, a UK-based independent think tank on ethnicity and cultural diversity, coined the term "Islamophobia" in 1997. In the report, titled *Islamophobia: A Challenge for Us All*, the term is used to refer to "unfounded hostility towards Islam" and "the practical consequences of such hostility in unfair discrimination against Muslim individuals and communities, and to the exclusion of Muslims from mainstream political and social affairs."[1] The term became widely accepted especially after the United Nations (UN) conference "Confronting Islamophobia: Education for Tolerance and Understanding," held in December 2004. Kofi Annan, then the secretary of the UN, stated: "Since the September 11 attacks on the United States, many Muslims, particularly in the West, have found themselves the objects of suspicion, harassment and discrimination ... many people see Islam as a monolith and as intrinsically opposed to the West" (quoted in Esposito 2011, 9).

Although many scholars use the term "Islamophobia," there is not a consensus on its definition. As Erik Bleich (2012, 180) notes, some scholars deploy it without defining it (Cole 2009; MacMaster 2003; Munzl 2007; Poynting and Mason 2007) while others define it in a way that is difficult to measure (Geisser 2003; Gottschalk and Greenberg 2008) or very narrowly (Abbas 2004; Lee et al. 2009; Semati 2010; Stolz 2005; Zúquete 2008). I use

[1] Runnymede Trust 1997, 4.

the term "to identify the history, presence, dimensions, intensity, causes, and consequences of anti-Islamic and anti-Muslim sentiments" (Bleich 2012, 17). Following Erik Bleich (2011), I define Islamophobia "as indiscriminate negative attitudes or emotions directed at Islam or Muslims." Negative assessments that generalize about Muslims or aspects of Islam are considered Islamophobic. In other words, when people are assessed based solely on their membership in a defined category, Islam in this case, I consider those assessments to be Islamophobia.

Measuring Islamophobia is a challenging task. Some scholars use anecdotal examples of violence directed at Muslims,[2] some look at socioeconomic disadvantages that Muslims face (Tausch et al. 2007), and some look at negative symbols to map out negative attitudes toward Muslims (Cole 2009; Shryock 2010). In this study, in addition to these ad hoc ways of demonstrating Islamophobic attitudes and behaviors, I rely on surveys conducted by other scholars or institutions and on unsolicited public statements made by members of the political elite.

Media representations of Islam and Muslims in the West offer a monolithic image of Islam as being in conflict with Western liberal values. Media coverage that is not nuanced about the rich diversity among Muslims creates "a breeding ground for Islamophobic sentiments and acts" (Kalin 2011, 52). Although the September 11, 2001, terrorist attacks played a crucial role in prompting the media's monolithic representation of Islam, Islamophobia was already increasing before 2001. As the European Union Monitoring Centre on Racism and Xenophobia noted in its 2002 report on Islamophobia, "Much of what occurred post–September 11 drew heavily upon pre-existent manifestations of widespread Islamophobic and xenophobic attitudes." The September 11 attacks merely "gave a pre-existent prejudice a much greater credibility and validity" (Allen 2010, 14). Three factors can help explain the roots of Islamophobia.

First, as Paul Silverstein (2008) argues, the origins of Islamophobia can be dated back to European colonialism of the Middle East and North Africa. To Silverstein, Islam served to explain two opposite characteristics of a supposed Arab personality in the colonial discourse: "on the one hand, its 'bellicose', 'hostile' nature, attributable to a religious 'fanaticism'; and, on the other, its 'inveterate laziness', resulting from a reverent 'fatalism'" (Silverstein 2008, 7). To justify colonization, colonizers developed two visions of the colonized. Some colonizers created hierarchies between races and considered the colonized as "less than human." Taking the colonized from their humanity made it easier for the colonizers to justify their mistreatment of indigenous populations and despoilment of local resources (Muhammed 2010, 96). Other colonizers developed the idea of a "civilizing mission" and justified their occupation of colonized land by claiming that they were helping indigenous people modernize.

---

[2] EUMC 2002, 13–30; EUMC 2006, 62–89.

In both visions, the superiority of the colonizers and the inferiority of the colonized were the underlying justification. The influence of colonization on Islamophobia continued in the post-colonial era in Europe. Populations from the colonized lands migrated to the countries of their former colonizers. The best example for this trend is perhaps the waves of immigration from North African countries to France in the post–World War II era. French assumptions about these people, inherited from the colonial period, fed mistrust, and far-right political parties capitalized on the presence of immigrants in their political discourse and perpetuated the rise of anti-Muslim sentiments in Europe.

Second, socioeconomic marginalization of immigrants in Western Europe led to discrimination against Muslims. The inflow of Muslim immigrants to meet the labor needs of postwar Europe in the 1950s and 60s and their family unifications in the 1970s increased the Muslim population in European countries such as the United Kingdom, Germany, and France. The number of Muslims in France increased from 400,000 in 1963 to 1.5 million in 1974 due to labor migration and family unifications. This demographic change stimulated a far-right reaction to the newcomers. More importantly, the increase in the numbers of urban poor as a result of this new immigration wave created new social challenges in European countries. In France, the increasing socioeconomic marginalization of immigrants in the 1980s and 90s created a protest movement (the Beur Movement) in metropolitan suburbs. This movement, which committed violence from time to time, found itself at odds with broader French society. The socioeconomic deprivation of North African immigrants and the violent demonstrations that resulted served to maintain anti-Muslim perceptions (Aichoune 1991; Jazouli 1992).

Third, international events between the 1970s and the 2000s have reinforced anti-Muslim sentiments globally and in Europe. The 1979 Iranian revolution and the following Iranian hostage crisis, in which American diplomats in the US Embassy in Tehran were held hostage for more than a year, stirred anti-Islamic sentiments in the West. Statements made by the Iranian leadership that targeted the West and circulated an idea of "revolutionary Islam" increased concerns about Islamic political activism (Esposito 2011, 11). In the 1990s, the Algerian Civil War, in which the secular state and the Islamist opposition had a bloody conflict, contributed to anti-Islamic characterizations in the Western media. Islamophobia grew stronger especially after the "war on terror" in Afghanistan and Iraq, which followed the September 11 terrorist attacks. In addition, controversies such as the Salman Rushdie affair, the murder of Theo van Gogh, and the protests against the publication of caricatures of the Prophet Mohammed, created supposition that Islam is incompatible with Western values of pluralism and freedom of the press.

The September 11 terrorist attacks fed the growing visibility of Islamophobia and the proliferation of anti-Muslim hate crimes (Bleich 2009, 380). The USA-led "war on terror" and its coverage in the media solidified anti-Muslim rhetoric and attitudes in Western societies (Fekete 2004, 3). The response of the USA and of European states to the terrorist attacks has been twofold. On the one hand, international interventions in Afghanistan and Iraq and the instability in these countries in the post-intervention era put "Muslim violence" at the forefront. On the other hand, Western states implemented new "counter-terrorism" policies that challenged the civil liberties of Muslim minorities in Western countries. These policies included "the suspension of habeas corpus (detention without trial), the undermining of the non-refoulement principle (no return to torture), house arrest (control orders), and the corroding effects of the use of secret evidence" (Fekete 2010, 64). In the wake of the September 11 attacks, the feelings of being under physical and cultural threat from Muslims peaked among many in the West (Ciftci 2012).

Because the USA was the direct target of the September 11 attacks, anti-Muslim sentiment gained momentum in the USA thereafter. The response of the media magnified the anti-Muslim impact of foreign policies toward Muslims (Kaplan 2006, 13). Without making any distinction between mainstream and extremist movements, leading scholars and commentators such as Bernard Lewis, Daniel Pipes, and Martin Kramer lumped Islamic social and political movements together under the category of "fundamentalism." These scholars characterized Islamic activism with stereotypical phrases such as "Islam against the West," "Islam's War with Modernity," and "Roots of Muslim Rage" (Esposito 2011, 13). These authors promoted the idea of a binary distinction between Islam and the West. This framing of Islam and Muslims facilitated further polarization in society and the increased hatred of Muslims.

Employing this "scholarship," right-wing columnists, bloggers, and talk show hosts such as Stephen Schwartz, Michael Savage, and Christopher Hitchens used the term "Islamofascism" to blur the distinction between Islam as a religion and Muslim extremists (Esposito 2011, 15). Although President George W. Bush drew a sharp distinction between Islam and extremists, his subsequent use of the term "Islamofascism" implied that "Islam, not just its misuse by extremists, is the root cause of the problem" (Esposito 2011, 14). Other politicians followed suit. Former US senator Rick Santorum stated, "We're at war with Islamic fascism ... These people are after us not because we've oppressed them, not because of the state of Israel ... It's because we stand for everything they hate" (quoted in Esposito 2011, 15). The rise of anti-Muslim discourse in politics and the media shifted the terms of debate about American Muslims. They became part of the public debate on terrorism, violence, and religious extremism. The final outcome was an increase in hostile perceptions of Muslims.

According to a 2006 *USA Today*/Gallup poll, 44 percent of Americans believed Muslims were extreme in their religious beliefs. Nearly one-quarter of Americans would not want a Muslim as a neighbor; only less than half believed that US Muslims were loyal to the United States and almost half favored heightened security measures against Muslims to prevent terrorism.[3] Steven Salaita (2006) shows that the September 11 attacks and the follow-up "war on terror" in Afghanistan and Iraq increased anti-Arab sentiments among Americans. In short, Islamophobia was on strong ground in the wake of the September 11 attacks, scholars introduced binary thinking about Muslims by using the categories of friend and foe, and bloggers and pundits reinforced these divisions.

Although the USA was the target of the September 11 attacks, anti-Muslim sentiments and policies in Europe increased even faster than they did in the USA following the attacks. European capitals showed alarm after 2001 and increased their pressure on Muslims. According to Jocelyne Cesari (2011, 24), EU states arrested more than twenty times the number of terrorist suspects than the USA arrested between 2001 and 2004. The September 11 attacks stimulated an anti-Muslim environment in social, political, and cultural realms in Western European countries. European countries passed new laws that enabled discrimination against Muslims in their social and economic lives. Intellectuals in various European countries produced an anti-Muslim discourse that presented barriers to dialogue between Muslims and broader society. Capitalizing on the increasing anti-Muslim environment, the far-right political parties scapegoated Muslims. As a result, Islamophobia prevailed in Europe and provided the backdrop for public debates on the treatment of Muslims.

In Britain, quantitative data cited in reports on Islamophobia show a dramatic increase in the number of negative stories in the media about Islam and Muslims after the September 11 attacks (Allen 2006, 52). Elizabeth Poole (2002), in a study of reporting on Islam in the British media, demonstrates how global events, particularly the September 11 terror attacks, led the British people to associate negative behaviors with Muslims without making any differentiation between British Muslims and Muslims in other countries. A study conducted by the Psychology Department of Leicester University in 2002 under the leadership of Lorraine Sheridan concluded that the September 11 attacks played a significant role in the rise of discrimination against the Muslim community in Britain (Sheridan 2002; 2006). Britain, a country that had been known for its openness to immigrants, gradually took a harsher stance against Muslims.

A bombing in the London underground rail system on July 7, 2005, contributed to the rise of Islamophobia in Britain. It not only facilitated anti-Muslim sentiments but also led to the passage of new law enforcement regulations that further increased the pressure on British Muslims (Githens-Mazer and Lambert 2010). Clive Field, through an examination of 104 surveys

---

[3] Lydia Saad, "Anti-Muslim Sentiments Fairly Commonplace," Gallup, August 10, 2006, available at www.gallup.com/poll/24073/AntiMuslim-Sentiments-Fairly-Commonplace.aspx (last accessed on June 21, 2017).

undertaken in Britain between 1988 and 2006, concluded that "A stereotypical picture of British Muslims in the eyes of the majority population has emerged, Muslims being seen as slow to integrate into mainstream society, feeling only a qualified sense of patriotism, and prone to espouse anti-Western values that lead many to condone so-called Islamic terrorism" (Field 2007, 447). Terrorism and the public response to it expanded the gap between Muslims and non-Muslims in Britain and made anti-Muslim state policies more likely.

In the wake of the September 11 and the 2005 attacks, the British government passed new antiterrorism laws that increased monitoring of and suspicion toward British Muslims. In November 2001, two months after the September 11 attacks, the government enacted the Anti-Terrorism, Crime and Security Act. The law increased the power of law enforcement authorities in dealing with issues related to terrorism. It allowed the state to detain foreign nationals for an indefinite time if the authorities concluded that it was not safe to deport them to their country of origin. It gave the state flexibility in the freezing and confiscation of funds associated with terrorism. According to the law, detention and interrogation would not depend on an act of violence being committed; an anticipation of violence would be enough to detain or interrogate a person.[4] In practice, this law made all British Muslims potential suspects because it was easy to be suspicious of a Muslim citizen given the Islamophobic environment that had emerged in the wake of the September 11 terror attacks.

After the London Underground bombing in 2005, the British state passed the Prevention of Terrorism Act to further increase the powers of law enforcement authorities in dealing with terrorism charges. The act criminalized the glorification of terrorism; granted the state the right to close places of worship used to foment extremism, to deport or deny entry to foreign nationals who "foster hatred," to refuse asylum to anyone who had links to a terrorist activity, and to strip citizenship from naturalized citizens engaged in terrorism; allowed 90-day pre-charge detention of terrorism suspects; and limited Muslim religious leaders in the topics they could preach in their religious lectures and sermons (Allen 2006, 66). A study conducted by the British Institute of Race Relations found that prosecutors used antiterrorism acts overwhelmingly against Muslim defendants in comparison with other defendants. Only a few arrests led to convictions, and most of the crimes that ended up with convictions turned out to be routine criminal acts and immigration violations (Cesari 2011, 25).

Within this anti-Muslim environment, the English Defense League, a far-right political group in Britain, became bolder and more aggressive against immigrants and Muslims. The group organized several street protests against Muslims across the country. These protests and similar demonstrations organized by other groups polarized the country and put Muslims in the spotlight.

---

[4] The law can be accessed at www.legislation.gov.uk/ukpga/2001/24/contents (last accessed on June 21, 2017).

The situation in continental Europe was not different. As with the USA and Britain, anti-Muslim attitudes and attacks in Germany increased noticeably after the September 11 terrorist attacks. According to a report of the European Union Monitoring Centre on Racism and Xenophobia, there was a significant increase in verbal abuse and physical attacks directed at women with headscarves and men with an Arabic appearance.[5] According to a longitudinal empirical study conducted by Wilhelm Heitmeyer (2005) on "Group Based Humanophobia," attitudes towards Muslims changed negatively in Germany in the years 2002 to 2004 (cited in Karakaşoğlu et al. 2006, 154). According to the report, in 2004, 70 percent of respondents did not think Muslim culture fit into Western society, 58 percent did not want to have Muslim neighbors, and 39 percent did not trust Muslims in general (Karakaşoğlu et al. 2006, 154).

Anecdotal evidence also supports this trend. The tragic murder of an Egyptian-born Muslim, Marwa El-Sherbani, in a Dresden courtroom symbolized the level of hatred of Muslims in Germany. El-Sherbani had sued a neo-Nazi man who insulted her for wearing a headscarf in a public park. While El-Sherbani was giving her testimony against him, the defendant stabbed El-Sherbani and killed her in the courtroom.[6] In the 2000s the far-right National Democratic Party of Germany organized several meetings, demonstrations, and street protests against immigrants, particularly Turkish Muslim immigrants, across Germany.

The increasing social distrust of Muslims was paralleled with state policies that singled out Muslims in limiting their civil liberties. Germany passed two comprehensive bills regarding law enforcement, combating terrorism, civil liberties, immigration regulations, and freedom of worship in September 2001 and January 2002. The new laws introduced amendments to twenty existing laws. With the amendments, the powers of law enforcement authorities were extended so that they had more control over personal data, such as transportation records, electronic and postal communications, and financial transactions. The authorities were allowed to use data-mining methods to identify potential terrorism suspects. The police were given authority for eavesdropping and wiretapping in the course of an investigation. The immigration regulations were amended and the issuing of residence permits for foreigners became more restricted (Karakaşoğlu et al. 2006, 154).

Islamophobia diffused into the cultural sphere as well. In late 2000s, Thilo Sarrazin (2009), a former member of the Executive Board of the Deutsche Bundesbank, published the controversial Islamophobic book, *Deutschland Schafft Sich Ab* (Germany Abolishes Itself). In the book, Sarrazin argued that since Muslim immigrants had genetically lower intelligence and higher fertility,

---

[5] EUMC 2002, 19.

[6] Kate Connolly and Jack Shenker, "The Headscarf Martyr: Murder in German Court Sparks Egyptian Fury," *Guardian*, July 7, 2009.

Germany would eventually become "a nation of dunces." The combination of media representations, state policies, the rise of far-right groups, and cultural productions reinforcing xenophobia created an environment that was dominated by Islamophobia.

The Netherlands experienced a sea change in its approach toward Muslims after the September 11 attacks. It departed from its decades-old multiculturalist policies and started to discuss radical policies toward Muslims including forbidding Islam, deporting Muslims, banning mosques that implemented gender segregation, and revoking state benefits to Muslim organizations (Maussen 2006; Prins 2002).[7] In the past, the Netherlands had used a system of pillarization (*verzuiling*) according to which the state provided resources to various segments of society to maintain their political, ethnic, or religious identities. Each segment of society had its own newspapers, televisions, schools, and civil society organizations that were supported by public funding. The state funded the establishment of schools, hospitals, and other institutions serving different communities (Spiecker and Steutel 2001). In the wake of the September 11 attacks, this system, which was already in decline, came completely to an end.

The reason for the sweeping change in the Netherlands was not only global acts of terror but also domestic developments that paralleled the worldwide rise of Islamophobia. In 2004, a radical Moroccan Muslim assassinated filmmaker Theo van Gogh because of a film that he produced. Attacks on mosques and Muslim associations followed. The increasing discourse of hate created fertile ground for the rise of far-right political parties. Politicians such as Geert Wilders, Rita Verdonk, and Ayaan Hirsi Ali openly spoke out against Islam and Muslims and translated their radical discourse into political opportunities (Maussen 2006, 123). Over the following years, far-right parties increased their influence on Dutch politics, culminating in the 2010 victory of Geert Wilder's fascist party, which became a coalition partner with 24 deputies in the parliament. Intellectuals such as Herman Philipse and Paul Cliteur publicly defended the view that Islam was incompatible with liberal Dutch values (Cesari 2006, 24).

Italy was not different from other European countries in this respect: anti-Muslim sentiments increased there after the September 11 attacks. Mina Liguori (2006), analyzing media representations of Islam after September 11, shows that many Italians considered martyrdom a fundamental aspect of Islam because of al-Qaeda's suicidal action on September 11. Many Italians identified Islam and Italian Muslims with negative ideas such as oppression of women, violence, being against freedom of speech, and other illiberal attitudes (Liguori 2006). The far-right Northern League party took a strong stance against immigration after 2001. The party called on the Italian state to leave the EU

---

[7] See also Jane Kramer, "The Dutch Model: Multiculturalism and Muslim Immigrants," *New Yorker*, April 3, 2006, 60–67.

in order to limit the free flow of people within Europe. The party was part of Silvio Berlusconi's coalition government in 2001–2006 and 2008–2011. In the cultural realm, famous Italian author Oriana Fallaci (2002) published a very critical book on Islam, *La Rage et l'orgueil* (The Rage and the Pride), in which she portrayed Muslims as members of a warlike religion destroying Italian society.

In September 2001, Italy's prime minister Silvio Berlusconi made an infamous comment arguing the superiority of Western civilization and the backwardness of Islam with the expectation that the former would supersede the latter.[8] In later years, the Italian government passed a bill to combat the threat of terrorism and extended the police authority for detention (Cesari 2011, 25). Under the conservative administrations of Berlusconi through most of the 2000s, the Italian state embraced a discriminatory rhetoric against Muslims.

Anti-Muslim sentiments increased in other Western European countries as well during this period. Far-right parties won significant shares of the vote in Sweden and Denmark. In 2009, Switzerland banned the construction of mosques with minarets after a referendum in which a majority of the population voted for the ban. These global trends had a strong influence on the formation of public opinion against Muslims in France. The deepening of Islamophobia and the rise of far-right politics prepared the groundwork for discriminatory state policies toward Muslims.

## ISLAMOPHOBIA AND THE RISE OF THE FAR RIGHT IN FRANCE

Islamophobia diffused into French politics and society with an accelerating speed after the bombings of the World Trade Center in 2001. The rise of Muslim populations in France throughout the 1960s and 1970s led to increased tensions in the later years as Muslims faced socioeconomic marginalization in French society. Furthermore, the deepening of EU connections and the transfer of some aspects of state sovereignty to a supranational structure alarmed far-right politicians and led to a nationalist backlash against Europeanization. Muslims found themselves between a transnational Islamophobia and the rise of populist right-wing politics in France.

In France, Muslims were often stereotypically portrayed in media reports as a devoutly religious and undifferentiated group sharing a fundamentalist vision of Islam. This image concealed major differences in religious beliefs and practices resulting from Muslims' different national, cultural, and religious backgrounds (cf. Bowen 2006, 155–181). The reasons for the rise of global Islamophobia that are examined in the beginning of this chapter—colonialism, marginalization, and international events—also largely explain the rise of

---

[8] Alasdair Palmer, "Is the West Really the Best?" *The Telegraph*, September 30, 2001.

Islamophobia in France. France's colonial relationship with North Africa influenced its approach toward immigrants coming from former colonial lands. The socioeconomic marginalization of immigrants in suburban neighborhoods led to further divisions in society. International events further exacerbated existing stereotypes against Muslims.

As Joan Scott (2007, 45–54), a well-known historian of France and feminist scholar, skillfully explained, the French colonization of North Africa and the bloody war of Algerian independence fueled prejudices against the North African immigrants in France. She argues that the French rulers and intellectuals of the nineteenth century legitimized the colonization of Africa and the Middle East with the concept of "civilizing mission" in which they put a hierarchical relationship between French culture and the cultures of the colonized. Novels and other cultural productions reinforced this image over the years. The war of Algerian independence (1954–1962), which left hundreds of thousands dead, reinforced stereotypes about people of North African descent in later periods (MacMaster 2003). Because of these historical legacies, Islam is seen as the religion of the colonized in France.[9]

The social marginalization of immigrants in suburban housing projects created issues of social disorder and chaos in the late 1990s and early 2000s. This chaotic environment led to anxiety among right-wing politicians and activists and further exacerbated negative attitudes toward North African immigrants, most of whom were Muslims (Silverstein 2008, 17). International events exacerbated existing prejudices: the Iranian revolution of 1979, the rise of Islamism in Algeria in the early 1990s, and the September 11 terrorist attacks consolidated already existing negative attitudes toward Muslims.

French Muslims are more likely to be unemployed than the rest of the French population. According to the National Institute for Statistics and Economic Studies in France, while 26.5 percent of university graduates of North African background were unemployed in 2004, this number is only 5 percent for the overall population.[10] Muslims are only half as likely to become executives in their places of work as compared to the broader population. A recent field experiment conducted by a team of political scientists showed the extent of Islamophobia in France (Adida et al. 2011). In their research, the team tested French behaviors toward a Senegalese Muslim, a Senegalese Christian, and a French Christian in social and business life. The French respondents did not typically treat a Senegalese Christian differently from a French Christian. However, a Senegalese Muslim faced discrimination in different settings, including being only one-third as likely to find a job as his or her Christian counterpart. The scholars concluded that anti-Muslim discrimination was holding back Muslim economic success in France (Adida et al. 2011). Jennifer

---

[9] Author's interview with Catherine de Wenden, Paris, France, July 24, 2007.

[10] "French Muslims Face Job Discrimination," *BBC News*, November 2, 2005, available at http://news.bbc.co.uk/2/hi/europe/4399748.stm (last accessed on June 21, 2017).

Fredette (2014), through interviews with members of France's Muslim minority, demonstrates the gap between French Muslims and the general public as well as the divide within the French Muslim community.

In addition to global causes of the rise of Islamophobia, the unique French experience with religion and secularism played a significant role in the rise of anti-Muslim attitudes and policies in France. As explored in Chapter 3, in France the contestations between Catholics and republicans shaped the formation of French national identity. In French official and public discourse, religions are often depicted as "backward ideologies used to control the masses, supposedly prone to hysteria and extremism" (Muhammed 2010, 96). Muslims are highly visible through their symbols, dress codes, and other physical manifestations, triggering long-lived antireligious hatred in France (Muhammed 2010, 96). The rise of the Muslim presence in the public sphere alarmed some secularists about the rising role of religion. This visibility, combined with international news stories on extremism, led to anti-Muslim sentiment among the French people.

Even before the September 11 attacks, after which Islamophobia became a greater concern, there was already an upward trajectory of anti-Muslim attitudes in France. Discussion of Islamic fundamentalism pervaded public discourse in France in the late 1980s. Gilles Kepel argues that debates around the Muslim presence in France increased notably after the rise of the Islamic Salvation Front in Algeria in 1989 and the events that followed French military intervention to prevent the party from coming to power. These developments, for Kepel, influenced not only the perceptions of the French people about Islamic movements, but also the perceptions of Muslim youth about France, in that it recalled colonial legacies (Kepel 1997, 151). Joan Scott also demonstrated the relationship between the events in Algeria in the early 1990s and domestic struggles in regard to Muslims' place in France by referencing the historical legacies of colonialism (Scott 2007, 42–89).

Media coverage of events contributed to the rise of Islamophobia. The media, most of the time, represented Muslims as a monolithic group of people resisting French values of republicanism and secularism. A study conducted by Lina Molokotos Liederman examines French representations of Muslims in the 1990s. Analyzing 1,174 newspaper articles published between 1989 and 1999 on the headscarf controversy in *Le Figaro, Le Monde, Libération, L'Humanité, La Croix,* and *Le Monde de l'éducation,* Liederman concludes that secularism (laïcité) and fundamentalism (intégrisme) were "the key defining elements" of the debates in France (Liederman 2000, 373). She writes that the wearing of the headscarf was "perceived and portrayed as a symbol of Islamic religious fundamentalism"; and it was thus seen as "a threat to *laïcité* and to the secular character of the French state schools" (Liederman 2000, 373–374). Liederman demonstrates that the French media characterized Muslim girls' wearing of headscarf as "being aggressive, provocative, and obstinate" (Liederman 2000, 375).

Joel Fetzer and Christopher Soper's research, which looks at Europeans' support for the accommodation of Islam in state-run schools, shows that public support for Muslims decreased after the events of September 11, 2001 (Fetzer and Soper 2003). Although Fetzer and Soper explain the anti-Muslim stance in France as resulting from the historical legacies of state–religion institutions, they acknowledge the influence of the September 11 attacks on the increasing animosity toward Muslims and the decreasing support for accommodating Muslims in France. A report released by the European Monitoring Centre on Racism and Xenophobia, a research center supported by the European Union, concluded that hostility and verbal and physical attacks against Muslims increased after September 11, 2001, in France. According to the report, this finding is parallel to findings in other European countries in which similar research was conducted.[11]

Alain Gresh (2004), in his work analyzing French perceptions of Muslims, conducted in-depth interviews with representatives of multiple organizations in France. Gresh identified three main perceptions about Islam and Muslims. First, to many French people, Islam was incompatible with French political ideals. To them, this was the major obstacle against Muslims' integration into French society. Second, many French citizens saw Islam as a threat to the French ideal of secularism. Defining secularism as a founding principle of French society, they were critical of Muslims who challenged it with their religious visibility in the public sphere and in French classrooms. Finally, a majority of French people had a very negative image of the Islamic headscarf. To many, the wearing of headscarves by Muslim women represented their submission to men. Very few of them considered the wearing of the headscarf as a religious duty that women fulfilled to meet their responsibility to God (Gresh 2004).

Gresh's study also examined the roots of these common perceptions about Muslims. His interviewees identified two main causes for their negative attitudes toward Muslims. First, for many respondents, concerns about "Islamic terrorism" were the leading reason for their negative perceptions. The French interviewees frequently mentioned the horrors of the Algerian Civil War in the 1990s and the September 11 attacks. Global extremist violence shaped their outlook toward Muslims, in most cases without differentiating French Muslims from others. Second, the interviewees mentioned the increasing number of Muslim immigrants in France. To many, the increasing visibility of religious symbols in the French public sphere was alarming (Gresh 2004). In my personal interview with him, Gresh mentioned that the backlash against France's integration with the EU also created a backlash against immigrants, including North African Muslims in France.[12]

---

[11] Nicolas Bourcier, "L'UE a connu une vague d'islamophobie en 2001," *Le Monde*, May 31, 2002.

[12] Author's interview with Alain Gresh, Paris, France, July 18, 2007.

Thomas Deltombe's study demonstrates how television news media contributed to Islamophobia in France. Scrutinizing French television news archives from the three decades prior to 2005, he showed "how the media have gradually built a real Islamophobia" (Deltombe 2005, 2). He argued that several of the news stories were manipulated to "stigmatize the 'other' Muslim" (Deltombe 2005, 4). To him, the selective presentation of Muslims, particularly at the time of political crisis, created the image that Muslims were a threat to French values of republicanism and secularism. Deltombe showed that the broadcasting media treated Muslims as a monolithic group threatening French values. The media gradually built "an imaginary Muslim" who was undermining the French political and cultural institutions.

Similarly, Pierre Tévanian (2005) analyzed media output before the passing of the headscarf ban. He showed how the media ignored the voices against the ban and published news and commentary that created an image of an overlapping consensus, what Tévanian called "Islamophobic consensus," over banning the headscarf in schools. He argued that the apparent consensus around the banning of the headscarf was not real, but it was deliberatively constructed by the media. In doing so, the media turned a blind eye to moderates in both camps and polarized French society along the lines of secularism and fundamentalism. Tévanian hold the media responsible for the portrayal of Muslims as a monolithic fundamentalist group by excluding from the debate those sociologists, teachers, and civil actors who opposed the ban.

Vincent Geisser (2003), in his *La Nouvelle Islamophobie* (The New Islamophobia), analyzed the role of the media and intellectuals in the formation of Islamophobic discourse in France (Geisser 2003, 23–51). Geisser accused the French media of selecting contents, images, and commentators to present Islam as a "potential threat." He wrote that the media focused only on "the risks of infiltration by Islamic terrorism" so as to reinforce the French audience's biases and fears. The media illustrated a conception of Islam as necessarily a potential threat. Geisser also argued that the media presented Islam as being an obstacle for immigrants' integration into French society. The media's narrative was that the only way for Muslims to integrate French society was to distance themselves from their religion (Geisser 2003, 40–42).

Surveys conducted before the passing of the headscarf law show the extent of Islamophobia in France. In a 2002 Pew Global Attitudes Survey, 50 percent of respondents in France believed that immigrants had a bad influence on the country while 46 percent believed that immigrants had a good influence.[13] In the same survey, 59 percent of respondents agreed that "the greatest danger to the world was religious and ethnic conflict."[14] In another Pew Global Attitudes

---

[13] Pew Research Centre, *What the World Thinks in 2002*, Pew Global Attitudes Survey, Washington, DC, December 4, 2002, 44, available at www.pewresearch.org/wp-content/uploads/sites/2/2002/12/2002-Report-Final-Updated.pdf (last accessed on April 6, 2019).

[14] Ibid., 48.

Survey conducted in June 2003, 51 percent of French respondents stated that North Africans who came to work in France were bad for the country.[15] In 2003, the left-wing Paris-based National Committee for Human Rights found that 18 percent of French respondents who said they had no problem with immigrants stated strong negative feelings about the practice of Islam by immigrants (Muhammed 2010, 99). In another research project, conducted just a few months after the passing of the headscarf law in the parliament (May 2004), the Monitoring Centre on Discrimination at the University of Paris sent out standard résumés with different names in response to 258 job advertisements for salespeople. It was found that a person who had a Muslim name had five times less of a chance of getting a positive reply than a person with a non-Muslim name (Amadieu 2004).

As in other European countries, the rise of Islamophobia among the French public was in parallel with restrictive changes in legal policies toward Muslims. France passed a new law two months after the September 11 terrorist attacks that increased the power of law enforcement authorities to contain terrorist activity. The law expanded police powers, making it easier to stop and search vehicles in the context of terrorism investigations. The law gave the police the ability to search unoccupied premises at night without notification. It made it easier for enforcement authorities to monitor and record electronic transactions of terrorism suspects. A follow-up immigration law passed in 2003 made it easier to deport individuals whose behavior threatened public order; it implemented increased penalties for illegal immigration and put limits on family reunification (Cesari 2011, 24). The victims of the new law were mostly Muslims; they became targets of longer detentions, police searches, and social isolation in their neighborhoods.

In 2003, the interior minister Nicolas Sarkozy increased official pressure on "clandestine" mosques and Islamic associations. He criminalized assembly in the basements and garages of housing projects in an effort to block means of radicalization (Silverstein 2008, 18). He threatened to expel imams who spread ideas that did not correspond to French values (Silverstein 2008, 19). Sarkozy encouraged the construction of large mosques in order to trace and constrain extremism among Muslims. Sarkozy helped Muslim groups to establish a federation with the aim of creating a French Islam that was more transparent and easier to monitor.

In addition to the backlash against globalization and the EU, the global and European context of rising Islamophobia led to the rise of the far right in France (Zúquete 2008). The National Front (FN), the major far-right political party in France, mostly voiced concerns about immigration. The FN, which was established by Jean-Marie Le Pen in 1972 and gained momentum in

---

[15] Pew Research Centre, *Views of a Changing World: June 2003*, Pew Global Attitudes Survey, Washington, DC, June 3, 2003, 12, available at www.pewresearch.org/wp-content/uploads/sites/2/2003/06/Views-Of-A-Changing-World-2003.pdf (last accessed on July 31, 2016).

the second half of the 1990s, offered a program based on French nationalism and economic protectionism.[16] Within its program, the party promoted Euroskepticism, xenophobia, a moralizing conservatism, an ultra-security discourse, and an anti-globalist foreign policy (Hainsworth 2004, 104). The FN leadership developed a political agenda against French membership of the EU, describing it as "programmed death for French sovereignty" (Hainsworth 2004, 105). The FN put law and order at the center of its domestic policy agenda. The issue of immigration gained priority within this context. The party program included draconian measures to stop immigration that includes "a total ban on immigration; tougher penalties on airline carriers and employers (if necessary); abrogation of family reunion rights/facilities; a clampdown on 'false tourism' and a target of zero immigration" (Hainsworth 2004, 105).

Starting in 1997, the FN gradually increased its vote share and became a significant actor in French politics. Increasing unemployment rates in France fed the nationalist and populist FN. The party leader Le Pen benefited from the post–September 11 climate in promoting his program, which was based on anti-immigration and law and order. In 2002, Le Pen finished the first round of presidential elections as the second candidate and competed against Jacques Chirac in the runoff elections.

The rise of the far right provoked the central parties to take a strict stance toward Muslims. The rise of Le Pen, especially in the 2002 presidential elections, led centrist parties to extend their appeal to more nationalistic political discourses. This is possibly one of the reasons that presidential candidates for the 2007 elections developed agendas mainly related to immigration[17] and why Le Pen's share of the vote decreased from its 2002 level.[18] Other parties appropriated his political agenda, which was based on order and xenophobia. Some scholars argue that President Chirac calculated that he could gain the support of both the secular left and the anti-Muslim right by introducing a law banning the wearing of headscarves in state schools. They argue that the law represented a strategy to counter Jean-Marie Le Pen's FN, rather than reflecting any real concern for the promotion of secularism (Idriss 2005, 284; Bell 2004, 543–545).

To Joan Scott (2007), the rise of the FN sharpened the French government's position towards Muslims. As she writes, Le Pen's strong showing in the presidential election of 1988 was followed by the expulsions of headscarf-wearing girls in Creil in 1989; the FN's gaining seats in the European Parliament in 1994 was followed by Bayrou's ministerial circular and the sixty-nine

---

[16] Marine Le Pen, Jean-Marie Le Pen's daughter, assumed the leadership of the party after 2011. The party changed its name to National Rally (Rassemblement national) in June 2018.

[17] David Rieff, "Battle Over the Banlieues," *New York Times*, April 15, 2007.

[18] In the first round of the 2002 presidential elections, Le Pen got 17 percent of the votes, compared to 11 percent in the 2007 presidential elections. For an elaborative work that analyzes the relationship between niche strategies and major political parties see Meguid 2005, and on the FN see especially page 356.

expulsions; and Chirac's headscarf law came shortly after he defeated Le Pen in the second round of the presidential election of 2002 (Scott 2007, 38). Scott argues that many leaders in centrist and leftist parties share Le Pen's attribution of France's social problems to immigrants, but they offer solutions different from expelling immigrants from France, such as only expelling them from schools (Scott 2005, 110).

The rise of Islamophobia in France allowed the supporters of anti-Muslim policies to push their policy agendas. Due to the rise of "concerns" about Islam in the French public sphere, the proponents of the headscarf ban were able to gain public support. They considered the headscarf ban to be a measure to stop fundamentalism rather than an issue of religious freedoms. In Chapter 7, I demonstrate how the proponents of the ban won public support and expanded their coalition to pass the ban. One question regarding the role of the international context in these events is whether there were any global reactions against the French state's limitations on Muslims, particularly the passing of the headscarf ban in 2004. If so, why did these groups fail to exert any influence on French policymakers? The next section deals with this question.

## INTERNATIONAL PRESSURE AGAINST THE HEADSCARF BAN

International pressure had only limited effect in discouraging the French government from banning the wearing of headscarves in public schools. The most important supranational body that could put pressure on France was the EU; however, the EU did not have supranational mechanisms monitoring state–religion relations in member states. Freedom of religion is considered an integral part of the basic principles of democracy, human rights, fundamental liberties, and the rule of law, to which the EU has attached special importance since the Maastricht Treaty in 1992.[19] The EU monitors state–religion relations if human rights issues are involved; and this has generally been the case for candidate countries.

Although the EU did not impose any policy on France, some individual European legislators criticized the ban. For example, Jean Lambert, a member of the Human Rights and Civil Liberties Committee of the European Parliament, stated that "banning the wearing of religious symbols is a clear human rights violation" (Wing and Smith 2006, 757). However, in terms of influencing the making of foreign policy, the statements as such did not make a difference. They even created a backlash; French nationalist deputies reacted

---

[19] The Maastricht Treaty, also known as the Treaty on European Union, was signed in February 1992 after final negotiations in December 1991 between the members of the European Community. The treaty, which entered into force in November 1993, created the European Union legally. The treaty specified the framework for monetary and political union among the member states.

to these statements by depicting them as encroachments on the sovereignty of France.

The only international pressure mechanism that could have created an obstacle to French policymakers passing the headscarf law would have been a ruling of the European Court of Human Rights (ECHR). However, the ECHR did not have a solid position on the issue of the wearing of headscarves. In previous cases, the ECHR had upheld the rulings of the national courts (Marshall 2006).[20] On issues related to state–religion relations, the ECHR gave special importance to the regulations and legal structures of national authorities. This preference of the court stems from the doctrine of the margin of appreciation, which allows the court to consider that the convention will be interpreted differently for different signatory states. Judges are obliged to take into account the cultural, historic, and philosophical differences between European standards and those of member states. The foundational principles and philosophies of member states are considered in the decision-making process of the court (McGoldrick 2006, 28–29).

The Stasi Commission took the compatibility of ECHR standards into account for a possible law prohibiting religious symbols in public schools.[21] The commission asked for advice from the ECHR before making its recommendation. The commission stressed that the ECHR makes final judgments according to "the traditions of each country, without seeking to impose a uniform model of the relationship between church and state."[22] The commission based its recommendation on the French tradition of secularism in order to comply with the ECHR.[23] A member of the commission, Patrick Weil, stated that the commission had addressed French traditions in the proceedings to emphasize national foundational characteristics of French secularism.[24] The margin of appreciation thus became a possible tool to avoid any judicial consequence from the ECHR. This would prevent schoolgirls who wear headscarves in public schools from successfully appealing to the ECHR.

During legislative debates in the French parliament, compatibility with the ECHR rulings was discussed in detail. Socialist deputies, asking to include all kinds of religious symbols in the law, opposed to the word "ostentatious" and suggested replacing it with "visible" in the bill. Prime Minister Raffarin indicated that the adjective "ostentatious" was necessary to make the bill

---

[20] Karaduman v Turkey, Application no. 16278/90, May 3, 1993; Dahlab v Switzerland, Application no. 42393/98, February 15, 2001.

[21] Commission de reflexion sur l'application du principe de laïcité dans la République 2003, 21.

[22] Ibid. For a detailed discussion of this issue, see Thomas 2006.

[23] Christian Joppke (2007, 326) writes that the reason for the choice of the word "ostentatious" over "visible" is to meet the requirements of ECHR standards. The word "ostentatious" is much more associated with public order, which would favor French legislatures in a possible application to the ECHR.

[24] Author's interview with Patrick Weil, Paris, France, July 27, 2007.

compliant with the European Convention on Human Rights.[25] Although it seems that international norms had exerted pressure on France to some extent, at least in the wording of the law, they did not change the ultimate outcome for the schoolgirls.

The USA also criticized the French initiative to ban headscarves in public schools, but it did not have any monitoring power over France. The chair of the United States Commission on International Religious Freedom (USCIRF), Michael K. Young, stated his concern over the French law on religious signs in public schools: "These restrictions, if enacted, may violate France's international commitments, including the European Convention on Human Rights, under which each individual is guaranteed the freedom to manifest religion or belief, in public as well as in private."[26] He indicated that many Muslims, Jews, and Sikhs consider it a religious obligation to cover their heads. He stated that the commission acknowledged immigration problems in France but "these challenges should be addressed directly, and not by inappropriately limiting the right to freedom of thought, conscience, religion, and belief." The commission also stated that "The French state's promotion of its understanding of the principle of secularism should not result in violations of the internationally recognized individual right to freedom of religion or belief." The commission called on the US government to urge the government of France "to ensure that any state regulations on public expression of religious belief or affiliation adhere strictly to international human rights norms."[27]

The US Department of State, in its annual religious freedom reports, criticized French policies on the wearing of headscarves in public schools before the law was passed. The issue was mentioned in the reports of 1999,[28] 2000,[29] 2003,[30] and 2004.[31] The 1999 and 2000 reports described the restrictions on the wearing of headscarves in some schools as a violation of

---

[25] Jean-Pierre Raffarin's speech in parliament on February 3, 2004, available at www.assemblee-nationale.fr/12/cra/2003–2004/148.asp#P201_50355 (last accessed on October 10, 2007).

[26] United States Commission on International Religious Freedom, "France: Proposed Bill May Violate Freedom of Religion," February 3, 2004, available at www.uscirf.gov/mediaroom/press/2004/february/02032004_france.html (last accessed on October 11, 2007).

[27] Ibid.

[28] U.S. Department of State, "Annual Report on International Religious Freedom for 1999: France," September 9, 1999, available at www.state.gov/www/global/human_rights/irf/irf_rpt/1999/irf_france99.html (last accessed on October 10, 2007).

[29] U.S. Department of State, "2000 Annual Report on International Religious Freedom: France," September 5, 2000, available at www.state.gov/www/global/human_rights/irf/irf_rpt/irf_france.html (last accessed on October 10, 2007).

[30] U.S. Department of State, "2003 Annual Report on International Religious Freedom: France," May 2003, available at www.state.gov/g/drl/rls/irf/2003/24357.htm (last accessed on October 10, 2007).

[31] U.S. Department of State, "2004 Annual Report on International Religious Freedom: France," May 2004, available at www.state.gov/g/drl/rls/irf/2004/35454.htm (last accessed on October 10, 2007).

human rights, while the 2003 and 2004 reports indicated that it was contested whether or not the practice of wearing headscarves in public school was a violation of human rights.

Despite the reactions of the USCIRF and the US Department of State's religious freedom reports, the USA did not have any effective mechanism for influencing the French state's policies on Muslims. The issue of the status of Muslims played a very minor role, if it played at all, in USA–French relations. The US presidents of the time did not make any statements about the increasing Islamophobia in France or the French state's increasingly restrictive policies toward Muslims. US policymakers did not take any action based on the reports prepared by the USCIRF and the Department of State.

Transnational nongovernmental organizations attempted to create pressure on France, but they did not have the power to deter France from passing the ban. Human Rights Watch (HRW) criticized the law in February 2004, characterizing it as a violation of the rights to freedom of religion and expression. The executive director of HRW, Kenneth Roth, said that "[t]he proposed law is an unwarranted infringement on the right to religious practice; for many Muslims, wearing a headscarf is not only about religious expression, it is about religious obligation."[32] In HRW's view, states could limit religious practices only when there was a compelling public safety reason, when the manifestation of religious beliefs would impinge on the rights of others, or when such limitations served a legitimate educational function. Muslim headscarves, Sikh turbans, Jewish skullcaps, and large Christian crosses "do not pose a threat to public health, order or morals; they have no effect on the fundamental rights and freedoms of other students; and they do not undermine a school's educational function."[33]

On February 9, 2004, the International Helsinki Federation for Human Rights[34] expressed its concern over the planned French law to ban Islamic headscarves from schools, claiming that it would violate international conventions. The federation's executive director, Aaron Rhodes, stated that "The law would contradict the conventions on human rights and violate the international standards that France has agreed to and sometimes contributed to create. Such a ban would bring the French state in collision with international human rights standards on freedom of religion." Instead of creating unity in French society under the banner of secularism, as Chirac's ruling conservative party promised, Rhodes said the move could be counter-productive and lead to "increased alienation and marginalization of Muslims living in France."[35]

---

[32] Human Rights Watch, "France: Headscarf Ban Violates Religious Freedom," February 27, 2004, available at http://hrw.org/english/docs/2004/02/26/france7666_txt.htm (last accessed on October 11, 2007).

[33] Ibid.     [34] This organization ceased to exist in November 2007.

[35] Agence France-Presse, "French Headscarf Ban Flouts International Accords: Helsinki Rights Group," *Agence France-Presse*, February 9, 2004.

In short, the international context of rising Islamophobia played a crucial role in the passing of legislation that limited the freedoms of Muslims in France. International advocates of human rights and religious freedoms were unable to exert enough pressure on France to deter it from passing the ban. Unlike Turkey, which was under strict monitoring by the EU during the relevant period, France was relatively immune from the pressure of international institutions and actors. The EU, the ECHR, the USA, and transnational human rights organizations did not play a noticeable role in the policymaking process that led to the passing of the headscarf ban in France.

## CONCLUSION

The terrorist attacks of September 11, 2001, increased anti-Muslim sentiments globally. Verbal and physical attacks against Muslims, monolithic representations of Muslims in the media as fundamentalist and inflexible, and constraining state policies toward Muslims increased in European countries. The legacies of European colonization that put Muslims and Westerners in a conflictual relationship, the increasing socioeconomic marginalization of Muslim immigrants in European countries, and the international events that sharpened the cultural and political differences between Muslims and European countries had all contributed to Islamophobia. The September 11 attacks built on these existing conditions and facilitated anti-Muslim sentiments globally and across Europe by catalyzing the existing social, economic, and political conditions.

The increasing Islamophobia shaped public debates in France in the early 2000s. The rise of the far right also contributed to the marginalization of Muslims. The debates around Muslims in the early 2000s were whether or not Muslims fit into French values of secularism and republicanism. The passing of laws that banned headscarves in 2004 and burqas in 2010 arose out of this rising anti-Muslim environment in France. The international and domestic context helped the proponents of the ban break the link between international norms and the wearing of headscarves in public schools by framing the headscarf as a symbol of Islamic fundamentalism threatening French republican values. There were international actors who criticized the passing of the restrictive laws; however, these pressures did not create the intended outcome due to those actors' lack of sanctioning capacity.[36]

---

[36] When I asked Bernard Godard, a French official responsible for Muslim affairs at the time of my fieldwork in 2007, about the French state's reaction to international responses, he told to me that those responses did not matter for France since those organizations did not understand the inner mechanisms of state–religion relations in France. He stated that France would take into consideration the decisions of the ECHR, since it was the only institution to which the French state is responsible. Author's interview with Bernard Godard, Ministry of Interior, Paris, France, July 25, 2007.

The rise of Islamophobia helped the proponents of the ban expand their support base, and their strategies in the domestic realm shaped the final decision on the headscarf law. The presence of actors ready to utilize Islamophobia differentiated France from other countries in Europe. These domestic actors linked their policies to the French values of secularism and republicanism in mobilizing support for the ban. In contrast to other European countries, political entrepreneurs in France used these public sentiments effectively to restrict the civil rights and liberties of Muslim minorities. In Chapter 7, I analyze the strategies used by these domestic actors in implementing their desired policies by using the rise of Islamophobia to expand their social base and coalition.

PART III

DOMESTIC ACTORS AND POLICY CHANGE

# 6

## Kemalists, Conservatives, and Christians in Turkey

In summer 2010 I met Louis Pelatre, the Catholic bishop responsible for churches in Turkey. I asked how he felt about the reforms that the Islamist Justice and Development Party (AKP, Adalet ve Kalkınma Partisi) had undertaken to address the problems that Christian minorities faced. He indicated that he was pleased with the reformist atmosphere, even though many of the problems were still unresolved. He then added, "They [the AKP] see themselves as the grandchildren of the Ottomans. The Christians were protected under the Ottoman Empire." The bishop was not suggesting bringing back the Ottoman monarchy to replace modern freedoms; rather, he was pointing out the limitations that Turkish secularism and nationalism have put on Christian minorities.[1] In a statement that he gave to an Italian Catholic monthly magazine, Bishop Pelatre said, "It's because of Turkish 'secularism' and not Islam, that the Church cannot officially exist."[2] What brought a Catholic bishop and an Islamist political party together in this case? It is the negative consequences of Turkish secularism, which aimed to put religion under state control. Due to European Union (EU) pressure, the reforms that constrained the authoritarian establishment in Turkey in the 2000s created room for Christian minorities. In this chapter, I analyze how domestic actors utilized EU pressure to open up space for themselves, which also helped expand the rights of the Christian minority.

As demonstrated in Chapter 2, the Turkish state had implemented discriminatory policies toward its Christian minority. Although the Treaty of Lausanne guaranteed the basic rights of non-Muslim minorities in Turkey, the strictly secularist and nationalist approach taken by the Turkish government led to the violation of their rights. However, in the 2000s, the Turkish government began a reform process that ameliorated several, though not all, of the issues faced by the Christian minority. As shown in Chapter 4, the main international

---

[1] Author's interview with Louis Pelatre, Istanbul, Turkey, May 26, 2010.
[2] Lorenzo Biondi, "Interview with Louis Pelatre: This New Air That One Breathes in Turkey," *30 Days*, June 2011, available at www.30giorni.it/articoli_id_77759_l3.htm (last accessed on June 23, 2017).

factor that enabled such a transformation was the increase in pressure from the EU. In the first decade of the 2000s, the EU put powerful pressure on Turkey that led to several political reforms in all walks of life, including religious rights for minorities. What enabled this external pressure to propel reform was the availability of domestic actors who would embrace a reformist agenda.

The driving force for these reforms was persistent, systematic, and intensive international pressure coming from international institutions, especially from the EU. This international pressure effectively empowered those domestic actors who supported the reforms (see Figure 6.1). In other words, international pressure structured the domestic configuration of power relationships in favor of the proponents of the reforms. International pressure pushed for religious liberties; however, the appropriation of international pressure by strong domestic actors was the key for the liberalization of state policies toward Christians.

The leading actors who opposed the reforms about the status of Christian minorities were certain state organs such as the military, the General Directorate of Foundations (GDF), some local administrators, nationalist political parties such as the Nationalist Action Party (MHP, Milliyetçi Hareket Partisi), and a number of Islamist political parties such as the Felicity Party (Saadet Partisi) and the Greater Turkey Party (Büyük Türkiye Partisi). The Republican People's Party (CHP, Cumhuriyet Halk Partisi), a secular nationalist party based on the ideology of Kemalism, opposed reform packages that would improve the status of Christians although they were supportive of many other reforms that the EU pushed for. The reforms were supported by Christian groups (Greek Orthodox Church, Armenian Orthodox Church, Syrian Orthodox Church, Roman Catholic groups, Protestant congregations, and others); by liberal groups, organizations, and individuals; and by some Islamic groups, including the Gülen movement and the governing AKP. Within the government, the Ministry of Foreign Affairs was an important supporter of the reforms because those reforms were helpful to Turkey in its negotiations with the EU.

Domestic actors with relatively broad social support contributed to the passing of the reforms. The Islamic actors and their allies developed strategies through which they were able to undermine the authoritarian bureaucracy and the repressive political environment created by the military in the late 1990s. These strategies increased the likelihood of the political survival of the Islamist actors. After coming to power in 2002, the AKP, the main Islamist political actor, implemented a policy agenda that prioritized EU-led reforms. Along with democratizing reforms that decreased the power of the military to control Turkish politics, the party instituted religious rights for Christians, an act that was among the conditions for Turkish membership of the EU. Social and political allies of the AKP – liberal groups, social democrats, and some Islamic groups – contributed to the passing of the reforms through civil society activism and interfaith engagements with religious minorities. In short, the passing of reforms in favor of Christian minorities became possible only after strong

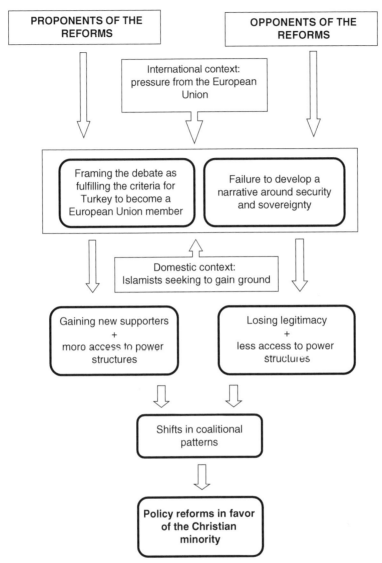

FIGURE 6.1 The flow of arguments: the state and Christians in Turkey

domestic actors appropriated those reforms for either instrumental or normative reasons.

In this chapter, I first examine the strategies and activities of the opponents of reform in their efforts to prevent the passing of laws enhancing rights for Christians. These groups voiced their opposition by referring to issues of security and sovereignty. They claimed that the new reforms, by increasing the influence of foreign powers over Turkey, would undermine Turkish sovereignty and threaten national security. Second, I examine how proponents of the reforms made their case for passing the laws in parliament. The convergence of interests between Christian minorities and Islamic political and social actors helped in the passing of the reforms. Liberal, social democrat, and some Islamic groups also contributed to the outcome thanks to their normative commitment to pluralism.

## THE EU AND THE OPPONENTS OF THE REFORMS

The opponents of the reforms for religious minorities in Turkey based their positions on the argument that such policy changes would undermine Turkey's security and sovereignty and increase the influence of international actors, particularly of the EU, on Turkish politics. They argued that the reforms would undermine Turkey's sovereignty in that they would leave Turkey in an inferior position with regard to the EU. The reforms, in their view, would also diminish Turkish security because they saw the Christian minorities as "foreign." While the state bureaucracy raised concerns about the issues of security, political parties voiced their opposition to the reforms on the basis of issues of both security and sovereignty.

The bureaucratic organs of the military and the GDF resisted the reform of legislation on the treatment of Christians. They impeded the implementation of the reforms even after the parliament had passed the laws related to the Christian minorities.[3] The bureaucratic organs formulated regulations with ambiguous language to allow more space for bureaucratic hurdles in the implementation of the laws (Goltz 2006, 177). They slowed down the paperwork, created new obstacles, and referred minority files from one office to another. For example, when the parliament amended the Law on Foundations to transfer the authority of approval from the Council of Ministers to the GDF in January 2003, the GDF issued a regulation to specify the procedures of how the community foundations would acquire and dispose of their properties and how they would register their unregistered properties under their names.[4] This regulation stated that the GDF would ask the opinion of relevant state bodies in cases where they thought it necessary to do so.[5] The

---

[3] The government during the first reform package (Law No. 4771) was constituted by three parties: the Democratic Left Party, MHP, and the Motherland Party. Among these parties, the MHP did not support the reforms enhancing the rights of Christian minorities. All other reforms were passed during the rule of the AKP.

[4] "Cemaat Vakıflarının Taşınmaz Mal Edinmeleri, Bunlar Üzerinde Tasarrufta Bulunmaları ve Tasarrufları Altında Bulunan Taşınmaz Malların Bu Vakıflar Adına Tescil Edilmesi Hakkında Yönetmelik," Official Gazette No. 25003, published on January 24, 2003, available at www .vgm.gov.tr/001_Menu/02_Mevzuat/03_Yonetmelik/cemaat-1.cfm (last accessed on June 5, 2008).

[5] Ibid.

implied state bodies were the police and intelligence agencies (Oran 2004, 106). By making this regulation, the GDF aimed to create new security-related obstacles in the registration of the properties of community foundations. This regulation provided the GDF the opportunity to turn down property claims made by community foundations. The GDF turned down several such claims in the first months after the passing of the law. For example, in May 2003, out of 1,813 claim applications made by community foundations for registration of real estate, 579 were found to be incomplete, 574 were refused, and 226 were returned as invalid (Oran 2007, 53).[6]

The National Security Council, controlled by the military at the time, played a major role in slowing down the implementation of the reforms. For example, in April 2003, the National Security Council asked the GDF to lengthen the procedures for the approval of the claims made by community foundations. The letter implicitly asked the GDF to create hurdles for the community foundations.[7] On another occasion, the National Security Council requested the GDF to limit the freedoms that the new law granted to only those religious minorities recognized by the Treaty of Lausanne, even though the law did not make any specific references to the treaty.[8] The National Security Council treated the issue of religious minorities not from a point of view of equal citizenship but largely from the perspective of security, law, and order. Bureaucracies in the local provinces also created hurdles for the implementation of the reforms passed in parliament. For example, a Presbyterian community spent one year attempting to open a small church in Ankara. The community leaders had to deal with both the governor's office and the mayor's office in order to get the necessary permissions. The problems were solved only after the minister of the interior intervened to facilitate the bureaucratic process.[9]

Opposition political parties, the CHP and the MHP, opposed the law by bringing up issues of security and sovereignty, arguing that the proposed law would diminish the Turkish state's capacity to govern itself independently. They criticized the law's supporters for their "submission" to international powers. The speeches made by opponents of the law demonstrate the strength of the EU's pressure on Turkey. During these legislative debates, parliamentarians from the opposition parties accused the governing party of being dependent on the EU.

Analysis of speeches made by CHP and MHP deputies during parliamentary deliberations on the Law on Foundations in 2008 reveals that both parties defended a more restrictive environment for religious minorities out of concerns for sovereignty and security: they saw religious minorities as agents

---

[6] İsmail Saymaz, "Vakıflar mülklerini alamadı," *Radikal*, May 5, 2003.
[7] İsmail Saymaz, "Yasayı delen karar," *Radikal*, May 6, 2003.
[8] Fatma Sibel Yüksek, "Vakıflara MGK Freni," *Radikal*, October 2, 2002.
[9] *Radikal*, "Bir kilisenin öyküsü," May 27, 2004.

or tools of great powers; they saw minorities as a threat to Turkish national unity; they defended the principle of reciprocity between Turkey and Greece in granting rights to minorities; and they saw reforms as an instrument for the Greek Orthodox patriarchate to gain official recognition as the ecumenical leader of Orthodox Christians worldwide.

The CHP opposed the Law on Foundations for a number of reasons that reveal the importance of the EU's role in the passing of the reforms.[10] First, CHP politicians perceived the passing of the law as an intrusion into Turkish sovereignty. They emphasized how foreign powers, especially the EU, the USA, and Greece, were pressuring Turkey to pass the reforms. Deputies such as Rahmi Güner, Birgen Keleş, Halil Ünlütepe, Ali Rıza Öztürk, Tayfun Süner, and Turgut Dibek referenced this issue in their speeches to the assembly. Güner stated that the government would be passing the bill due to pressure from the EU and the USA, even though the law was to the detriment of Turkish national interests. Ünlütepe criticized the government for preparing a bill based on the EU's requests to Turkey (as expressed in the EU's progress reports) rather than the real need on the ground. Süner, Dibek, and Keleş questioned the EU's conditionality of passing a law about non-Muslim community foundations. Süner suggested that what should have mattered to the EU was not group rights given to non-Muslim minorities but individual rights given to each member of minority groups. Dibek pointed out that within the EU only Greece had legal regulations on community foundations and that the regulations in Greece were not as progressive as those proposed in Turkey. Keleş stated that "no state has the right to ask Turkey to pass a law that is not in its legal system." The fiercest speech came from the CHP's Öztürk: he accused the AKP of submitting to the imperialist demands of great powers and of acting as if the party's politicians were the heroes of democracy and freedom in Turkey. He rejected claims the CHP had been illiberal and authoritarian in its handling of minority rights; the CHP was only protecting Turkey's dignity.

Presenting the second of their reasons for objecting to the proposed law, a number of CHP representatives – such as Güner, Keleş, Ünlütepe, Atila Emek, İsa Gök, and Tansel Barış – characterized the law as a blow to the unity of the Turkish nation. These representatives argued that the law offered many concessions to non-Muslims that were against the Treaty of Lausanne. Güner stated, "It is a shame to bring this bill to the national assembly," as it threatened Turkey's integrity. Gök questioned the law on the basis that it gave a special status to foundations established by specific religious and ethnic groups. To Gök, this was against the founding principles of the Turkish Republic and would open a path to the territorial disintegration of the country. He likened the law to the Sèvres Treaty, which the Ottoman Empire signed after the First

---

[10] The speeches referenced here are drawn from the parliamentary proceedings of the Turkish Grand National Assembly on January 30 and 31 and February 13, 14, and 20, 2008. The proceedings are available at www.tbmm.gov.tr (last accessed on December 12, 2018).

World War. The treaty proposed the establishment of many states in Anatolia by various ethnic and religious groups.

Keleş directed attention to the article of the law that allowed non-Muslim minority foundations to acquire property. She warned that the Greek Orthodox patriarchate could, with the help of financial support from abroad, purchase large areas of land in Istanbul in order to establish an independent state with a similar status to the Vatican. Barış criticized the law's proposition to allow community foundations to be involved in commercial activities. He suggested that this would provide the community foundations with immense economic power that could be used against Turkish unity. Gök dealt with the proposition of the bill that would allow community foundations to cooperate with international associations and foreign foundations. He raised concerns that this proposition would threaten Turkey's national identity.

Ünlütepe shifted the discussion to the potential activities of foreign foundations being allowed to establish branches in Turkey. He gave examples of how foreign foundations had destabilized political regimes in Eastern Europe, Central Asia, and the Middle East. Ünlütepe accused the AKP of providing foreign foundations with the opportunity to function freely in Turkey. Güner and Keleş then brought up the issue of missionaries, accusing the AKP of making it easier for community foundations and foreign associations to cooperate, which could increase the number of missionaries in Turkey. They suggested that agents, disguised as members of the clergy, would come to Turkey to prepare conditions for the nation's disintegration.

The third main argument for opposing the law, raised by the CHP, was that Greece, an EU member, did not have a similar law for its Turkish Muslim minority. The CHP deputies stated that the Treaty of Lausanne required reciprocity between Turkey and Greece; that is, both countries are to grant similar rights to their respective minorities – Greek Christians in Turkey and Turkish Muslims in Greece. A number of politicians addressed a new law that the Greek parliament passed in February 2008 to regulate the Greek state's relationships with Turkish community foundations. The CHP deputies argued that the Greek law did not grant similar rights to the Muslim minority. Barış pointed out that the Greek state could appoint the *mufti* (religious leader) of Turkish Muslims in Greece, and that Greek provincial governors could lead the executive committees of the Turkish Muslim foundations, if they wished. Ali İhsan Köktürk summed up the CHP's position on reciprocity in the following words:

Greece, which is an EU member, implements both EU law and domestic law. The EU should first go to Greece and see what rights are granted to the Turkish Muslim minority there. Only after that, they should come to Turkey and say: "Greece, an EU member, grants to the Muslim minority this set of rights. You should do the same for the non-Muslim minority." This is our position.

In making a fourth argument, a number of CHP speakers raised the concern that the new law was against secularism, one of the fundamental principles of the

Turkish republic. These deputies based their argument on three points. First, Keleş claimed that the law would give legal personality to religious communities. In her view, this development would be detrimental to Turkish secularism, which does not recognize religious communities as legal entities. Second, Köktürk argued that the community foundations were established under Ottoman law, which was based on Islamic teachings that recognized religious identities. He suggested that maintaining legal protection for foundations in the republic would reinforce Islamic law and challenge secularism. Finally, Ünlütepe argued that a proposition of the law that required having a representative from non-Muslim communities in the executive committee of the GDF would be against secularism, because the religious identity of that person would be considered in the appointment process.

Finally, the CHP representatives described the law as a concession that would prepare the ground for the Greek Orthodox Church in Istanbul to be recognized as the "ecumenical patriarchate." The Turkish state officially rejects the title "ecumenical" for the patriarch, even though the internal church teachings of Orthodox Christians says the reverse. Güner said that allowing community foundations to purchase property would increase the Greek Orthodox Church's economic and political power, thereby helping the patriarch gain recognition as "ecumenical patriarch." Köktürk criticized the prime minister and the foreign minister for stating that whether or not the title "ecumenical" was used was up to the internal decision of the Orthodox people. He accused the AKP of bringing back the ideology of Ottomanism, which defended the cohabitation of Muslims and non-Muslims within Ottoman territories.

The MHP, which puts Turkish nationalism at the center of its political discourse (Dural 2011), shared the concerns of the CHP in its opposition to the Law on Foundations.[11] First, like the CHP politicians, the MHP deputies accused the government of increasing the influence of external powers on Turkey. They argued that the government had brought the issue to the attention of the parliament because of international pressure. Deputies such as Rıdvan Yalçın, Mehmet Şandır, Metin Çobanoğlu, and İsmet Büyükataman made reference to government representatives' meetings with the USA, the EU, and Greek authorities at which the issue of community foundations was also discussed. Yalçın said that there were no legal regulations about community foundations in the EU, and thus the EU did not have the right to request Turkey to pass a law on the status of community foundations. Büyükataman claimed that the EU was making Greek demands part of the EU's conditionality and treating the demands as if they were required legal amendments for accession.

---

[11] The speeches referenced here are drawn from the parliamentary proceedings of the Turkish Grand National Assembly on January 30 and 31 and February 13, 14, and 20, 2008. The proceedings are available at www.tbmm.gov.tr (last accessed on December 12, 2018).

Çobanoğlu went further and charged the government with treason for submitting to the demands of imperialist powers. He claimed that this attitude of the government had encouraged the EU to push Turkey to make as many concessions as possible. Şandır gave historical examples of how foreign powers used the issue of non-Muslim minorities to influence politics and economy in the late Ottoman Empire. He said that Ottoman reforms in the treatment of minorities facilitated the fall and disintegration of the empire, and that the new reforms would do the same in modern Turkey.

A further argument made by the MHP deputies was that they viewed the Law on Foundations as a serious threat to the survival and unity of the Turkish nation. Many MHP deputies – including Yalçın, Çobanoğlu, Büyükataman, Şandır, Erkan Akçay, Faruk Bal, Süleyman Çirkin Turan, Hasan Çalış, Osman Ertuğrul, Ertuğrul Kumcuoğlu, and Behiç Çelik – repeatedly referred to the law as treasonous, divisive, imperialist, and heinous. The arguments that the MHP made with regard to the law's influence over Turkish national unity were similar to the CHP's arguments. Ertuğrul and Yalçın criticized the law for reinforcing communitarian identities based on religion. They stated that individuals were free to establish whatever associations they wished but that extending this right to communities would divide the country along religious and ethnic lines.

Akçay, Büyükataman, and Turan criticized the law on the basis that it could cause the establishment of a Vatican-like Greek Orthodox state in Istanbul, because non-Muslims would have the right to acquire as much land as they wished. They argued that Greek Christians, with financial support from the West, could expand their territory and prepare the conditions for an independent state within Turkey. Akçay questioned the law on the basis that it would allow foreign foundations to open branches in Turkey and become involved in economic activities. Like his CHP counterparts, he pointed out that these foundations might gain enormous economic power and promote their own political interests. Büyükataman suggested that foreign foundations, through their commercial companies, might destroy Turkish firms and gain control of the Turkish economy. Bal addressed the possible political activities of foreign foundations if they had the opportunity to function in Turkey. He expressed concerns that these foundations could destabilize Turkey just as they had helped revolutionary groups in Ukraine, Kyrgyzstan, and Georgia. The MHP deputies also suggested that the new law would help Christian missionary organizations thrive in Turkey. Büyükataman went even further and claimed that the missionaries, by abusing the law, would prepare the ground for the establishment of many Christian states on Turkish territories. Çelik presented the law as an EU plot against Turkey to Christianize the Turkish nation.

Like their CHP counterparts, several MHP deputies brought up the issue of reciprocity between Turkey and Greece regarding state policies toward religious minorities. Ertuğrul, Bal, and Yalçın compared the law to the one that Greece had passed in February 2008 to regulate Turkish Muslim foundations. They questioned the government's intention to expand the space in favor of non-Muslim minorities at a time when Greece, an EU member, was placing limitations on its Muslim minority. The MHP representative Şenol Bal said that the status of minorities in Greece and Turkey was no different according to the Treaty of Lausanne, which included the principle of reciprocity. What makes the principle of reciprocity significant, he claimed, was the ethnic and religious affinity between Turkish and Greek minorities and the majorities in Turkey and Greece respectively.

Finally, in line with the CHP, representatives from the MHP also raised the issue of the ecumenical title of the Greek Orthodox patriarch and argued that the law would encourage the patriarch to push for official recognition of his ecumenical title. Büyükataman, for example, stated that the law would boost the economic power of the Greek Orthodox Church, open the way to the establishment of a semi-independent Greek state in Turkey, and give the patriarch more power to claim global leadership over Orthodox Christians.

Kemalist intellectuals also perceived the reforms as a threat to Turkey's national sovereignty and security. Oktay Ekşi, an ardent secularist, raised the principle of reciprocity in the discussions about minority rights, especially regarding the reopening of the Theological School of Halki.[12] He argued that the Treaty of Lausanne contained the principle of equality among all Turkish citizens including Christian minorities, and reopening the Theological School of Halki would violate the principle of equality in favor of the Greek Orthodox minority.[13] Although many Islamic groups did not oppose the reforms, nationalist-religious groups stated their opposition to the law on the grounds of security and sovereignty.[14]

By creating a backlash against international powers, EU pressure played a significant role in strengthening the opposition of the bureaucracy, local administrators, opposition parties (CHP and MHP), and secular and nationalist intellectuals to the reforms aimed at expanding the religious freedom of Christians. They did not perceive the issue from an equal citizenship perspective; they considered religious minorities to be "agents" of foreigners. Ironically, equal citizenship was also not the emphasis for the proponents of the reforms. Like their rivals, they presented the reforms as the requirements of being a member of the EU. In other words, international pressure also defined the terms of the debate for the proponents of the reforms.

## THE EU AND THE PROPONENTS OF THE REFORMS

Pressure from the EU played a significant role in the passing of the reforms in the Turkish parliament. The bills about religious minorities were justified by the

---

[12] Oktay Ekşi, "Bu imtiyaz talebidir ... " *Hürriyet*, December 4, 2005; Oktay Ekşi, "Patriğin şikáyetleri," *Hürriyet*, June 1, 2007.
[13] Oktay Ekşi, "Bu imtiyaz talebidir ... " *Hürriyet*, December 4, 2005.
[14] Murat Çabas, "Patrikhane ve Ruhban Okulu," *Yeni Mesaj*, December 2, 2004.

necessity of compliance with EU regulations. The Christian minority lobbied not only Turkish policymakers but also the representatives of international institutions, particularly EU representatives, to put pressure on Turkey. Christian leaders, notably the Greek patriarch Bartholomew, took advantage of their close relationship with Greece in pushing Turkey toward a reformist stance. Of the political parties in the parliament, only the Kurdish nationalist Democratic Society Party (Demokratik Toplum Partisi) and the Islamist AKP supported the bill on religious minorities. The Kurdish party took an equal citizenship stance, referring to the EU values as universal standards. The AKP used the EU pressure as leverage for passing reforms to open up space for the party in Turkish politics. Liberals, social democrats, and some Muslim groups contributed to the process by promoting the reforms from a normative point of view.

An examination of legislative debates on the reforms demonstrates that the Turkish parliament passed several reforms under the pressure of the EU; in most cases the proponents of the reforms used the prospect of EU membership as a reason to pass the bills improving the status of Christians. The proponents of the reforms emphasized that the reforms were necessary to lift Turkey to the level of European standards. To them, the reforms were the requirements of complying with international norms on religious liberty.

The justification for the amendments to the Law on Foundations and the 2002 law on the uses of languages other than Turkish (Law No. 4771) was stated as follows: "Both Turkey and Europe have mutual obligations on the road toward full membership to the European Union." After making this statement, the justification of the law indicated that Turkey needed to adapt the provisions of international treaties to its domestic legal system. The justification referred to both the International Declaration of Human Rights and the European Convention on Human Rights as the international treaties that the proposed law would comply with.[15]

The legislative debates on this law, conducted on August 2, 2002, demonstrated the influence of the EU. The deputies sponsoring the law pointed out Turkey's obligations toward the EU membership process in explaining the necessity of passing the bill. Yekta Açıkgöz, a deputy from the Democratic Left Party, a coalition partner at the time, stated that "if we want to join to the EU, we have to fulfill their criteria. We, as Democratic Left Party, support the EU project, which is a modernization project. So, we support this law." Mehmet Sağlam, a deputy from the True Path Party, an opposition party at the time, stated the necessity of the passing of the law to fulfill the EU membership criteria.[16] A deputy from another coalition partner, the

---

[15] The commission report on the bill (Law No. 4771). It is available on the official website of the Turkish parliament at www.tbmm.gov.tr/sirasayi/donem21/yilo1/ss890m.htm (last accessed on June 22, 2017).

[16] Mehmet Sağlam's speech in parliament, "Türkiye Büyük Millet Meclisi Genel Kurul Tutanağı 21. Dönem 4. Yasama Yılı 125. Birleşim," August 2, 2002, available at the

Motherland Party, Nejat Arseven, asked the parliament to support the law because it included one of the most important criteria of becoming an EU member: fulfillment of minority rights.[17]

The AKP government initiated the reforms making reference to Turkey's bid for membership of the EU. Abdullah Gül, then the minister of foreign affairs, stated in May 2004 that the government would pass the reforms so as not to leave the EU any excuse for excluding Turkey from membership.[18] Cemil Çiçek, spokesperson for the government, justified the reforms by indicating their positive contribution to Turkey's progress toward becoming an EU member.[19] AKP members used EU conditionality to justify their support for passing reforms. The AKP was able to do so because at the time there was strong popular support for Turkey's membership to the EU.

Similar debates occurred during the passing of the Law on Foundations (Law No. 5737) in 2006 and 2008.[20] The government first brought the law to the agenda of the parliament after receiving pressure from EU officials, especially from the EU enlargement commissioner, Olli Rehn.[21] After the veto of the president, parliament brought the bill back to its agenda in February 2008. The speeches in parliament demonstrate that the motivation for the government proposing the bill was to fulfill the standards required to become a member of the EU. During the legislative debates in 2008, an AKP deputy, Mehmet Tunçak, justified the bill by stating that Turkey had to demonstrate to the world that it considered its citizens as equal before the law. Another AKP deputy, Mehmet Salih Erdoğan, gave examples of different foundations within the EU and pointed out the necessity of catching up with the world. He suggested that the law would also allow the Turkish state to be more active in protecting Turkish heritage abroad. Hayati Yazıcı, the cabinet member responsible for community foundations, argued that the bill was not a violation of the Treaty of Lausanne and that, on the contrary, it would make implementation of the treaty possible.[22]

Christian minorities in Turkey, aware of the usefulness of playing the EU card, followed a two-pronged strategy to facilitate reform, approaching both

website of the Turkish parliament: www.tbmm.gov.tr/develop/owa/tutanak_g_sd.birlesim _baslangic?P4=8070&P5=B&PAGE1=1&PAGE2=145 (last accessed on June 22, 2017).

[17] Nejat Arseven's speech in parliament, "Türkiye Büyük Millet Meclisi Genel Kurul Tutanağı 21. Dönem 4. Yasama Yılı 125. Birleşim," August 2, 2002, available on the website of the Turkish parliament: www.tbmm.gov.tr/develop/owa/tutanak_g_sd.birlesim _baslangic?P4=8070&P5=B&PAGE1=1&PAGE2=145 (last accessed on June 22, 2017).

[18] *Radikal*, "Gül: AB'ye hiçbir bahane bırakmayacağız," May 24, 2004.

[19] *Radikal*, "AB yumurtası kapıya dayandı," May 25, 2004.

[20] As stated earlier in the chapter, this law came before the parliament twice: in 2006 and 2008. In 2006 the president vetoed the law. The law was included in the parliament's agenda again in 2008 after the presidential election.

[21] Yurdagül Şimşek, "Vakıflara yeni tanım," *Radikal*, June 14, 2006.

[22] The speeches referenced here are drawn from the parliamentary proceedings of the Turkish Grand National Assembly on February 12, 13, and 14, 2008. The proceedings are available at www.tbmm.gov.tr (last accessed on June 22, 2017).

domestic and international actors. First, they communicated with Turkish politicians and state officials to request relevant legislative and administrative changes to ameliorate their status. The reformist agenda of the government helped the Christians to adopt a relatively assertive stance in their quest for rights. The frequency of these meetings with government officials increased in the 2000s, when Turkey began to reform the position of the Christian minorities. When the issue first came to the parliament in early 2002, the patriarch of Turkish Armenians, Mesrob Mutafyan, met with the leader of the AKP, Recep Tayyip Erdoğan, to inform him about their problems. He informed Erdoğan of the inequalities faced by Christians and the drawbacks of the law proposed by the government.[23] The Greek Orthodox patriarch Bartholomew made repeated requests to the Turkish government to reopen the Theological School of Halki. He repeated his appeal in a meeting with Prime Minister Erdoğan on August 28, 2003 (Yannas 2007, 67).

On September 23, 2003, representatives of the Christian minorities in Turkey sent a joint open letter, titled "On the Question of the Religious Needs of Christian and Non-Muslim Minorities in Turkey," to the Human Rights Commission of the Turkish parliament.[24] In this letter, the representatives summarized their problems and asked the commission to pass legislation to solve them. The letter cited the lack of legal personality, the implementation problems of the law on property rights, problems related to the training of clergy and the approval of work permits for foreign clergy, and the difficulties of opening of places of worship. The leaders sent the letter to other state institutions, including the Prime Ministry, the Interior Ministry, the Foreign Ministry, the ministry responsible for religious affairs, and the GDF (Oehring 2004, 47).

A group of non-Muslim community leaders and intellectuals issued a declaration in September 2006 as a response to parliamentary debates on the Law on Foundations.[25] In this declaration, they stated that their demands were the minimum requirements of living in a democratic republican regime. They criticized both the government and the opposition parties. They criticized the government for defending the law due only to the Turkey's EU membership application and not on the principle of equal citizenship. They criticized the opposition parties for raising the argument of the principle of reciprocity, such that rights would be given to Christian minorities only if Greece granted the same rights to Turks in Greece. The declaration stated that non-Muslims did not want to be treated as hostages either to Turkey's EU membership or to the granting of rights to the Turkish minority in Greece. The declaration ended with

---

[23] *Zaman*, "Ermeni Patriği Erdoğan'dan destek istedi," January 16, 2002.

[24] The religious groups that signed the letter were the Greek Orthodox Patriarchate, the Armenian Orthodox Patriarchate of Istanbul, the Syrian Orthodox Church, and the Catholic Church.

[25] The signatories of the declaration included the press advisor of the Greek Orthodox Church, Dositheos Anagnostopulos; the editor-in-chief of the Armenian newspaper *Agos*, Hrant Dink; and other journalists and intellectuals such as Raffi A. Hermonn, Karin Karakaşlı, Etyen Mahçupyan, Sarkis Seropyan, and Nazan Maksudyan.

an invitation to the deputies to treat non-Muslim minorities equally, as a basic principle of a democratic republic.[26]

When the new bill for the Law on Foundations passed from the preparatory commission and moved to the parliamentary assembly, the Christian minorities warned the government about the pitfalls of the bill. The Armenian Orthodox patriarch Mesrob Mutafyan, for example, sent a letter to the speaker of the parliament, Bülent Arınç, the prime minister, Recep Tayyip Erdoğan, and the minister of foreign affairs, Abdullah Gül, to emphasize the principle of equality. Mutafyan stated in his letter that the principle of reciprocity could not be accepted. He wrote in the letter that Christian minorities were citizens of Turkey and they needed to be compared with other Turkish citizens, not with the citizens of other countries. He sent his suggestions for revising the bill to help solve the problems of Christian minorities.[27]

One difficulty that the Christian minorities faced in their lobbying was the negative societal stereotypes of them, especially of missionaries. These stereotypes prevented the Christian minority from reaching out to the public to gain their support. A Catholic priest in Istanbul, Guiseppe Giorgis, mentioned that they limited their charity work to Christians and could not help the Muslim poor in the city because they were being accused of converting Muslims to Christianity.[28] Similarly, priest Felice Suriano complained that the people knew little about Christianity and always approached their religious activities with suspicion.[29]

The other prong of the Christian minorities' efforts involved lobbying in international institutions, especially in the EU, to put pressure on Turkey for the amelioration of their status. For example, in July 2002, the Vatican sent a letter to the ambassadors of the member states of the EU "On the Situation of the Catholic Church in Turkey." The letter raised the issues that Catholics had to cope with: the lack of legal personality, the violations of property rights, the issues about training clergy, and the problems of foreign church employees (Oehring 2004, 48). The Vatican sent a similar letter to the ambassadors in September and asked them to use Turkey's EU negotiations as a catalyst for the resolution of these problems. The Vatican expected Turkey to respect "cultural and religious diversity" and "to consummate its legal reforms by explicitly recognizing all the religious minorities on its soil, and granting them the legal status" (quoted in Oehring 2004, 48).[30]

---

[26] İsmail Saymaz, "Azınlıklar bildirisi: Rehine değiliz," *Radikal*, September 26, 2006.
[27] *Hürriyet*, "Ermeni Patriği Vakıflar Yasa Tasarısına karşı," October 19, 2006.
[28] Author's interview with Guiseppe Giorgis, Istanbul, Turkey, May 28, 2010.
[29] Author's interview with Felice Suriano, Istanbul, Turkey, June 15, 2010.
[30] International nongovernmental organizations associated with the Christian churches in Turkey have also lobbied for the advancement of religious rights for Christian minorities in Turkey. For example, the Pontifical Mission Society has published a number of reports on Turkish policies toward Christian minorities. In one of its reports, the Pontifical Mission Society compares the Turkish legal system with European norms in regard to religious rights, and identifies problems (Oehring 2004, 50).

The Greek Orthodox patriarch Bartholomew met with several EU representatives to discuss the issue of Christian minorities. In September 2006, in his meeting with European journalists just before the pope's visit to Turkey, he asked the help of the pope and the EU in improving Christian minority rights in Turkey. He said that "it is impossible to reconcile the discrimination that we face in Turkey with Turkey's passion to become a member of the European family."[31] In January 2007, in his speech to the Council of Europe, Patriarch Bartholomew spoke about the violations of religious rights in Turkey.[32] In December, the patriarch met with the members of the European People's Party[33] and informed them about the difficulties of the Greek Orthodox Church in Turkey.[34] In January 2008, he met with the president of European Commission, José Manuel Barroso, and the European commissioner of enlargement, Olli Rehn, to communicate the problems related to religious minorities.[35]

The Greek Orthodox patriarch sought the support of Greece, which is an EU member state, in putting pressure on Turkey. The patriarch met with the Greek prime minister Kostas Karamanlis several times both in Turkey and in Greece during the reform process.[36] In the meetings, the patriarch asked for Greece's support not only for minority rights in Turkey but also for Turkey's EU membership bid, the engine of the reform process. Since each EU member state could block membership negotiations of a candidate country, the patriarch's relations with Greece was significant in putting pressure on Turkey.

Christian minorities put additional pressure on Turkey by applying to the European Court of Human Rights (ECHR) for redress of the violation of their rights by the Turkish state. In the mid-2000s, the Greek and Armenian Orthodox communities of Turkey applied to the ECHR on the grounds that the Turkish state had violated their property rights. In both cases the ECHR ordered the government of Turkey to return the properties of Greek Orthodox[37] and Armenian Orthodox[38] community foundations.

---

31 *Yeni Şafak*, "AB ve Papa bize yardımcı olacak," September 29, 2006.
32 *Milli Gazete*, "Bartholomeos'tan küstahlık," January 25, 2007.
33 This is the umbrella organization for Christian Democrat parties in the European Parliament.
34 *Turkish Daily News*, "Euro Parliamentarians Meet with Patriarchate Representatives," December 4, 2007.
35 Macit Soydan, "Tapınak Şövalyeleri," *Yeniçağ Gazetesi*, April 12, 2008; Zeynel Lüle, "AİHM'nin türban kararları," *Hürriyet*, September 23, 2007.
36 Bedia Ceylan Güzelce, "Barışçıl liderler'e Patrik duası," *Sabah*, January 26, 2008; *Radikal*, "Karamanlis'ten Fener ziyareti," June 28, 2004; *Sabah*, "Patrik'ten Atina'ya: Türkiye'nin AB yolunu destekleyin," October 19, 2006; *Milliyet*, "En iyi büyükelçi Ekümenik Patrik!" January 27, 2008.
37 "Fener Rum Erkek Lisesi Vakfı vs Turkey," Application No. 34478/97, January 9, 2007, available at http://cmiskp.echr.coe.int/tkp197/view.asp?item=1&portal=hbkm&action=html&highlight= turkey%20%7C%2034478/97&sessionid=9077090&skin=hudoc-pr-en (last accessed on June 10, 2008).
38 "Affaire Yedikule Surp Pırgiç Ermeni Hastanesi Vakfı c. Turquie," Application No. 50147/99 and 51207/99, June 26, 2007, available at http://cmiskp.echr.coe.int/tkp197/view.asp?

In addition to mobilizing European institutions, the Christian minority also lobbied in the USA to advance its status. Greek Orthodox churches in the USA lobbied on behalf of the patriarchate, especially about the reopening of the Theological School of Halki. These groups lobbied in Congress and the White House to put additional external pressure on Turkey.[39]

Another group that supported the reforms was the Kurdish party in the parliament, the Democratic Society Party.[40] Deputies from the party, particularly Hasip Kaplan, supported the bill with strong statements in the parliament. The deputies addressed concepts such as "justice," "equal citizenship," "democracy," and "fairness" in their speeches, in contrast with the speeches by the CHP and MHP representatives, who mostly perceived the matter as being an issue of law and order. In terms of EU pressure, the Democratic Society Party deputies also referred to EU documents to justify their position, but their perspective in doing so was that of elevating Turkey's standards of human rights and democracy to match universal standards rather than merely meeting EU conditionality.[41]

The key to passing the reforms in the parliament was the support of the AKP government. The AKP supported the improvement of Christian minority rights even though there were ups and downs in the reform process after the party came to power in November 2002. The party intervened in bureaucratic processes in cases when the bureaucrats had failed to implement the provisions of the reforming laws. In the process, there were several instances of tension between the Ministry of Foreign Affairs and the GDF. The former had to intervene to prevent the latter's neglect of the minority rights. The Ministry of Foreign Affairs was a significant actor of the reform process due mostly to the crucial role of the reforms in the progress toward Turkish membership in the EU.[42]

The leaders of the AKP supported the laws reforming the state's approach toward Christian minorities between 2002 and 2010. The party balanced its constituency's response by not recognizing the Greek Orthodox patriarch as the "ecumenical patriarch."[43] When faced with security and sovereignty questions, the leaders raised human rights issues and stated that those security and

---

item=1&portal=hbkm&action=html&highlight=&sessionid=9077029&skin=hudoc-en    (last accessed on June 10, 2008).

[39] Author's interview with Dositheos Anagnostopulos, press advisor of the Greek Orthodox Church, Istanbul, Turkey, June 4, 2014.

[40] Once it was closed by the constitutional court, the party members later established a new Peace and Democracy Party (Barış ve Demokrasi Partisi) in 2008. In 2014, the Peace and Democracy Party joined the newly established People's Democracy Party (Halkın Demokrasi Partisi).

[41] The speeches referenced here are drawn from the parliamentary proceedings of the Turkish Grand National Assembly on January 30 and 31 and February 13, 14, and 20, 2008. The proceedings are available at www.tbmm.gov.tr (last accessed on December 12, 2018).

[42] Hilal Köylü, "Vakıflar'ın inadı inat," *Radikal*, March 7, 2005.

[43] *Zaman*, "Abdullah Gül: Patrikhanenin statüsü değişmeyecek," June 27, 2005.

sovereignty concerns were baseless. For example, when Prime Minister Recep Tayyip Erdoğan was asked whether the reforms would open the path for the establishment of an Orthodox state under the patriarch, he asked, "Is it possible to establish a state on 80-meter square grounds?"[44] Along the same lines, Mehmet Ali Şahin, the minister of state responsible for community foundations, during the legislative debates on the Law on Foundations in November 2006 stated that "we will give the confiscated properties back to the community foundations. This neither divides our country nor undermines our sovereignty. This only glorifies our state."[45] Hayati Yazıcı, who became the state minister responsible for community foundations in September 2007, said: "this law acknowledges their [the non-Muslims'] rights. Look! Justice is the foundation of a state. If you do not provide justice, and human rights, and if you ignore property rights and freedom of expression, you destroy the foundations of the state. If someone has the right, as a state, you should grant it to him. If these rights include property rights, you should grant them as well."[46]

Why did the AKP, coming from an Islamist, anti-Western background, support the reforms that improved the status of Christian minorities? The political context of the late 1990s and early 2000s made the AKP support for the reforms possible (Kılınç 2014a). In June 1996 the Islamist Welfare Party, in coalition with the center-right True Path Party, came to power. The military and its civilian allies took a strong opposition to the new coalition government on the grounds that the government was a threat to Turkish secularism. By early 1997 the military had increased its pressure on the government, which was forced to resign in June. Between June 1997 and April 1999, the new military-supported government suppressed political and social Islamic groups in Turkey. The Welfare Party was closed down by the Constitutional Court, Islamic movements were strictly monitored, their financial resources were decreased, state employees affiliated with religious groups were fired, and female university students wearing the Islamic headscarf were dismissed (Kılınç 2014b; Kuru 2012).

Faced with these threats to their political survival after 1997, the Islamic political actors changed their strategies. Unlike their predecessors, who had tried to find a compromise with the military, these Islamic actors took a strong position against the military and became supporters of democratic reforms to minimize the role of the military in politics. To this end, Islamic actors supported Turkey's EU membership process with the aim of restructuring the

---

[44] *Radikal*, "Hükümet azınlık okulları ve 40 bin Ermeni için adım atamadı," September 27, 2006.
[45] *Zaman*, "Vakıflar Yasası tamam, azınlık vakıflarının mallarına iade yolu açıldı," November 10, 2006.
[46] Hayati Yazıcı's speech in parliament, "Türkiye Büyük Millet Meclisi Genel Kurul Tutanağı 23. Dönem 2. Yasama Yılı 67. Birleşim," February 20, 2008, available on the website of the parliament: www.tbmm.gov.tr/develop/owa/tutanak_ss.birlesim_baslangic?P4=17665&P5=B&web_user_id=5573538&PAGE1=1&PAGE2=149 (last accessed on June 10, 2008).

Turkish legal system so as to protect their political survival (Driessen 2014, 199–202; Yildirim 2013). This move represented a reversal of attitudes toward the EU. For example, when he was a Welfare Party deputy in the mid-1990s, Abdullah Gül had opposed Turkey's membership of the EU, considering it an economic threat to Turkey that would weaken national industry (Taniyici 2003, 471). However, by November 2000 he considered EU membership to be a vehicle for the internal struggle for democracy (Mufti 2010, 10). Ali Bulaç, an influential intellectual among Islamists who had been a Euroskeptic in the past, openly supported EU membership in the 2000s on the grounds that it would transform the Turkish political system and lead to more civil and political liberties for religious groups.[47] He wrote, "the events [after the 1997 military intervention] that turned many people's [lives] into a nightmare led the people to see the EU as a savior" (quoted in Dagi 2004, 146).[48]

In short, Islamic actors might not have embraced the EU project without a serious threat to their survival from the military. In this case, external pressure might have deprived a strong domestic ally of further political reform. In the presence of a threat to its survival, the AKP supported the EU's reform proposals in the 2000s and openly declared its strong support for Turkey's EU membership.[49] After coming to power in 2002, the AKP government supported and passed various democratizing reforms based on EU requirements, including religious rights for Christian minorities. Several EU reforms were implemented between 2002 and 2007.[50]

Liberals and a few social Islamic groups, by enhancing the domestic popular legitimacy of the reforms, lent support to the drive for religious rights for Christian minorities. They propagated the view that being a democratic country necessitated the implementation of human rights in all arenas. They asked for state neutrality toward the Christian minorities, emphasizing the relationship between the demands of Christian minorities and international norms on human rights. They strongly criticized the appeal to the principle of reciprocity on the grounds of equal citizenship.

The Association for Liberal Thinking organized several conferences and projects in support of the reforms. In the early 2002, within the framework of its European Commission–funded project, "Interreligious Affairs: Search for a Framework for a Peaceful Coexistence in a Secular and Democratic System," the association prepared several reports outlining the violations of religious freedoms in Turkey, published books to increase awareness on religious freedoms, and organized panels and conferences which gathered academics

---

[47] Ali Bulaç, "Niçin AB," *Zaman*, December 11, 1999.

[48] A. Kadir Yildirim argues that the ideological transformation of the AKP was an outcome of the economic liberalization model that the Turkish state implemented after the 1980 military coup: see Yildirim 2009; 2015; 2016. See also Karakaya and Yildirim 2013; Sokhey and Yildirim 2013; Yildirim and Lancaster 2015.

[49] Ergun Aksoy, "Ve Bir Ampül Yandı," *Radikal*, August 15, 2001.

[50] For a study that examines Turkey's transformation in this period, see Kuru and Stepan 2012.

and religious leaders together.[51] Another important organization with social democratic leanings, the Turkish Economic and Social Studies Foundation (Türkiye Ekonomik ve Sosyal Etütler Vakfı), organized conferences and published research on the issue of Christian minorities.[52] The foundation's reports were widely publicized and attracted significant media attention.

Liberal intellectuals supported the reform process and criticized the drawbacks of the reform packages.[53] They emphasized that a citizenship regime that took equality as its principle could not implement the principle of reciprocity.[54] Other intellectuals wrote that granting rights to Christian minorities was among the minimum constituent standards of being a democratic republican state that respected its citizens.[55] Still others recommended that those who embraced the idea of reciprocity should look at other European countries such as Germany and see the rights that the Turkish community living abroad enjoyed.[56]

Several Islamic groups supported the reforms. For example, the president of an Islamic human rights organization, MAZLUMDER, stated that "the rights of our minority citizens cannot be sacrificed to the fears and doubts of history. It is impossible to change what happened in the past, but we have a chance toward a more positive path."[57] MAZLUMDER published reports on violations of religious freedoms. In addition to the problems faced by Muslims, these reports included detailed descriptions of the violations of religious liberties that non-Muslim minorities confronted.[58] A conservative journalist wrote that the Christian minorities should not have paid the price for those who rebelled against the Ottoman Empire years ago. The same author stated that the Muslim democrats should have worked with the Christian minorities who had suffered under the authoritarian state for years.[59]

Turkey's influential Islamic movement at the time, the Gülen movement, supported religious freedoms for non-Muslim minorities.[60] Fethullah Gülen,

---

[51] For more information see the associations website at www.liberal-dt.org.tr/index.php?lang=en&message=dinlerarasi2 (last accessed on June 10, 2008).

[52] For more information on the activities of TESEV concerning the issue of Christian minorities, see www.tesev.org.tr/etkinlik/azinlik_dilleri.php (last accessed on June 10, 2011).

[53] Turgut Tarhanlı, "Nasıl bir iyileştirme," *Radikal*, August 1, 2002; Yıldırım Türker, "O da mı Ermeni Çıktı?" *Radikal*, February 29, 2004.

[54] Bekir Berat Özipek, "Azınlık hakları, Ruhban Okulu ve birlikte yaşam formülü!" *Zaman*, August 26, 2004; Mehmet Ali Birand, "Azınlıklardan neden korkuyoruz?" *Hürriyet*, March 9, 2005.

[55] Etyen Mahçupyan, "Meramsız iyi niyet," *Zaman*, June 27, 2005; Etyen Mahçupyan, "Vatandaşı hazmedemeyen cumhuriyet olur mu?" *Zaman*, October 1, 2006.

[56] Murat Belge, "Gayrimüslim vakıflar (1)," *Radikal*, February 22, 2008.

[57] Yılmaz Ensarioğlu, "Gayrimüslim vakıfları … " Zaman, May 28, 2002.

[58] MAZLUMDER 2010.

[59] Leyla İpekçi, "Asıl gayrimüslimler çekti bu ittihatçı zihniyetten!" *Zaman*, May 6, 2008.

[60] During the reform years, 2002–2010, the Gülen movement and the AKP were political allies. However, their relationship deteriorated later, especially after 2013. In July 2016, the

the leader of the movement, met with leaders of non-Muslim communities in the mid-1990s and stated his support for freedoms for Christian minorities, including the reopening of the Theological School of Halki.[61] The Journalists and Writers Foundation, an organization affiliated with the Gülen movement, supported the reforms through its lectures, conferences, and interfaith activities. Christian minorities and their leaders participated in events and meetings organized by the foundation. The movement's interfaith activities in Turkey and abroad helped in the legitimization of an environment that is tolerant toward Christian minorities.

Discussions known as Abant workshops, organized by the Journalists and Writers Foundation, served as a platform for the legitimation of pluralism in Turkey among conservatives. In the Abant workshops, journalists, academics, and politicians from different backgrounds met to discuss issues such as religious freedom, secularism, pluralism, democracy, and globalization. In their final declarations, the workshops declared compatibility, if not a friendly relationship, between Islam and pluralism. Many AKP politicians were regular participants in the Abant workshops, including Abdullah Gül, Bülent Arınç, Cemil Çiçek, Mehmet Aydın, Hüseyin Çelik, Burhan Kuzu, and Ali Coşkun (Kuru 2007b; Uğur 2007). In short, liberal and Islamic groups, through their activism to support religious liberties, increased awareness in Turkish society and contributed to the formation of a reform-friendly environment among conservative people. In contrast to the animosity toward non-Muslims that was prevalent among Islamists in the 1990s, local leaders in the AKP provincial offices approached the reforms on Christian minorities as "a necessity to fulfill justice"[62] and as "protecting the Ottoman legacies in our lands."[63]

EU pressure structured Turkish domestic politics in strategic and normative ways to enable reforms in the treatment of Christian minorities. Strategically, EU pressure provided Christian groups with the power to transform domestic politics. Even though the Christian minority in Turkey constituted a tiny proportion of the Turkish population and they did not have strong political representation, they were able to apply pressure for policy change through European mechanisms. The AKP government used EU pressure strategically. With the stated aim of preparing Turkey for EU membership, the government enabled the Turkish political system to exercise more power than traditional bureaucratic authoritarian institutions would have allowed. With the reforms that constrained the military and the bureaucracy, the AKP leadership passed

---

government hold the Gülen movement responsible for the failed coup attempt. By December 2018, the movement had been criminalized in Turkey.

[61] Basri Doğan, "Freedom Award Recipient Bartholomew Praises Gülen's Peace Efforts." *Today's Zaman*, May 13, 2012.

[62] Author's interview with a local AKP leader in Şanlıurfa, Turkey, June 30, 2012.

[63] Author's interview with a local AKP leader in Erzurum, Turkey, May 27, 2014.

legislation reforming treatment of the Christian minority. Normatively, EU pressure activated groups such as liberals, social democrats, and some Islamic groups committed to the values of human rights, freedoms, and democracy. By influencing public debate, the EU increased the legitimacy in Turkey of values that expanded the rights of the Christian minority.

## CONCLUSION

Despite unfavorable historical institutions, Turkey passed a number of reforms ameliorating the conditions of Christian minorities in the first decade of the twenty-first century. The EU had a radical impact on these policy changes; however, it alone could not have produced the outcome. Turkey had an active relationship with European institutions since the 1950s, but this did not propel reforms to expand the rights of the Christian minority until the early 2000s, when a leading domestic actor appropriated the EU-led reforms. Although international pressure played a major role in changing domestic institutions, the actors facilitated the process due to the convergence of interests among weak actors and relatively stronger actors, and the increasing popular legitimacy of international norms brought about by the national and international activities of liberals and some Islamic groups.

The AKP's embrace of the reform of Christian minority rights in Turkey cannot be explained independent from the party's interests in Turkey's possible membership of the EU. The need for reforms in order to continue on the path to membership constrained the military and the bureaucracy and increased the balance of power among domestic actors. The EU-led reforms redesigned Turkish political institutions so as to increase opportunities for the political actors. In the end, the political actors empowered their positions vis-à-vis the bureaucratic establishment. Despite their weakness in domestic politics, the Christian minorities exploited the AKP's sympathetic position toward the EU reforms and lobbied both in Turkey and abroad to put pressure on the government. Considering the historical institutions, the reforms passed in the 2000s on the status of Christian minorities were revolutionary.

Liberals, social democrats, and some Islamic groups embraced the process because they saw the transformation as being in line with their normative commitments. EU pressure and resources allowed these groups to organize lectures, talks, symposiums, and community engagement programs that prepared the groundwork for the AKP's reforms. In terms of Christian minority rights, these normative entrepreneurs educated the AKP constituency to make such reforms more possible. Despite their Islamist background, the constituency was welcoming to the new reforms and the expansion of the rights of the Christian minority.

The alliance of Islamists, liberals, and social democrats, which became possible due to EU pressure, made it increasingly difficult for opponents to block the passing of the bills improving the status of Christians. Secularist and nationalist opposition in Turkey did not support the expansion of liberties for non-Muslim minorities. Both the CHP and the MHP approached the question of minorities from a security and sovereignty angle. They did not consider the issue to be one of religious freedom, property rights, or human rights. While the ideological differences between the parties might lead one to expect different reactions from them on the question of non-Muslim minorities, they instead displayed almost identical responses to the reforms. The strategic thinking of the AKP, in their efforts to gain ground in Turkish politics, and the normative support of other groups undermined the opposition to the reforms.

# 7

# Radical Right, Liberals, and Muslims in France

On December 16, 2003, a group of Muslim demonstrators gathered in Paris and marched through the city to protest against the French parliament's plan to ban the wearing of headscarves in public schools. During the protests, Muslim girls waved the French flag and wore blue, white, and red scarves matching the French flag "to show that we are French and Muslim and proud of it." During their four-hour march, the protestors chanted "Where is France? Where is tolerance? The veil is my choice." An Algerian-born Muslim woman, Kawthar Fawzy, said, "When I came here, they told me France was the land of human rights. I found out it is the opposite."[1] In this protest, Muslim girls aimed to give the message that wearing headscarves was their own choice and doing so did not contradict their duties of French citizenship. By demonstrating symbols of both Islam and France, the girls wanted to challenge the polarization in which Muslim girls' wearing of headscarves was presented as a threat to French republicanism and secularism. Despite protests like this, this message did not appeal to the French people. The view of a binary divide between Islam and secularism prevailed, and those who defended the headscarf ban in the public schools had no difficulty in gaining popular support. In this chapter, I analyze why this was the case. The supporters of the headscarf ban in schools took advantage of the global rise of Islamophobia to define the terms of the debate in France. The global and national rise of anti-Muslim sentiments provided the proponents of the ban with the necessary instruments to gain supporters for their own policy agendas and form a coalition that made the passing of the ban possible.

The French parliament passed the ban on the wearing of headscarves in public schools in early 2004. Prior to the passing of the headscarf ban, the proponents of the ban in France were the major parties in France (the Union for a Popular Movement and the Socialist Party), secularist organizations such as the Association for Republican Secularism (Comité laïcité république),

---

[1] Bootie Cosgrove-Mather, "Protests vs Muslim Headscarf Ban," *CBS News*, December 17, 2003, available at www.cbsnews.com/news/protests-vs-muslim-head-scarf-ban (last accessed on May 26, 2018).

feminists, and intellectuals such as Henri Pena Ruiz and Regis Debray. The opponents of the ban were Muslim, Jewish, and Christian organizations, a few liberal organizations such as the League of Education, and a handful of intellectuals such as Jean Bauberot and Alain Gresh. Since the parliament was the main decision maker in this process, the proponents of the ban accessed the center parties to get their support for it. A majority of French parliamentarians supported the ban, while only a few of them were against it.

As Chapter 3 showed, French secularism, which was shaped during the Third Republic and remained after that except for a short period of Vichy rule during the Second World War, both protected religious minorities and constituted a threat for them. It protected religious minorities because it provided them with constitutional state neutrality and equality of treatment toward religions. It threatened them because the strong emphasis on secularism in France made it not only a legal principle but also a national identifier. Secularism played a significant role in the formation of the political identity of the French republic when the republican elite mobilized the masses against the religious establishment. Although neutrality and the egalitarian aspects of French secularism protected Muslims' religious liberties in France until the 2000s, the rise of global Islamophobia, which was demonstrated in Chapter 5, changed the trajectory of French state policies. The strict secularist groups in France utilized the secularist sensitivities of the French people and the new international environment to mobilize the public against the visibility of Muslim symbols. They portrayed Muslims as a threat to the French values of secularism and republicanism and sought to limit their symbols at public schools. The rise of Islamophobia also yielded the path for the rise of far-right politics in France.

The interaction of the international context and domestic actors made the decision to ban the headscarf easier (see Figure 7.1). The rise of Islamophobia provided the proponents of the ban with several advantages. First, Islamophobia allowed them to portray headscarves as a symbol of "Islamic fundamentalism" that was based on the rejection of French secularism, one of the most important pillars of the republic. In the minds of the proponents of the ban, protecting French secularism meant protecting the French republic. The headscarf ban, then, would be a remedy to the rise of "Islamic fundamentalism." This point was ubiquitous in public debates, in the statements of statesmen, and in legislative debates in the parliament. Second, the rise of Islamophobia facilitated access to policymakers for the proponents of the ban. Increased concerns about the rise of Islam at both public and elite levels helped the ban's proponents enhance the pro-ban coalition. The decision makers were heavily influenced by the binary framing of secularism and fundamentalism that the proponents offered by capitalizing on rising Islamophobia. Third, the rise of Islamophobia prevented the opponents of the ban from developing a rights-based argument in defending the rights of

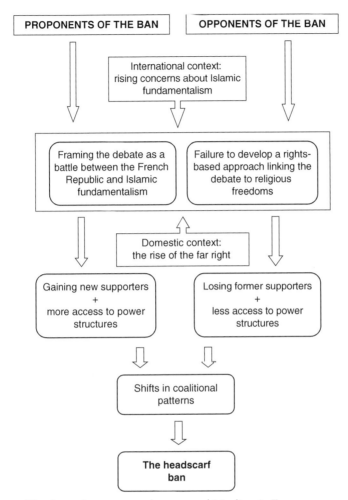

FIGURE 7.1 The flow of arguments: the state and Muslims in France

headscarf-wearing girls in public debates. It also prevented them from pushing for their policy agendas based on universal norms of religious freedoms. The dominant anti-Muslim attitudes prevented the opponents of the ban from establishing institutional and corporate connections to policymakers because politicians were reluctant to be affiliated with Muslims, wishing to avoid stigmatization within an increasingly polarized public.

As French society polarized along the lines of republicanism and Islamism, the nuances of the debate were lost. Many intellectual, social, and political groups who opposed the ban in the past became its supporters. This polarization changed the coalitional structures to favor the proponents of the ban, and these shifts in coalitions led to the passing of the ban in the parliament.

In this chapter, I demonstrate how proponents of the French headscarf ban exploited Islamophobia in pushing their policy agendas while opponents failed to counter the increasing pro-ban coalition.

## ISLAMOPHOBIA AND THE ADVOCATES OF THE HEADSCARF BAN

Due to the rising concerns about Islamic fundamentalism, anti-Muslim groups were able to frame the headscarf ban as a significant move to protect French secularism. The advocates of the ban were able to put the policy changes into the context of French principles of republicanism and secularism. Civil society groups who were against the wearing of the headscarf at school mobilized a strong public movement for the ban and eventually reached out to politicians to execute their policy agendas. By framing public debates as a fight between Islamic fundamentalism and French secularism, the advocates of the ban formed a large coalition to support their policy agenda. Many politicians gradually arrived at the decision to support the ban. It was this large coalition that made the headscarf ban possible.

### Islamophobia and Civil Society Activism for the Headscarf Ban

In public debates, social actors such as the Teachers Union and secularist intellectuals defended the ban, arguing that the headscarf was a symbol of the rejection of the French republic and secularism. They portrayed those who wore the headscarf as the agents, or at least subjects, of Islamic fundamentalists. They described the headscarf as a symbol of Islamic fundamentalism and saw it as a threat to French republican ideals. Some proponents, especially feminist groups, associated the headscarf with the oppression of women by familial and community pressures, a manifestation of the Islamic threat to French values of equality. Thus, according to proponents of the ban, the headscarf constituted a threat against French principles of secularism and equality. The headscarf, then, symbolized the rise of Islamic fundamentalism, which "had spread to the heart of France" (Idriss 2005, 276). For many, the headscarf represented "the ultimate symbol of Islam's resistance to modernity" (Scott 2007, 2). In short, proponents of the headscarf ban framed the issue as a battle between republicanism and Islamic fundamentalism.

Although some had associated the headscarf with Islamic fundamentalists since the first headscarf debate in 1989, the framing of fundamentalism versus republicanism gained dominance in the early 2000s. This binary framing found a suitable environment after the September 11 attacks, which led to the rise of Islamophobia. A review of how civil society advocates of the ban portrayed the headscarf from 1989 reveals the transformation in French public attitudes toward the headscarf.

In the first headscarf affair in 1989, Eugène Chenière, the principal of the high school in which the headscarf-wearing girls were dismissed, legitimized his decision by refering to the principle of secularism. He claimed that he was protecting the principle of secularism from what he later called "insidious jihad" (Scott 2007, 22), symbolized by the wearing of the headscarf. For Chenière, "it is laïcité [secularism] that has allowed the public school to be the melting pot in which, through education, differences vanish so that the nation emerges."[2] For him, Islamic fundamentalists created differences and inequalities to the detriment of girls; these inequalities could disseminate through the school, which he regarded as the "neutral" space of the Republic.

At the time, support for Chenière's line of argument was limited and marginal. Five famous left-wing intellectuals published a declaration against the wearing of headscarves in schools in 1989. They were asking for a ban, arguing that the French model of democracy was under threat. They argued that the school was the fundamental place for reproducing republican persons. They described tolerance for headscarves in schools as something like the appeasement policies of European states toward Hitler in 1930s.[3] The response of the far-right National Front (FN, Front national) was similar. The party saw Islam as a threat to the French way of life and republican ideals. To the party, a Muslim civilization was implanting itself in France symbolically by the wearing of the headscarf in schools. They asked the question: "should France adapt her principles to those of immigrants, or should immigrants adapt their customs to the laws of our country?" (Freedman 2004, 13). However, these voices did not get support from mainstream political actors in 1989.

The argument about the Islamic fundamentalist threat continued in 1994 during the second headscarf controversy in France when the minister of education issued a circular to ban headscarves at schools after nationwide teachers' protests. In its cover story on headscarves, *L'Express* featured a staunchly secularist intellectual, André Glucksmann, calling the headscarf a terrorist emblem of Islamic radicals operating against French republican ideals. For him, the headscarf was a refusal of French citizenship and an acknowledgement of religious fundamentalism.[4]

The framing of the headscarf issue as a battle between the republic and religious fundamentalism reached its highest point after the September 11 terrorist attacks, particularly during the headscarf debates in 2003 prior to the passing of the law. After 2001, the advocates of the ban gained popular support for their policy agenda mainly because the public became more prone to accept the portrayal of the issue as a fight between Islamic fundamentalism and secularism in the wake of the September 11 terrorist attacks.

---

[2] Michel Gonod, "La Riposte: Pourquoi ce principal de collège s'oppose à l'offensive des religieux," *Paris-Match*, November 9, 1989, 61.

[3] Elisabeth Badinter, Régis Debray, Alain Finkielkraut, Elisabeth de Fontenay, and Catherine Kintszler, "Profs, ne capitulons pas," *Le Nouvel observateur*, November 2–8, 1989.

[4] *L'Express*, "Foulard – Le Complot – Comment les islamistes nous infiltrent," November 7, 1994.

Intellectuals such as Michèle Tribalat, who had in the past expressed opposition to the dismissal of girls from schools for wearing headscarves, took a hostile position toward the headscarf in 2003. In May 2003, similarly to the 1989 letter against the headscarf mentioned above, four influential intellectuals, including Tribalat, made a declaration in favor of banning the headscarf. These intellectuals, in their declaration calling for a law to ban all religious signs in schools, claimed that the school must be free from the pressure of any politico-religious group. They defined the school as a place where "French citizens" are formed; and they saw the intervention of dogmatic ideas into this "sacred place" as detrimental to the republic. They ended their declaration by a call: "Prohibit by law all religious signs in public schools and any sign of discrimination; people should be required not to define a priori a sense of belonging."[5] Similarly, the well-known French philosopher Régis Debray, who was also a member of the Stasi Commission, said in late 2003 that "the absence of a law would be worse: it is not a sign of tolerance, but one of weakness, an incentive for fanatics" (Wing and Smith 2006, 771).

Feminist writers Caroline Fourest and Fiammette Venner, after examining the rise of religious movements in France, wrote that veiling was not an issue in itself.[6] For them, "the authorization of the veil in school is just one step in the agenda of fundamentalist associations who want to test secularism." They supported the headscarf ban, saying "we must serve to reaffirm a particularly ambitious vision of secularism at a time when it is more than ever threatened by the rise of fundamentalism" (Fourest and Venner 2003, 31).

The Association of Republican Secularism, an established secularist organization and one of the ardent supporters of the ban, also contributed to the debate by making a binary distinction between republicanism and fundamentalism. In its statement in late 2003, the association defined the school as a "sacred place" where students learn to become citizens. This, for them, constituted the basis for banning the wearing of headscarves in public schools: because the school should remain a "sanctuary of secularism" not subject to pressure from communitarian fundamentalists.[7]

As Cécile Laborde puts it, to many secularists "headscarves, as ostensible signs of religious belief, infringe on the neutrality and civic purpose of schools" (Laborde 2008, 53). Headscarves played such a role by introducing "signs of private difference and religious divisiveness into the public sphere,"

---

[5] Catherine Kintzler, Pierre-André Taguieff, Bernard Tepe, and Michèle Tribalat, "Une loi pour interdire tout signe religieux à l'école: L'école publique doit être soustraite à la pression des groupes politico-religieux," *Libération*, May 6, 2003.

[6] These writers were recognized by the French parliament. The French National Assembly awarded Caroline Fourest a prize for the best political book of the year for *La Tentation obscurantiste* (2005), which was about the rise of the Islamic threat in France. The book incorporates Fourest's writings on the headscarf issue written during the public controversy in late 2003 and early 2004.

[7] For the statement, see the organization's website at www.laicite-republique.org/IMG/pdf/APPEL-NI-CROIX.pdf (last accessed on November 1, 2007).

symbolizing "the primacy of the believer over the citizen," infringing on equality between the students, and undermining "the civic mission of schools" (Laborde 2008, 53–54). Riva Kastoryano, a French political sociologist, thought of the French public sphere as an ideologically driven arena in which the introduction of the headscarf issue revived debates on secularism.[8]

The proponents of the ban also brought up the issue of gender equality in framing the headscarf issue as a battle between the republic and Islamism. The wearing of headscarves, for them, was a sign of the violation of the principle of gender equality, an important constituting principle of French national identity. This argument portrayed Muslim schoolgirls as victims of inequality and repression because it was assumed that they were being forced to wear the headscarf by their parents. The ban was justified on the basis of guaranteeing social equality among men and women. The ban, then, would protect schoolgirls from familial and religious pressure; it would also protect those who did not wear the headscarf from the social pressure of those who did so (Idriss 2005, 277).

The argument of gender equality found many supporters among schoolteachers. French teachers' unions, which traditionally had good access to politicians (Gaziel and Taub 1992), participated in the public debates. The majority of teachers opposed the wearing of headscarves in classrooms. The National Union of Secondary Education (Syndicat nationale enseignement secondaire) was the most assertive organization in the public debates.[9] It organized a number of strikes to put pressure on legislators for the passing of the headscarf ban. According to a survey conducted in January 2004, 79 percent of the teachers thought that wearing of a headscarf in classrooms was incompatible with the values of the republican education.[10] The extent of this support becomes evident when one considers that popular support for the bill was about 70 percent when the parliament passed it.[11] The words of a history teacher during a BBC discussion program immediately after the passing of the law summarize the attitude of most French teachers toward the headscarf: "This law is here to protect those girls who are compelled to do things they don't want to do – not to be forced into marriage, not to wear the veil."[12]

---

[8] Author's interview with Riva Kastoryano, Paris, France, July 17, 2007.

[9] Other significant organizations are the Federation of National Education (Fédération de l'éducation nationale), the National Union of Elementary Schoolteachers (Syndicat nationale des instituteurs), and Teachers of General Education in High Schools (Professeurs de l'enseignement général des collèges).

[10] Sondages CSA. 2004. "Les Enseignants des collèges et lycées et la laïcité" Paris, January 24, 2004, available at www.csa-tmo.fr/dataset/data2004/opi20040124c.htm (last accessed on November 1, 2007).

[11] *The Economist*, "The War of the Headscarves," February 7, 2004. The survey was conducted in January 2004 by CSA.

[12] Elizabeth Jones, "Muslim Girls Unveil their Fears," *BBC News*, March 28, 2005, available at http://news.bbc.co.uk/2/hi/programmes/this_world/4352171.stm (last accessed on June 24, 2017).

Feminist organizations also voiced their opposition to the wearing of headscarves on the grounds of gender inequality. Among the feminist organizations that lobbied for the ban, the most vocal one was the organization named Neither Whores nor Submissives (Ni Putes, ni soumises). The organization was established in 2002 to protest physical violence against women perpetrated in the name of Islam.[13] From its foundation it developed a close relationship with the French political parties, both socialists and conservatives.[14] In a widely circulated petition campaign, organized just before the passing of the headscarf law, the organization supported the ban on headscarves because "the Islamic veil subjects all of us, Muslim and non-Muslim alike, to an intolerable discrimination against women."[15] The leader of the group, Fadela Amera, co-authored a book to support the ban. The book describes the activism for a headscarf ban as a fight against the oppression of women (Amara and Zappi 2003).

Another leading feminist organization, Les Pénélopes, supported the ban by arguing that veiled women represented the supremacy of men over women, and girls should be emancipated from this supremacy.[16] A prominent feminist organization, the Chiennes de garde, also called for the ban, claiming that the headscarf was "the symbol of the oppression of women, of a demonization of the body and women's sexuality."[17] Another one, the Feminist Reforms Study Group (Cercle d' étude de réformes féministes), organized a huge petition campaign supporting the headscarf ban.[18] These organizations tended to see the Muslim girl wearing the headscarf as "an unwilling victim of sexist familial or community pressures" (Thomas 2006, 247). At the height of the debates on the headscarf issue in December 2003, a group of women published an open letter in *Elle* magazine calling for the banning of the headscarf in public schools on the grounds that the wearing of the headscarf discriminated against women. Several prominent women including the actor Isabelle Adjani, the historian Elisabeth Badinter, the writer Catherine Millet, the fashion designer Sonia Rykiel, and the founder of Ni Putes ni soumises, Fadela Amara, signed the letter.[19]

---

[13] For more information, see the organization's website at www.niputesnisoumises.com (last accessed on November 3, 2007).

[14] Fadela Amara, the president of the organization, became a cabinet member in François Fillon's center-right government in May 2007.

[15] The petition can be seen at www.niputesnisoumises.com/mouvement.php?section=petition_eng (last accessed on November 3, 2007).

[16] Marie-Thérèse Martinelli, "Voilées / Dévoilées – Deux facettes d'une même domination," *Les Pénélopes*, January 3, 2004, available at www.penelopes.org/xarticle.php3?id_article=4573 (last accessed on October 6, 2007).

[17] Bureau des chiennes de garde, "Voile: Le Symbole et l'acte," March 7, 2005, available at http://chiennesdegarde.org/article.php3?id_article=383 (last accessed on November 3, 2007).

[18] For more information about the organization, see www.c-e-r-f.org (last accessed on June 23, 2017).

[19] Elaine Sciolino, "Ban Religious Attire in School, French Panel Says," *New York Times*, December 12, 2003.

Caroline Fourest and Fiammetta Venner, the editors of the feminist journal *Pro-Choix*, played a prominent role in the public debates.[20] In issue 25 of *Pro-Choix*, a special issue titled *Veil: School and Secularism – Are They in Danger?* (*Voile: L'École et laïcité sont-elles en danger?*), Fourest and Venner denied the liberal arguments on the headscarf, which supported the headscarf-wearing girls for the sake of equality among students. They stated that "Respect for the lifestyle involves seeing them as individuals having the free will to choose," and for them, the wearing of the headscarf was not a decision made by the free will of the students. They further wrote that "we feel that the only way to fight today for an equal world is to claim an ambitious secularism" (Fourest and Venner 2003, 31).

Two other prominent feminists, Anne Vigerie, a member of the Feminist Reforms Study Group, and Anne Zelensky, president of the League of Women's Rights (Ligue du droit des femmes), went even further, stating that the ban should be expanded to colleges and business places. They suggested expanding the ban even to the streets to protect the rights of women and the secular identity of the nation. The headscarf symbolized the place of women in Islam, which, for them, was "shadows, relegation, and submission to men." To Vigerie and Zelensky, "freedom to wear a headscarf must stop, where social, moral, or physical violence against those who do not wear starts."[21] On another occasion, Anne Vigerie identified the headscarf as a "flag on the head" (*le drapeau sur la tête*) that confirmed the underdeveloped status of women in Islam (quoted in Wing and Smith 2006, 769).

In short, feminists considered the headscarf to be a symbol of paternalistic pressure over schoolgirls. As summarized in Laborde (2008, 118), to secularist feminists, "Families cannot be trusted to provide autonomy-promoting education to their children; the state, with its public commitment to autonomy and citizenship, is a more reliable paternalist agent." Instead of a particularistic worldview of family and religious communities, school was to provide an environment in which children were "thoroughly socialized into forms of autonomous behavior and thought appropriate to modern individualistic societies" (Laborde 2008, 124). These feminists saw the headscarf ban as a move toward the realization of women's autonomy.

Due to rising Islamophobia in Europe and France, the social groups and activists who supported the banning of the headscarf successfully undermined the idea that the wearing of headscarf was a religious freedom. Framing the issue along republican and Islamic lines with reference to French values of secularism and equality helped the proponents receive support from politicians to pursue their policy agendas.

---

[20] As indicated earlier in the chapter, Caroline Fourest had very close relationships with the legislators. These relationships allowed her to shape ongoing policymaking with regard to the headscarf ban in France.

[21] Anne Vigerie and Anne Zelensky, "Laïcardes, puisque féministes," *Le Monde*, May 30, 2003.

### From Civil Society Activism to Political Change

Although the social groups that favored a ban on the headscarf in public schools had access to policymakers since the controversy first arose in 1989, there was not at that time enough support to pass a bill in the French parliament. When the issue came to the attention of the deputies, a majority of conservatives and socialists did not support it. However, after the September 11 terrorist attacks, increased support for the ban made its passing possible in 2004.

The proponents of the ban organized a strong political campaign to gain support from legislators. Prior to 2003, teachers' unions staged several strikes to demonstrate their support for the law.[22] Feminist groups established strong relationships with both right- and left-wing parties. Caroline Fourest was given an award by the French parliament for her book, which included several of her writings on the headscarf issue (Fourest 2005). Fadela Amera, another feminist leader who had been very active in anti-headscarf demonstrations, served in the government in later years. These actors' access to politicians strengthened legislative support for the ban. The transformation of the perspectives of politicians from 1989 to 2004 demonstrates this change at the political level.

In 1989, centrist parties did not support the banning of the headscarf in schools. The Socialist Party was in power at the time; the party did not issue even a circular to limit the wearing of headscarves in public schools. Although there was pressure from teachers' unions, the party did not offer a single proposal for the ban. Lionel Jospin, the minister of education at the time, approached the issue as a matter of freedom (Idriss 2005, 272).

In 1994 the center-right government, in response to teachers' demands, issued a circular banning the headscarf in public schools. Events in Algeria at the time influenced French domestic politics and made politicians more vigilant toward Islamic organizations. François Bayrou, who issued the circular that banned the wearing of the headscarf, referred to republican values in justifying his decision on the ban. He defined school as a space where all children learn and live together with respect for one another. He considered religious signs as indications of the undermining of equality among schoolchildren. He equated the banning of the headscarf with an attempt to vindicate the status of the republican school based on the perpetuation of French ideals (McGoldrick 2006, 78).

Bayrou did not support a ban on headscarves in 1989, arguing that it was up to students to wear whatever they wanted in school. However, in 1994, he argued that the school had to exclude differences to integrate all students. When describing his change in attitude, Bayrou said that in 1989 he had seen the wearing of a headscarf as a personal form of religious expression. Later, he

---

[22] Olivier Bertrand, "Un foulard déclenche une grève dans un lycée de Lyon," *Libération*, March 13, 2003; Catherine Simon, "Le Voile est un piège, qui isole et marginalize," *Le Monde*, December 17, 2001; Luc Bronner, "Les Professeurs d'un lycée de Seine-Saint-Denis en grève contre l'islamisme," *Le Monde*, March 25, 2002.

claimed, he discovered the real meaning of the headscarf for fundamentalists. By banning it, Bayrou wanted to stop the influence of Islamic religio-political groups at schools (Freedman 2004, 14–15). Another member of the government, Charles Pasqua, then minister of the interior, associated wearing headscarves with religious fundamentalism. To him, the headscarf symbolized a total submission to religious fundamentalism that was foreign to the French traditions of secularism and gender equality (Freedman 2004, 15).

This executive response to the headscarf in 1994 did not translate into legislative action. Many socialists were against the ban. The Council of State revoked the Bayrou circular on the ground that it was unconstitutional. However, the situation radically changed in the early 2000s. In 2004, the ban received support from the majority of deputies. Perceptions about Islamic fundamentalism played a major role in this transformation. Reports from governmental agencies and politicians' statements of the time demonstrate this point.

The Debré and Stasi Commissions were established to investigate the implementation of the principle of secularism in France. These commissions based their recommendations on the assumption that the republic was under threat from Islamic fundamentalism, manifested as the wearing of headscarves in public schools. The Debré Commission, formed by the parliament, reviewed the threats coming from "religious fundamentalists" and recommended that "the authorities must be vigilant to strictly enforce the principle of secularism more than ever."[23] The commission advised that a law would end the subordination of girls by their fathers, brothers, and religious communities. The Debré report stated that it was up to the state to prepare necessary conditions for the emancipation of girls suffering from external pressures. The chair of the commission, Jean-Louis Debré, referenced the "fundamentalist threat" to explain the rationale behind the commission's recommendation to ban the headscarf. He said that secularism guaranteed freedom of religion, and France "respects all religions," but "we ask those who want to live their faith to do so within the boundaries of the Republic."[24] In his speech during the parliamentary session in which the law was discussed, Debré reaffirmed that the law was a "clear affirmation that public school is a place for learning, not for militant activity or proselytism."[25]

The report of the presidential Stasi Commission justified the headscarf ban on the grounds that there should be no negotiation over the principle of secularism with extremists who are "testing the resistance of the republic and pushing some young people to reject its values."[26] The report rejected any kind of negotiation

---

[23] Debré 2003.

[24] Sophie Hunt, "Debré: Je préfère le mot visible a ostensible," *Le Figaro*, January 9, 2004.

[25] Jean-Louis Debré's speech in parliament on February 3, 2004, available at www.assemblee-nationale.fr/12/cra/2003-2004/148.asp#P201_50355 (last accessed on June 24, 2017).

[26] Stasi 2004, 6.

with the religious extremists, who "targeted the values of the republic to replace them with their dogmatic principles."[27] The Stasi report identified the wearing of headscarves as humiliation of women and found a ban necessary since "the space of the school must remain for students a place of liberty and emancipation; not a place of suffering and humiliation."[28] Bernard Stasi, the chair of the commission, linked the ban with a concern to protect the republic. He stated that women who wore the veil displayed their religious and community affiliation, and this display harmed the unity of the French republic.[29] In my personal interview, Patrick Weil, a member of the Stasi Commission, described the ban as a necessary measure to confront the threat against French republican values.[30]

The government supported the ban at the highest level with the same concern – protecting republican principles against Islamists. President Jacques Chirac, Prime Minister Jean-Pierre Raffarin, and Minister of Education Luc Ferry explicitly stated their support for the ban. In a speech to the National Assembly, Chirac said that the law would protect schools from breaking down along ethnic lines. He said "school must remain a privileged place for the transmission of the republican principles and a melting pot for equal opportunity. Choosing to ban conspicuous signs [of religious affiliation] in schools is a decision that respects our history, our customs and our values."[31]

Prime Minister Raffarin reaffirmed the same position in his interview just before the National Assembly passed the law: "I tell fundamentalists that there is no question of them attacking our Republic's foundations. The Republic must defend itself and adopt the means to ensure it is respected, including at the level of the law."[32] In his opening speech in the parliamentary assembly at which the headscarf bill was debated, Raffarin emphasized the importance of the ban in protecting republicanism and secularism. He said that "secularism is the center of our Republic. It is both a tradition and a promise of freedom. We must now, together, give it more strength. That is why I solemnly ask you, whatever your political choices, you gather around the text, which symbolizes our confidence in the Republic and our national will to live together."[33]

---

[27] Ibid., 9.    [28] Ibid., 47.

[29] Isabelle de Gaulmin and Bernard Gorce, "L'Intégration à l'épreuve du voile," *La Croix*, November 13, 2003.

[30] Author's interview with Patrick Weil, Paris, France, July 27, 2007.

[31] Jacques Chirac, "Statement made by Jacques Chirac, President of the Republic," Paris, January 28, 2004, available at www.info-france-usa.org/news/statmnts/2004/chirac_secular-ismo12804.asp (last accessed on November 24, 2007).

[32] Interview given by Jean-Pierre Raffarin to *Le Journal du dimanche* newspaper, Paris, January 25, 2004, available at www.info-france-usa.org/news/statmnts/2004/raffarin_secularism_012504 .asp (last accessed on November 5, 2007).

[33] Jean-Pierre Raffarin's speech in parliament on February 3, 2004, available at www.assemblee-nationale.fr/12/cra/2003-2004/148.asp#P201_50355 (last accessed on June 24, 2017).

Luc Ferry, the minister of national education, also defended the law on the basis of protecting French secularism from religious extremists: "the law will keep classrooms from being divided up into militant religious communities."[34] On another occasion, he identified the aim of the law as rescuing girls from religious pressures. In an article in the French daily *Le Figaro*, Ferry stated that there were girls who asked their teachers to ban headscarves in school to get rid of the pressure coming from their parents and the community.[35]

An analysis of the speeches delivered during the parliamentary proceedings on the headscarf bill reveals that the deputies widely believed that Islam threatened French values, with the headscarf being its most prominent representative symbol. The point of protecting republican values was repeated by speaker after speaker in the parliamentary session. The leader of the Socialists at the time, Jean-Marc Ayrault, argued that the law would protect schools from the pressure of politico-religious groups. With regard to foreign criticisms made against France, Ayrault said that "We were also told: 'France is isolated.' Yes, it is . . . For a hundred years! France is the only nation in Europe having a secular constitution."[36] Ayrault identified secularism as "a light for women prisoners of obscurantism" and "a hope for the oppressed minorities."[37] Ayrault claimed that the law, by strengthening the principle of secularism, would be a shield for "oppressed women."[38]

The Socialist member Gilbert Le Bris stated that the politico-religious fanaticism of Islamists was replacing French values. Muslims wanted "to penetrate the secular schools with the veil. Any weakness would be betrayal of our ancestors and contempt for our children."[39] Another Socialist member of parliament, Jean-Yves Le Déaut, stated that "we believe that school should be a place of integration rather than the affirmation of differences."[40] Another Socialist, Michel Charzat, supported the ban, saying "There should be a halt to these forces that want to test the ability of our country to promote its republican ethics, and in this struggle between secular democracy and theocracy, France is not far behind, it is ahead." He stated that with his decision to support the ban, he refused to subcontract with fundamentalists and communalists.[41]

[34] Luc Ferry's speech in parliament on February 5, 2004, available at www.assemblee-nationale.fr /12/cra/2003-2004/153.asp (last accessed on June 24, 2017).

[35] Luc Ferry, "L'équipe éducative a fait son devoir degrees," *Le Figaro*, October 13, 2003.

[36] Jean-Marc Ayrault's speech in parliament on February 3, 2004, available at www.assemblee-nationale.fr/12/cra/2003-2004/148.asp#P201_50355 (last accessed on June 24, 2017).

[37] Ibid.   [38] Ibid.

[39] Gilbert Le Bris's speech in parliament on February 5, 2004, available at www.assemblee-nationale.fr/12/cra/2003-2004/153.asp (last accessed on June 24, 2017).

[40] Jean-Yves Le Déaut's speech in parliament on February 5, 2004, available at www.assemblee-nationale.fr/12/cra/2003-2004/153.asp (last accessed on June 24, 2017).

[41] Michel Charzat speech in parliament on February 5, 2004, available at www.assemblee-nationale.fr/12/cra/2003-2004/153.asp (last accessed on June 24, 2017).

Dominique Paillé, one of the leading figures of the conservative Union for a Popular Movement, legitimized his decision to support the law by reference to protecting the republic: "the republic must reaffirm its principles loud and clear."[42] Another deputy from the same party, Etienne Mourrut, stated in the parliamentary debates that the headscarf undermined women's rights "by placing women in an inferior position compared to men" and by "confining women in exclusion." For him, it was upon the shoulders of the state to protect "all those women who bravely resisted the pressure."[43]

The far-left supporters of the ban developed their arguments on the grounds of gender equality rather than secularism. Although these groups had supported the headscarf-wearing girls in the past, many of the far-left representatives voted for the 2004 law. For example, the members of the Workers' Struggle (Lutte ouvrière) party voted for the ban in the parliament. In their speeches prior to the parliamentary debates, they stated that they would vote in the name of the denial of the "oppression of women" by religious fanatics, which was symbolized by the wearing of a headscarf.[44] Another far-left party, the Revolutionary Communist League (Ligue communiste révolutionnaire) did not support the ban, but they did criticize the wearing of headscarves, which, in their view, represented the oppression of women.[45]

Other deputies justified the law on the ground of defending the principle of secularism, which they considered to be

"French specificity" (Clément), "principle of living together in the republican way" (Asensi), "constitutive of our collective history" (Bur), "principal factor of the moral or spiritual unity of our nation, ... our social contract, ... heart of the republican pact" (Vaillant), "sacred value ... of our Republic" (Gerin), "cornerstone of republican values" (Brard), "essential part of our common national patrimony" (Paul), "founding principle of our Republic" (Dionis du Sejour) and so forth. (quoted in Joppke 2007, 326)

The increasing support for the ban in the early 2000s shifted the coalitional dynamics and made the passing of the headscarf ban easier. The framing of the issue by the proponents of the ban as a struggle between republic and fundamentalism contributed to the polarization of French society between two narrowly defined pacts: "defenders of the republic" and "supporters of the fundamentalists." Public debates consolidated this polarity. For example,

---

[42] Dominique Paillé's speech in parliament on February 5, 2004, available at www.assemblee-nationale.fr/12/cra/2003-2004/153.asp (last accessed on June 24, 2017).

[43] Etienne Mourrut's speech in parliament on February 5, 2004, available at www.assemblee-nationale.fr/12/cra/2003-2004/153.asp (last accessed on June 24, 2017).

[44] Caroline Monnot and Xavier Ternisien, "L'Exclusion de deux lycéennes voilées divise l'extrême gauche," *Le Monde*, October 9, 2003.

[45] This position of the Revolutionary Communist Party, which is known as "ni loi ni voile" (neither law nor veil), divided the party; some left the party because of its tolerant approach to the wearing of the headscarf. See Caroline Monnot, "Le Voile fait aussi désordre à l'extrême gauche," *Le Monde*, February 7, 2004.

Caroline Fourest blamed well-known journalists of *Le Monde*, Henri Tincq and Xavier Ternisien, for dividing the secular camp by using terms such as "camp ultralaïque" (ultra-secular camp) (Fourest 2003, 41). According to Fourest, a person was a secular or antisecular; and those who did not define themselves within the secular camp were cooperating with religious fundamentalists within the antisecular camp. Some strict secularist feminists developed an intolerant approach towards those feminists who opposed the headscarf ban and considered the wearing of the headscarf to be an individual right. Acherar and Fourest criticized those feminists who opposed the ban as being under the influence of Islamists (Acherar and Fourest 2004, 64).

As society became more polarized, former opponents of the ban shifted their positions and supported the ban. In November 1989 a group of intellectuals, including the sociologist Alain Touraine, had described those who supported the expulsion of girls from the school as "secular fanatics" and suggested that it was impossible to integrate Muslims into the French social and political system without recognizing and tolerating their differences. In their open letter titled "For an Open Secularism," these intellectuals opposed the expulsion of girls from school, claiming that the school had to respect differences in order to achieve better integration of immigrants.[46] The signatories' support for the Muslim girls diminished in the following years. Alain Touraine became a member of the Stasi Commission in 2003 and voted in favor of a ban in the schools. Another signatory of the 1989 letter, Harlem Désir, the president of France's well-known anti-racist organization SOS Racisme, supported the headscarf ban in 2004.

Similarly, the Socialist Party, along with other left-wing groups who had supported the headscarf-wearing girls in the past, gave strong support for the ban in 2004. Jack Lang, the former Socialist education minister, sparked the debates in April 2003 by stating that "My position on the issue of the veil has changed because the situation nationally and internationally itself has changed. Islamism has grown, especially in the ghettos; the territorial and social apartheid that we allowed enclosed millions of people in poverty and cultural communitarianism."[47] He also stated that there should be a unanimous vote in the parliament to make a strong statement about the French republic and its republican teachers.[48]

In sum, the alliance of strict republicans, secularist intellectuals, and feminists succeeded in framing the headscarf as a symbol of Islamic fundamentalism and oppression of women. This framing dissociated the wearing of headscarves in public schools from the discourse on religious freedoms. The framing also polarized French society and changed coalitional

---

[46] Joëlle Brunerie-Kaufmann, Harlem Désir, René Dumont, Gilles Parrault, and Alain Touraine, "Pour une laïcité ouverte," *Politis*, November 9–15, 1989.
[47] Eric Conan, "Jack Lang: 'Interdire tout signe religieux'," *L'Express*, April 30–May 6, 2003.
[48] Ibid.

patterns in favor of the proponents of the ban. Domestic actors who were against the ban failed to build a strong coalition. They could have made strong appeals to universal human rights norms and religious liberties in developing a counter-strategy against the proponents of the ban; however, the strength of the republican alliance left little room for alternative groups to have a notable influence in French public debates. The next section discusses the political activism and strategies of opponents of the headscarf ban to explain why they failed to prevent its passing.

## ISLAMOPHOBIA AND THE OPPONENTS OF THE HEADSCARF BAN

French Muslims failed to form a unified anti-ban coalition around the idea that wearing the headscarf was a manifestation of a religious liberty. Although there were groups opposed to the ban, their lack of unified action, combined with their weakness in the domestic political setting, made their access to power structures difficult. Without such access, they could not get the support of the legislators who made the final decision. Only a small number of deputies opposed the ban, for varying reasons.

### Islamophobia and Failure to Mobilize Civil Activism Against the Ban

The rise of Islamophobia deepened the differences among Muslim associations and created further obstacles for a possible liberal coalition between Muslims and non-Muslims against the headscarf ban. Muslims were not able to develop a unified strategy to defy the headscarf ban. Muslims in France did not oppose the ban uniformly. Surveys show that more than 40 percent of Muslims were against the wearing of headscarves in public schools.[49] Further, as Carolyn Warner and Manfred Wenner argue, because of the decentralized structure of Islam and the obstacle of overcoming entrenched national identities, "the possibilities for broad-based collective action on religious grounds are limited" (Warner and Wenner 2006, 458). Even those Muslim groups who opposed the ban did not develop a strategy to prevent the law from passing. Notable Muslim organizations opposed the ban, but they did not form a strong unified front against it, acting as they were within an environment in which the rise of Islamophobia led to the vilification of Muslim activism.

The French Council of the Muslim Religion (Conseil français du culte musulman), the umbrella organization for French Muslim groups, made

---

[49] For example, according to a survey conducted one month before the passing of the ban in parliament, 42 percent of the Muslim population of France supported the ban. See *The Economist*, "The War of the Headscarves," February 7, 2004. The survey was conducted in January 2004 by CSA, France's well-known survey company. For a demonstration of the diversity of Muslim views on the headscarf in France, see Philippe Bernard, "Ces musulmans de France hostiles au port du foulard à l'école," *Le Monde*, October 14, 2003.

a statement against the law; however, it did not mobilize its constituent organizations against it. According to the secretary of the organization, the Council did not want to take a strong position against the state, which had helped in its formation. The organization tried to solve the problem "without creating a provocative move against the state."[50] Dalil Boubakeur, the president of the French Council of the Muslim Religion at the time, stated that the law would be a great mistake. Boubakeur stated that the headscarf was a religious requirement and banning it would be a violation of international human rights treaties. Boubakeur called on the legislators to implement the opinions of the Council of State in public schools.[51] It was difficult to reconcile the positions of the organizations constituting the French Council of the Muslim Religion.

The Algerian-dominated Great Mosque of Paris (Grande Mosquée de Paris), which is known for its closeness to the French state, stated its discontent with the law; but it did not mobilize its followers against the ban. The Great Mosque of Paris demanded the implementation of the Council of State's decisions, which it considered a balance between religious freedoms and the republican order (Adrian 2006, 104). Similarly, the Moroccan-dominated National Federation of Muslims of France (Fédération nationale des musulmans de France) protested against the law but did not promote widespread mobilization against it. Organizations closely linked to the Turkish state's Directorate of Religious Affairs (Diyanet İşleri Türk İslam Birliği) remained silent about the ban. Even though the Turkish association did not support the ban, it did not make any public declarations against it. According to Haydar Demiryürek, the secretary of the French Council of the Muslim Religion and the president of Turkish association at the time, the close connections of the Muslim associations with the states of Algeria, Morocco, and Turkey prevented these organizations from actively engaging in the anti-ban protests.[52]

The most active group against the ban was the Union of Islamic Organizations of France (Union des organisations islamiques de France), known for its loose association with the Egyptian-originated Muslim Brotherhood. The union, in cooperation with other associations tied to an influential Geneva-based Islamic philosopher, Tariq Ramadan, organized a number of demonstrations in mid-January[53] and mid-February 2004,[54] before the adoption of the law in the National Assembly and its approval in

---

[50] Author's interview with Haydar Demiryürek, Secretary-General of the French Council of the Muslim Religion, Paris, France, July 17, 2007.

[51] Xavier Ternisien, "L'UOIF, principale organisation musulmane, defend le port du voile mais souhaite une loi l'interdisant à l'école," *Le Monde*, October 14, 2003.

[52] Author's interview with Haydar Demiryürek, Secretary-General of the French Council of the Muslim Religion, Paris, France, July 17, 2007.

[53] Cécilia Gabizon and Dalil Kenz, "Quelque 20 000 musulmans favorables au port du voile à l'école publique ont défilé à Paris et en province," *Le Figaro*, January 19, 2004.

[54] Marc Burleigh, "Muslims Hold Rallies in France Against Anti-headscarf Law for Schools," *Agence France-Presse*, February 14, 2004.

the Senate. About 25,000 Muslims marched throughout France. They protested against the law with the claim that it prevented Muslims from manifesting their religious practices. To demonstrate that being French and being a devout Muslim are compatible, some protestors donned headscarves in the red, white, and blue stripes of the French flag. The president of the Union of Islamic Organizations of France, Lhaj-Thami Breze, stated that the majority of devout Muslims in France "want to practice their religion in peace and in total respect for the law. But when you persecute, when you make fun of, when you refuse, when you don't respect beliefs, what is the consequence? The consequence is radicalization."[55]

The Union of Islamic Organizations of France opposed the headscarf ban on several occasions, but it did not develop a consistent argument based on human rights. Some members of the organization even stated that they supported the ban from an Islamic law perspective. Xavier Ternisien of the *Le Monde* reported that people from the leadership of the Union of Islamic Organizations of France said "We do not want to remain in ambiguity. If the headscarf was banned, it would be easier to ask the girls to remove the headscarf at the door of the school; because, theologically, the rules may be abandoned if there is oppression."[56]

There was no consensus on the headscarf among Muslim intellectuals. A large number of them supported the ban. For example, public intellectual Malek Chebel[57] stated his opposition to the wearing of a headscarf by portraying the veil as the oppression of women.[58] The arguments of those Muslim intellectuals who supported the headscarf-wearing students reflect how the rise of Islamophobia defined the debate on the headscarf in France. For example, Dounia Bouzar and Saïda Kada, two prominent Muslim women who actively opposed the ban, based their arguments on the grounds that wearing headscarves should be allowed to encourage healthy integration. Their argument rested on the domestic concerns about the integration of Muslim immigrants. Bouzar, an anthropologist and member of the French Council of the Muslim Religion, argued that wearing the headscarf was a means for the girls to stay close to their families, while challenging other traditions such as arranged marriages. The headscarf enabled girls to go "public" and discover their individual autonomy. Wearing a headscarf as a religious symbol increased the integration of Muslim girls, in that religion could replace ethnic origin, facilitating self-identification with the French state.[59] Saïda Kada, the founder of French Muslim Women in Action

---

[55] Jon Henley, "French MPs Vote for Veil Ban in State Schools," *The Guardian*, February 11, 2004.

[56] Xavier Ternisien, "L'UOIF, principale organisation musulmane, defend le port du voile mais souhaite une loi l'interdisant à l'école," *Le Monde*, October 14, 2003.

[57] Malek Chebel is well known for his studies on Islam and Muslims in France, in some of which he also states his views on the headscarf issue: see Chebel 2002, 2005, 2007.

[58] Pierre Ysmal, "Le Voile est une regression," *L'Humanité*, January 24, 2004.

[59] Xavier Ternisien, "Il n'y a que 150 cas conflictuels, selon la médiatrice de l'éducation nationale," *Le Monde*, May 10, 2003.

(Femmes françaises et musulmanes engagées), opposed the ban, arguing that "the ban fans the flames of extremism" that made Muslims' integration difficult (Fekete 2006, 17). In their co-authored book *One Veiled, the Other Not* (*L'une voilée, l'autre pas*), Bouzar and Kada argued for the compatibility of being a French citizen and a devout Muslim (Bouzar and Kada 2003, 91).

There were Muslim attempts to create a movement against the ban by relying on a human rights perspective; however, their attempts proved unsuccessful due to the international and domestic context of the period. The rise of Islamophobia globally and the the rise of the far right in domestic politics limited the capabilities of Muslim groups to develop a rights-based argument in countering their opponents. In the logic of a polarized political context, their efforts to reconcile Islamic practice and French republican ideals failed.

Some Muslim women challenged perceptions that they wore the headscarf because of familial and community pressures; they aimed to demonstrate that they wore the headscarf as their personal decision. Headscarf-wearing girls used different public forums to explain that veiling was their own choice and that they considered it a religious duty.[60] In the environment of Islamophobia, the French media did not pay attention to these voices.

In their 2003 book, Bouzar and Kada attempted to show the agency of the Muslim women, arguing that young women, veiled or not, sought access to modernity. They argued that many Muslim girls stood up against commonly held misconceptions about the role of a husband, divorce, etc.; in short, they opposed injustice set by patriarchal structures (Bouzar and Kada 2003, 6). For them, women donned the headscarf as one of the steps taken in the formation of their spiritual relationships (Bouzar and Kada 2003, 16). However, these analyses did not get the attention of the media at all, the dominant description in the media equating the wearing of headscarves with an affiliation to Islamic fundamentalist movements.

The media controversy around the sisters Alma and Lila Lévy in the autumn of 2003 elaborates how Islamophobia silenced Muslim voices who defended the wearing of headscarf from a rights-based perspective. In October 2003, Alma and Lila were expelled from their high school in Aubervilliers, five miles away from the center of Paris, on the ground that they were wearing headscarves on school premises.[61] Their background contested the argument that headscarves symbolized the oppression and submission of women. Their father was a communist lawyer of Jewish origin. He worked for the leftist anti-racist organization Movement against Racism and for Friendship among Peoples (Mouvement contre le racisme et pour l'amitié entre les peuples). Their mother, a teacher from the Kabylia, a Berber region in Algeria, was raised as

---

[60] Elizabeth Jones, "Muslim Girls Unveil Their Fears," *BBC News*, March 28, 2005, available at http://news.bbc.co.uk/2/hi/programmes/this_world/4352171.stm (last accessed on June 24, 2017).

[61] Marie-Joâlle Gros, "Statu quo au lycée d'Aubervilliers," *Libération*, September 30, 2003.

a Catholic but became an atheist (Giraud 2004). The girls' expulsion attracted extensive media coverage. A book consisting of interviews with the two girls became a bestsellers in France (Lévy and Lévy 2004). The father, Laurent Lévy, characterized the attitude of the teachers as "hysterical madness of some of ayatollahs of secularism." He stated that he was not offending against secularism, but defending the right of his children to go to school.[62] Throughout the book, these girls tried to show the lack of family and social pressure influencing their decision to veil; however, the mainstream media described them as the victims of fundamentalist Islam in France, even though they strongly denied their links to fundamentalist movements.[63]

A number of empirical studies showed different interpretations of the wearing of headscarves, but the dominant perceptions about Islam filtered the conclusions of these studies in the public debate. One such study, a widely cited work, suggested that Muslims perceived the headscarf to be an autonomous expression of their identity. The book based its conclusions on interviews conducted with Muslim women (Gaspard and Khosrokhavar 1995). The study concluded that a headscarf was a means for Muslim girls to integrate in modernity: "If one accepts the postulate that the royal road to liberation is through education," the study indicated, "then to reject girls with veils is ... to penalize them ... by denying them the possibility of becoming modern" (Gaspard and Khosrokhavar 1995, 210).[64]

The international and domestic context of Islamophobia prevented Muslims from getting the support of the broader public. A well-known Muslim scholar Tariq Ramadan, for example, developed a reconciliatory rhetoric for Muslims in France and Europe. Ramadan mainly argued that it was possible for Muslims both to integrate into European societies and to keep their Islamic identity. He developed the concept of "European Muslims" in general or "French Muslims" in the national context. The idea behind this conceptualization was to invite Muslims to integrate into European societies, instead of living secluded within their own national cultures (Ramadan 1998; 2004; 2007). Ramadan was marginalized by the strict secularists in France; he was accused of using different languages in different contexts.[65] Several newspapers in late 2003 cited him as an accomplice of Islamic fundamentalists in France. These publications even associated Ramadan with terrorist activities organized by radical religious groups.[66] The severest criticism to Ramadan came from Caroline Fourest, who accused him of using a dual language in his writings.

---

[62] Xavier Ternisien, "Deux lycéennes d'Aubervilliers, filles d'un avocat du MRAP, exclues pour port du voile," *Le Monde*, September 25, 2003.

[63] *Le Monde*, "Foulard: Lila Lévy dément toute manipulation," 15 October 2003.

[64] Another study showed that most young women between the ages of eighteen and twenty-two who wore the headscarf adopted it out of personal religious conviction (Killian 2003).

[65] Pascal Virot, "Affaire Tariq Ramadan: Les Socialistes isolés à gauche," *Libération*, October 28, 2003.

[66] *Le Parisien*, "Tariq Ramadan, cible des services secrets européens," November 14, 2003.

In her book *Brother Tariq* (*Frère Tariq*), which is a collection of her writings on Ramadan, Fourest argued that Ramadan's ingenious rhetoric was a Trojan horse, fostering the anti-Semitic and anti-Christian values of fundamentalist Islam in Western Europe (Fourest 2004; for English translation, see Fourest 2007).[67]

There was a notable non-Muslim liberal opposition to the headscarf law, but this opposition did not create a broad-based movement to challenge the ban, mostly because of the polarizing impact of the rise of Islamophobia. Non-Muslim groups opposed the ban for various reasons. Religious groups such as Christian and Jewish organizations opposed the ban on the grounds that it was against religious liberty. Some liberals opposed the ban because they thought expelling the girls from schools was a violation of their educational rights. Others believed that the wearing of headscarves had to be allowed because the girls had the individual right to wear headscarves. Still others opposed the ban because they believed that it would become an obstacle against the integration of Muslims into French society.

Jewish and Christian religious organizations developed arguments against the headscarf ban on the grounds that the ban would violate religious freedoms guaranteed by the principle of secularism. These organizations took a position for the improvement of religious liberties by reasoning that limits on religious freedoms would eventually influence them.[68] Indeed, the law would also ban the wearing of large crosses and skullcaps in public schools. Chief Rabbi Joseph Sitruk stated his discontent with the law on several occasions, indicating that it would limit religious liberties for all living in France.[69]

The Catholic Church in France has supported the headscarf-wearing girls since the first headscarf affair erupted in 1989. Cardinal Aaron Lustiger, the leader of the French Catholic Church between 1981 and 2005, warned the legislators not to pass the law: "Do not touch: it would reopen Pandora's box."[70] The Archbishop of Strasbourg, Monsignor Joseph Doré, stated his discontent with the law indicating that the law would revive "frontal anticlericalism" of the past, and would break the compromise between the state and religions.[71] In November 2003, Archbishop Jean-Pierre Ricard,

---

[67] Others, like Olivier Roy, saw double language as something positive for Muslims' integration into French society. He argued that "Dual language is, in fact, a recognition of two spaces, that of religion and that of the order of the world, even if this is done with a longing for unity" (Roy 2007, 10).

[68] Elaine Sciolino, "Ban Religious Attire in School, French Panel Says," *New York Times*, December 12, 2003.

[69] Xavier Ternisien and Nicolas Weill, "M. Chirac annonce la création d'une autorité indépendante de lutte contre la discrimination," *Le Monde*, May 24, 2003.

[70] Besma Lahouri and Eric Conan, "Ce qu'il ne faut plus accepter: La laïcité face à l'Islam," *L'Express*, September 18–24, 2003.

[71] Xavier Ternisien, "Le Débat sur la place de l'Islam fait craindre aux évêques 'une régression de la liberté religieuse'," *Le Monde*, November 11, 2003.

president of the Bishops' Conference of France (Conférence des évêques de France), stated that "vigilance [of the State in terms of secularism] must not lead to mistrust." The regulations should acknowledge that "different spiritual and religious families in our society live together in peace." To him, a law banning religious signs in schools would be "a setback for religious freedom."[72]

Other Christian groups denounced the law on the grounds of protecting religious freedoms in France. On the day that the Stasi Commission report was released, the Council of Christian Churches in France, consisting of Catholic, Protestant, and Orthodox churches, sent an open letter to President Chirac. In their letter, they stated that the 1905 law guaranteed religious liberties for all in France and warned that any law banning the Islamic headscarf "would be felt as discriminatory." They predicted that secularism would quickly turn to an intolerant constitutional principle if the state denied the place of religion in society. They ended their letter by saying "It is our conviction that it is not through legislation that the current difficulties can positively be resolved."[73]

Many liberal organizations and intellectuals who opposed the ban criticized it based on the claim that excluding girls from school would prevent their integration into French society. Although most of these groups did not support the practice of wearing headscarves on their own terms, they resisted what they saw as the punishment of the schoolgirls. They argued that excluding the girls from public school would never serve their emancipation. In the view of these groups, this would leave the girls to the hands of fundamentalists. In the words of one scholar, the headscarf was "a partial window to modernity" from an oppressive patriarchal culture (Cesari 1994, 157).

The League of Education (Ligue de l'enseignement), one of the most important and influential actors focusing on the debates around secularism (Kuru 2009, 116),[74] delivered several declarations against the headscarf ban, arguing that it would curtail liberties and the scope of secularism in France. In its declaration in June 2003, the league stated that the law was contrary to the French constitution and international agreements ratified by France, since it would limit the liberties of a segment of society. The league emphasized the importance of a democratic debate rather than imposing a ban on the headscarves, which, according to the league, would feed radicalism in France. The league criticized the assumption that wearing a headscarf symbolized radicalism: "The wearing of headscarves is subject to a wide variety of motivations and it is urgent that the supporters of the law devote more time and energy to enrich their knowledge of the diversity of developments among

---

[72] Ibid.

[73] Jean-Pierre Ricard, Jean-Arnold de Clermont, and Archbishop Emmanuel, "L'Enjeu du débat est la réussite de l'intégration," *La Croix*, December 9, 2003.

[74] The league's very dynamic website, www.laicite-laligue.org, is considered one of the most important public forums about secularism in France (last accessed on June 24, 2017).

Muslims in France today." The declaration ended with an emphasis on the free will of the students: "We must let the girls decide for themselves what is good for them."[75]

In a later declaration in January 2004, the league strongly expressed its opposition to the law. The league stated that "the adoption of a law to ban 'conspicuous' religious symbols in the school is a bad solution"[76] to the problems reported by the proponents of the ban. The Commission of Islam and Secularism (Commission Islam et Laïcité), initiated by the League of Education in 1997 with the aim of bringing people of various backgrounds together to discuss issues related to the integration of Muslims in France, stated its discomfort with the law at the height of debates in late 2003 and early 2004.[77]

A group of influential French intellectuals opposed the ban for similar reasons. In a letter published in *Libération* in May 2003, five well-known French intellectuals stated their opposition to a possible headscarf law: "We are not 'proponents of the véil,' we are simply advocates of a secular school that works for the emancipation of all, and not for exclusion." They argued that "neutrality, as defined by the laws of 1881, 1882 and 1886, is an obligation for premises, curriculum, and teachers, not for the students." They portrayed schoolgirls as victims. To them, regardless of whether the headscarf was a choice or an imposition, the girls should not be treated as criminals. Girls should not pay the price. In all cases, they continued, it was the secular school that could help them emancipate themselves and gain the means of autonomy.[78]

Other leading intellectuals employed similar arguments in their support for the girls. The philosopher Étienne Balibar, for example, criticized the logic of the law: "by banishing them from school, i.e., making them personally – in their lives, their futures, their flesh – bear the penalty for the injustice of which they are the 'victims,' is sending them back to the communitarian space dominated by precisely this religious sexism" (Balibar 2004, 354). Françoise Gaspard, a former Socialist deputy and a prominent sociologist, came out publicly against the headscarf ban, claiming that "it would keep the daughters of Islamist families from getting to go to school at all, and they would end up

---

[75] Statement by the league's secretary-general on the league's website: "Une loi serait inopportune" – Pierre Tournemire, Secrétaire général de la Ligue de l'enseignement dans le N°110 des Idées en Mouvement, June 2003, available at http://ww1.laicite-laligue.org/index.php?option=com_docman&task=doc_download&gid=47 (last accessed on November 7, 2007).

[76] Statement by the league's president: "Une loi qui sanctionnerait les victimes" – Jean-Michel Ducomte, Président de la Ligue de l'enseignement dans le N°115 des Idées en Mouvement, January 2004, available at http://ww1.laicite-laligue.org/index.php?option=com_docman&task=doc_download&gid=48 (last accessed on November 7, 2007).

[77] See the official website of the commission at www.islamlaicite.org (last accessed on June 24, 2017).

[78] Etienne Balibar, S. Bouamama, F. Gaspard, C. Lévy, and P. Tevanian, "Oui à la laïcité, non aux lois d'exception," *Libération*, May 20, 2003. For an expanded version, see Pétition 2003.

'martyrs' to the Islamist cause."[79] Farhad Khosrokhavar, a leading sociologist, said "even those who do not wear the headscarf are likely to feel offended because it is a denial of personal rights. Instead of fighting against Islamic radicalism it might encourage it, precisely because of this feeling of stigmatization."[80] Marwan Bishara criticized the expulsion of girls in the name of secularism and equality: "The same girls who are coerced by men to put on the veil in public will now be forced by other men to take it off in the public schools. France must urgently reverse its social and economic discrimination against millions of French Muslims as a way of integrating them into a state of all its citizens."[81] Jean Baubérot, an authority on French secularism and the only member of the Stasi Commission who was against the headscarf ban, questioned the link between headscarves and familial and social pressure: "no social scientific evidence for this existed, so that the representative nature of these testimonies could not be corroborated" (quoted in Joppke 2007, 324).

Alain Gresh considered the state position toward Muslims as a backlash against integration with the EU. The headscarf-wearing girls, according to Gresh, should not pay the price of the problems of European integration. The rise of Islamophobia allowed many to find an easier answer to many problems that country faced: limiting Muslims in the public sphere.[82] Similarly, Olivier Abel, a French philosopher, considered the debate around the headscarf ban to be a response to the increasing number of Muslims in France. Anti-Muslim sentiments provoked the historical debate on secularism, and the headscarf ban provided a solution to comfort many in the French public.[83]

The rise of Islamophobia marginalized these liberal voices who tried to reconcile the conflicting ideas of strict secularists and Muslims on various issues. For example, the feminist sociologist Leïla Babès criticized the League of Education for inviting Tariq Ramadan to their workshop series on Islam and secularism. The League of Education's workshop, led by Alain Gresh, aimed to bring various people from secularist and Islamist camps to find a middle ground in the resolution of the issues of state–religion relations. Babès wrote that "Scheduled to facilitate the emergence of a secular Islam, the workshop has in fact served mainly as a Trojan horse to Islamists such as Tariq Ramadan" (Babès 2004, 34). This polarizing rhetoric deepened the division in society and made it difficult for opponents of the ban to build a large coalition.

---

[79] Jane Kramer, "Taking the Veil: How France's Public Schools Became the Battleground in a Culture War," *New Yorker*, November 22, 2003, p. 67.

[80] Jon Henley, "French MPs Vote for Veil Ban in State Schools," *The Guardian*, February 11, 2004.

[81] Marwan Bishara, "The Headscarf Debate: Lifting the Veil in France," *International Herald Tribune*, December 20, 2003.

[82] Author's interview with Alain Gresh, Paris, France, July 18, 2007.

[83] Author's interview with Olivier Abel, Paris, France, July 29, 2007.

Although there were important voices against the headscarf ban, neither Muslims nor their liberal supporters had access to the politicians, whose ideas were mostly shaped by the bifurcation between Islamism and republicanism.

## Muslims' Limited Access to Political Power

The opponents of the ban had limited access to power structures. Muslims did not have the power to influence politics. As part of their protests in March 2004, before approval of the ban in the Senate, they sought to intimidate the parties by not voting for them in 2004 regional elections. Because 70 percent of the French population supported the ban,[84] this threat was relatively uninfluential. Further, as another constraint, Muslims also lacked a corporate relationship with the political parties like the teachers' unions had. The global rise of Islamophobia increased the vilification of liberal voices who supported the headscarf-wearing girls in public. Politicians avoided taking sides with these voices in an environment in which attitudes against Islam were becoming increasingly negative.

A few of the groups that opposed the ban had limited corporate relationships with a small number of politicians. Their opposition to the law did not make a difference. The Christian organizations' relationship with a few deputies of the Union for a Popular Movement party did not change the outcome. Only a few of them, such as Jean-Marc Nesme, opposed the ban. Nesme voted against the bill, expressing the concern that it was against religious freedoms that French secularism was supposed to guarantee. Nesme stated in his speech that the International Convention on the Rights of the Child provided parents the right to raise their children in their own way. He reminded his listeners that the Charter of Fundamental Rights of the European Union referred to "religion" in four sections, and guaranteed the freedom to manifest religion or belief, in public or private. Nesme argued that it is "certainly the responsibility of the State to defend freedom of conscience, to ensure the peaceful social coexistence between all segments of society, and to oppose any form of violence to impose a faith in society."[85]

Liberal and left-wing intellectuals had links to a number of politicians. The Schools for All (Écoles pour tous et toutes) movement served as an umbrella organization for most of the leftist groups opposed to the headscarf ban (Roy 2007, 5). This group defended the right to wear headscarves in school in the name of individual rights and free choice.[86] The Greens were the most notable

[84] *The Economist*, "The War of the Headscarves," February 7, 2004. The survey was conducted in January 2004 by CSA, France.

[85] Jean-Marc Nesme's speech in parliament on February 5, 2004, available at www.assemblee-nationale.fr/12/cra/2003-2004/153.asp (last accessed on June 24, 2017).

[86] John Mullen, "Islamophobia Divides the Left in France," *Socialist Unity Network*, September 2004. Available at, http://john.mullen.pagesperso-orange.fr/0904headscarf.html (last accessed on September 12, 2018).

political group to oppose the headscarf ban. Green Party leader Alain Lipietz, who was also a European parliamentarian at the time, opposed the law, arguing that the school had to offer services to the children of different backgrounds to teach them tolerance and mutual respect. Expelling girls from schools, for Lipietz, was leaving them uneducated, which would eventually make their full integration into French society more difficult (Lipietz 2003, 130). Another Green member, Yves Contassot, opposed the ban, stating that "It is more important to ensure that children attend all classes."[87]

A few deputies from the Communist Party opposed the ban because of their relationship with socialist civil society organizations that were part of the Schools for All movement. The Communist Party deputy Alain Bocquet stated that the law would exclude citizens of immigrant origin by stripping their individual rights and would "set things on fire rather than calm them down."[88] Another communist deputy, Marie-George Buffet, voted against the bill, saying "Your act will increase tensions, reduce the scope of secularism, and thus democracy, and disrupt the educational process."[89] A few Socialist Party deputies opposed the headscarf ban, among them Gilles Cocquempot, who said that the law was against the neutrality of the state by violating the individual rights of Muslim students. He stated, "We must give full meaning to secularism, and make it a political project reminding the world that France remains an area of freedom, equality and fraternity. Muslims of France have their rightful place in our country, as well as Jews, Catholics, Protestants, and Orthodox Christians."[90]

The support for the headscarf among parliamentarians was minimal. In the national assembly, only 36 members voted against the ban while 494 voted for it; in the Senate, only 20 senators voted against the ban while 276 voted for it. The opponents' access to power structures was limited. The rise of Islamophobia created an environment in which those opposing the ban were marginalized. The successful issue-framing by the proponents of the ban, who portrayed the headscarf as a threat to the French Republic, shifted coalitional patterns, and increased the support for the ban. The coalitional shifts advantaged the proponents in accessing power structures and made the headscarf ban easier to pass.

## CONCLUSION

In France, the parliament passed the headscarf ban despite the fact that it was a departure from France's historically established norms on religious freedoms.

---

[87] Eric Aeschimann and Emmanuel Davidenkoff, "Le Gouvernement ne hisse pas le voile," *Libération*, April 23, 2003.

[88] Elaine Sciolino, "French Assembly Votes to Ban Religious Symbols in Schools," *New York Times*, February 11, 2004.

[89] Marie-George Buffet's speech in parliament on February 3, 2004. Available at www.assemblee-nationale.fr/12/cra/2003-2004/148.asp#P201_50355 (last accessed on June 24, 2017).

[90] Gilles Cocquempot's speech in parliament on February 5, 2004, available at www.assemblee-nationale.fr/12/cra/2003-2004/153.asp (last accessed on June 24, 2017).

The pro-ban groups overcame historical institutions by framing the issue as being about the protection of the French republic and French secularism from Islamic fundamentalism. The pro-ban groups exploited the rise of Islamophobia to counter the arguments that presented the wearing of the headscarf as an issue of religious freedom. The proponents' use of republicanism as the main cause marginalized the headscarf-wearing Muslims and contributed to their portrayal as fundamentalists challenging French secularism. The practice of wearing a headscarf was also presented as a symbol of oppression of women in Islam. The proponents successfully simplified "the many meanings of the headscarf into one" (Scott 2007, 137), which for them was an Islamic fundamentalist rebellion against French republicanism and secularism. Proponents gained the support of several groups who had in the past opposed a possible headscarf ban.

The increasing polarization of French society along the lines of republicanism and Islamic fundamentalism obliterated the Muslim groups' effort to develop counter-strategies to challenge the secularist depictions of the wearing of the headscarf. The discourse of secularism gained even more strength when issues around Islam were publicly debated. According to sociologist Nilüfer Göle, the debate around Muslims reshaped French secularism and made it more nationalist and populist.[91] Within this growing populist nationalism, Muslims' efforts to demonstrate the ability of the schoolgirls to make independent decisions, and to develop a rights-based language challenging the secularist arguments, failed to generate a notable influence in the media. Muslims were unable to mobilize a movement against the secularist coalition: the Islamophobic political environment did not leave room for such a movement to thrive.

In 2010, six years after the passing of the headscarf law, the French parliament banned the wearing of burqas, full-face veils, in the streets with the same motivations, to protect French secularism from "fundamentalist ideas" and to implement gender equality (Heider 2012). While the state recognized religious and cultural associations established by Muslims and tolerated, even encouraged, the construction of larger mosques, it developed a negative attitude toward the manifestation of religious symbols in public. On the surface, we see "a greater willingness by local governments to help local Islamic groups to construct a mosque" (Bowen 2009b, 447) and a greater willingness by the central government to help Muslims create larger organizations. However, at the root, the rise of Islamophobia was still the main determinant in these government initiatives. Through its support for the founding of a Muslim federation, the government aimed "to domesticate and incorporate the Muslim population, substituting a French identity for their transnational one" (Maxwell 2011, 116). Constraining Muslims in the manifestation of religious symbols but helping them in building mosques and institutions may seem to be contradictory. However, the theoretical framework

---

[91] Author's interview with Nilüfer Göle, Paris, France, July 3, 2007.

that I have developed in this book shows that this is not a contradiction. By recognizing mosques and associations, the state seeks to regulate Islam. By limiting religious symbols, the state wants to create a less threatening "French Islam." The rise of Islamophobia provides an analytical background to explain the new trend to grant state recognition to more visible Islamic associations and institutions.

# CONCLUSION

# 8

# Testing the Argument Beyond the Scope of the Study

As demonstrated throughout this book, the interaction of international context and domestic actor strategies structured state policies toward religious minorities in Turkey and France during the period discussed. Throughout the 2000s, Turkey implemented relatively reformist policies toward Christians because of European Union (EU) pressure and the Islamists' need to expand the political sphere in their own favor. On the other hand, France implemented relatively restrictive policies toward Muslims because of the global rise of Islamophobia and the activism of actors who took advantage of the new international environment and supported the ban on the headscarf. In this chapter, I discuss how the argument developed in this book account for other issues beyond the scope of this study. First, I evaluate more recent developments in the treatment of religious minorities in Turkey and France, discussing state policies toward Christians in Turkey and Muslims in France in the post-2010 period. Then, I explore whether my argument can explain state policies toward other minorities in both countries, focusing on policies toward the Jewish minority in Turkey and toward sects in France. Finally, I briefly discuss a few illustrative examples to examine the extent to which the argument can account for other cases beyond Turkey and France.

## STATE POLICIES TOWARD CHRISTIANS IN TURKEY AFTER 2010

In Turkey, the conditions that produced the reformist moment between 2000 and 2010 radically changed in the 2010s. In contrast to expectations of many, the Justice and Development Party (AKP, Adalet ve Kalkınma Partisi) government reversed its liberal policies in the 2010s and took an authoritarian path. The changing international environment enabled the AKP government to shift toward an authoritarian direction. The new international and domestic environment negatively affected the status of Christian minorities, and the freedoms that they had gained in the previous decade came under threat. Rising populist Islamism made non-Muslim minorities a target at both discursive and policy levels.

## International Context

In the wake of the Arab uprisings, Turkey–EU relations moved out of a euphoric era and into a deep crisis. Once the AKP government had established its political position vis-à-vis the bureaucratic establishment, its enthusiasm for EU membership faded. The AKP no longer needed the EU to guarantee its political survival. Further, the Arab uprisings, when they started in 2011, created the possibility that Islamists would come to power in several Middle Eastern countries. This expectation revived the Islamist identity of the AKP with the consideration that Turkey would play a key role in the anticipated new Middle East. Turkey's departure from Western orientation increased the authoritarian tendencies of the party.

The Arab Spring substantially affected domestic political development in Turkey and became a turning point for the rise of authoritarianism. In a nutshell, the Arab Spring led to the decrease of Western leverage over Turkish democratization and revived the Islamist ideology of the AKP. That the Arab Spring came at a time when the AKP had weakened the military's influence over politics facilitated the establishment of an authoritarian regime in Turkey.

The Arab uprisings influenced democratic political development in Turkey in three ways. First, they decreased Western leverage over Turkey. When the AKP began to pursue authoritarian policies starting from 2013, the USA did not react to these moves, because the USA had many other priorities shaped by the Arab uprisings. The USA needed Turkey particularly in its fight against the Islamic State of Iraq and Syria. Turkey's long border with Syria and Iraq made Turkey indispensable for US national security policy. Although human rights and democracy had played a significant role in the EU's relations with Turkey until the Arab uprisings, the international displacement of millions of Syrian refugees following the uprising in 2011 transformed the EU's priorities. EU officials tried to keep as many Syrian refugees as possible in Turkey and remained silent on the human rights violations of the AKP.

Second, the Arab uprisings led the AKP leadership to revise their ideological position. The weakening of Western leverage and the taming of the military gave the AKP more room for maneuver. While the AKP's leadership promoted a secular democratic model for the new Middle East in the immediate aftermath of the Arab uprisings, this position was gradually replaced by an authoritarian Islamist model especially after late 2012 and early 2013. The possibility that groups affiliated with the Muslim Brotherhood would take over the governments in countries such as Egypt, Tunisia, and Syria led the AKP to polish its Islamist credentials and bury its democratic ideas over time. A popular-style Islamism replaced the ideology of conservative democracy that the AKP claimed to have embraced between 2001 and 2012. By reverting back to Islamism, the AKP aimed to become a regional player in the imagined new Middle East.

Finally, the Arab uprisings helped the AKP leadership increase and justify state repression, which became instrumental in the suppression of protests after summer 2013. The AKP utilized the unleashing of chaos and instability in Arab countries as an excuse to repress domestic opposition in Turkey. When thousands took to the streets to protest plans to convert a city park into a shopping mall in Istanbul in summer 2013, the government harshly repressed them. To justify the repression, the AKP claimed that the protestors, following the example of protestors in the Arab streets, aimed to overthrow the government.

Arab uprisings created these outcomes in interaction with the structural conditions in Turkey. The Arab Spring came at a time when the AKP leadership had been emboldened to make radical changes in the political field. By the start of the Arab uprisings, the military was no longer strong enough to constrain the AKP power. Further, Turkey had had consistent economic growth over almost a decade prior to the Arab uprisings, which provided the AKP with strong popular support. Finally, although Turkey was at the verge of strong democratic governance by the start of 2010s, the state institutions that the 1982 constitution put in place to control Turkish society were still functioning. Building on this advantageous position, the AKP leadership chose to establish a political hegemony by using these institutions instead of converting them into vehicles of a more pluralistic system.

## Domestic Changes

Because of the domestic transformations that the Arab uprisings led to, the AKP followed a more authoritarian trajectory. From 2012, the AKP increasingly had a hostile stance toward dissent. Following the government's repression of peaceful protest in summer 2013, mentioned in the previous section, a corruption probe against four ministers in December 2013 was another turning point for the authoritarian trend. When prosecutors initiated a corruption probe that included four high-level cabinet members, the AKP blamed the Gülen movement for attempting a coup against the government through its affiliates in the judiciary and police. After the incident, the AKP quickly tightened its control over the judiciary by creating special courts with politically appointed judges and prosecutors, and by redesigning the entire bureaucracy. Through state-appointed trustees, the government indirectly seized control of television channels and newspapers that were critical of the government. When the government lost its majority in parliament in the June 2015 elections, it targeted Kurdish groups in order to create a more nationalistic environment that helped the AKP win the snap elections of November 2015. From 2015, the AKP drifted away from negotiations it had started with the Kurdistan Workers Party (PKK), which was recognized as a terrorist organization by Turkey and the USA along with many countries. The AKP implemented a military strategy that unleashed a cycle of violence.

Authoritarianism in Turkey reached its peak after the failed coup in July 2016. The AKP announced a state of emergency and targeted a number of journalists, academics, and opposition figures. After the coup attempt, almost 200,000 people were detained, more than 60,000 were arrested, more than 150,000 were dismissed from their public jobs, thousands of academics were fired, and hundreds of journalists were put in prison. The government blamed the soldiers affiliated with the Gülen movement for the coup but imprisoned several thousands of others including businessmen, teachers, doctors, and even housewives. Erdoğan used the post-coup attempt environment to change the political system in Turkey from a parliamentary democracy to a presidential system. In a referendum in April 2017, Turkey shifted its system to a presidential one in which president had sweeping powers vis-à-vis the legislative and judiciary. In June 2018, Erdoğan was elected as the president of the new system. This move decreased the power of the legislative and increased the executive powers of Erdoğan.

In justifying authoritarianism for the eyes of the public, Erdoğan employed a strong populist nationalist/Islamist rhetoric. The AKP leadership emphasized its pro-Islamic foreign policy. In addition, the supporters of the government used conspiracy theories and portrayed any actor who was critical of the government as a traitor and collaborator with international powers that did not want to see a rising Turkey and a strengthening Muslim world. These narratives were widely circulated in local, presidential, and parliamentary elections in 2014, 2015, and 2018 as well as in the referendum of 2017. Further, the AKP government employed the Directorate of Religious Affairs to justify its policies and to demonize antigovernment religious groups, particularly the Gülen movement. Having control over mosques in Turkey, the directorate arranged for sermons in Friday prayers to serve the political positions taken by the government.[1] The directorate also organized events in which pro-government religious scholars were given awards. Through benefits and the use of state resources, the government co-opted several Islamic communities. Immediately before the local elections of March 2014, the presidential elections of August 2014, and the parliamentary elections of June 2015, pro-government religious groups ran full-page newspaper ads supporting the government.[2]

## Policies toward Christians

The rise of populist Islamism left little room for non-Muslim groups to participate in the Turkish political realm. The rising Islamist discourse put the AKP's relationship with the Christian minority into a religious framework. In its milder state, the AKP leadership had considered Christians to be "a legitimate

---

[1] *Radikal*, "Diyanet'ten Cok Tartisilan Cuma Hutbesi," March 28, 2014.
[2] *Sabah*, "Sivil Dayanisma Platformun'ndan Gazetelere Saglam Irade Ilani," January 5, 2015.

yet inferior community under the ruling Sunni elite" (Sandal, 2013, 650). The liberal citizenship framework that treated Christians as equal citizens with the other groups gradually gave way to a more religion-based discourse.[3]

In its harsher discourse, the AKP leadership regarded the Christian minority as collaborators with foreign powers that aimed to redesign Turkish politics and to undermine Islamism. This outlook gained more prominence when a US priest, Andrew Brunson, was arrested after the coup attempt for collaborating with the Gülen movement to overthrow the government. Brunson was also blamed for being in close connection with the Kurdish militant group PKK. Between Brunson's arrest in 2016 and his release in October 2018, government-controlled media published controversial stories about his relationship with the "terrorists." At the root of these stories, Christians were depicted as working in collaboration with foreign powers aiming to undermine the Turkish government. When the USA imposed sanctions on Turkey in summer 2018 to force Turkey to release Brunson, Turkish politicians blamed the USA for undervaluing the Turkish lira in order to destroy the Turkish economy. The media published various conspiracy theories about the USA, Brunson, and Christian minorities, particularly evangelicals, in Turkey.[4]

The marginalization of the Gülen movement after 2013, and its criminalization after the July 2016 coup attempt, influenced Turkish state attitudes toward Christians. After July 2016, every single institution affiliated with the Gülen movement was closed down by the government. The closing of the Journalists and Writers Foundation, which played a key role in establishing interfaith relations in Turkey, and the imprisoning of certain divinity school professors who had promoted interfaith dialogue in their writings and activities, led to a slowdown in minorities' access to power structures (Ilgit 2017, 82). Further, because the Gülen movement worked closely with minorities, the government-controlled media implied that the movement had a hidden agenda of undermining Turkey's Muslim identity.[5] Fethullah Gülen, the leader of the movement, had met with several religious leaders including the Greek Orthodox patriarch Bartholomew in April 1996, Pope John Paul II in February 1998, and the Sephardi chief rabbi of Israel Eliyahu Bakshi-Doron in 1999. The movement had established several interfaith organizations globally, including the Dialogue Society in London and the Rumi Forum in Washington, DC (Ilgit 2017, 77–88). As Antuan Ilgit (2017, 83) writes, the criminalization of the Gülen movement "raises some questions relating to the Vatican and religious orders like the Franciscans, Capuchins, Dominicans, and Jesuits

---

[3] Süleyman Önsay, "Ehli Kitap Müşriktir," *Yeni Akit*, October 14, 2016.

[4] *Yeni Şafak*, "Kim Daha Casus?," April 18, 2018; *A Haber*, "Trump'ın Serbest Bırakılsın Dediği Rahip Brunson'un Günah Defteri Kabarık," May 17, 2017, available at www.ahaber.com.tr/gundem/2017/05/17/trumpin-serbest-birakilsin-dedigi-rahip-brunsonin-gunah-defteri-kabarik (last accessed on October 26, 2018).

[5] *Türkiye*, "Asıl Hedefi İslamiyet'i Tahrip Etmek," July 15, 2017.

present in Turkey, which have been involved at different levels in Muslim–Christian dialogue with Gülen and some of his followers." Some indictments portrayed the Gülen movement as paragons of Christianity. For example, a public prosecutor described the volunteers of the Gülen movement as helpers of the Jesuits in their efforts to implant Christianity in Turkey and beyond.[6]

Within the context of the new political environment, the process of reforming the status of Christian minorities in Turkey stalled. Unresolved issues around the status of Greek Orthodox Church, the lack of legal personality for religious organizations, and the reopening of the Theological School of Halki were omitted from public discussion. While the government had taken some initiatives toward the resolution of these issues in the 2000s, the issues lost priority and were left unaddressed in the 2010s. The religious communities that were not recognized as minorities in the Lausanne Treaty, such as the Syriac Orthodox, Chaldean, and Romanic communities, still lack the community rights accorded to the recognized minorities. The government's approach toward minorities fluctuated based on international developments (Bishku 2017). For example, when the German parliament passed a resolution in 2016 recognizing the Armenian Genocide, Erdoğan threatened to expel non-citizen Armenians residing in Turkey.[7]

In short, the international environment that had made the reforms possible in the first decade of 2000s was replaced by an environment that boosted Turkey's authoritarian shift in the 2010s. The Arab Spring, combined with the Turkish government's desire to control the political realm, led to a context in which reforms in favor of religious minorities stalled.

## STATE POLICIES TOWARD MUSLIMS IN FRANCE AFTER 2010

In France, the conditions that led to anti-Muslim policies between 2000 and 2010 did not change in the 2010s. The international context that had produced anti-Muslim attitudes got worse in the 2010s. With the rise of new extremist movements in the 2010s, Islamophobia continued to gain ground. Further, the socioeconomic marginalization of Muslim immigrants in the French suburbs persisted. The radical right grew even stronger from 2010. The leader of the National Front (FN, Front national), Marine Le Pen, became a front-runner in the 2017 presidential elections. In contrast with the early 2000s, though, when the center-right and center-left parties had shifted toward an anti-immigrant stance to compete for the favor of the gradually more nationalistic public, in the 2017 elections Emmanuel Macron, who had defended a pro-immigrant and pro-EU stance, won the runoff. However, Marine Le Pen won one-third of the votes in those elections. This indicates that Islamophobia and the anti-

[6] Mert İnan, "Örgüt modeli Cizvit sembolü ise Halley," *Milliyet*, September 7, 2016.
[7] *Agos*, "Erdoğan Threatens Armenian Citizens Once Again," June 4, 2016.

immigrant social base was growing in France. All in all, as of February 2019, neither international nor domestic factors appeared to dictate a rapid change in policies toward Muslims in France. An analysis of the international and domestic contexts of French policies toward Muslims makes this point clear.

## International Context

The September 11 terrorist attacks prompted the rise of anti-Muslim attitudes in Europe and helped the supporters of anti-Muslim policies to pass restrictive laws about Muslims. In the 2010s, anti-Muslim sentiments gained even more dominance not only in Europe but also globally. The events that followed the Arab uprisings unleashed the spread of Muslim extremist groups in the Middle East and Europe. The unstable political environment in Iraq after the withdrawal of American troops in 2011 and the lack of central political authority in Syria in the wake of the Syrian Civil War led to the emergence of fundamentalist terrorist organizations in the Middle East. One such group, the Islamic State of Iraq and Syria, became particularly influential after summer 2014 when it took control of Mosul, the second-largest city in Iraq. This group not only created an environment of violence and terror in the territories that it controlled but also instigated terrorist attacks in Western countries including France.

Between 2014 and 2016, the Islamic State of Iraq and Syria conducted or inspired more than 140 terrorist attacks in 29 countries other than Iraq and Syria, where it originated. These attacks killed at least 2,043 people and injured thousands more.[8] Of these attacks, eighteen were conducted in European countries, with France undergoing seven attacks. Three of the attacks in France attracted global media attention and boosted anti-Muslim sentiments in France and more widely in Europe. On January 7, 2015, two French gunmen with Algerian origins attacked the offices of the satirical magazine *Charlie Hebdo* claiming to revenge the Prophet Mohammed, of whom the magazine had published caricatures. The gunmen killed twelve people in the attack. On November 13, 2015, a series of terrorist attacks in Paris killed 130 people and wounded more than 350 others. The attackers targeted six locations including a soccer match and a concert hall. On July 14, 2016, in Nice, a French-Tunisian man drove a truck into crowds celebrating France's national day. The attacker killed eighty-four people, including ten children, and injured many others.[9] A related global development that put Muslims on the spot in public discussions was the outflow of millions of refugees from Syria after a civil war

---

[8] Tim Lister, Ray Sanchez, Mark Bixler, Sean O'Key, Michael Hogenmiller, and Mohammed Tawfeeq, "ISIS Goes Global: 143 Attacks in 29 Countries Have Killed 2043," *CNN*, February 12, 2018, available at www.cnn.com/2015/12/17/world/mapping-isis-attacks-around-the-world/index.html (last accessed on October 29, 2018).

[9] Ibid.

erupted in the aftermath of the Syrian uprising of March 2011. Those who had mobilized the supporters of the headscarf ban utilized the new environment to maintain their support base for more restrictive policies toward Muslims.

These developments contributed to the rise of far-right populism in Europe and elsewhere in the 2010s, when new movements against Muslims formed in several European countries. In 2014 an anti-Islamic movement, Patriotic Europeans against the Islamization of the West (PEGIDA), was founded in Dresden, Germany (Holmes and Castaneda 2016, 15). In the wake of the Paris attacks in November 2015, the far-right prime minister of Hungary, Viktor Orban, said that "terrorists have exploited mass migration by mingling in European societies."[10]

A quick overview of the changes in vote share of far-right parties over the last few years shows the extent of the rise of radical right in Europe. In the UK, the far-right United Kingdom Independence Party received 26.8 percent of the votes in European parliamentary elections and became an important actor in the EU parliament.[11] In September 2017, Germany's Alternative for Germany party became the first far-right group to enter the German parliament, winning 94 parliamentary seats out of 709 and forcing the German chancellor Angela Merkel to form a coalition government with left-wing parties.[12]

The rise of the far right in European countries was part of a global rise in populism around the world. In line with this trend, the British people held a referendum in June 2016 and decided to leave the EU. In the USA, Donald Trump based his presidential campaign on a nationalist and anti-immigrant discourse. During the campaign period anti-Muslim sentiments increased in the country. Further, after Trump won the presidential race in November 2016 his government imposed a travel ban on some Muslim-majority countries, restricting visa issuance to the citizens of the countries listed in the ban. All in all, the global environment led to more Islamophobia in the world and in Europe in the 2010s.

The rise of Islamophobia and the increasing appeal of the far right changed the terms of the political game in European countries. The shift of political discourses on immigrants led centrist parties to extend their appeal using more nationalistic discourses. The upward trajectory of far-right parties made the development of inclusive policies more difficult, as mainstream political parties have been concerned to lose their social base to their far-right

---

[10] Michelle Chen, "European Countries' Closing Their Borders to Refugees Is Collective Punishment," *The Nation*, November 18, 2015, available at www.thenation.com/article/european-countries-closing-their-borders-to-refugees-is-collective-punishment/ (last accessed on December 20, 2018).

[11] Amanda Taub, "The Terrifying Rise of the Far Right in the UK, Explained in One Chart," *Vox*, November 6, 2014, available at www.vox.com/2014/11/6/7163375/ukip-conservative-right-europe (last accessed on December 20, 2018).

[12] Jon Henley, "German Elections 2017: Angela Merkel Wins Fourth Term but AfD Makes Gains – as It Happened," *The Guardian*, September 24, 2017.

competitors. The presence of a hawkish alternative makes the mainstream parties stricter than they have traditionally been. This has had a transformative impact on the stance of mainstream parties on refugees in the direction of more restrictive policies. With the rise of the far right and growing Islamophobia, politicians have shifted their attention from human rights to xenophobia to get the support of a public that has become increasingly anti-immigrant. This international sentiment surrounded the French domestic political setting.

## Domestic changes

In line with global rise of populism, the far right in France gained momentum in the 2010s. In the 2012 presidential election, the leader of the FN, Marine Le Pen, came in third, with 17.90 percent of the vote in the election's first round. In 2014, the FN won 24 of France's 74 seats in the European Parliament, becoming France's largest party there.[13] In the 2017 presidential elections Marine Le Pen became the front-runner, with 21.3 percent of the vote in the first round of the elections.[14] While Le Pen lost the elections in the runoff race, she was able to gain 33.9 percent of the vote. This is a significant increase from 2002, when the FN leader Jean-Marie Le Pen (Marine Le Pen's father) had taken only 17 percent of the vote in his runoff elections against Jacques Chirac. When Jean-Marie Le Pen took part in the runoff in 2002, hundreds of thousands of French people went out on the streets and protested against him; however, such a broad based protest did not happen when Marine Le Pen was in the runoff in 2017. Far-right politicians became gradually more acceptable in French politics. The FN received almost 11 million votes in the 2017 election, becoming the main opposition bloc in France. In the 2017 election campaign, Le Pen capitalized on a nationalist and anti-immigrant rhetoric. She prioritized the sovereignty and security of France, implicating immigrants as a big concern for national security and the EU as a major threat to French security. She promoted exit from the eurozone, suggested protectionist economic policies, and targeted Muslim immigrants in France.[15]

Although Le Pen's opponent, Emmanuel Macron, offered a pro-immigrant, pro-European stance and won the elections, the main cleavage in France became between globalism and nationalism. The traditional center-right and center-left parties lost their influence. None of the candidates from those parties made the runoff in 2017. The rise of the National Front, renamed National Rally (Rassemblement national) in 2018, transformed the

---

[13] Stefan Schmid, "The Rising Power of France's Front National," *The National*, March 30, 2015, available at www.thenational.scot/world/the-rising-power-of-frances-front-national.1529 (last accessed on December 20, 2018).

[14] The National Front changed its name to National Rally (Rassemblement national) in June 2018.

[15] *Le Figaro*, "Présidentielle: Qui sont les 11 candidats sur la ligne de départ," March 18, 2017.

conventional run of politics in France and the made globalist–nationalist cleavage the main thrust of political debates. Laurent Wauquiez, the new leader of France's traditional center-right Republicans party (les Républicains), is taking the party further toward the right. Wauquiez is a Euroskeptic and against immigration. The two slogans that Wauquiez used in a recent election show his stance on these issues: "immigration, that's enough" and "Brussels, that's enough."[16] By embracing a strong right-wing discourse, Wauquiez aims to become the main challenger to Macron in the 2022 elections. Because of the recent surge of far-right politics in France, using a strong right-wing discourse is the only way to challenge Macron, who is considered a globalist leader in France.

Although National Rally is the main actor in far-right politics in France, the rise of populism generated several other far-right political movements there in the 2010s. Groups such as Bloc Identitaire, Resistance Républicaine, and Riposte Laïque demand radical measures to restrict Muslims in France. The political agendas of these groups include outlawing Islam in France, stopping immigration from Muslim-majority countries, and forcing Muslims to migrate to Muslim-majority countries (Lucas 2011, 26). The popularity of far-right discourse went so far that some members of the FN left the party on the grounds that it was not supporting the anti-European and anti-immigrant agenda sufficiently. Florian Philippot, the former vice president of the FN, left the party and established his own far-right political movement, the Patriots (les Patriotes), in September 2017. Taking a nationalist and Euroskeptic position, Philippot aligned with other Euroskeptic parties in the European parliament.[17] In short, political developments in France in the 2010s created an environment in which passing anti-Muslim policies became easier than ever before.

## Policies toward Muslims

French policies toward the Muslim minority became more discriminatory in the 2010s. Previously, the debate had been mostly limited to whether or not to ban headscarves in public schools. In the 2010s, however, widespread bans on face-covering on the street, halal food in schools, etc. were proposed and in some cases implemented. The 2010 burqa ban set the stage for policies toward Muslims in France in the 2010s. While previous policies had limited the manifestations of religious symbols in public schools, the new policies put far-reaching limits on Muslims. Further, support for the limitations on Muslims

---

[16] Owen Barnell and Alcyone Wemaere, "Laurent Wauquiez: The Hardliner Leading France's Les Républicains Farther Right," *France 24*, December 13, 2017, available at www.france24.com/en/20171211-laurent-wauquiez-center-margins (last accessed on October 31, 2018).

[17] Cole Stangler, "Can France's Far-Right Reinvent Itself?" *The Atlantic*, January 14, 2018, available at www.theatlantic.com/international/archive/2018/01/france-national-front-far-right/550484/ (last accessed on October 31, 2018).

expanded to almost all political groups in France. The burqa ban was initiated by far-left members of parliament and the law was passed almost unanimously, with majorities of 335 to 1 in the French National Assembly and 246 to 1 in the Senate.[18] The European Court of Human Rights upheld the burqa ban in 2014 on the grounds that the French authorities were aiming to preserve the idea of living together.[19] In summer 2016, some French cities banned the wearing of full-body swimwear (the burkini) on public beaches. Despite a higher administrative court's ruling that mayors did not have authority to ban clothing on beaches, some cities continued to implement the ban.[20]

After every terrorist attack, French policies toward Muslims became more restrictive. In the wake of the *Charlie Hebdo* terrorist attacks, the French parliament passed a bill in May 2015 which allowed officials to monitor emails and phone calls of potential suspects without court authorization. After the terrorist attacks in November 2015, the French government declared a state of emergency to "give security forces expanded powers to conduct warrantless house raids, seize personal data, and place people on house arrest – all without an authorization from a judge."[21] During the state of emergency, the police raided thousands of homes and businesses owned by Muslims, and placed hundreds of suspects under house arrest on tenuous grounds. The French public was strongly supportive of the state of emergency: according to a poll conducted in January 2016, 77 percent of the French population supported it.[22] Although the state of emergency ended in November 2017, the French parliament passed a new bill that made some of the emergency provisions into ordinary laws. The new bill, passed in October 2017, increased the administrative measures that the Ministry of the Interior could take in countering terrorism "in cases where there was not sufficient evidence to open a criminal investigation."[23] These measures included restrictions on freedom of movement, enhanced stop-and-search powers, house searches, and the closing of places of worship.

[18] Steven Erlanger, "Parliament Moves France Closer to a Ban on Facial Veils," *New York Times*, July 14, 2010.

[19] Kim Willsher, "France's Burqa Ban Upheld by Human Rights Court," *The Guardian*, July 1, 2014.

[20] Sheena McKenzie, "French Mayors Maintain Burkini Bans Despite Court Ruling," *CNN*, August 29, 2016, available at www.cnn.com/2016/08/29/europe/french-mayors-refuse-lift-burkini-ban/index.html (last accessed on November 4, 2018).

[21] Amar Toor, "France's Anti-terrorism Laws Leave Muslims in a State of Fear," *The Verge*, January 29, 2016, available at www.theverge.com/2016/1/29/10860964/france-state-of-emergency-muslim-paris-attacks (last accessed on November 3, 2018).

[22] Geoffroy Claver, "Sondage: Deux mois après, l'état d'urgence jugé justifié par 77% des français," *Huffington Post*, January 13, 2016, available at www.huffingtonpost.fr/2016/01/13/sondage-etat-durgence-justifie-77-francais-exclusif_n_8968278.html (last accused on November 3, 2018).

[23] Amnesty International, "France: 2017/2018," 2018, available at www.amnesty.org/en/countries/europe-and-central-asia/france/report-france/ (last accessed on November 3, 2018).

The state's efforts to control Islam continued throughout the 2010s. Manuel Valls, the prime minister of France between 2014 and 2016 under François Hollande's presidency, blamed Islam for violence in France.[24] As of February 2019, Emmanuel Macron was also working on a plan to domesticate Islam in France. Among other things, Macron was aiming to make sure that French Muslims were less connected to the Muslim-majority countries that support Islamic organizations in France. In this regard, Macron was suspicious of Muslims' links to Algeria, Morocco, and Turkey in their provision of religious education and services.[25] In January 2018, the French National Assembly passed a bill to ban members of parliament from wearing religious symbols in the parliament. Although the ban did not specifically target Muslims, many observers related the passing of the law to increasingly anti-Muslim attitudes in France.[26] These moves indicate that the French state has retained its motivation to control Islam in the public sphere, as was the case in the 2000s.

In short, the international environment that produced anti-Muslim policies in the 2000s continued to structure French domestic politics. High levels of Islamophobia went hand in hand with the rise of far-right politics in France in the 2010s. The interaction of Islamophobia in the international environment and the far-right's dominance of domestic politics continued to limit Muslims in France throughout the 2010s.

## STATE POLICIES TOWARD JEWS IN TURKEY

Jews have been present in Turkey for centuries, but the rise of the Jewish population in significant numbers dates back to 1492, when Sultan Bayazid II of the Ottoman Empire welcomed Jews who had escaped from Spain during the inquisition. About 50,000 Jews were relocated to several cities across the Ottoman Empire (Toktas 2008, 512). Under Ottoman rule, Jews, along with Greeks and Armenians, gained official minority status, and Jews were thus regarded as one of the *millet* groups that had legal autonomy in return for paying a special tax.

The minority status of the Jews was retained under the new republic. Along with Christians, Jews were recognized as a minority in 1923 by the Treaty of Lausanne. Accordingly, the Turkish state recognized the chief rabbi in Istanbul as the leader of Turkish Jewry. Although Jews had a minority status, there were

---

[24] Mathilde Siraud, "Le Problème de l'Islam: Manuel Valls crée la polémique," *Le Figaro*, November 22, 2017.

[25] Hervé Gattegno and David Revault d'Allonnes, "Islam de France: Ce que veut faire Macron," *Journal du dimanche*, February 11, 2018, available at www.lejdd.fr/politique/islam-de-france-ce-que-veut-faire-macron-3571067 (last accessed on November 4, 2018).

[26] Pascal-Emmanuel Gobry, "Secular is a French Word for Anti-Muslim," *Bloomberg*, February 23, 2018, available at www.bloomberg.com/opinion/articles/2018-02-23/france-s-emmanuel-macron-isn-t-fighting-ant-muslim-bias (last accessed on November 4, 2018).

intensive Turkification efforts such as language campaigns that forced minorities to speak Turkish. The state had the aim of homogenizing the nation along nationalist and secularist lines. Non-Muslim minorities, including Jews, were dismissed from positions in bureaucracies and state-owned enterprises in the early republican era (Toktas 2005: 398). In July 1934, there was an anti-Semitic campaign that resulted in attacks against Jews living in cities in the Thrace region of Turkey such as Çanakkale, Edirne, Kırklareli, and Tekirdağ (Toktas 2005: 402).

Although the Jewish minority faced various difficulties in Turkey in the early republican period, they were considered more integrated than the Christian minorities until the establishment of the state of Israel. While Greeks and Armenians were considered a threat to Turkish national identity under the early republic, Jews were seen as loyal citizens. Because of Turkey's war with Greece and the possibility of the establishment of an Armenian state in eastern Turkey during the First World War, the state kept a distance from its Greek and Armenian citizens. However, the republic's founding fathers did not feel threatened by the Jewish presence in the nation (Toktas 2005, 396). Turkey supported European Jewry during the Holocaust and the Second World War, invited some Jewish citizens of Nazi Germany to settle in Turkey. Several Jewish professors who fled from Germany played key roles in the development of the Turkish university system (Bishku 2017, 441). Even the establishment of the state of Israel did not influence the state's relations with Jews initially. Turkey was one of the first nations to recognize Israel as an independent state. However, the wars between Israel and the Palestinians turned Turkish public perceptions against Israel and negatively influenced the Turkish state's relations with its own Jewish citizens.

Today, there are about 20,000 Jews living in Turkey. The vast majority, about 17,500, live in Istanbul, and about 1,500 in Izmir. The number of Jews in other cities is insignificant. Turkish Jews publish an eight-page weekly magazine, with seven pages written in Turkish and one page in Ladino (a Judeo-Spanish language traditionally used by Turkish Jews).[27]

The problems that the Jewish minority had in republican Turkey were similar to the issues that Christian minorities faced. Like Christians, Jews were protected under the terms of the Treaty of Lausanne. The state appropriated properties owned by the Jewish minority and prevented them from acquiring or disposing of real estate until new laws were enacted between 2000 and 2010. The Jewish minority had lost properties after the 1970s. In places where the

---

[27] There are various estimates of the size of the Jewish population in Turkey. The U.S. State Department, in its 2017 International Religious Freedom Report, estimates the Jewish population as 16,000. I came up with the figure given here by sifting through various estimates available online. See U.S. Department of State, "Turkey 2017 International Religious Freedom Report," available at www.state.gov/documents/organization/281212.pdf (last accessed on December 19, 2018).

Jewish population had decreased, the foundations that owned properties did not continue. In those cases, the state appropriated the properties. The new reforms allowed the Jewish minority to regain those lost properties from the state.[28]

Although the legal framework regarding religious education affected Jews and Christians equally, the Jewish minority did not lobby for the establishment of schools to train clergy. The opening of institutions of religious education has not become an issue between the Turkish state and the Jewish community. With regard to the use of their own language, the Jewish community also did not have a problem. Because Jews were a recognized minority, they were able to publish and broadcast in their own language, Ladino. Because existing places of worship were sufficient to meet the needs of the decreasing Jewish population, the issue of opening new places of worship did not arise for Jews in Turkey. The 2003 law that allowed the opening of places of worship for non-Muslims also gave the Jewish minority that right. Like all religious groups in Turkey, the Jewish minority does not have a legal personality for their religious institutions. Organizing around religion is not legally permitted in Turkey.

The dynamics that produced reforms for the benefit of the Christian minority in the 2000s were also at play in the formation of state policies toward the Jewish minority. Most of the reforms targeted non-Muslim minorities regardless of the specific religious beliefs of the people that benefited from the changes. EU pressure targeted discrimination against non-Muslim minorities including the Jews, and the resulting improvements advanced the status of both Christians and Jews equally. The EU provided a permissive international context for reform, while the AKP utilized this reformist context to expand its sphere of influence in domestic politics. While the Christian minority used international forums to exert pressure on Turkey, the Jewish minority preferred to work with the Turkish state and avoided lobbying against Turkey in the international forums. As Rıfat Bali wrote, the Jews in Turkey preferred to solve their problems in close coordination with the state without using public forums (Bali 1998, 85). Further, the Jewish community lobbied for Turkey in international forums to advance Turkish state interests. Thanks to close connections with Jewish organizations in the USA, Turkish Jews lobbied on Turkey's behalf with the US Congress on several issues (Yıldız 2015, 275).

After the AKP's turn to authoritarianism and the embrace of a populist Islamist path, two developments influenced policies toward the Jews. First, an anti-Semitic discourse proliferated in Turkey in the 2010s. Anti-Semitic discourses have been widely employed in the political rhetoric of various circles from Islamists to leftists, but this gained more acceptance at state level in the 2010s. Both Islamist intellectuals such as Abdurrahman Dilipak and left-

---

[28] *Mynet Haber*, "Moris Levi: Üzerinde Yaşadığımız Toprakları Çok Kültürlülük Beslemiştir," August 2, 2018, available at www.mynet.com/moris-levi-uzerinde-yasadigimiz-topraklari-cok-kulturluluk-beslemistir-110104307010 (last accessed on December 19, 2018).

wing intellectuals such as Yalçın Küçük and Soner Yalçın have transmitted conspiracy theories about Jews in general and a certain group of people called the Dönme in particular (Nefes 2015, 573). Dönmes are seen as hidden Jews living in Turkey. Dönmes were originally the followers of Rabbi Shabbatai Tzevi, who started a Jewish sect in the seventeenth century. When the Ottoman Empire found Tzevi's activities suspicious, he was arrested; later, he converted to Islam. Those of his followers who publicly converted to Islam but privately kept their religious beliefs are called Dönme. Many Islamist circles in Turkey believes that the Dönmes were involved in the toppling of Abdulhamid II and played a significant role in the establishment of the Turkish republic. According to these theories, the Dönmes dethroned Abdulhamid II because he refused to give land to the Jews in Palestine (Baer 2013, 551). Anti-Semitic discourses gained acceptance even at presidential level in the recent years. For example, in November 2018, President Erdoğan accused George Soros, describing him as "a Hungarian Jew," of being behind the street protests in 2013 "to overthrow the government."[29]

Second, the AKP, in line with its Islamist turn, used Israel's attacks against Palestinians as a tool to consolidate its social support, and this strategy created a social environment in which Jews have been stigmatized by the public. Whenever there is an international issue related to Israel, the loyalty of Turkish Jews to the Turkish state becomes a point of debate (Toktas 2005, 421). For example, in 2014, the governor of Edirne province delayed the opening of a recently restored historical synagogue with the excuse that Israel had attacked Palestinians in Gaza and East Jerusalem (Yıldız 2015, 281). During the 2014 Israeli attacks against Gaza, attacks against Jewish places of worship and the vilification of Jews in the media proliferated in Turkey (Yıldız 2015, 282). Even though these attacks were mostly at the societal level, the discourse of the politicians and their inaction in the face of these incidents facilitated their circulation.

The interaction of domectic actor strategies and international context structured state policies toward Jews in Turkey. While Turkey's bid for EU membership and the AKP's relatively more democratic domestic strategy led to the implementation of reforms in favor of the Jewish minority, the authoritarian turn of the AKP after the Arab uprisings and Israeli action against the Palestinians unleashed an anti-Semitic discourse in Turkey and increased the concerns of the Jewish minority.

## STATE POLICIES TOWARD SECTS IN FRANCE

French policies toward sects have also been shaped by the interaction of international context and domestic political configuration. International

---

[29] Onur Ant, "Turkey's Erdogan Joins in Vilification of Soros," *Bloomberg*, November 21, 2018, available at www.bloomberg.com/news/articles/2018-11-21/erdogan-joins-vilification-of-soros -with-gezi-protests-claim (last accessed on December 19, 2018).

events created fears about sects, and anti-sect activists built on this fear and mobilized policymakers toward more restrictive policies. Eventually, France became "the first country in the world to introduce specific legislation aimed at controlling the activities of cults."[30] The French public was already unsympathetic toward sects such as Scientology, the Children of God, the Unification Church, Raelism, and the Solar Temple Order, but international events made it easier for anti-sect groups to advance their policy agendas. While anti-sect activists and their allies in the state considered such sects to be criminal organizations exploiting people in the guise of legitimate religious groups, members of these sects and their supporters considered state action against their groups to be discriminatory and fed by prejudice. To them, state policies created an environment of intolerance and exclusion toward minority religious groups.

International events in 1994 and 1995 triggered public discussion of the sects in France. The first of such events was the tragic mass suicide committed by the members of the Solar Temple Order in Canada and Switzerland in October 1994. These mass suicides took 53 lives in the villages of Cheiry and Salvan in Western Switzerland and in Morin Heights, Quebec, in Canada. Of these people, 15 people committed suicide with poison, 30 were killed with bullets, and the rest were killed by other causes (Mayer and Siegler 1999, 173). In March 1995, a similar cultic incident happened in Japan. Members of the cult of the Aum Shinrikyo attacked the Tokyo subway with sarin gas, killing 13 people, seriously injuring 54, and affecting thousands (Brackett 1996). Within a few months of the Solar Temple and Tokyo subway tragedies, the French National Assembly voted unanimously to appoint a commission "to study the sect phenomenon" (Palmer 2011, 10). The influential Guyard report listing "dangerous" sects immediately followed this committee work. While the Guyard report did not have any legal status, it had "an enormous impact on the social status of minority religions and their adherents" (Palmer 2011, 11). The political environment shaped by international events helped the anti-sect activists pass their policy agenda without much resistance.

In July 1995, the French National Assembly formed a commission, the Parliamentary Commission on Cults in France (Commission d'enquête parlementaire sur les sectes en France), to investigate the status of cults. The commission released a report in December 1995 that warned the French public about the degenerative impact of the sects. Further, the commission prepared a list of sects that were undermining the safety and security of French citizens. The list included 173 sects operating in France. The parliamentary commission used two sets of criteria to include any group on the list. The first set of criteria were used to show the threats that sects posed to the people. According to the commission, the listed sects posed threats to mental stability, physical integrity, financial status, and family unity, and dangers including the indoctrination of

---

[30] Jon Henley, "France Arms Itself with Legal Weapon to Fight Sects," *Guardian*, May 31, 2001.

children. The second set of criteria identified threats to community. These threats included public disorder, antisocial speech, judicial involvement, diversion of economic relations, and infiltration of public offices.[31] In preparing a list of sects, the commission held various hearings with former members of the cults and members of anti-sect associations and gained information from the French secret police. Not surprisingly, the report prompted criticisms from the representatives of several new religious movements. These critics pointed out ambiguities in the criteria that permitted the listing of a religious movement as a sect in the list. Representatives of these movements were not allowed to see the documents that led to their inclusion on the list. Further, the committee did not listen to anyone who was affiliated with the religious movements included in the list (Palmer 2002, 176–177).

In May 1996, following the release of the report on the sects, the French state established a bureaucratic body to coordinate government monitoring of the sects, the Interministerial Observatory of Sects (Observatoire interministériel sur les sectes). Between 1996 and 1998, this body organized training and awareness programs for the police, prosecutors, judges, and teachers about sects and their impact on society (Palmer 2011, 17). In 1998, this body was replaced by another interministerial organization, the Interministerial Mission for the Fight Against Cults (Mission interministérielle de lutte contre les sectes). Alain Vivien, an anti-cult activist, was appointed director of the new organization, signaling that the state intended to increase its pressure on the sects (Palmer 2011, 17). The new organization defined its function as "the constant surveillance of the sectarian landscape" and took an active role in curtailing the impact of sects in France (Hervieu-Léger 2001, 249).

The government detailed its plan for work against the sects in the following years. In 1999, the French parliament formed another commission specifically focusing on the financial status of sects in France. It aimed to investigate the financial, tax-related, and economic activities of the sects. The report singled out Jehovah's Witnesses and the Church of Scientology as the richest cults in France and added new sects to the 1995 list. The 1999 report pointed out the negative impact of these sects on the French financial and economic system.[32] The French parliament passed a law in May 2001, known as the About-Picard law, to further consolidate state pressure on sects. The law allowed prosecutors to investigate sects for abusing the weaknesses of their followers who "might be harmed by charismatic leaders – fraud, physical abuse, sexual exploitation,

---

[31] Assemblée Nationale, *Au Nom de la Commission d'enquête sur les sectes*, December 22, 1995, available at www.assemblee-nationale.fr/rap-enq/r2468.asp (last accessed on November 7, 2018).

[32] Assemblée Nationale, *Les Sectes et l'argent*, June 10, 1999, available at www.assemblee-nationale.fr/dossiers/sectes/sommaire.asp (last accessed on November 7, 2018).

incitement to mass suicide, denial of medical treatment, or the illegal practice of medicine" (Palmer 2011, 22).

These moves, as well as the assertive stance of the Interministerial Mission for the Fight Against Cults led by an anti-cult activist, created furor and criticism of the French government by domestic and international human rights groups. In response to this growing concern, the French government implemented new policies in the 2000s. First it disbanded the Interministerial Mission in the Fight Against Cults and replaced it with a new organization, the Interministerial Mission for Monitoring and Combating Cultic Deviances (Mission interministérielle de vigilance et de lutte contre les dérives sectaires) in 2002.[33] The new office would inform the public about sects that were undermining fundamental individual liberties or that threatened public order and law. The office would also conduct research and analysis into the sects and share this information with relevant offices in the state bureaucracy.[34] The office was intended to develop "a more reasonable approach to deal with the 'cult problem'" (Palmer 2011, 19). While the former office had "engaged in a head-on fight" against the sects, the new office had "a more circumspect and apparently sophisticated mission" of "vigilance and fight against sectarian deviance" (Palmer, 2008, 205). Second, in May 2005, Prime Minister Jean-Pierre Raffarin issued a circular and ordered French civil servants not to be bound by the list prepared by the parliament in 1995. The circular recommended that civil servants apply criteria in consultation with the Interministerial Mission for Monitoring and Combating Cultic Deviances.[35]

In 2006, the French National Assembly created a new parliamentary commission focusing on the influence of cults on minors, particularly on the physical and mental health of children. The commission released a report that identified practices through which sects had influenced minors' physical and mental development. The report particularly emphasized the weakness of the children and the sects' "brainwashing" practices in controlling them. The report called upon state officials to take measures in monitoring sects and preventing the exposure of minors to their influence. The report criticized the "moderate approach" that the government had taken toward sects in the previous years and called for more restrictive policies.[36]

---

[33] For more information, see the website of the organization: www.derives-sectes.gouv.fr (last accessed on November 7, 2018).

[34] Ibid.

[35] The circular, "Circulaire du 27 mai 2005 relative à la lutte contre les dérives sectaires," is available at www.legifrance.gouv.fr/affichTexte.do?cidTexte=JORFTEXT000000809117&dateTexte= &categorieLien=id (last accessed on December 20, 2018).

[36] The report of the Assemblée Nationale, "L'Influence des mouvements à caractère sectaire et aux conséquences de leurs pratiques sur la santé physique et mentale des mineurs," December 12, 2006, is available at www.assemblee-nationale.fr/12/pdf/rap-enq/r3507-rapport.pdf (last accessed on November 8, 2018).

The bills and organizations to fight sects came after the international incidents previously mentioned, but the fervent campaigns of the anti-sect activists also mobilized people toward these policies. The French public in general had very negative perceptions of the sects in question. In a poll conducted in 2000, 73 percent of the respondents indicated that sects were a threat to French democracy and 66 percent said that sects were a threat to their family and friends. In the same poll, 86 percent of the respondents supported legislation monitoring the sects.[37] Anti-cult organizations such as the National Union of Associations for the Defense of Families and the Individual Victims of Cults (Union nationale des associations de défense des familles et de l'individu victimes de sectes) used this sentiment in mobilizing the public against sects (Richardson and Introvigne 2001, 143). The international incidents provided these organizations with "a visible symbol for discussion and debate" (Jenkins 1996, 170).

The reports prepared by the parliamentary commissions increased public fears about sects because those reports were prepared using the testimony of former members of the sects, anti-cult activists, and the security officials. Active members of the sects were not invited to testify in the parliamentary commissions. The anti-cult activists made the point that the cults were a threat not only to children but also to adults, in that they use various brainwashing and mind-controlling methods. Denis Barthélemy, the secretary of the French Interministerial Mission in the Fight Against Cults, accused the sects of exploiting people's sentiments "against their wish" through their mind-control methods (Richardson and Introvigne 2001, 163). Sarah Palmer (2002) identifies six mechanisms of discriminating against sects: labeling as deviant, exerting financial pressure, publicly humiliating the leaders, ostracizing sect members from public spaces, prosecuting members of the sects, and exposing professionals as members of cults in their workplaces.

Members of the sects and religious freedom groups criticized these French policies, but their voices remained weak in an environment in which the main narrative about sects was woven around the security and safety of French citizens. When the About-Picard law was enacted in 2001, a group called Coordination of Associations and Individuals for the Freedom of Conscience (Coordination des associations et particuliers pour la liberté de conscience) was founded. The group released a report, "Report on Discrimination against Spiritual and Therapeutical Minorities in France," and criticized the French state for witch-hunting its own citizens. The report said that the state "should not specify groups as 'sectarian' or 'cultic' as, in a democracy, all individuals and groups should be treated

---

[37] Commission Nationale des Sondages, "Les Français et les sectes," February 15, 2000, available at www.csa-tmo.fr/dataset/data2K/opi20000215b.htm (last accessed on August 22, 2013).

equally and in the same manner."[38] However, the framing of the issue in a security perspective undermined the impact of such groups.

International organizations such as the US Commission on International Religious Freedom criticized the discriminatory French policies toward sects. The commission addressed French sect policies in its annual reports beginning in 2000. In its 2000 report, the commission indicated that the environment created by French policymakers had unleashed intolerance toward these sects, especially toward those identified as "threatening" in the parliamentary reports.[39] After each major bill about the sects passed in the French parliament, the US commission addressed the concerns of members of minority religious groups in its annual reports.

As was the case with the headscarf ban, international events facilitated the campaign of the anti-sect activists and helped them frame the public debate about sects around the issues of safety and security. The protection of religious freedoms lost ground within the context of the new framework. The stereotypes and public images of the sects helped the anti-sect activists in pushing their own agendas. It was the interaction of international context and domestic actors that led to the anti-sect political environment and policies in France.

## STATE POLICIES TOWARD RELIGIOUS MINORITIES IN OTHER CONTEXTS

How can the argument developed in this book help explain the expansion or limitation of freedoms for religious minorities in other cases? Further research is required to systematically analyze the impact of the interaction between international context and domestic actors on liberties for religious minorities. However, it is instructive to give a few illustrative examples from different contexts.

In the late 1990s and early 2000s, reformists in Bulgaria used European pressure to institute religious liberties for the Turkish Muslim minority. Muslims, with a population of about 600,000, constitute about 10 percent of Bulgarians. While they had been under oppression in the last years of the Communist regime in the late 1980s, their status progressed in the post-Communist era. In the 1990s, the Bulgarian state granted religious freedom rights for the Muslim minority. Bulgaria's bid to become an EU member played a significant role in the reform process. The reforms continued in the 2000s

---

[38] Coordination des associations et particuliers pour la liberté de conscience, _Report on Discrimination against Spiritual and Therapeutical Minorities in France_, October 2001, available at www.coordiap.com/Gtem000.htm (last accessed on December 4, 2018).

[39] United States Commission on International Religious Freedom, "The Annual Report of the United States Commission on International Religious Freedom," 2000, available at www.uscirf.gov/sites/default/files/resources/stories/pdf/Annual_Report/2000annual report.pdf (last accessed on December 5, 2018).

when Bulgaria became an EU member (Ivanova 2017). However, as in many other European countries, the rise of Islamophobia in recent years increased pressure on Muslims in Bulgaria. The far-right parties ignited xenophobia by bringing up the issues of refugees and immigration in public debates. On September 30, 2016, the Bulgarian parliament passed a law that outlawed the burqa (full-face veil) for its citizens.[40]

When President Donald Trump indirectly attacked Muslims during his electoral campaign in 2016, there were two significant factors that were considered as guarantors of Muslims' rights: the constitutional significance of religious freedoms in the USA, and the strategic alliances between the USA and major Muslim-majority countries. Notwithstanding these factors, President Trump was able to capitalize on global discourses of Islamophobia to gain ground in the electoral process. After coming to power, the Islamophobic discourse helped him execute some of his promises. He banned visas for a number of Muslim-majority countries.[41] However, the USA's strategic relationship with countries such as Pakistan and Saudi Arabia prevented the expansion of the ban to these countries. The strong constitutional tradition in the USA prevented the president from expanding limitations on Muslims.

In the 1980s and 1990s, progressive political forces in Mexico utilized US pressure to guarantee religious liberties for Protestant minorities, who constitute about 7 percent of Mexicans. After the 1982 economic crisis in Mexico, religious leaders put pressure on the government to expand these liberties. The urgent necessity of economic trade with the USA encouraged the state to implement more religion-friendly policies. The state wanted to attract Protestant immigrants who might facilitate economic relations between the USA and Mexico (Gill 2008, 159–161). The increased pressure to expand relations between the USA and Mexico led to constitutional amendments in 1992 that ended the decades-old state hostility to religion. Although these changes did not only target the expansion of minority rights, they did allow for more religious liberties. The strategies of domestic actors to facilitate public dissent against government policies and the availability of the US markets for further economic development led to more permissive policies toward religion, including minority religions.

Jordan's historically friendly relationship with the USA had an impact on Christians' relatively better status compared to other Middle Eastern contexts. In Jordan, the legal framework provided ample space for religious freedoms for Christians. Issues such as marriage, divorce, inheritance, and child custody are dealt with in the ecclesiastical courts of Christian minorities. Christians are fairly represented in government positions. They regularly serve as cabinet

---

[40] Siobhan Fenton, "Bulgaria Imposes Burqa Ban and Will Cut Benefits of Women Who Defy It," *The Independent*, October 1, 2016.
[41] Rick Gladstone and Satoshi Sugiyama, "Trump's Travel Ban: How It Works and Who Is Affected," *New York Times*, July 1, 2018.

ministers. There are nine seats reserved for Christians in the 150-seat parliament. The state reserves positions in the upper levels of the military for Christians. The kingdom of Jordan grew with the support of Britain during the mandate regime after the First World War and continued its friendly relations with Western powers thereafter (Wilson 1988). Jordan's close collaboration with the USA contributed to the regime's good relations with Christian minorities.

When it first came to power in 2012, the Muslim Brotherhood in Egypt invested energy in developing a warmer relationship with the Christian minority in an effort to demonstrate its moderate position to Western audiences concerned with the movement's Islamist agenda. Although there were attacks against Christian churches in that period, President Mohammed Morsi ordered investigations into the attacks and tried to address the issue in an effort to soothe Western critics of his government, which needed strong legitimacy.[42] Similarly, Abdel Fatah al-Sissi, who staged a military coup and was involved in several human rights violations, condemned an attack against Christian pilgrims in 2018 and ordered further investigation.[43] He used the issue as an instrument to prove his commitment to pluralism to his Western audiences. The case was used to stifle criticism of the violation of human rights in Egypt. Policies toward Christians was used to further the legitimacy of the government in the global context.

## CONCLUSION

The argument developed throughout this book explains the cases covered in this chapter. The changing international context after the Arab uprisings of 2011 and the shifting preferences of the AKP created a new environment for Christian minorities in Turkey after 2010. In this period, reforms stopped, and issues around Christian minorities were buried in the new populist/Islamist discourse of the Turkish government. In France, Islamophobia continued to grow, especially after the rise of extremism in the Middle East in the wake of the Arab uprisings. Anti-Muslim groups took advantage of this global context and pushed for further limitations on Muslims after 2010. State policies toward Jews in Turkey were similar to state policies toward Christians because these two minorities shared a similar status. However, Israeli policies toward Palestinians in occupied territories and the rise of anti-Semitic discourses after the AKP's populist turn created a relatively restrictive environment for the Jewish minority in the 2010s. State policies toward sects in France followed a similar path as state policies toward Muslims. International events around

---

[42] David D. Kirkpatrick, "Coptic Christian Leader in Egypt Criticizes Government over Violence," *New York Times*, April 9, 2013.

[43] Sudarsan Raghavan and Heba Farouk Mahfouz, "Gunmen in Egypt Attack Bus Carrying Christians, Killing at Least 8 and Wounding 13," *Washington Post*, November 2, 2018.

sects sparked fears at the public level, and anti-sect activists utilized the new environment to push for restrictive policies toward sects.

In other contexts, such as Bulgaria, the USA, Mexico, Jordan, and Egypt, international context and domestic actor strategies interacted to producing various policies toward religious minorities. International pressure may not always be present to enable certain policies to be passed. Reformists in Turkey were lucky to have systematic international pressure from the EU in the 2000s. Anti-Muslim activists in France found a supportive international environment of global Islamophobia that enabled them to execute their policy agendas. The same level of pressure might not be easy to create in other contexts, but domestic actors' ability to utilize existing international pressure can still facilitate reform. Ultimately, the interaction of international context and domestic actors shapes the status of religious minorities.

# 9

# Conclusion

Religious minorities have never been out of the headlines. In the 2010s, some European countries passed laws to restrict the public manifestation of Muslim religious symbols. Likewise, the Arab uprisings and political instability that followed led to concerns about the future of Christian minorities in the Middle East. Across the globe, there has been a plethora of evidence of ongoing changes in policies addressing religious minorities. Yet our understanding of why states change their policies toward religious minorities remained incomplete. This book attempted to contribute to theorizing on state policies toward religious minorities using in-depth case studies of the Christian minority in Turkey and the Muslim minority in France between 2000 and 2010. The book demonstrated that one needs to take seriously the interaction between international context and domestic politics in order to arrive at a complete understanding of changes to state policies toward religious minorities. In this chapter, I first summarize the main findings of the book. Second, I make broader conclusions on the relationship between historical institutions, international context, domestic politics, and state–religion relations. Finally, I assess the relationship between political context and theory development that can be deduced from the intellectual endeavor in the book.

## CHANGING POLICIES TOWARD RELIGIOUS MINORITIES
## IN TURKEY AND FRANCE

In the 2000s, the Turkish parliament passed a number of laws expanding Christian minority rights, such as rights concerning religious property, religious education, and the construction of houses of worship. Most of these reforms were instituted under the rule of the AKP, a party with Islamist roots, but the reforms stalled when the Turkish government took a strong authoritarian path in the 2010s. In the 2000s, the French parliament passed laws constraining Muslim minority rights, especially in the public manifestation of religious symbols including the wearing of the Islamic headscarf in public schools. These bans received strong support from diverse ideological camps in the French parliament including the Socialists, a group with a solid pro-immigrant track record. This book explained why Turkish legislators passed laws enhancing religious liberties for Christians between 2000 and 2010 while their French counterparts passed laws limiting religious freedoms for Muslims in the same period. While answering this empirical question in the book, I offered a more general theory of state policies toward religious minorities.

Scholars of political science have offered diverse explanations to account for the degree of religious freedoms accorded to minority groups. In explaining liberties for minority religions, modernization theorists refer to macro-level social trends toward secularization, leaving religious minorities more room for maneuver. However, the reforms in Turkey came at a time when the influence of Islamists, the proponents of the majority religion, over politics increased in parallel with an increasing industrialization. On the other hand, the restrictions in France occurred when there were no major changes in industrialization and secularization in the country.

Historical institutionalists focus on the formation of state–religion relations within specific historical conditions over a long period of time and explain the freedoms for religious minorities based on the space provided by historically established regimes. In the Turkish and French cases, though, we see a clear departure from such historical patterns. The Turkish state departed from historically established discriminatory policies toward Christians and implemented new reforms that expanded liberties. The French state shifted from its traditional position that allowed Muslims to entertain their religious freedoms and implemented exclusionary policies.

Scholars focusing on ideology examine ideological competition in a given country to account for religious freedoms. Religious minorities operate in a more permissible environment when inclusivist ideologies dominate in a particular country. Such theories of ideology can explain why the weakening of the state ideology of secular nationalism created opportunities for Christians in Turkey and the rise of anti-Muslim sentiments restricted Muslims in France; however, it has limited power to explain the reasons for these ideological shifts in both countries.

Rational choice theorists explain religious freedoms by looking at the strategic interaction between political and religious actors. The examination of actor strategies plays a significant role in explaining the political outcomes in both Turkey and France. In Turkey, Islamists supported the rights of Christian minorities because doing so helped them to stay in power; the reforms came as a package with other political reforms that empowered Islamists vis-à-vis secularists. Similarly, politicians in France supported discriminatory policies toward Muslims because doing so helped them appeal to increasingly Islamophobic voters. However, rational choice theory is blind to the dynamic that forced both Turkish Islamists and French politicians to change their strategies: the interaction of international context and domestic politics. In both countries, the global context shaped the terms of domestic political struggles among actors.

Although previously existing explanations provided valuable insights to explain state policies toward religious minorities, they fall short of fully accounting for the variation in religious freedoms for minorities in Turkey and France. I have argued that the change in religious freedoms in Turkey and France can be explained by the interaction between the international context and the strategies of domestic political actors. The book has shown that policy change becomes possible only when strong domestic actors find a suitable international context that help them execute their policy agendas. Islamist actors in Turkey utilized the EU membership bid to strengthen their position against the bureaucratic establishment. French right-wing politicians utilized the international environment of rising Islamophobia in the wake of the September 11 terrorist attacks and formed a coalition to pass anti-Muslim laws in the French parliament.

Using the data gathered from legal documents of international institutions on religious freedoms, reports of governmental and nongovernmental organizations on religious liberties, parliamentary proceedings, court decisions, newspaper archives, and my interviews with officials, politicians, and leaders of religious minorities during frequent visits for field research to Istanbul and Paris between 2007 and 2015, I developed this argument in three steps.

First, I showed that long-term historical development is integral to the formation of state policies toward religious minorities in both Turkey and France. I looked at how ideological battles between various actors during certain historical epochs in each country gave birth to particular regimes of state–religion relations and how states approached religious minorities within these historically established regimes. I also showed the deviations from this historical pattern in the time period analyzed. Both Turkey and France established secularism as a constitutional principle and championed a secular identity that excluded religion from the public sphere. They however followed different policies toward religious minorities: the Turkish state highly regulated religious minorities, while the French state marginalized minorities without direct intervention in the religious field. The recent policies are deviations from this pattern, as Turkey passed new reforms to empower Christians while France imposed new bans to control how Muslims manifest religion in the public sphere.

In the Treaty of Lausanne, the Turkish state not only guaranteed equal treatment to non-Muslim minorities but also recognized their rights as minorities, allowing them to open educational institutions in their mother tongues and to manage the functions of their religious, social, and charitable institutions. However, over the course of modern Turkish history, Christian minorities have been treated as if they were "foreigners." Turkish nationalism and secularism have contributed to the inferior status of the Christian minority. The founding fathers of modern Turkey imagined a homogenous nation that was based on Turkish ethnic and Sunni Islamic identities. This understanding of nationalism left little room for Christians to take part in the nationalist project. Turkish secularism, which aimed to put religion under state control, limited the freedom of religion for Christian minorities. They were not able to establish legal religious entities as the state did not allow religion to grow independent from the state.

As a result of its nationalist and secularist outlook, the Turkish state did not fulfill its obligations stemming from the Treaty of Lausanne, and thus Turkey violated the rights of the Turkish Christian minority for most of its modern history. Among other issues, four major problems stood out. First, the state took over the properties of the Christian minority through small legal technicalities and created obstacles to returning the properties of non-Muslim community foundations to their original owners. Further, the state did not allow non-Muslims to acquire new properties or dispose of their existing real estate. Second, the Christian minority faced difficulties in opening their own schools to train clergy. They had difficulties in propagating religion in their own languages and even sometimes in Turkish. Third, the state did not allow the Christian minority to open new places of worship. In addition to social obstacles that Christians faced, the state created political and bureaucratic obstacles to prevent the opening of churches. Finally, the state does not recognize religious associations legally.

The Turkish government passed new reforms in the first decade of the 2000s and relaxed some of the restrictions on the Christian minority. Christian community foundations can acquire new properties and dispose of their existing ones. They are permitted to cooperate with international organizations in their religious and social activities. The state agreed to give back the properties that had been taken over in the past. For the cases in which those properties were transferred to third parties, the state agreed to pay the value of those properties to the community foundations. The Turkish state passed new regulations that made possible the use of non-Turkish mother tongues for religious education, broadcasting, and media. New regulations made the opening of places of worship easier. Despite these improvements, the state did not pass laws or regulations to make the training of clergy easier or to allow religious groups act with a legal personality.

In France, secularism gained most of its shape in the Third Republic, when republicans set the rules of state–religion relations thanks to their consecutive election victories. In addition to being a constitutional principle, secularism became a significant part of the French national identity. The 1905 law on secularism allowed religious liberties and prevented religious groups from taking control of the state. The French policies toward the Muslim minority followed the structure set by the principle of secularism. The state took a neutral position toward Muslims and protected their religious freedoms. In line with the principle of secularism, French Muslims entertained their religious liberties and did not get any support from the state. However, this started to change in the first decade of the 2000s.

The French state shifted its policies of neutrality toward increasing state control over Muslims. One can detect this qualitative shift in the issues that defined the state's relationship with Muslims in the 2000s. In opposition to its supposed neutrality, the state led the establishment of a Muslim federation that would coordinate major Muslim associations in France and their relationship with the state. Due to the quotas given to the Interior Ministry in the selection of administrators for the federation, the French state has a direct control over the association. Similarly, the state encouraged and supported the building of large mosques in an effort to monitor the activities of Muslims easier. Instead of having numerous small mosques that operate unofficially, the state wanted to support the formation of large mosques that operate transparently. Despite the state's strong support for a Muslim federation and larger mosques, it has been reluctant to establish contract relationships with Muslim schools. Other than a few schools, the state did not issue permits for Muslim schools. This policy is in line with the trend of state control over Muslims. Because of the lack of state-contracted Muslims schools, Muslims would send their children to either Catholic or public schools. The state preferred this path to facilitate Muslim integration into the French society.

In the issue of the public manifestation of religious symbols, the state's regulatory policies toward Muslims have been more visible. Although the state continued to allow Muslim girls to wear headscarves in schools after the issue first gained prominance in French public debates in 1989, it changed its direction in the early 2000s. In 2004, the French parliament passed laws that changed the state neutrality clause in French secularism. The state banned the wearing of headscarves in public schools. The state enlarged the ban on religious symbols in 2010 and forbade the wearing of the burqa on the streets.

In the second step of my argument, I discussed the extent to which the international context structures the changes in state policies toward religious minorities given historical state–religion patterns. Turkey's process of negotiation for membership of the EU constituted the international context for reform toward the Christian minority, while increasing concerns about political violence and Islamization in Europe helped frame policy changes toward France's Muslim minority. The European Commission's progress reports, resolutions passed in the European parliament, and official statements of European leaders on Christians influenced domestic policy discourses in Turkey as domestic actors used them to advance their positions. The rise of Islamophobia globally shifted the terms of the public debate about Muslims in France. In the new climate, Muslims have been portrayed as a threat to the French ideals of republicanism and secularism.

Turkey's membership negotiations with the EU provided an opportunity for those actors who sought to improve the status of Christian minorities. This international push for reform structured domestic politics in a way that empowered the reformists vis-à-vis their opponents in strategic and normative ways. By putting intensive, persistent, and systematic pressure for the policy change, the EU helped the reformers defend their policy agendas. Further, the wider democratization agenda of the EU boosted the normative value attached to the reports in the public debates. Because of Turkey's EU reform packages, Christian community foundations gained the rights to acquire and dispose of properties, improvements in their freedom to use their own languages, and ameliorations in their ability to open places of worship.

The EU was not the only international actor that promoted religious freedoms for Christian minorities in Turkey. The UN, the USA, and international nongovernmental organizations also pushed for further reforms; however, their impact remained limited because their pressure did not have sanctions attached to it. Strategic priorities and the alliance between Turkey and the USA was another reason for the limited influence of US pressure for reform.

In France, the international context operated on a different plane. Islamophobia peaked globally after the September 11 terrorist attacks in 2001. The discourse against Muslims facilitated a monolithic understanding of Muslims defined by inflexibility, fundamentalism, and violence. In France, the environment that formed in the wake of the September 11 attacks built on existing prejudices against Muslims that stemmed from the legacies of French colonization in North Africa, the socioeconomic marginalization of Muslim immigrants of North African descent, and the aftershocks of the Algerian Civil War in the 1990s. Increasing anti-Muslim sentiments created a suitable environment for the passing of laws that increased state surveillance of Muslims' institutions and personal lives. Those who defended laws to restrict Muslims' liberties used the global and national rise of Islamophobia as an opportunity to broaden their support base. It was in this atmosphere that French legislators passed the headscarf ban, which aimed to limit Muslim visibility in public schools, and the burqa ban, which aimed to restrict ultra-conservative Muslim dress on the streets.

In the final step of my argument, I showed how international pressure and domestic groups align to implement changes in state policies towards religious minorities. The Turkish Islamists, who were dominated by the secular elite, used Turkey's EU membership bid as an opportunity to constrain bureaucratic authoritarian institutions, including the military, and liberalized the Turkish political system. They built a broad social coalition with liberals, social democrats, and minorities in passing democratic reforms, using Europeanization as an instrument. This coalition, which included the Christians, facilitated the passing of reforms in favor of religious minorities. In France, the radical right and strict secularists utilized rising Islamophobia in Europe to restrict the public manifestation of Islamic religious symbols. By using anti-Islamic discourse, these domestic actors portrayed Islamic activism and Islamic religious symbols as threats to French secularism and republicanism, and they built a broad coalition, which included conservatives and socialists, to ban Muslim religious symbols in the public sphere.

In Turkey, starting from the mid-1990s, the military constrained Islamist actors and limited their ability to function in the domestic political scene. The AKP utilized the EU pressure to help the party liberalize the political institutions to allow more ground for Islamists. Although Turkey had a long-lasting relationship with the EU, its impact created concrete policy change only after the AKP, a leading domestic actor with a strong popular base, used its transforming capacity to materialize gains vis-à-vis the secular elite. In doing so, the party allied with other actors who opposed bureaucratic authoritarianism. The new coalition of social and political actors instituted several liberal reforms, including rights for religious minorities, with the excuse of bringing Turkey closer to the EU.

By justifying certain policies over others, the EU empowered the otherwise weaker actors and increase the possibility of passing the reforms. Further, the norm entrepreneurs used both the legitimizing power of European values and the material resources that the EU provided to spread liberal ideas in an effort to prepare a conducive environment for reform. Although Christian minorities did not have enough political weight to change the status quo, the impact of the EU and the material interests of the AKP, which were tightly linked to EU reforms, created an opportunity for them to gain more freedoms. Christian leaders exploited EU conditionality and lobbied for reforms in domestic and international politics to create a strong external push for the passing of religious freedoms. Secularist and nationalist opposition to the new laws expanding Christian religious freedoms, based on an evaluation of the status of Christian minorities from a security and order perspective, were not able to resist the changes in the face of the new broad-based social coalition for reform.

In France, the external condition of the rise of Islamophobia structured domestic actor strategies to produce the passing of laws that limited the freedoms of the Muslim minority. The proponents of the headscarf ban used Islamophobia to frame their policy agendas as a remedy to the rising "Islamist threat" to the French values of republicanism and secularism. Creating a binary distinction between secularism and fundamentalism in an environment of anti-Muslim sentiments in which the nuances of the debate could easily be lost, the proponents of the ban expanded their social base for their policy agendas. Although there was a considerable opposition to the ban from Muslim, Christian, and Jewish organizations, and from liberals, these groups were not successful in challenging the proponents of the ban within an increasingly Islamophobic public. They failed to develop a rights-based discourse that would balance the newly emerging policies in an atmosphere in which Muslim activism was highly stigmatized. The new coalitional dynamics led to the banning of headscarves in public schools in 2004.

The emergence of other French policies toward Muslims can also be attributed to domestic actors' engagement with rising Islamophobia. The state, with the motivation of scrutinizing Muslim organizations in a more transparent way, led the establishment of a Muslim federation that could develop a corporatist relationship with the state. It encouraged the building of larger mosques in which state surveillance would be easier. The state showed reluctance to fund Muslim schools, which it considered to be an obstacle for the integration of Muslims into broader French society. Concerns about the rise of Islam in Europe played a significant role in the formation of state policies toward Muslims in these areas. However, it was the actors' engagement with these attitudes that created the final policies.

After the 2010s, reform process stalled in Turkey and the restrictions toward Muslims increased in France. In Turkey, after the Arab uprisings, EU pressure no longer structured Turkish politics in favor of Christian minorities and the Turkish Islamists took an authoritarian path. In France, the impact of Islamophobia deepened with the rise of religious extremism globally, and far-right politicians continued to exploit the new environment to expand restrictive policies toward Muslims. In other issue areas, international context and domestic actors interacted in producing policies toward religious minorities. Turkey followed a similar policy toward its Jewish minority as that toward Christians, although Israel's actions in the Middle East and the rise of anti-Semitic discourses were additional factors in the shaping of Turkish policies toward Jews. French policies toward sects were influenced by the interaction of global developments that undermined the legitimacy of the sects and the activism of the anti-sect actors. The interaction of international context and domestic actors also structured state policies toward minorities in other contexts such as Bulgaria, the USA, Mexico, Jordan, and Egypt.

## HISTORICAL INSTITUTIONS, INTERNATIONAL CONTEXT, AND DOMESTIC POLITICS

What broader conclusions does this study permit about the interaction of international and domestic factors in the formation of state policies toward religions minorities? The general focus of the book has been specifying the ways through which international contexts change state policies toward religious minorities. Based on the analysis developed throughout the book, one can make conclusions around three main questions about the relationship between international context, domestic politics, and state–religion relations.

The first question is on the role of historical institutions. Is change in state-religion regimes restricted by historical institutions? Historical institutions structure domestic change by either shifting power relations or privileging certain ideological positions over others. First, they structure the power relationship between various domestic groups, which in turn influence the institutional setting. Those groups who are favored by the founding principles of the state are privileged over others. Institutional structures, from legal regulations to bureaucracy, base their workings on the founding principles. In

Turkey, the secularist orientation of the military, the bureaucracy, and the higher judiciary was shaped by the historical trajectories. One-party rule until 1950 and military interventions in 1960, 1971, 1980, and 1997 designed the political system so as to keep the Kemalist/secularist orientation within the state apparatus. The bureaucracy's resistance to the reforms enhancing rights for Christian minorities reflects this secularist orientation. The strength of state institutions and the relative weakness of the politicians and the parliament had been structured by historical events. The situation in France is different from Turkey. Secularism constituted an important place in French political history; it is also an important national identifier in France; and it is diffused into France's state institutions. However, the emphasis given to the freedom of religion has been stronger in the French version of secularism than in Turkey. State institutions had emphasized "freedom" over protection of the state for several years. Although history in the French case also played an important role in structuring politics, it influenced domestic institutions through the employment of ideas.

Historically privileged ideas help domestic actors mobilize the people around a certain policy agenda. Domestic groups employ historically relevant ideas in instituting their policy agendas, a practice that allows them to reach out to larger populations. In Turkey, the opponents of the reforms enhancing Christian minority rights addressed the founding treaties of the Turkish Republic and the role of the minorities during the First World War to justify their opposition. The courts, universities, and bureaucrats in Turkey justified their discriminatory policies with reference to these historically shaped ideas. In France, the proponents of the headscarf ban employed the principles of secularism and republicanism to institute their policy agenda. French republican history privileged these two principles.

However, history's influence has its own limits. Contrary to many historical institutionalist arguments, history does not necessarily determine ongoing change, and actors do not need to wait until another critical juncture to change domestic institutions. Domestic historical change is still possible against the stream of history through incremental changes. Often, incremental change comes out of the renegotiations between various domestic actors as a reflection of changing power relationships. In Turkey, international pressure helped the Christian minorities to challenge historically shaped institutions, which had systematically discriminated against non-Muslim minorities. Empowered by the international pressure, they cooperated with those who challenged the authoritarian state to change domestic institutions. Although French historical institutions did not give strategic dominance to the proponents of the headscarf ban, its proponents capitalized on the global rise of Islamophobia to mobilize the masses so as to gain parliamentary support for the ban.

The second question concerns the influence of international context on domestic institutional change. To what extent do international institutions and discourses influence domestic change? International institutions and discourses influence domestic policy change in instrumental and normative ways. Instrumentally, by exerting international pressure on states, international institutions restructure the domestic power relationship. International pressure strengthens some groups over others, empowering pro-norm groups to create norm-friendly institutions or policies. Turkey's ongoing membership negotiations with the EU forced Turkey to change its policies toward Christian minorities. EU pressure empowered the tiny Christian minority. International discourses, in this case the rise of Islamophobia, helped the proponents of the headscarf ban in France shape the public debates around the binary distinction of secularism and fundamentalism, and expand their coalition in support of the ban.

Normatively, international context influences domestic politics by increasing the legitimacy of certain ideas over others. Ideas represented by international organizations diffuse into domestic structures through the activities of norm entrepreneurs. The EU, with the ideas that it claims to represent, has an enormous impact on European member and candidate countries through mobilizing the people around the ideas of human rights and democracy. Turkey's relationship with the EU helped the emergence of a movement supporting democratization in Turkey. Civil society organizations and intellectuals in Turkey organized numerous activities for the spread of liberal ideas. The EU supported many of these activities in the form of financial assistance and logistical support. In France, the global context of rising Islamophobia promoted normative judgments about Muslims and boosted stereotypes, helping the proponents of the ban gain more legitimacy for their policy agendas in the public debates.

However, the impact of the international context is contingent. The extent of its impact depends on the strength of historical institutions on a certain issue area, and the domestic configuration of power. On issues in which strong historical institutions are involved, the impact of international organizations is limited if they work against domestic institutions. This can be seen in the reforms that Turkey implemented under EU pressure. Although Turkey implemented several reform packages related to Christian minorities, the reforms did not expand to include the issues of the legal personality for religious organizations. The non-recognition of religious associations has been a defining characteristic of Turkish secularism, mainly to block the emergence of Islamic movements outside the purview of state control. Another important factor that determines the extent of the impact of international institutions is the nature of the relationship between a specific country and an international organization. If an international organization has significant sanctioning power, its impact on domestic institutional change increases. This is why the EU was able to create domestic institutional change in Turkey on the issue of

Christian minority rights, while other international organizations had a limited impact. Turkey was under the supervision of the EU due to its candidacy status. Turkey's membership of the EU was conditional on strict criteria, and Turkey, by signing accession partnership treaties, promised to fulfill these criteria. Similarly, the global rise of Islamophobia created restrictive policies toward Muslims in France while it did not necessarily do so in countries such as the United Kingdom, where a more liberal state–religion regime prevailed. Because secularism is a stronger element of national identity in France than it is in Britain, domestic actors were more easily able to relate anti-Muslim sentiments to their policy agendas than might have been the case elsewhere. The historical significance of secularism differentiated France from other European countries and led the state to implement more restrictive policies toward Muslims.

The final question examines the role of domestic groups in institutional change. To what extent do domestic actors control the direction and pace of policy change? Domestic actors' ability to change policies depends on the historical institutions and international context. The rules of the game in both Turkey and France were put in place by historical developments. Anti-reform groups in Turkey addressed historical events in mobilizing their supporters to block the passing of laws that granted Christian minorities religious rights. The proponents of the headscarf ban in France capitalized on the strength of secularist identity in France. International context influences the ability of domestic actors to create institutional change by supporting certain types of actors over others. Ideas promoted by international forces may also be used in mobilizing people around particular policy agendas. The success of Christian minorities and the emergence of a movement supporting democratization in Turkey cannot be explained without reference to the international context shaped by Turkey's EU relationship. Similarly, the success of the proponents of the headscarf ban in reaching out to a broad public to execute their policy preferences cannot be thought of as independent from the global rise of Islamophobia. In addition, the organizational capabilities of domestic actors matter in utilizing the resources (whether historical, international, or domestic) available to them. This is why the opponents of the headscarf ban in France were unable to develop a sound strategy in the face of pro-norm historical institutions, while the proponents of reforms for Christian minorities in Turkey succeeded in forming a strong coalition in support of their policy choices.

## POLITICAL CONTEXT AND THEORY DEVELOPMENT

Although this research is based on a systematic and in-depth comparison of Turkish and French cases, it provides generalizable conclusions and contributes to the theoretical debates specifically on relations between states and religious minorities, and more broadly on the interaction of international context and domestic politics. Synthesizing the insights of previous literature within the context of international and domestic interactions, I have attempted to explain certain changes in state policies toward religious minorities. This intellectual endeavor is significant for a number of reasons.

First, this study shows that the diffusion of international norms is closely linked to important material interests, but that they are not easily reducible to those interests (Fearon and Wendt 2002; Jupille et al. 2003; Weber 1948). At one extreme, scholars tend to see ideas as epiphenomenal to material interests (Schelling 1960; Goldstein et al. 1993; McNamara 1998); at the other, they see ideas as being the engine of political outcomes in defining actor identities and interests (Geertz 1973; Scott 1998). The framework that I used in the book contends that there is no necessary contradiction between the two (Adler 1997; Bleich 2003; Checkel 1997; Laitin 1986; Sewell 1992). The relationship between ideas, interests, and identities is highly complex and needs to be explored with reference to historical context and exogenous effects. As explored throughout the book, the complex interaction between ideas, interests, and institutional change requires scholars not to subscribe to narrow explanations but to be attentive to context.

Second, by developing a dynamic model that explored domestic actors' interaction with international and domestic structures, this study demonstrated that both actors and structural factors matter in explaining political outcomes. As opposed to structuralism, which posits that social forces determine social reality and individual behaviors, and an agency-centered approach, which posits that the individual has the full capacity to construct social reality, structure and agency are complementary forces: human behavior is influenced by social structures; however, humans can also change the structures within which they operate (Dessler 1989; Sewell 1992; Wendt 1987; Berger and Luckmann 1990; Bhaskar 1989, 1998; Bourdieu 1990; Giddens 1984). The interaction between structure and agency should be seen as a constitutive process which is determined by the impact of the two. The task of the theory is to specify the working conditions of each factor and the interactions between the two.

Finally, rather than relying on a general theory which is valid at all times in all places, I developed a middle-range theory that explores causal mechanisms and their scope conditions. Mechanisms are "recurrent processes linking specified initial conditions and a specific outcome" (Hedström and Swedberg 1998, 32–33). Explorations of causal mechanisms operate at an analytical level below that of a more general theory; and they increase the theory's credibility by offering more fine-grained explanations (Tilly 2001; Elster 1989a, 1989b; Jelen and Tamadonfar 2011). In theory development, I consider the "context" within which the social phenomena occur. "Context" should not be dismissed for the sake of parsimony, because "what is easily dismissed as 'context' may in fact be absolutely crucial to understanding important social processes" (Pierson 2004, 169). This is why causal mechanisms serve as a framework to integrate the "context" into theory development. Within this framework, I refined the ways that international institutions and discourses influence domestic policy change. I developed a theory by borrowing insights from competing theoretical traditions and specify the conditions under which certain mechanisms work while others do not. I demonstrate the impact of international context, historical institutions, and domestic power struggles in the process of norm diffusion. Theoretically, the middle ground I stake out will not satisfy some. Empirically, however, it best captures the complex reality of political change. In short, although I do not develop a general theory, this argument can be extended to similar contexts in different regions and issue areas.

# Bibliography

## INTERVIEWS

Alain Gresh, journalist, Paris, France, July 18, 2007.
Bernard Godard, officer, Ministry of Interior Affairs, Paris, France, July 25, 2007.
Catherine de Wenden, academic, Paris, France, July 24, 2007.
Dositheos Anagnostopulos, Press Advisor of Greek Orthodox Church, Istanbul, Turkey, June 4, 2014.
Elçin Macar, academic, Istanbul, Turkey, June 27, 2012.
Felice Suriano, religious leader, Istanbul, Turkey, June 15, 2010.
Guiseppe Giorgis, religious leader, Istanbul, Turkey, May 28, 2010.
Haydar Demiryürek, Secretary-General, French Council of the Muslim Religion, Paris, France, July 17, 2007.
Louis Pelatre, religious leader, Istanbul, Turkey, May 26, 2010.
Nilüfer Göle, academic, Paris, France, July 3, 2007.
Olivier Abel, academic, Paris, France, July 29, 2007.
Patrick Weil, academic, Paris, France, July 27, 2007.
Rinaldo Marmara, academic, Istanbul, Turkey, June 4, 2010.
Riva Kastoryano, academic, Paris, France, July 17, 2007.
Unidentified politician, a local AKP leader in Erzurum, Turkey, May 27, 2014.
Unidentified politician, a local AKP leader in Şanlıurfa, Turkey, June 30, 2012.
Zeki Basatemir, President, Istanbul Syriac Foundation, Istanbul, Turkey, June 22, 2012.

## PUBLICATIONS

Abbas, Tahir. 2004. "After 9/11: British South Asian Muslims, Islamophobia, Multiculturalism, and the State." *American Journal of Islamic Social Sciences* 21(3): 26–38.
Acherar, Leïla, and Caroline Fourest. 2004. "Voici venu le temps des féministes pro-voile." *ProChoix* 28: 62–73.
Adida, Claira, David Laitin, and Marie-Anne Valfort. 2011. "'One Muslim Is Enough!' Evidence from a Field Experiment in France." IZA Discussion Paper Series, IZA DP No. 6122.
Adler, Emanuel. 1997. "Seizing the Middle Ground: Constructivism in World Politics." *European Journal of International Relations* 3(3): 319–363.
Adrian, Melanie. 2006. "Laïcité Unveiled: A Case Study in Human Rights, Religion, and Culture in France." *Human Rights Review* 8(1): 102–114.

Aeschimann, Eric, and Emmanuel Davidenkoff. 2003. "Le Gouvernement ne hisse pas le voile." *Libération*, April 23.

Agence France-Presse. 2004. "French Headscarf Ban Flouts International Accords: Helsinki Rights Group." *Agence France-Presse*, February 9.

Agence France-Presse. 2004. "French Senate Votes Ban on Religious Insignia in State Schools." *Agence France-Presse*, March 3.

Agence France-Presse. 2012. "French Court Agrees Permit for Marseille Mega-mosque." *Hurriyet Daily News*, June 19.

Ahmad, Feroz. 1993. *The Making of Modern Turkey*. London: Routledge.

Aichoune, Farid. 1991. *Nés en banlieue*. Paris: Ramsey.

Akkan, Serhan. 2008. "El Yakan Ödev." *Tercüman*, May 8.

Aksoy, Ergun. 2001. "Ve Bir Ampül Yandı." *Radikal*, August 15.

Aktar, Ayhan. 1996. "Cumhuriyetin İlk Yıllarında Uygulanan Türkleştirme Politikaları." *Tarih ve Toplum* 156: 4–18.

Allen, Chris. 2006. "United Kingdom." In *Securitization and Religious Divide in Europe: Muslims in Western Europe after 9/11*, ed. Jocelyne Cesari. Brussels: European Commission, 49–99.

Allen, Chris. 2010. "Contemporary Islamophobia before 9/11: A Brief History." *Arches Quarterly* 4(7): 14–22.

Amadieu, Jean-François. 2004. *Enquête testing sur CV-Adia/ Paris I- Observatoire des discriminations*. Paris: Centre d'études et de recherches sur la gestion des organisations et des relations sociales.

Amara, Fadela, and Sylvia Zappi. 2003. *Ni Putes ni soumises*. Paris: Découverte.

Amnesty International. 2018. *France: 2017/2018*, available at www.amnesty.org/en/countries/europe-and-central-asia/france/report-france/ (last accessed on November 3, 2018).

Andonova, Liliana B. 2004. *Transnational Politics of the Environment: The European Union and Environmental Policy in Central and Eastern Europe*. Cambridge, MA: MIT Press.

Ant, Onur. 2018. "Turkey's Erdogan Joins in Vilification of Soros." *Bloomberg*, November 21, available at www.bloomberg.com/news/articles/2018–11-21/erdogan-joins-vilification-of-soros-with-gezi-protests-claim (last accessed on December 19, 2018).

Asalıoğlu, İbrahim. 2003. "Bartholomeos, Ruhban Okulu İçin Resmi Müracaatını Yaptı." *Zaman*, October 31.

Assemblée nationale. 1995. *Au nom de la Commission d'enquête sur les sectes*, December 22, available at www.assemblee-nationale.fr/rap-enq/r2468.asp (last accessed on November 7, 2018).

Assemblée nationale. 1999. *Les Sectes et l'argent*, June 10, available at www.assemblee-nationale.fr/dossiers/sectes/sommaire.asp (last accessed on November 7, 2018).

Assemblée nationale. 2006. *L'Influence des mouvements à caractère sectaire et aux conséquences de leurs pratiques sur la santé physique et mentale des mineurs*, December 12, available at www.assemblee-nationale.fr/12/pdf/rap-enq/r3507-rapport.pdf (last accessed on November 8, 2018).

Assemblée nationale. 2010. *Au nom de la Mission d'information sur la pratique du port du voile intégral sur le territoire national*, January 10, available at www.assemblee-nationale.fr/13/pdf/rap-info/i2262.pdf (last accessed on November 8, 2018).

Babès, Leïla. 2004. "La Ligue des amis de 'l'Islam' et la laïcité." *ProChoix* 28: 73–82.

Badinter, Elisabeth, Régis Debray, Alain Finkielkraut, Elisabeth de Fontenay, and Catherine Kintszler. 1989. "Profs, ne capitulons pas." *Nouvel Observateur*, November 2–8.

Baer, Marc D. 2013. "An Enemy Old and New: The Donme, Anti-Semitism, and Conspiracy Theories in the Ottoman Empire and the Turkish Republic." *Jewish Quarterly Review* 103(4): 523–555.

Baer, Marc. 2015. "The Double Bind of Race and Religion: The Conversion of the Dönme to Turkish Secular Nationalism." *Comparative Studies in Society and History* 46(4): 682–708.

Bali, Rıfat N. 1998. "Cumhuriyet Döneminde Azınlıklar Politikası." *Birikim* 115: 80–90.

Balibar, Etienne. 2004. "Dissonances within Laïcité." *Constellations* 11(3): 353–367.

Balibar, Etienne, S. Bouamama, F. Gaspard, C. Lévy, and P. Tevanian. 2003. "Oui à la laïcité, non aux lois d'exception." *Libération*, May 20.

Barkey, Karen, and George Gavrilis. 2016. "The Ottoman Millet System: Non-territorial Autonomy and Its Contemporary Legacy." *Ethnopolitics* 15(1): 24–42.

Barnell, Owen, and Alcyone Wemaere. 2017. "Laurent Wauquiez: The Hardliner Leading France's Les Républicains Farther Right." *France 24*, December 13, available at www.france24.com/en/20171211-laurent-wauquiez-center-margins (last accessed on October 31, 2018).

Başgil, Ali Fuat. 2003 [1942]. *Din ve Laiklik*. Istanbul: Yağmur Yayınları.

Baubérot, Jean. 2003. "Secularism and French Religious Liberty: A Sociological and Historical View." *BYU Law Review* 2003(2): 451–464.

Baubérot, Jean, and Micheline Milot. 2011. *Laïcité sans frontiers*. Paris: Seuil.

Baume, Maïne de la. 2011. "France: Court Cancels Permit for Grand Mosque of Marseille." *New York Times*, October 27.

Bayoumi, Moustafa. 2000. "Shadows and Light: Colonial Modernity and the *Grande Mosquée* of Paris." *Yale Journal of Criticism* 13(2): 267–292.

Bayrou, François. 1994. "Le Texte du ministre de l'éducation nationale." *Le Monde*, September 21.

BBC News. 2005. "French Muslims Face Job Discrimination." *BBC News*, November 2, available at http://news.bbc.co.uk/2/hi/europe/4399748.stm (last accessed on June 21, 2017).

Belge, Murat. 2008. "Gayrimüslim Vakıflar (1)." *Radikal*, February 22.

Bell, David S. 2004. "Parliamentary Democracy in France." *Parliamentary Affairs* 57(3): 533–549.

Berger, Peter. 1969. *The Sacred Canopy*. Garden City, NY: Doubleday.

Berger, Peter L., and Thomas Luckmann. 1990. *The Social Construction of Reality: A Treatise in the Sociology of Knowledge*. New York: Anchor Books.

Berkan, Ismet. 2004. "İki Kilise Öyküsü." *Radikal*, November 29.

Berkes, Niyazi. 1964. *The Development of Secularism in Turkey*. Montreal: McGill University Press.

Bernard, Philippe. 2003. "Ces musulmans de France hostiles au port du foulard a l'école." *Le Monde*, October 14.

Bernard, Philippe, and Sylvie Kauffmann. 2004. "Voile: Les États d'âme de quatre 'sages' de la commission Stasi." *Le Monde*, February 3.

Bertrand, Olivier. 2003. "Un foulard déclenche une grève dans un lycée de Lyon." *Libération*, March 13.

Bhaskar, Roy. 1989. *Reclaiming Reality: A Critical Introduction to Contemporary Philosophy*. London and New York: Verso.

Bhaskar, Roy. 1998. *The Possibility of Naturalism: A Philosophical Critique of the Contemporary Human Sciences*, 3rd ed. London and New York: Routledge.

Biondi, Lorenzo. 2011. "Interview with Louis Pelatre: This New Air that One Breathes in Turkey." *30 Days*, June, available at www.30giorni.it/articoli_id_77759_l3.htm (last accessed on June 23, 2017).

Birand, Mehmet Ali. 2005. "Azınlıklardan Neden Korkuyoruz?" *Hürriyet*, March 9.

Bishara, Marwan. 2003. "The Headscarf Debate: Lifting the Veil in France." *International Herald Tribune*, December 20.

Bishku, Michael B. 2017. "The Interactions and Experiences of Armenians and Jews in the Ottoman Empire and Republic of Turkey from the Young Turk Revolution of 1908 to the Present." *Nationalism and Ethnic Politics* 23(4): 431–452.

Bleich, Erik. 2003. *Race Politics in Britain and France: Ideas and Policymaking since the 1960s*. New York: Cambridge University Press.

Bleich, Erik. 2009. "Where do Muslims Stand on Ethno-racial Hierarchies in Britain and France? Evidence from Public Opinion Surveys, 1988–2008." *Patterns of Prejudice* 43(3–4): 379–400.

Bleich, Erik. 2011. "What Is Islamophobia, and How Much Is There? Theorizing and Measuring an Emerging Comparative Concept." *American Behavioral Scientist* 55: 1581–1600.

Bleich, Erik. 2012. "Defining and Researching Islamophobia." *Review of Middle East Studies* 46(2): 179–188.

Boli, John, and George M. Thomas. 1999. *Constructing World Culture: International Nongovernmental Organizations since 1875*. Stanford, CA: Stanford University Press.

Bourcier, Nicolas. 2002. "L'UE a connu une vague d'islamophobie en 2001." *Le Monde*, May 31.

Bourdieu, Pierre. 1990. *The Logic of Practice*. Cambridge: Polity Press

Bouzar, Dounia, and Saïda Kada. 2003. *L'Une voilée, l'autre pas*. Paris: A. Michel.

Bowen, John Richard. 2004. "Does French Islam Have Borders? Dilemmas of Domestication in a Global Religious Field." *American Anthropologist* 106(1): 43–55.

Bowen, John Richard. 2006. *Why the French Don't Like Headscarves: Islam, the State, and Public Space*. Princeton, NJ: Princeton University Press.

Bowen, John Richard. 2009a. *Can Islam Be French? Pluralism and Pragmatism in a Secularist State*. Princeton, NJ: Princeton University Press.

Bowen, John R. 2009b. "Recognising Islam in France after 9/11." *Journal of Ethnic and Migration Studies* 35(3): 439–452.

Brackett, D. W. 1996. *Holy Terror: Armageddon in Tokyo*. New York: Weatherhill.

Braude, Benjamin, and Bernard Lewis, eds. 1982. *Christians and Jews in the Ottoman Empire: The Functioning of a Plural Society*. Teaneck, NJ: Holmes & Meier Publications.

Bremmer, Ian. 2015. "These 5 Facts Explain the Worrying Rise of Europe's Far-Right." *Time*, October 15.

Brockett, Gavin D. 2011. *How Happy to Call Oneself a Turk: Provincial Newspapers and the Negotiation of a Muslim National Identity*. Austin, TX: University of Texas Press.

Bronner, Luc. 2002. "Les Professeurs d'un lycée de Seine-Saint-Denis en grève contre l'islamisme." *Le Monde*, March 25.

Brubaker, Rogers. 1992. *Citizenship and Nationhood in France and Germany*. Cambridge, MA: Harvard University Press.

Bruce, Steve. 1992. *Religion and Modernization: Sociologists and Historians Debate the Secularization Thesis*. Oxford: Oxford University Press.

Brunerie-Kaufmann, Joëlle, Harlem Désir, René Dumont, Gilles Parrault, and Alain Touraine. 1989. "Pour une laïcité ouverte." *Politis*, November 9–15.

Bulaç, Ali. 1999. "Niçin AB." *Zaman*, December 11.

Bunzl, Matti. 2007. *Anti-Semitism and Islamophobia: Hatreds Old and New in Europe*. Chicago: Prickly Paradigm Press.

Burleigh, Marc. 2004. "Muslims Hold Rallies in France Against Anti-Headscarf Law for Schools." *Agence France presse*, February 14.

Burley, Anne-Marie, and Walter Mattli. 1993. "Europe Before the Court: A Political Theory of Legal Integration." *International Organization* 41(1): 41–76.

Byrnes, Joseph F. 2005. *Catholic and French Forever: Religious and National Identity in Modern France*. University Park, PA: Pennsylvania State University Press.

Çabas, Murat. 2004. "Patrikhane ve Ruhban Okulu." *Yeni Mesaj*, December 2.

Çavdar, Gamze. 2006. "Islamist New Thinking in Turkey: A Model for Political Learning?" *Political Science Quarterly* 121(3): 477–497.

Cengiz, Orhan Kemal. 2004. "Temel Sorun: Tüzel Kişilik." *Radikal*, May 27.

Cesari, Jocelyne. 1994. *Être musulman en France: Associations, militants et mosquées*. Paris: Karthala.

Cesari, Jocelyne. 2004. *When Islam and Democracy Meet: Muslims in Europe and in the United States*. New York: Palgrave Macmillan.

Cesari, Jocelyne. 2011. "Islamophobia in the West: A Comparison between Europe and America." In *Islamophobia and the Challenges of Pluralism in the 21st Century*, ed. John Esposito and Ibrahim Kalin. Washington, DC: Georgetown University Press, 18–41.

Çetin, Fethiye. 2000. "Yerli Yabancılar." In *Ulusal, Ulusalüstü, ve Uluslararası Hukukta Azınlık Hakları*, ed. İ. Kaboğlu. Istanbul: İstanbul Barosu İnsan Hakları Merkezi, 70–81.

Chadwick, Kay. 1997. "Education in Secular France: (Re)defining Laïcité." *Modern and Contemporary France* 5(1): 47–59.

Chebel, Malek. 2002. *Le Sujet en Islam*. Paris: Seuil.

Chebel, Malek. 2005. *L'Islam et la raison: Le Combat des idées*. Paris: Perrin.

Chebel, Malek. 2007. *L'Esclavage en terre d'Islam: Un tabou bien gardé*. Paris: Fayard.

Checkel, Jeffrey T. 1997. *Ideas and International Political Change: Soviet/Russian Behavior and the End of the Cold War*. New Haven, CT: Yale University Press.

Checkel, Jeffrey T. 1999. "Norms, Institutions, and National Identity in Contemporary Europe." *International Studies Quarterly* 43(1): 83–114.

Chen, Michelle. 2015. "European Countries' Closing their Borders to Refugees is Collective Punishment." *The Nation*, November 18, available at www.thenation.com/article/european-countries-closing-their-borders-to-refugees-is-collective-punishment/ (last accessed on December 20, 2018).

Ciftci, Sabri. 2012. "Islamophobia and Threat Perceptions: Explaining Anti-Muslim Sentiment in the West." *Journal of Muslim Minority Affairs* 32(3): 293–309.

Çınar, Alev. 2005. *Modernity, Islam, and Secularism in Turkey: Bodies, Places, and Time*. Minneapolis: University of Minnesota Press.

Cizre, Ümit. 1999. *Muktedirlerin Siyaseti: Merkez Sağ-Ordu-İslamcılık*. Istanbul: İletişim Yayınları.

Cizre, Ümit, and Menderes Çınar. 2003. "Turkey 2002: Kemalism, Islamism, and Politics in the Light of the February 28 Process." *South Atlantic Quarterly* 102(2/3): 309–332.

Clavel, Geoffroy. 2016. "Sondage: Deux mois après, l'état d'urgence jugé justifié par 77% des français." *Huffington Post*, January 13, available at www.huffingtonpost.fr/2016/01/13/sondage-etat-durgence-justifie-77-francais-exclusif_n_8968278.html (last accessed on November 3, 2018).

Cobb, Roger W., and Charles D. Elder. 1983. *Participation in American Politics: The Dynamics of Agenda Building*, 2nd ed. Baltimore, MD: Johns Hopkins University Press.

Cole, Mike. 2009. "A Plethora of 'Suitable Enemies': British Racism at the Dawn of the Twenty-First Century." *Ethnic and Racial Studies* 32(9): 1671–1685.

Collier, Ruth Berins, and David Collier. 1991. *Shaping the Political Arena: Critical Junctures, the Labor Movement, and Regime Dynamics in Latin America*. Princeton, NJ: Princeton University Press.

Commission de reflexion sur l'application du principe de laïcité dans la république. 2003. *Rapport au Président de la République*. Paris: La Documentation française, available at http://lesrapports.ladocumentationfrancaise.fr/BRP/034000725/0000 .pdf (last accessed on October 10, 2007).

Conan, Eric. 2003. "Jack Lang: 'Interdire tout signe religieux'." *L'Express*, April 30–May 6.

Connolly, Kate, and Jack Shenker. 2009. "The Headscarf Martyr: Murder in German Court Sparks Egyptian Fury." *The Guardian*, July 7.

Coordination des associations et particuliers pour la liberté de conscience. 2001. *Report on Discrimination against Spiritual and Therapeutical Minorities in France*, October, available at www.coordiap.com/Gtemooo.htm (last accessed on December 4, 2018).

Cortell, Andrew P., and James W. Davis. 1993. "How Do International Institutions Matter? The Domestic Impact of International Rules and Norms." *International Studies Quarterly* 40(4): 451–478.

Cortell, Andrew P., and James W. Davis. 2000. "Understanding the Domestic Impact of International Norms: A Research Agenda." *International Studies Review* 2(1):65–87.

Cosgrove, Michael. 2011. "How Does France Count Its Muslim Population?" *Le Figaro*, April 7.

Cosgrove-Mather, Bootie. 2003. "Protests vs Muslim Headscarf Ban." *CBS News*, December 17, available at www.cbsnews.com/news/protests-vs-muslim-head-scarf-ban (last accessed on May 26, 2018).

Cowles, Maria Green, James A. Caporaso, and Thomas Risse-Kappen. 2001. *Transforming Europe: Europeanization and Domestic Change*. Ithaca, NY: Cornell University Press.

Dagi, Ihsan D. 2004. "Rethinking Human Rights, Democracy and the West: Post-Islamist Intellectuals in Turkey." *Critique: Critical Middle Eastern Studies* 13(2): 135–151.

Dağı, İhsan D. 2005. "Transformation of Islamic Political Identity in Turkey: Rethinking the West and Westernization." *Turkish Studies* 6(1): 21–37.

Dağı, İhsan. 2006. "The Justice and Development Party: Identity, Politics, and Human Rights Discourse in the Search for Security and Legitimacy." In *The Emergence of a New Turkey: Democracy and the AK Parti*, ed. Hakan Yavuz. Salt Lake City: University of Utah Press, 88–106.

Davison, Andrew. 1998. *Secularism and Revivalism in Turkey: A Hermeneutic Reconsideration*. New Haven, CT: Yale University Press.

Davison, Andrew. 2003. "Turkey, a Secular State? The Challenge of Description." *South Atlantic Quarterly* 102(2/3): 333–350.

Debré, Jean-Louis. 2003. *La Laïcité à l'école: Un principe républicain à réaffirmer, Rapport No 1275*. Paris: Assemblée nationale.

De Groot, Alexander H. 2003. "The Historical Development of the Capitulatory Regime in the Ottoman Middle East from the Fifteenth to the Nineteenth Centuries." *Oriente moderno* 22(3): 575–604.

Deltombe, Thomas. 2005. *L'Islam imaginaire: La Construction médiatique de l'islamophobie en France, 1975–2005*. Paris: Découverte.

Desch, Michael C. 1999. *Civilian Control of the Military: The Changing Security Environment*. Baltimore, MD: Johns Hopkins University Press.

Dessler, David. 1989. "What Is at Stake in Agent–Structure Debate?" *International Organization* 43(3): 441–473.

Doğan, Basri. 2012. "Freedom Award Recipient Bartholomew Praises Gülen's Peace Efforts." *Today's Zaman*, May 13.

Douglas, Mary. 1982. "The Effects of Modernization on Religious Change." *Daedalus* 111(1): 1–19.

Downing, Brian M. 1992. *The Military Revolution and Political Change: Origins of Democracy and Autocracy in Early Modern Europe*. Princeton, NJ: Princeton University Press.

Dressler, Markus. 2015. *Writing Religion: The Making of Turkish Alevi Islam*. New York: Oxford University Press.

Driessen, Michael D. 2014. *Religion and Democratization: Framing Religious and Political Identities in Muslim and Catholic Societies*. New York: Oxford University Press.

Dumont, Antoine. 2008. "Representing Voiceless Migrants: Moroccan Political Transnationalism and Moroccan Migrants' Organizations in France." *Ethnic and Racial Studies* 31(4): 792–811.

Dural, Baran. 2011. *Pratikten Teoriye Milliyetçi Hareket*. Istanbul: Bilge Karınca Yayınları.

Durham Jr., W. Cole. 1997. "Perspectives on Religious Liberty: A Comparative Framework." In *Religious Human Rights in Global Perspective: Legal Perspectives*, ed. Johan D. van der Vyver and John Witte Jr. The Hague: Martinus Nijhoff Publishers, 1–44.

Eder, Mine. 2003. "Implementing the Economic Criteria of EU Membership: How Difficult Is It for Turkey?" In *Turkey and the European Union: Domestic Politics, Economic Integration and International Dynamics*, ed. A. Çarkoğlu and B. Rubin. New York: Frank Cass, 219–244.

Ekşi, Oktay. 2005. "Bu İmtiyaz Talebidir … " *Hürriyet*, December 4.

Ekşi, Oktay. 2007. "Patriğin Şikáyetleri." *Hürriyet*, June 1.

Elster, Jon. 1989a. *The Cement of Society: A Study of Social Order*. New York: Cambridge University Press.

Elster, Jon. 1989b. *Solomonic Judgements: Studies in the Limitations of Rationality.* New York: Cambridge University Press.

Ensarioğlu, Yılmaz. 2002. "Gayrimüslim Vakıfları … " *Zaman,* May 28.

Erdem, Gazi. 2008. "Religious Services in Turkey: From the Office of Şeyhülislam to Diyanet." *Muslim World* 98(2): 199–215.

Erdoğan, Mustafa. 2005. "1982 Anayasasında Din Özgürlüğü." In *Türkiye'de Din ve Vicdan Hürriyeti: Çeşitlilik, Çoğulculuk, Barış,* ed. M. Yılmaz. Ankara: Liberal Düşünce Topluluğu, 23–25.

Ergin, Sedat. 2004. "Milli Güvenlik Siyaset Belgesi Değiştiriliyor." *Hürriyet,* November 24.

Erlanger, Steven. 2010. "Parliament Moves France Closer to a Ban on Facial Veils." *New York Times,* July 14.

Erlanger, Steven. 2011. "France Enforces Ban on Full-Face Veils in Public." *New York Times,* April 12.

Erol, Su. 2015. "The Syriacs of Turkey: A Religious Community on the Path of Recognition." *Archives de sciences sociales des religions* 60(171): 59–80.

Ertman, Thomas. 1997. *Birth of the Leviathan: Building States and Regimes in Medieval and Early Modern Europe.* New York: Cambridge University Press.

Esposito, John. 2011. "Introduction." In *Islamophobia: The Challenge of Pluralism in the 21st Century,* ed. John Esposito and Ibrahim Kalin. New York: Oxford University Press, 9–17.

EUMC. 2002. *Summary Report on Islamophobia in the EU after 11 September 2001.* Vienna: European Union Monitoring Center on Racism and Xenophobia.

EUMC. 2006. *Muslims in the European Union: Discrimination and Islamophobia.* Vienna: European Union Monitoring Centre on Racism and Xenophobia.

European Commission. 1998. "1998 Regular Report from the Commission on Turkey's Progress towards Accession," available at http://ec.europa.eu/enlargement/archives/pdf/key_documents/1998/turkey_en.pdf (last accessed on June 20, 2017).

European Commission. 1999. "1999 Regular Report from the Commission on Turkey's Progress towards Accession," October 13, available at http://ec.europa.eu/enlargement/archives/pdf/key_documents/1999/turkey_en.pdf (last accessed on June 20, 2017).

European Commission. 2000. "2000 Regular Report from the Commission on Turkey's Progress towards Accession," November 8, available at http://ec.europa.eu/enlargement/archives/pdf/key_documents/2000/tu_en.pdf (last accessed on June 20, 2017).

European Commission. 2001. "2001 Regular Report from the Commission on Turkey's Progress towards Accession," November 13, available at http://ec.europa.eu/enlargement/archives/pdf/key_documents/2001/tu_en.pdf (last accessed on June 20, 2017).

European Commission. 2002. "2002 Regular Report from the Commission on Turkey's Progress towards Accession," October 9, available at http://ec.europa.eu/enlargement/archives/pdf/key_documents/2002/tu_en.pdf (last accessed on June 20, 2017).

European Commission. 2003. "2003 Regular Report from the Commission on Turkey's Progress towards Accession," available at http://ec.europa.eu/enlargement/archives/pdf/key_documents/2003/rr_tk_final_en.pdf (last accessed on June 20, 2017).

European Commission. 2004. "2004 Regular Report from the Commission on Turkey's Progress towards Accession," October 6, available at http://ec.europa.eu/

enlargement/archives/pdf/key_documents/2004/rr_tr_2004_en.pdf (last accessed on June 20, 2017).

European Commission. 2005. "2005 Regular Report from the Commission on Turkey's Progress towards Accession," November 9, available at http://ec.europa.eu/enlargement/archives/pdf/key_documents/2005/package/sec_1426_final_progress_report_tr_en.pdf (last accessed on June 20, 2017).

European Commission. 2006. "Turkey 2006 Progress Report," November 8, available at http://ec.europa.eu/enlargement/pdf/key_documents/2006/nov/tr_sec_1390_en.pdf (last accessed on June 20, 2017).

European Commission. 2007. "Turkey 2007 Progress Report," November 6, available at http://ec.europa.eu/enlargement/pdf/key_documents/2007/nov/turkey_progress_reports_en.pdf (last accessed on June 20, 2017).

European Commission. 2008. "Turkey 2008 Progress Report," November 5, available at http://eur-lex.europa.eu/legal-content/EN/TXT/PDF/?uri=CELEX:52008SC2699&from=EN (last accessed on June 20, 2017).

European Commission. 2009. "Turkey 2009 Progress Report," October 14, available at http://eur-lex.europa.eu/legal-content/EN/TXT/PDF/?uri=CELEX:52009SC1334&from=EN (last accessed on June 20, 2017).

European Commission. 2010. "Turkey 2010 Progress Report," November 9, available at http://eur-lex.europa.eu/legal-content/EN/TXT/PDF/?uri=CELEX:52010SC1327&rid=3 (last accessed on June 20, 2017).

European Commission. 2011. "Turkey 2011 Progress Report," October 12, available at http://ec.europa.eu/enlargement/pdf/key_documents/2011/package/tr_rapport_2011_en.pdf (last accessed on June 20, 2017).

Fallaci, Oriana. 2002. *La Rage et l'orgueil*. Rome: Plon.

Favell, Adrian. 1998. *Philosophies of Integration: Immigration and the Idea of Citizenship in France and Britain*. New York: St. Martin's Press.

Fearon, James, and Alexander Wendt. 2002. "Rationalism vs Constructivism: A Skeptical View." In *Handbook of International Relations*, ed. W. Calsneas, T. Risse and B. A. Simmons. Thousand Oaks, CA: Sage Publications, 52–72.

Fekete, Liz. 2004. "Anti-Muslim Racism and the European Security State." *Race and Class* 46(1): 3–29.

Fekete, Liz. 2006. "Enlightened Fundamentalism? Immigration, Feminism and the Right." *Race and Class* 48(2): 1–22.

Fekete, Liz. 2010. "The New McCarthyism in Europe." *Arches Quarterly* 4(7): 64–68.

Fenton, Siobhan. 2016. "Bulgaria Imposes Burqa Ban and Will Cut Benefits of Women Who Defy It." *Independent*, October 1.

Fernando, Mayanthi. 2005. "The Republic's 'Second Religion': Recognizing Islam in France." *Middle East Report* 235: 12–17.

Ferry, Luc. 2003. "L'Équipe éducative a fait son devoir." *Le Figaro*, October 13.

Fetzer, Joel S., and J. Christopher Soper. 2003. "The Roots of Public Attitudes toward State Accommodation of European Muslims' Religious Practices Before and After September 11." *Journal for the Scientific Study of Religion* 42(2): 247–258.

Fetzer, Joel S., and J. Christopher Soper. 2005. *Muslims and the State in Britain, France, and Germany*. New York: Cambridge University Press.

Field, Clive D. 2007. "Islamophobia in Contemporary Britain: The Evidence of the Opinion Polls, 1988–2006." *Islam and Christian–Muslim Relations* 18(4): 447–477.

Finke, Roger, and Rodney Stark. 1992. *The Churching of America, 1776–1990: Winners and Losers in Our Religious Economy*. New Brunswick, NJ: Rutgers University Press.

Finkel, Caroline. 2005. *Osman's Dream: The History of the Ottoman Empire*. Cambridge, MA: Basic Books.

Finnemore, Martha, and Kathryn Sikkink. 1998. "International Norm Dynamics and Political Change." *International Organization* 52(4): 887–917.

Florini, Ann. 1996. "The Evolution of International Norms." *International Studies Quarterly* 40(3): 363–389.

Fourest, Caroline. 2003. "'Le Monde' à l'envers: À propos des convictions anti-laïques diffusées par H. Tincq et X. Ternisien." *ProChoix* (26–27): 37–61.

Fourest, Caroline. 2004. *Frère Tariq: Discours, stratégie et méthode de Tariq Ramadan*. Paris: B. Grasset.

Fourest, Caroline. 2005. *La Tentation obscurantiste*. Paris: Grasset.

Fourest, Caroline. 2007. *Brother Tariq: The Doublespeak of Tariq Ramadan*. New York: Encounter Books.

Fourest, Caroline, and Fiammetta Venner. 2003. "Les Enjeux cachés du voile à l'école." *ProChoix* (25): 19–31.

Fox, Jonathan. 2008. *A World Survey of Religion and the State*. New York: Cambridge University Press.

Fox, Jonathan, and Shmuel Sandler, eds. 2004. *Bringing Religion into International Relations*. New York: Palgrave MacMillan.

France 24. 2013. "France's First Private Muslim School Tops Ranks." *France 24*, March 29, available at www.france24.com/en/20130329-france-first-private-muslim-school-tops-ranks-averroes (last accessed on April 4, 2019).

Frank, David John, and John W. Meyer. 2002. "The Profusion of Individual Roles and Identities in the Postwar Period." *Sociological Theory* 20(1): 86–105.

Fraser, Christian. 2010. "Marseille's Muslims Eye Long-Awaited Mosque." *BBC News*, July 6, available at www.bbc.co.uk/news/10508069 (last accessed on June 20, 2017).

Fredette, Jennifer. 2014. *Constructing Muslims in France: Discourse, Public Identity, and the Politics of Citizenship*. Philadelphia: Temple University Press.

Freedman, Jane. 2004. "Secularism as a Barrier to Integration? The French Dilemma." *International Migration* 42(3): 5–27.

Frieden, Jeffry A., and Ronald Rogowski. 1996. "The Impact of the International Economy on National Policies: An Analytical Overview." In *Internationalization and Domestic Politics*, ed. R. O. Keohane and H. V. Milner. Cambridge, UK, and New York: Cambridge University Press, 25–47.

Gabizon, Cécilia, and Dalil Kenz. 2004. "Quelque 20 000 musulmans favorables au port du voile à l'école publique ont défilé à Paris et en province." *Le Figaro*, January 19.

Gaspard, Françoise, and Farhad Khosrokhavar. 1995. *Le Foulard et la République*. Paris: Découverte.

Gattegno, Hervé, and Revault d'Allonnes, David. 2018. "Islam de France: Ce que veut faire Macron." *Journal du dimanche*, February 11, available at www.lejdd.fr/politique/islam-de-france-ce-que-veut-faire-macron-3571067 (last accessed on November 4, 2018).

Gaulmin, Isabelle de, and Bernard Gorce. 2003. "L'Intégration a l'épreuve du voile." *La Croix*, November 13.

Gaziel, Haim H., and David Taub. 1992. "Teachers Unions and Educational Reform – A Comparative Perspective: The Cases of France and Israel." *Educational Policy* 6(1): 72–86.

Gedikli, Yusuf. 2002. "Heybeliada Ruhban Okulu Açılmalı mı?" *Ufuk Ötesi*, August 23–29.

Geertz, Clifford. 1973. *The Interpretation of Cultures: Selected Essays*. New York: Basic Books.

Geisser, Vincent. 2003. *La Nouvelle Islamophobie*. Paris: Découverte.

George, Alexander L., and Andrew Bennett. 2005. *Case Studies and Theory Development in the Social Sciences*. Cambridge, MA: MIT Press.

Giddens, Anthony. 1984. *The Constitution of Society: Outline of the Theory of Structuration*. Cambridge: Polity Press.

Gill, Anthony James. 2008. *The Political Origins of Religious Liberty*. New York: Cambridge University Press.

Gill, Anthony, and Arang Keshavarzian. 1999. "State Building and Religious Resources: An Institutional Theory of Church–State Relations in Iran and Mexico." *Politics and Society* 27(3): 431–465.

Giraud, Veronique. 2004. "Cover Up: Alma and Lila Levy." *Index on Censorship* 33(4): 117–125.

Githens-Mazer, Jonathan, and Robert Lambert. 2010. *Islamophobia and Anti-Muslim Hate Crime: A London Case Study*. Exeter: University of Exeter European Muslim Research Centre.

Gladstone, Rick, and Satoshi Sugiyama. 2018. "Trump's Travel Ban: How It Works and Who Is Affected." *New York Times*, July 1.

Gobry, Pascal-Emmanuel. 2018. "Secular Is a French Word for Anti-Muslim." *Bloomberg*, February 23, available at www.bloomberg.com/opinion/articles/2018-02-23/france-s-emmanuel-macron-isn-t-fighting-ant-muslim-bias (last accessed on November 4, 2018).

Goertz, Gary. 1994. *Contexts of International Politics*. New York: Cambridge University Press.

Gökaçtı, M. Ali. 2004. *Nüfus Mübadelesi: Kayıp Bir Kuşağın Hikâyesi*. Istanbul: İletişim Yayınları.

Goldstein, Judith, and Robert O. Keohane. 1993. *Ideas and Foreign Policy: Beliefs, Institutions, and Political Change*. Ithaca, NY: Cornell University Press.

Göle, Nilüfer. 1997. "Secularism and Islamism in Turkey: The Making of Elites and Counter-Elites." *Middle East Journal* 51(1): 46–58.

Goltz, Gabriel. 2006. "The Non-Muslim Minorities and Reform in Turkey." In *Turkey Beyond Nationalism: Towards Post-Nationalist Identities*, ed. H.-L. Kieser. New York: I.B. Tauris, 175–182.

Gonod, Michel. 1989. "La Riposte: Pourquoi ce principal de collège s'oppose à l'offensive des religieux." *Paris Match*, November 9, 60–63.

Gottschalk, Peter, and Gabriel Greenberg. 2008. *Islamophobia: Making Muslims the Enemy*. Lanham, MD: Rowman & Littlefield.

Gourevitch, Peter Alexis. 1978. "The Second Image Reversed: International Sources of Domestic Politics." *International Organization* 32(4): 881–912.

Gözaydın, İştar. 2009. *Diyanet: Türkiye Cumhuriyeti'nde Dinin Tanzimi*. Istanbul: İletişim Yayınları.

Gresh, Alain. 2004. *L'Islam, la République et le monde*. Paris: Fayard.

Grim, Brian J., and Roger Finke. 2010. *The Price of Freedom Denied: Religious Persecution and Conflict in the Twenty-First Century.* New York: Cambridge University Press.

Gros, Marie-Joâlle. 2003. "Statu quo au lycée d'Aubervilliers." *Libération,* September 30.

Guerlac, Othon. 1908. "The Separation of Church and State in France." *Political Science Quarterly* 23(2): 259–296.

Gündem. 2008. "AKP'nin Ruhban Okulu Aşkı." *Ortadoğu,* January 27.

Güngör, Dilek. 2004. "Ruhban için kavga." *Radikal,* June 20.

Gunn, T. Jeremy. 2004. "Religious Freedom and Laïcité: A Comparison of the United States and France." *BYU Law Review* 2004(2): 419–506.

Gurowitz, Amy. 1999. "Mobilizing International Norms: Domestic Actors, Immigrants, and the Japanese State." *World Politics* 51(3): 413–445.

Güven, Dilek. 2006. *Cumhuriyet Dönemi Azınlık Politikaları ve Stratejileri Bağlamında 6–7 Eylül Olayları.* Istanbul: İletişim Yayınları.

Güzelce, Bedia Ceylan. 2008. "Barışçıl Liderler'e Patrik Duası." *Sabah,* January 26.

Hainsworth, Paul. 2004. "The Extreme Right in France: The Rise and Rise of Jean-Marie Le Pen's National Front." *Representation* 40(2): 101–114.

Hale, Dana S. 2008. *Races on Display: French Representations of Colonized People, 1886–1940.* Bloomington, IN: Indiana University Press.

Hall, Peter. 2003. "Aligning Ontology and Methodology in Comparative Politics." In *Comparative Historical Analysis in the Social Sciences,* ed. J. Mahoney and D. Rueschemeyer. New York: Cambridge University Press, 373–406.

Hall, Peter A., and Rosemary Taylor. 1996. "Political Science and Three New Institutionalisms." *Political Studies* 44(5): 936–957.

Hanioğlu, M. Şükrü. 1995. *Young Turks in Opposition.* New York: Oxford University Press.

Hanioğlu, Şükrü. 2008. *A Brief History of the Late Ottoman Empire.* Princeton, NJ: Princeton University Press.

Hansen, Randall. 2003. "Migration to Europe since 1945: Its History and Its Lessons." *Political Quarterly* 74(1): 25–38.

Haut Conseil à l'intégration. 2000. *L'Islam dans la République.* Paris: La Documentation française.

Hedström, Peter, and Richard Swedberg. 1998. *Social Mechanisms: An Analytical Approach to Social Theory.* New York: Cambridge University Press.

Heider, Jennifer. 2012. "Unveiling the Truth Behind the French Burqa Ban: The Unwarranted Restriction of the Right to Freedom of Religion and the European Court of Human Rights." *Indiana International and Comparative Law Review* 22: 95–135.

Heitmeyer, Wilhelm. 2005. "Gruppenbezogene Menschenfeindlichkeit. Die theoretische Konzeption und empirische Ergebnisse aus den Jahren 2002, 2003 und 2004." In *Deutsche Zustände,* Series 3, ed. Wilhem Heitmeyer. Frankfurt am Main: Suhrkamp, 13–34.

Henley, Jon. 2001. "France Arms Itself with Legal Weapon to Fight Sects." *The Guardian,* May 31.

Henley, Jon. 2004. "French MPs Vote for Veil Ban in State Schools." *The Guardian,* February 11.

Henley, Jon. 2017. "German Elections 2017: Angela Merkel Wins Fourth Term but AfD Makes Gains – as It Happened," *The Guardian,* September 24.

Herbst, Jeffrey Ira. 2000. *States and Power in Africa: Comparative Lessons in Authority and Control.* Princeton, NJ: Princeton University Press.

Hervieu-Léger, Danièle. 2001. "France's Obsession with the Sectarian Threat." *Nova Religio: The Journal of Alternative and Emergent Religions* 4(2): 249–257.

Higgins, Andrew. 2009. "Defending the Faith: Battle over a Christian Monastery Tests Turkey's Tolerance of Minorities." *Wall Street Journal,* March 7.

Hoffmann, Stanley. 1963. "Paradoxes of the French Political Community." In *In Search of France,* ed. S. Hoffmann, C. P. Kindleberger, L. Wylie, J. R. Pitts, J.-B. Duroselle and F. Goguel. Cambridge, MA: Harvard University Press, 1–117.

Holmes, Seth M., and Heide Castaneda. 2016. "Representing the European Refugee Crisis in Germany and Beyond: Deservingness and Difference, Life and Death." *American Ethnologist* 43(1): 12–24.

Hooghe, Liesbet, and Gary Marks. 2001. *Multi-level Governance and European Integration.* Lanham, MD: Rowman & Littlefield.

Huggler, Justin. 2016. "Germany's Far-Right AfD Party 'Has More Public Support than Ever'." *The Telegraph,* May 5.

Human Rights Watch. 2002. *World Report 2002: Events of 2001.* New York: Human Rights Watch, available at www.hrw.org/legacy/wr2k2/ (last accessed on December 12, 2018).

Human Rights Watch. 2004. "France: Headscarf Ban Violates Religious Freedom," February 27, available at http://hrw.org/english/docs/2004/02/26/france7666_txt .htm (last accessed on October 11, 2007).

Human Rights Watch. 2006. *World Report 2006: Events of 2005.* New York: Human Rights Watch, available at www.hrw.org/legacy/wr2k6/ (last accessed on December 12, 2018).

Hunt, Sophie. 2004a. "Debré: Je préfère le mot visible à ostensible." *Le Figaro,* January 9.

Hunt, Sophie. 2004b. "Jean-Pierre Raffarin veut un débat sur le voile Islamique." *Le Figaro,* April 30.

Hurd, Elizabeth Shakman. 2009. *The Politics of Secularism in International Relations.* Princeton, NJ: Princeton University Press.

İçduygu, Ahmet, and B. Ali Soner. 2006. "Turkish Minority Rights Regime: Between Difference and Equality." *Middle Eastern Studies* 42(3): 447–468.

Idriss, Mohammad Mazher. 2005. "Laïcité and the Banning of the 'Hijab' in France." *Legal Studies* 25(2): 260–295.

Ilgıt, Antuan. 2017. *Muslim and Catholic Perspectives on Disability in the Contemporary Context of Turkey: A Proposal for Muslim–Christian Dialogue.* PhD dissertation, Boston College, Boston, MA.

İnan, Mert. 2016. "Örgüt Modeli Cizvit Sembolü İse Halley." *Milliyet,* September 7.

International Helsinki Federation for Human Rights. 1999. "Annual Report 1999: Turkey," available at www.ihf-hr.org/viewbinary/viewhtml.php?doc_id=3831 (last accessed on June 15, 2008).

İpekçi, Leyla. 2008. "Asıl Gayrimüslimler Çekti Bu İttihatçı Zihniyetten!" *Zaman,* May 6.

İpekçioğlu, Kaan. 2003. "Ruhban Okuluna Vize." *Yeni Şafak,* August 9.

Ivanova, Evgenia. 2017. "Islam, State and Society in Bulgaria: New Freedoms, Old Attitudes?" *Journal of Balkan and Near Eastern Studies* 19(1): 35–52.

Jazouli, Adil. 1992. *Les Années banlieues.* Paris: Seuil.

Jelen, Ted G. 2005. "Ambivalence and Attitudes toward Church–State Relations." In *Ambivalence, Politics, and Public Policy*, ed. Stephen C. Craig and Michael D. Martinez. London: Palgrave Macmillan, 127–144.

Jelen, Ted G. 2010. "Religion, State, and Society: Jefferson's Wall of Separation in Comparative Perspective." *Journal of Church and State* 52(2): 367–369.

Jelen, Ted G., and Mehran Tamadonfar. 2011. "Islam and Roman Catholicism as Transnational Political Phenomena: Notes for a Comparative Research Agenda." *Religions* 2(4): 536–548.

Jelen, Ted G., and Clyde Wilcox, eds. 2002. *Religion and Politics in Comparative Perspective: The One, the Few, and the Many*. New York: Cambridge University Press.

Jenkins, Philip. 1996. *Pedophiles and Priests: Anatomy of a Contemporary Crisis*. New York: Oxford University Press.

Jeon, Yongjoo, and Donald P. Haider-Markel. 2001. "Tracing Issue Definition and Policy Change: An Analysis of Disability Issue Images and Policy Response." *Policy Studies Journal* 29(2): 215–231.

Jones, Elizabeth. 2005. "Muslim Girls Unveil Their Fears." *BBC News*, March 28, available at http://news.bbc.co.uk/2/hi/programmes/this_world/4352171.stm (last accessed on June 24, 2017).

Joppke, Christian. 1999. *Immigration and the Nation-State: The United States, Germany, and Great Britain*. New York: Oxford University Press.

Joppke, Christian. 2007. "State Neutrality and Islamic Headscarf Laws in France and Germany." *Theory and Society* 36(4): 313–342.

Judge, Harry. 2004. "The Muslim Headscarf and French Schools." *American Journal of Education* 111(1): 1–24.

Jupille, Joseph, and James A. Caporaso. 1999. "Institutionalism and the European Union: Beyond International Relations and Comparative Politics." *Annual Review of Political Science* 2: 429–444.

Jupille, Joseph, James A. Caporaso, and Jeffrey T. Checkel. 2003. "Integrating Institutions: Rationalism, Constructivism, and the Study of European Union." *Comparative Political Studies* 36(1–2): 7–40.

Kalin, Ibrahim. 2011. "Islamophobia and the Limits of Multiculturalism." In *Islamophobia: The Challenge of Pluralism in the 21st Century*, ed. John Esposito and Ibrahim Kalin. New York: Oxford University Press, 50–61.

Kalkan, Ersin. 2002. "Azınlık Vakıflarında Kaybedilmiş Eşeği Bulmanın Sevinci." *Hürriyet*, August 10.

Kalyvas, Stathis N. 1996. *The Rise of Christian Democracy in Europe*. Ithaca, NY: Cornell University Press.

Kaplan, Jeffrey. 2006. "Islamophobia in America? September 11 and Islamophobic Hate Crime." *Terrorism and Political Violence* 18(1): 1–33.

Kara, İsmail. 2004. "Diyanet İşleri Başkanlığı: Devletle Müslümanlar Arasında Bir Kurum." In *Modern Türkiye'de Siyasi Düşünce 6: İslamcılık*, ed. Y. Aktay. Istanbul: İletişim Yayınları, 178–200.

Karakas, Cemal. 2007. *Turkey: Islam and Laicism between the Interests of State, Politics, and Society*. Frankfurt: Peace Research Institute Frankfurt.

Karakaşoğlu, Yasemin, Sigrid Luchtenberg, Frank Peter, and Riem Spielhaus. 2006. "Germany." In *Securitization and Religious Divide in Europe: Muslims in Western Europe after 9/11*, ed. Jocelyne Cesari. Brussels: European Commission, 143–194.

Karakaya, Suveyda, and A. Kadir Yildirim. 2013. "Islamist Moderation in Perspective: Comparative Analysis of the Moderation of Islamist and Western Communist Parties." *Democratization* 20(7): 1322–1349.

Karpat, Kemal. 2001. *The Politization of Islam: Reconstructing Identity, State, Faith and Community in the Late Ottoman State.* New York: Oxford University Press.

Kastoryano, Riva. 2002. *Negotiating Identities: States and Immigrants in France and Germany.* Princeton, NJ: Princeton University Press.

Katırcıoğlu, Erol. 2007. "The Economic Challenges of the Accession Process: The Matter in Question." In *Turkey and the European Union: Prospects for a Difficult Encounter,* ed. E. LaGro and K. E. Jørgensen. New York: Palgrave Macmillan, 111–125.

Katznelson, Ira. 1998. "The Doleful Dance of Politics and Policy: Can Historical Institutionalism Make a Difference?" *American Political Science Review* 92(1): 191–197.

Keck, Margaret E., and Kathryn Sikkink. 1998. *Activists Beyond Borders: Advocacy Networks in International Politics.* Ithaca, NY: Cornell University Press.

Kelley, Judith Green. 2004a. *Ethnic Politics in Europe: The Power of Norms and Incentives.* Princeton, NJ: Princeton University Press.

Kelley, Judith Green. 2004b. "International Actors on the Domestic Scene: Membership Conditionality and Socialization by International Institutions." *International Organization* 58(3): 425–457.

Kepel, Gilles. 1997. *Allah in the West: Islamic Movements in America and Europe.* Stanford, CA: Stanford University Press.

Keskin, Adnan, and Tarık Işık. 2004. "Kilise Açabilirsiniz Demek Dile Kolay." *Radikal,* May 26.

Keyman, E. Fuat. 2007. "Modernity, Secularism and Islam: The Case of Turkey." *Theory, Culture and Society* 24(2): 215–234.

Keyman, E. Fuat, and Senem Aydın Düzgit. 2007. "Europeanization, Democratization and Human Rights in Turkey." In *Turkey and the European Union: Prospects for a Difficult Encounter,* ed. E. LaGro and K. E. Jørgensen. New York: Palgrave Macmillan, 69–89.

Kılınç, Ramazan. 2014a. "International Pressure, Domestic Politics and Dynamics of Religious Freedom: Evidence from Turkey." *Comparative Politics* 46(2): 127–145.

Kılınç, Ramazan. 2014b. "Critical Junctures as Catalysts in Democratic Consolidation: The Case of Turkey." *Political Science Quarterly* 129(2): 293–318.

Killian, Caitlin. 2003. "The Other Side of the Veil: North African Women in France Respond to the Headscarf Affair." *Gender and Society* 17(4): 567–569.

Kingdon, John W. 1995. *Agendas, Alternatives, and Public Policies,* 2nd ed. New York: HarperCollins College.

Kintzler, Catherine, Pierre-André Taguieff, Bernard Tepe, and Michèle Tribalat. 2003. "Une loi pour interdire tout signe religieux à l'école: L'École publique doit être soustraite à la pression des groupes politico-religieux." *Libération,* May 6.

Kırbaki, Yorgo. 2010. "AİHM: Rum Yetimhanesi Patrikhane'ye Verilsin." *Hürriyet,* June 16.

Kirkpatrick, David D. 2013. "Coptic Christian Leader in Egypt Criticizes Government over Violence." *New York Times,* April 9.

Koenig, Matthias. 2007. "Europeanising the Governance of Religious Diversity: An Institutionalist Account of Muslim Struggles for Public Recognition." *Journal of Ethnic and Migration Studies* 33(6): 911–932.

Kotsovilis, Spyridon. 2006. "Between Fedora and Fez: Modern Turkeys's Troubled Road to Democratic Consolidation and the Pluralizing Role of Erdoğan's Pro-Islam government." In *Turkey and the European Union: Internal Dynamics and External Challenges*, ed. J. S. Joseph. New York: Palgrave Macmillan, 42–70.

Köylü, Hilal. 2004. "Ruhban Okuluna Formül Bulundu." *Radikal*, June 24.

Köylü, Hilal. 2005a. "AB: Din Notu Zayıf." *Radikal*, July 19.

Köylü, Hilal. 2005b. "AB: Uygulama Zayıf." *Radikal*, March 8.

Köylü, Hilal. 2005c. "Vakıflar'ın İnadı İnat." *Radikal*, March 7.

Köylü, Hilal. 2006. "Kretschmer: Bu, Kriz Değil." *Radikal*, June 12.

Kramer, Jane. 2004. "Taking the Veil: How France's Public Schools Became the Battleground in a Culture War." *New Yorker*, November 22, 58–71.

Kramer, Jane. 2006. "The Dutch Model: Multiculturalism and Muslim Immigrants." *New Yorker*, April 3, 60–67.

Krasner, Stephen. 1988. "Sovereignty: An Institutional Perspective." *Comparative Political Studies* 21(1): 66–94.

Krasner, Stephen D. 1999. *Sovereignty: Organized Hypocrisy*. Princeton, NJ: Princeton University Press.

Kratochwil, Friedrich V. 1989. *Rules, Norms, and Decisions: On the Conditions of Practical and Legal Reasoning in International Relations and Domestic Affairs*. New York: Cambridge University Press.

Kubicek, Paul, ed. 2003. *The European Union and Democratization*. London and New York: Routledge.

Küçükşahin, Şükrü. 2004. "Sessiz Azınlık Devrimi." *Hürriyet*, February 23.

Kuru, Ahmet T. 2007a. "Passive and Assertive Secularism: Historical Conditions, Ideological Struggles, and State Policies toward Religion." *World Politics* 59(4): 568–594.

Kuru, Ahmet T. 2007b. "Changing Perspectives on Islamism and Secularism in Turkey: The Gülen Movement and the AK Party." In *Muslim World in Transition: Contributions of the Gülen Movement*, ed. İhsan Yılmaz. London: Leeds Metropolitan University Press, 140–151.

Kuru, Ahmet T. 2008. "Secularism, State Policies, and Muslims in Europe: Analyzing French Exceptionalism." *Comparative Politics* 41(1): 1–19.

Kuru, Ahmet T. 2009. *Secularism and State Policies toward Religion: The United States, France, and Turkey*. New York: Cambridge University Press.

Kuru, Ahmet T. 2012. "The Rise and Fall of Military Tutelage in Turkey: Fears of Islamism, Kurdism, and Communism." *Insight Turkey* 14(2): 37–57.

Kuru, Ahmet T., and Alfred Stepan, eds. 2012. *Democracy, Islam and Secularism in Turkey*. New York: Columbia University Press.

Laborde, Cécile. 2008. *Critical Republicanism: The Hijab Controversy and Political Philosophy*. New York: Oxford University Press.

LaGro, Esra. 2007. "The Economics of the Accession Process: A Multidimensional and Policy-Oriented Approach for Turkey." In *Turkey and the European Union: Prospects for a Difficult Encounter*, ed. E. LaGro and K. E. Jørgensen. New York: Palgrave Macmillan, 90–110.

Lahouri, Besma, and Eric Conan. 2003. "Ce qu'il ne faut plus accepter: La Laïcité face à l'Islam." *L'Express*, September 18–24.

Laitin, David D. 1986. *Hegemony and Culture: Politics and Religious Change among the Yoruba*. Chicago: University of Chicago Press.

Larkin, Maurice. 1974. *Church and State after the Dreyfus Affair: The Separation Issue in France*. New York: Barnes & Noble.

Larkin, Maurice. 2003. "Religion, Anticlericalism, and Secularization." In *The Short Oxford History of France: Modern France*, ed. J. McMillan. New York: Oxford University Press, 203–227.

Laronche, Martine. 2004. "Le Conseil supérieur de l'éducation a adopté la circulaire sur le voile." *Le Monde*, May 19.

Laurence, Jonathan, and Justin Vaisse. 2006. *Integrating Islam: Political and Religious Challenges in Contemporary France*. Washington, DC: Brookings Institution Press.

Laurence, Jonathan. 2012. *The Emancipation of Europe's Muslims: The State's Role in Minority Integration*. Princeton, NJ: Princeton University Press.

Leane, Geoffrey W. G. 2011. "Rights of Ethnic Minorities in Liberal Democracies: Has France Gone Too Far in Banning Muslim Women from Wearing the Burka?" *Human Rights Quarterly* 33(4): 1032–1061.

Lee, Sherman A., Jeffrey A. Gibbons, John M. Thompson, and Hussam S. Timani. 2009. "The Islamophobia Scale: Instrument Development and Initial Validation." *International Journal for the Psychology of Religion* 19(2): 92–105.

Le Figaro. 2017. "Présidentielle: Qui sont les 11 candidats sur la ligne de départ." *Le Figaro*, March 18.

Legro, Jeffrey W. 1997. "Which Norms Matter? Revisiting the Failure of Internationalism." *International Organization* 51(1): 31–63.

Le Monde. 2003. "Foulard: Lila Lévy dément toute manipulation." *Le Monde*, 15 October.

Le Parisien. 2003. "Tariq Ramadan, cible des services secrets européens." *Le Parisien*, November 14.

Lévy, Alma, and Lila Lévy. 2004. *Des filles comme des autres: Au delà du foulard*. Paris: Découverte.

Lewis, Bernard. 1968. *The Emergence of Modern Turkey*. New York: Oxford University Press.

L'Express. 1994. "Foulard – Le Complot – Comment les islamistes nous infiltrent." *L'Express*, November 7.

Liederman, Lisa Molokotos. 2000. "Religious Diversity in Schools: The Muslim Headscarf Controversy and Beyond." *Social Compass* 47(3): 367–381.

Liguori, Mina. 2006. "Italy." In *Securitization and Religious Divide in Europe: Muslims in Western Europe after 9/11*, ed. Jocelyne Cesari. Brussels: European Commission, 301–323.

Linden, Ronald Haly, ed. 2002. *Norms and Nannies: The Impact of International Organizations on the Central and East European States*. Lanham, MD: Rowman & Littlefield.

Lipietz, Alain. 2003. "Le Débat sur le foulard … " *ProChoix* (26–27): 121–130.

Lister, Tim, Ray Sanchez, Mark Bixler, Sean O'Key, Michael Hogenmiller, and Mohammed Tawfeeq. 2018. "ISIS Goes Global: 143 Attacks in 29 Countries have Killed 2043." *CNN*, February 12, available at www.cnn.com/2015/12/17/world/mapping-isis-attacks-around-the-world/index.html (last accessed on October 29, 2018).

Lucas, Marieme Helie. 2011. "Understanding the French Ban on the Veil." *Economic and Political Weekly* 46(18): 25–27.

Lüle, Zeynel. 2007. "AİHM'nin Türban Kararları." *Hürriyet*, September 23.

Lyttle, Charles. 1933. "Deistic Piety in the Cults of the French Revolution." *Church History* 2(1): 22–40.

Macar, Elçin. 2003. *Cumhuriyet Döneminde İstanbul Rum Patrikhanesi.* Istanbul: İletişim Yayınları.

Macar, Elçin. 2004a. "Çözüm Gibi Bir Çözüm Şart." *Radikal*, July 13.

Macar, Elçin. 2004b. "Patrikhane Sorununu Anlamak." *Radikal*, March 15.

Macar, Elçin, and Mehmet Ali Gökaçtı. 2006. *Heybeliada Ruhban Okulunun Geleceği Üzerine Tartışmalar ve Öneriler.* Istanbul: TESEV Yayınları.

MacMaster, Neil. 1997. *Colonial Migrants and Racism: Algerians in France, 1900–1962.* New York: St. Martin's Press.

MacMaster, Neil. 2003. "Islamophobia in France and the 'Algerian Problem'." In *The New Crusades: Constructing the Muslim Enemy*, ed. E. Qureshi and M. A. Sells. New York: Columbia University Press, 288–313.

Mahçupyan, Etyen. 2005. "Meramsız İyi Niyet." *Zaman*, June 27.

Mahçupyan, Etyen. 2006. "Vatandaşı Hazmedemeyen Cumhuriyet Olur Mu?" *Zaman*, October 1.

Mahoney, James. 2000. "Path Dependence in Historical Sociology." *Theory and Society* 29(4): 507–548.

March, James G., and Johan P. Olsen. 1989. *Rediscovering Institutions: The Organizational Basis of Politics.* New York: Free Press.

Mardin, Serif. 1991. *Türk Modernleşmesi.* Istanbul: İletişim Yayınları.

Mardin, Şerif. 2000 [1962]. *The Genesis of Young Ottoman Thought: A Study in the Modernization of Turkish Political Ideas.* Syracuse, NY: Syracuse University Press.

Mardin, Serif. 2006. *Religion, Society, and Modernity in Turkey*, 1st ed. Syracuse, NY: Syracuse University Press.

Marquis, Christopher. 2003. "U.S. Chides France on Effort to Bar Religious Garb in Schools." *New York Times*, December 19.

Marshall, Jill. 2006. "Freedom of Religious Expression and Gender Equality: Sahin v Turkey." *Modern Law Review* 60: 452–461.

Martinelli, Marie-Thérèse. 2004. "Voilées / Dévoilées – Deux facettes d'une même domination." *Les Pénélopes*, January, available at www.penelopes.org/xarticle .php3?id_article=4573 (last accessed on October 6, 2007).

Maussen, Marcel. 2006. "The Netherlands." In *Securitization and Religious Divide in Europe: Muslims in Western Europe after 9/11*, ed. Jocelyne Cesari. Brussels: European Commission, 100–142.

Maxwell, Morgan. 2011. "The Belltowers of the Future: Mosque Financing and French Laïcité." In *The Financial Crisis of 2008: French and American Responses*, Proceedings of the 2010 Franco-American Legal Seminar, ed. Martin A. Rogoff, Michael Dixon, and Eric Bither. Portland, ME: University of Maine School of Law and Rennes: Faculté de droit et de science politique – Université de Rennes 1, 109–134.

Mayer, Jean-François, and Elijah Siegler. 1999. "Our Terrestrial Journey Is Coming to an End: The Last Voyage of the Solar Temple." *Nova Religio: The Journal of Alternative and Emergent Religions* 2(2): 172–196.

MAZLUMDER. 2010. *Türkiye'de Dini Ayrımcılık Raporu.* Istanbul: Mazlumder.

McAdam, Doug, Sidney Tarrow, and Charles Tilly. 2001. *Dynamics of Contention.* New York: Cambridge University Press.

McGoldrick, Dominic. 2006. *Human Rights and Religion: The Islamic Headscarf Debate in Europe.* Portland, OR: Hart.

McKenzie, Sheena. 2016. "French Mayors Maintain Burkini Bans Despite Court Ruling." *CNN*, August 29, available at www.cnn.com/2016/08/29/europe/french-mayors-refuse-lift-burkini-ban/index.html (last accessed on November 4, 2018).

McManners, John. 1972. *Church and State in France, 1870–1914*. New York: Harper and Row.

McNamara, Kathleen R. 1998. *The Currency of Ideas: Monetary Politics in the European Union*. Ithaca, NY: Cornell University Press.

Meguid, Bonnie M. 2005. "Competition Between Unequals: The Role of Mainstream Party Strategy in Niche Party Success." *American Political Science Review* 99(3): 347–359.

Meyer, John W., and W. Richard Scott. 1992. *Organizational Environments: Ritual and Rationality*, updated ed. Newbury Park, CA: Sage Publications.

Meyer, John W., John Boli, George M. Thomas, and Francisco O. Ramirez. 1997. "World Society and the Nation-State." *American Journal of Sociology* 103(1): 144–181.

Milner, Helen V. 1998. "Rationalizing Politics: The Emerging Synthesis among International Politics and American and Comparative Politics." *International Organization* 52(4): 759–786.

Ministry of Foreign Affairs of Turkey. 2001. "2001 National Programme of Turkey for the Adoption of the EU Acquis," available at www.ab.gov.tr/_195_en.html (last accessed on December 12, 2018).

Ministry of Foreign Affairs of Turkey. 2003. "2003 National Programme of Turkey for the Adoption of the EU Acquis," available at www.ab.gov.tr/_196_en.html (last accessed on December 12, 2018).

Ministry of Foreign Affairs of Turkey. 2008. "2008 National Programme of Turkey for the Adoption of the EU Acquis," available at www.ab.gov.tr/42260_en.html (last accessed on December 12, 2018).

Modood, Tariq, and Riva Kastoryano. 2006. "Secularism and the Accommodation of Muslims in Europe." In *Multiculturalism, Muslims and Citizenship: A European Approach*, ed. T. Modood, A. Triandafyllidou and R. Zapata-Barrero. New York: Routledge, 162–178.

Monnot, Caroline, and Xavier Ternisien. 2003. "L'Exclusion de deux lycéennes voilées divise l'extrême gauche." *Le Monde*, October 9.

Monnot, Caroline. 2004. "Le Voile fait aussi désordre à l'extrême gauche." *Le Monde*, February 7.

Monsma, Stephen V., and J. Christopher Soper. 1997. *The Challenge of Pluralism: Church and State in Five Democracies*. Lanham, MD: Rowman & Littlefield.

Mufti, Malik. 2010. "The Many-Colored Cloak: Evolving Conceptions of Democracy in Islamic Political Thought." *American Journal of Islamic Social Sciences* 27(2):1–27.

Müftüler Baç, Meltem. 2005. "Turkey's Political Reforms and the Impact of the European Union." *South European Society and Politics* 10(1): 16–30.

Muhammed, Marwan. 2010. "Islamophobia: A Deep-Rooted Phenomenon." *Arches Quarterly* 4(7): 96–101.

Mullen, John. 2004. "Islamophobia Divides the Left in France." *Socialist Unity Network*, September, available at http://john.mullen.pagesperso-orange.fr/0904headscarf.html (last accessed on September 12, 2018).

Navaro-Yashin, Yael. 2002. *Faces of the State: Secularism and Public Life in Turkey*. Princeton, NJ: Princeton University Press.

Naxidou, Eleonora. 2012. "Nationalism versus Multiculturalism: The Minority Issue in Twenty-First Century Bulgaria." *Nationalities Papers* 40(1): 85–105.

Nicolet, Claude. 1995. *L'Idée républicaine en France*. Paris: Messageries du Livre.

Nilsson, Per-Erik. 2015. "'Secular Retaliation': A Case Study of Integralist Populism, Anti-Muslim Discourse, and (Il)liberal Discourse on Secularism in Contemporary France." *Politics, Religion and Ideology* 16(1): 87–106.

Norris, Pippa, and Ronald Inglehart. 2004. *Sacred and Secular: Religion and Politics Worldwide*. New York: Cambridge University Press.

North, Douglass Cecil. 1990. *Institutions, Institutional Change, and Economic Performance*. New York: Cambridge University Press.

Ocak, Ahmet Yaşar. 1999. *Türkler, Türkiye ve İslam: Yaklaşım, Yöntem ve Yorum Denemeleri*. Istanbul: İletişim Yayınları.

Oehring, Otmar. 2004. *Human Rights: Turkey on the Road to Europe – Religious Freedom?* Aachen: Missio.

Öniş, Ziya. 2003. "Domestic Politics, International Norms and Challenges to the State: Turkey–EU Relations in the Post-Helsinki Era." In *Turkey and the European Union: Domestic Politics, Economic Integration and International Dynamics*, ed. A. Çarkoğlu and B. Rubin. New York: Frank Cass, 8–31.

Önsay, Süleyman. 2016. "Ehli Kitap Müşriktir." *Yeni Akit*, October 14.

Onuf, Nicholas Greenwood. 1989. *World of Our Making: Rules and Rule in Social Theory and International Relations*. Columbia, SC: University of South Carolina Press.

Oran, Baskın. 2004. *Türkiye'de Azınlıklar: Kavramlar, Lozan, İç Mevzuat, İçtihat, Uygulama*. Istanbul: TESEV Yayınları.

Oran, Baskın. 2007. "The Minority Concept and Rights in Turkey: The Lausanne Peace Treaty and Current Issues." In *Human Rights in Turkey*, ed. Z. F. K. Arat. Philadelphia: University of Pennsylvania Press, 35–56.

Özdalga, Elisabeth. 1998. *The Veiling Issue: Official Secularism and Popular Islam in Modern Turkey*. Richmond, Surrey: Curzon.

Özipek, Bekir Berat. 2004. "Azınlık Hakları, Ruhban Okulu ve Birlikte Yaşam Formülü!" *Zaman*, August 26.

Özyürek, Esra. 2006. *Nostalgia for the Modern: State Secularism and Everyday Politics in Turkey*. Durham, NC: Duke University Press.

Palmer, Alasdair. 2001. "Is the West Really the Best?" *The Telegraph*, September 30.

Palmer, Susan J. 2002. "France's Anti-Sect Wars." *Nova Religio: The Journal of Alternative and Emergent Religions* 6(1): 174–182.

Palmer, Susan J. 2011. *The New Heretics of France: Minority Religions, la République, and the Government-Sponsored War on Sects*. New York: Oxford University Press.

Payne, Daniel P. 2010. "Spiritual Security, the Russian Orthodox Church, and the Russian Foreign Ministry: Collaboration or Cooptation?" *Journal of Church and State* 52(4): 712–727.

Penicaut, Nicole. 2003. "Laïcité et voile: Raffarin noie le poisson." *Libération*, April 30.

Pétition. 2003. "Oui à la laïcité, non aux lois d'exception." *ProChoix* (25): 14–18.

Petito, Fabio, and Pavlos Hatzopoulos, eds. 2003. *Religion in International Relations: The Return from Exile*. New York: Palgrave MacMillan.

Pew Research Centre. 2002. *What the World Thinks in 2002*. Pew Global Attitudes Survey, December 4. Washington, DC: Pew Research Centre, available at www.pewresearch.org/wp-content/uploads/sites/2/2002/12/2002-Report-Final-Updated.pdf (last accessed on April 6, 2019).

Pew Research Centre. 2003. *Views of a Changing World: June 2003.* Pew Global Attitudes Survey, June 3. Washington, DC: Pew Research Centre, available at www.pewresearch.org/wp-content/uploads/sites/2/2003/06/Views-Of-A-Changing-World-2003.pdf (last accessed on April 6, 2019).

Philpott, Daniel. 2000. "The Religious Roots of Modern International Relations." *World Politics* 52(2): 206–245.

Pierson, Paul. 2000. "Increasing Returns, Path Dependence, and the Study of Politics." *American Political Science Review* 94(2): 251–267.

Pierson, Paul. 2004. *Politics in Time: History, Institutions, and Social Analysis.* Princeton, NJ: Princeton University Press.

Piser, Karina. 2018. "A New Plan to Create an Islam of France." *The Atlantic*, March 29, available at www.theatlantic.com/international/archive/2018/03/islam-france-macron/556604/ (last accessed on November 4, 2018).

Poole, Elizabeth. 2002. *Reporting Islam: Media Representations of British Muslims.* New York: I. B. Tauris.

Pope, Hugh. 2004. "Rahibin Kilise Çilesi." *Radikal*, November 29.

Poulat, Émile. 1987. *Liberté, laïcité: La Guerre des deux France et le principe de la modernité.* Paris: Cerf & Cujas.

Powell, Walter W., and Paul DiMaggio. 1991. *The New Institutionalism in Organizational Analysis.* Chicago: University of Chicago Press.

Poynting, Scott, and Victoria Mason. 2007. "The Resistible Rise of Islamophobia." *Journal of Sociology* 43(1): 61–86.

Pridham, Geoffrey. 1991. *Encouraging Democracy: The International Context of Regime Transition in Southern Europe.* New York: St. Martin's Press.

Prins, Baukje. 2002. "The Nerve to Break Taboos: New Realism in the Dutch Discourse on Multiculturalism." *Journal of International Migration and Integration* 3(3–4): 363–380.

Raghavan, Sudarsan, and Heba Farouk Mahfouz. 2018. "Gunmen in Egypt Attack Bus Carrying Christians, Killing at Least 8 and Wounding 13." *Washington Post*, November 2.

Ramadan, Tariq. 1998. *Les Musulmans dans la laïcité: Responsabilités et droits des musulmans dans les sociétés occidentales,* 2nd ed. Lyon: Tawhid.

Ramadan, Tariq. 2004. *Western Muslims and the Future of Islam.* New York: Oxford University Press.

Ramadan, Tariq. 2007. *In the Footsteps of the Prophet: Lessons from the Life of Muhammad.* New York: Oxford University Press.

Ravitch, Norman. 1967. "Liberalism, Catholicism, and the Abbé Grégoire." *Church History* 36(4): 419–439.

Ravitch, Norman. 1990. *The Catholic Church and the French Nation, 1589–1989.* New York: Routledge.

Rémond, René. 1999. *Religion and Society in Modern Europe.* Oxford: Blackwell.

Reyna, Yuda, and Yusuf Şen. 1994. *Cemaat Vakıfları ve Sorunları.* Istanbul: Gözlem Yayınları.

Ricard, Jean-Pierre, Jean-Arnold de Clermont, and Archbishop Emmanuel. 2003. "L'Enjeu du débat est la réussite de l'intégration." *La Croix*, December 9.

Richardson, James T., and Massimo Introvigne. 2001. "Brainwashing Theories in European Parliamentary and Administrative Reports on Cults and Sects." *Journal for the Scientific Study of Religion* 40(2): 143–168.

Rieff, David. 2007. "Battle Over the Banlieues." *New York Times*, April 15.

Risse, Thomas. 2000. "Let's Argue: Communicative Action in World Politics." *International Organization* 54(1): 1–39.

Risse-Kappen, Thomas. 1995. *Bringing Transnational Relations Back In: Non-state Actors, Domestic Structures, and International Institutions*. New York: Cambridge University Press.

Risse-Kappen, Thomas, Maria Green Cowles, and James A. Caporaso. 2001. "Europeanization and Domestic Change: Introduction." In *Transforming Europe: Europeanization and Domestic Change*, ed. M. G. Cowles, J. A. Caporaso and T. Risse-Kappen. Ithaca, NY: Cornell University Press, 1–19.

Risse-Kappen, Thomas, Steve C. Ropp, and Kathryn Sikkink. 1999. *The Power of Human Rights: International Norms and Domestic Change*. New York: Cambridge University Press.

Roy, Olivier. 2007. *Secularism Confronts Islam*. New York: Columbia University Press.

Rumford, Chris. 2013. *New Perspectives on Turkey–EU Relations*. London: Routledge.

Runnymede Trust. 1997. *Islamophobia: A Challenge for Us All*. London: Runnymede Trust.

Saad, Lydia. 2006. "Anti-Muslim Sentiments Fairly Commonplace." *Gallup*, August 10, available at www.gallup.com/poll/24073/AntiMuslim-Sentiments-Fairly-Commonplace.aspx (last accessed on June 21, 2017).

Sakallıoğlu, Ümit Cizre. 1996. "Parameters and Strategies of Islam–State Interaction in Republican Turkey." *International Journal of Middle East Studies* 28(2): 231–251.

Salaita, Steven G. 2006. "Beyond Orientalism and Islamophobia: 9/11, Anti-Arab Racism, and the Myths of National Pride." *New Centennial Review* 6(2): 245–266.

Sandal, Nukhet A. 2013. "Public Theologies of Human Rights and Citizenship: The Case of Turkey's Christians." *Human Rights Quarterly* 35(3): 631–650.

Sandal, Nukhet, and Jonathan Fox. 2013. *Religion in International Relations Theory: Interactions and Possibilities*. London: Routledge.

Sarkissian, Ani. 2012. "Religious Regulation and the Muslim Democracy Gap." *Politics and Religion* 5(3): 501–527.

Sarkissian, Ani. 2015. *The Varieties of Religious Repression: Why Governments Restrict Religion*. New York: Oxford University Press.

Sarkissian, Ani, Jonathan Fox, and Yasemin Akbaba. 2011. "Culture vs. Rational Choice: Assessing the Causes of Religious Discrimination in Muslim States." *Nationalism and Ethnic Politics* 17(4): 423–446.

Sarkozy, Nicolas. 2004. "Les Musulmans ne doivent pas avoir plus de droits. Veillons à ce qu'ils n'en aient pas moins." *Le Monde*, October 26.

Sarrazin, Thilo. 2009. *Deutschland Schafft Ab*. Munich: Deutsche Verlags-Anstalt.

Saymaz, İsmail. 2003a. "Vakıflar Mülklerini Alamadı." *Radikal*, May 5.

Saymaz, İsmail. 2003b. "Yasayı Delen Karar." *Radikal*, May 6.

Saymaz, İsmail. 2006. "Azınlıklar Bildirisi: Rehine Değiliz." *Radikal*, September 26.

Schelling, Thomas C. 1960. *The Strategy of Conflict*. Cambridge, MA: Harvard University Press.

Schimmelfennig, Frank. 2002. "Introduction: The Impact of International Organizations on the Central and Eastern European States – Conceptual and

Theoretical Issues." In *Norms and Nannies: The Impact of International Organizations on the Central and East European States*, ed. R. H. Linden. Lanham, MD: Rowman & Littlefield, 1–29.

Schimmelfennig, Frank, and Ulrich Sedelmeier. 2005. *The Europeanization of Central and Eastern Europe*. Ithaca, NY: Cornell University Press.

Schmid, Stefan. 2015. "The Rising Power of France's Front National." *The National*, March 30, available at www.thenational.scot/world/the-rising-power-of-frances-front-national.1529 (last accessed on December 20, 2018).

Schmidt, Vivien A., and Claudio M. Radaelli. 2004. "Policy Change and Discourse in Europe: Conceptual and Methodological Issues." *West European Politics* 27(2): 183–210.

Schofield, Hugh. 2016. "Jewish Dad Backs Headscarf Daughters." *BBC News*, October 1, available at http://news.bbc.co.uk/2/hi/europe/3149588.stm (last accessed on June 20, 2017).

Sciolino, Elaine. 2003. "Ban Religious Attire in School, French Panel Says." *New York Times*, December 12.

Sciolino, Elaine. 2004. "French Assembly Votes to Ban Religious Symbols in Schools." *New York Times*, February 11.

Scott, James C. 1998. *Seeing Like a State: How Certain Schemes to Improve the Human Condition Have Failed*. New Haven, CT: Yale University Press.

Scott, Joan W. 2005. "The Banning of Islamic Headscarves in French Public Schools." *French Politics, Culture and Society* 23(3): 106–127.

Scott, Joan Wallach. 2007. *The Politics of the Veil*. Princeton, NJ: Princeton University Press.

Scott, W. Richard, and John W. Meyer. 1994. *Institutional Environments and Organizations: Structural Complexity and Individualism*. Thousand Oaks, CA: SAGE Publications.

Semati, Mehdi. 2010. "Islamophobia, Culture and Race in the Age of Empire." *Cultural Studies* 24(2): 256–275.

Sewell, William H. 1992. "A Theory of Structure: Duality, Agency, and Transformation." *American Journal of Sociology* 98(1): 1–29.

Shadid, Wasif, and Sjoerd van Koningsveld. 2005. "Muslim Dress in Europe: Debates on the Headscarf." *Journal of Islamic Studies* 16(1): 35–61.

Shaw, Stanford J., and Ezel Kural Shaw. 1976. *History of the Ottoman Empire and Modern Turkey*, 2 volumes. New York: Cambridge University Press.

Sheridan, Lorraine P. 2002. *Effects of the Events of September 11th on Discrimination and Implicit Racism in Five Religious and Seven Ethnic Groups*. Leicester: University of Leicester.

Sheridan, Lorraine P. 2006. "Islamophobia Pre- and Post–September 11th, 2001." *Journal of Interpersonal Violence* 21(3): 317–336.

Shryock, Andrew, ed. 2010. *Islamophobia/Islamophilia: Beyond the Politics of Enemy and Friend*. Bloomington, IN: Indiana University Press.

Silverstein, Paul. 2008. "The Context of Antisemitism and Islamophobia in France." *Patterns of Prejudice* 42(1): 1–26.

Simon, Catherine. 2001. "Le Voile est un piège, qui isole et marginalise." *Le Monde*, December 17.

Şimşek, Yurdagül. 2006. "Vakıflara yeni tanım." *Radikal*, June 14.

Siraud, Mathilda. 2017. "Le Problème de l'Islam: Manuel Valls crée la polémique." *Le Figaro*, November 22.

Şişman, Cengiz. 2015. *The Burden of Silence: Sabbatai Sevi and the Evolution of the Ottoman-Turkish Dönmes*. New York: Oxford University Press.

Skocpol, Theda. 1979. *States and Social Revolutions: A Comparative Analysis of France, Russia, and China*. New York: Cambridge University Press.

Smith, Christian, ed. 2003. *The Secular Revolution: Power, Interests, and Conflict in the Secularization of American Public Life*. Oakland, CA: University of California Press.

Sokhey, Sarah Wilson, and A. Kadir Yildirim. 2013. "Economic Liberalization and Political Moderation: The Case of Anti-System Parties." *Party Politics* 19(2): 230–255.

Sondages CSA. 2004. "Les Enseignants des collèges et lycées et la laïcité," January 24, available at www.csa-tmo.fr/dataset/data2004/opi20040124c.htm (last accessed on November 1, 2007).

Soucek, Svatopluk. 2004. "Naval Aspects of the Ottoman Conquests of Rhodes, Cyprus and Crete." *Studia Islamica* 98/99: 219–261.

Soydan, Macit. 2008. "Tapınak Şövalyeleri." *Yeniçağ Gazetesi*, April 12.

Spiecker, Ben, and Jan Steutel. 2001. "Multiculturalism, Pillarization and Liberal Civic Education in the Netherlands." *International Journal of Educational Research* 35(3): 293–304.

Stangler, Cole. 2018. "Can France's Far-Right Reinvent Itself?" *The Atlantic*, January 14, available at www.theatlantic.com/international/archive/2018/01/france-national-front-far-right/550484/ (last accessed on October 31, 2018).

Stark, Rodney, and Larry L. Iannaccone. 1994. "A Supply-Side Reinterpretation of the 'Secularization' of Europe." *Journal for the Scientific Study of Religion* 33(3): 230–252.

Stasi, Bernard. 2004. *Laïcité et République: Rapport de la Commission de réflexion sur l'application du principe de laïcité dans la République remis au Président de la République le 11 décembre 2003*. Paris: Documentation française.

State Department Bureau of Democracy, Human Rights, and Labor. 2001. "2001 International Religious Freedom Report," May, available at www.state.gov/g/drl/rls/irf/2001/5694.htm (last accessed on June 20, 2017).

State Department Bureau of Democracy, Human Rights, and Labor. 2002. "2002 International Religious Freedom Report," May, available at www.state.gov/g/drl/rls/irf/2002/13986.htm (last accessed on June 20, 2017).

State Department Bureau of Democracy, Human Rights, and Labor. 2003. "2003 International Religious Freedom Report," May, available at www.state.gov/g/drl/rls/irf/2003/24438.htm (last accessed on June 20, 2017).

State Department Bureau of Democracy, Human Rights, and Labor. 2004. "2004 International Religious Freedom Report," May, available at www.state.gov/g/drl/rls/irf/2004/35489.htm (last accessed on June 20, 2017).

State Department Bureau of Democracy, Human Rights, and Labor. 2005. "2005 International Religious Freedom Report," May, available at www.state.gov/g/drl/rls/irf/2005/51586.htm (last accessed on June 20, 2017).

State Department Bureau of Democracy, Human Rights, and Labor. 2006. "2006 International Religious Freedom Report," May, available at www.state.gov/g/drl/rls/irf/2006/71413.htm (last accessed on June 20, 2017).

State Department Bureau of Democracy, Human Rights, and Labor. 2007. "2007 International Religious Freedom Report," May, available at www.state.gov/g/drl/rls/irf/2007/90204.htm (last accessed on June 20, 2017).

Stolz, Jörg. 2005. "Explaining Islamophobia: A Test of Four Theories Based on the Case of a Swiss City." *Swiss Journal of Sociology* 31(3): 547–566.

Stone, Deborah A. 1989. "Causal Stories and the Formation of Policy Agenda." *Political Science Quarterly* 104(2): 281–300.

Swidler, Ann. 1986. "Culture in Action: Symbols and Strategies." *American Sociological Review* 51(2): 273–286.

Tafolar, Meriç. 2012. "Bozdağ: Türkiye'de 349 Kilise Var." *Milliyet*, October 1.

Tamadonfar, Mehran, and Ted G. Jelen, eds. 2013b. *Religion and Regimes: Support, Separation, and Opposition.* Boulder, CO: Lexington Books.

Tamadonfar, Mehran, and Ted G. Jelen. 2013a. "Religion and Regime Change in Iran and Poland." In *Religion and Regimes: Support, Separation, and Opposition*, ed. Mehran Tamadonfar and Ted G. Jelen. Boulder, CO: Lexington Books, 213–240.

Taniyici, Saban. 2003. "Transformation of Political Islam in Turkey: Islamist Welfare Party's Pro-EU Turn." *Party Politics* 9(4): 463–483.

Tarhanlı, Turgut. 2002a. "Azınlıklar ve Vakıflar." *Radikal*, January 22.

Tarhanlı, Turgut. 2002b. "Nasıl Bir İyileştirme." *Radikal*, August 1.

Taub, Amanda. 2014. "The Terrifying Rise of the Far Right in the UK, Explained in One Chart." *Vox*, November 6, available at www.vox.com/2014/11/6/7163375/ukip-conservative-right-europe (last accessed on December 20, 2018).

Tausch, Arno, Christian Bischof, Tomaz Kastrum, and Karl Mueller. 2007. *Against Islamophobia: Muslim Communities, Social-Exclusion, and the Lisbon Process in Europe.* New York: Nova Science Publishers.

Tekay, Mebuse. 2002. "Yerli Yabancılarımız." *Radikal*, January 15.

Ternisien, Xavier. 2003a. "Deux lycéennes d'Aubervilliers, filles d'un avocat du MRAP, exclues pour port du voile." *Le Monde*, September 25.

Ternisien, Xavier. 2003b. "Il n'y a que 150 cas conflictuels, selon la médiatrice de l'éducation nationale." *Le Monde*, May 10.

Ternisien, Xavier. 2003c. "L'UOIF, principale organisation musulmane, défend le port du voile mais souhaite une loi l'interdisant a l'école." *Le Monde*, October 14.

Ternisien, Xavier. 2003d. "Le Débat sur la place de l'Islam fait craindre aux évêques 'une régression de la liberté religieuse'." *Le Monde*, November 11.

Ternisien, Xavier, and Nicolas Weill. 2003. "M. Chirac annonce la création d'une autorité indépendante de lutte contre la discrimination." *Le Monde*, May 24.

Tévanian, Pierre. 2005. *Le Voile médiatique – un faux débat: L'Affaire du foulard islamique.* Paris: Éditions Raisons d'Agir.

The Economist. 2004. "The War of the Headscarves," *The Economist*, February 7.

Thelen, Kathleen Ann. 1999. "Historical Institutionalism in Comparative Politics." *Annual Review of Political Science* 2: 369–404.

Thelen, Kathleen Ann. 2003. "How Institutions Evolve: Insights from Comparative Historical Analysis." In *Comparative Historical Analysis in the Social Sciences*, ed. J. Mahoney and D. Rueschemeyer. New York: Cambridge University Press, 208–240.

Thelen, Kathleen Ann. 2004. *How Institutions Evolve: The Political Economy of Skills in Germany, Britain, the United States, and Japan.* New York: Cambridge University Press.

Thomas, Elaine R. 2006. "Keeping Identity at a Distance: Explaining France's New Legal Restrictions on the Islamic Headscarf." *Ethnic and Racial Studies* 29(2): 237–259.

Thomas, George M. 1987. *Institutional Structure: Constituting State, Society, and the Individual.* Newbury Park, CA: Sage Publications.

Thomas, George M. 1989. *Revivalism and Cultural Change: Christianity, Nation Building, and the Market in the Nineteenth-Century United States.* Chicago: University of Chicago Press.

Thomas, George M. 2004. "Constructing World Civil Society through Contentions over Religious Rights." *Journal of Human Rights* 3(2): 239–251.

Thomas, Scott. 2005. *The Global Resurgence of Religion and the Transformation of International Relations: The Struggle for the Soul of the Twenty-First Century.* New York: Palgrave MacMillan.

Tilly, Charles. 1992. *Coercion, Capital, and European States, AD 990–1992.* Cambridge, MA: Blackwell.

Tilly, Charles. 2001. "Mechanisms in Political Processes." *Annual Review of Political Science* 4: 21–41.

Tilly, Charles, and Gabriel Ardant. 1975. *The Formation of National States in Western Europe.* Princeton, NJ: Princeton University Press.

Toft, Monica Duffy, Daniel Philpott, and Timothy Samuel Shah. 2011. *God's Century: Resurgent Religion and Global Politics.* New York: WW Norton & Company.

Toktaş, Şule. 2005. "Citizenship and Minorities: A Historical Overview of Turkey's Jewish Minority." *Journal of Historical Sociology* 18(4): 394–429.

Toktaş, Şule. 2008. "Cultural Identity, Minority Position and Immigration: Turkey's Jewish Minority vs. Turkish-Jewish Immigrants in Israel." *Middle Eastern Studies* 44(3): 511–525.

Toktaş, Şule, and Bülent Aras. 2009. "The EU and Minority Rights in Turkey." *Political Science Quarterly* 124(4): 697–720.

Toor, Amaar. 2016. "France's Anti-Terrorism Laws Leave Muslims in a State of Fear." *The Verge*, January 29, available at www.theverge.com/2016/1/29/10860964/france-state-of-emergency-muslim-paris-attacks (last accessed on November 3, 2018).

Toprak, Binnaz. 1981. *Islam and Political Development in Turkey.* Leiden: Brill.

Törüner, Yaman. 2006. "Avrupa Parlamentosu Bizden Ne İstiyor?" *Milliyet*, October 23.

Tribalat, Michèle. 2011. "L'Islam reste une menace." *Le Monde*, October 13.

Tuduk, Mine. 2011. "Azınlıklara Çifte Bayram." *Radikal*, August 29.

Turam, Berna. 2007. *Between Islam and the State: The Politics of Engagement.* Stanford, CA: Stanford University Press.

Türker, Yıldırım. 2004. "O da mı Ermeni Çıktı?" *Radikal*, February 29.

Türkmen, Füsun, and Emre Öktem. 2013. "Foreign Policy as a Determinant in the Fate of Turkey's Non-Muslim Minorities: A Dialectical Analysis." *Turkish Studies* 14(3): 463–482.

Ugur, Etga. 2007. "Religion as a Source of Social Capital? The Gülen Movement in the Public Sphere." In *Muslim World in Transition: Contributions of the Gülen Movement*, ed. İhsan Yılmaz. London: Leeds Metropolitan University Press, 152–162.

Uğur, Mehmet. 2006. "The Economic Dimension of Turkey's EU Membership: A Stock-Taking Exercise at the Start of Accession Negotiations." In *Turkey and the European Union: Internal Dynamics and External Challenges*, ed. J. S. Joseph. New York: Palgrave Macmillan, 16–41.

UN Human Rights Commission. 2000. "Interim report of the Special Rapporteur of the Commission on Human Rights on the elimination of all forms of intolerance and of discrimination based on religion or belief," available at www.unhchr.ch/Huridocda/Huridoca.nsf/0/c2fe53d6c1416863c125697e00500a6b/$FILE/N0060496.pdf (last accessed on June 20, 2008).

United States Commission on International Religious Freedom. 2000. "The Annual Report of the United States Commission on International Religious Freedom," available at www.uscirf.gov/sites/default/files/resources/stories/pdf/Annual_Report/ 2000annualreport.pdf (last accessed on December 5, 2018).

United States Commission on International Religious Freedom. 2004. "France: Proposed Bill May Violate Freedom of Religion," February 3, available at www .uscirf.gov/mediaroom/press/2004/february/02032004_france.html (last accessed on October 11, 2007).

United States Commission on International Religious Freedom. 2007. "Annual Report 2007," May 1, available at www.uscirf.gov/images/AR_2007/annualreport2007.pdf (last accessed on June 20, 2017).

U.S. Department of State. 2000. "2000 Annual Report on International Religious Freedom: France," September 5, available at www.state.gov/www/global/ human_rights/irf/irf_rpt/irf_france.html (last accessed on October 10, 2007).

U.S. Department of State. 2003. "2003 Annual Report on International Religious Freedom: France," May, available at www.state.gov/g/drl/rls/irf/2003/24357.htm (last accessed on October 10, 2007).

U.S. Department of State. 2004. "2004 Annual Report on International Religious Freedom: France," May, available at www.state.gov/g/drl/rls/irf/2004/35454.htm (last accessed on October 10, 2007).

U.S. Department of State. 2016. "International Religious Freedom Report 2015: Turkey," available at www.state.gov/documents/organization/256463.pdf (last accessed on June 24, 2017).

U.S. Department of State. 2017. "International Religious Freedom Report 2016: Turkey," available at www.state.gov/documents/organization/269120.pdf (last accessed on June 24, 2017).

U.S. Department of State. 2018. "Turkey 2017 International Religious Freedom Report," available at www.state.gov/documents/organization/281212.pdf (last accessed on December 19, 2018).

Vachudová, Milada Anna. 2005. *Europe Undivided: Democracy, Leverage, and Integration after Communism.* New York: Oxford University Press.

Vigerie, Anne, and Anne Zelensky. 2003. "Laïcardes, puisque féministes." *Le Monde,* May 30.

Virot, Pascal. 2003. "Affaire Tariq Ramadan: Les Socialistes isolés à gauche." *Libération,* October 28.

Warner, Carolyn M. 2000. *Confessions of an Interest Group: The Catholic Church and Political Parties in Europe.* Princeton, NJ: Princeton University Press.

Warner, Carolyn M., and Manfred W. Wenner. 2006. "Religion and the Political Organization of Muslims in Europe." *Perspectives on Politics* 4(3): 457–479.

Weber, Eugene. 1976. *Peasants into Frenchmen: The Modernization of Rural France, 1870–1914.* Stanford, CA: Stanford University Press.

Weber, Max. 1948. "The Social Psychology of the World Religions." In *From Max Weber: Essays in Sociology,* ed. H. H. Gerth and C. W. Mills. London: Routledge, 267–301.

Weill, Nicolas. 2006. "What's in a Scarf? The Debate on Laïcité in France." *French Politics, Culture and Society* 24(1): 59–73.

Weitz, Eric D. 2008. "From the Vienna to the Paris System: International Politics and the Entangled Histories of Human Rights, Forced Deportations and Civilizing Missions." *American Historical Review* 113(5): 1313–1343.

Wendt, Alexander. 1987. "The Agent–Structure Problem in International Relations Theory." *International Organization* 41(3): 335–370.

Wenner, Manfred W. 1980. "The Arab/Muslim Presence in Medieval Central Europe." *International Journal of Middle East Studies* 12(1): 59–79.

Whitehead, Laurence. 1996. *The International Dimensions of Democratization: Europe and the Americas.* New York: Oxford University Press.

Willsher, Kim. 2014. "France's Burqa Ban Upheld by Human Rights Court." *The Guardian*, July 1.

Wilson, Bryan R. 1982. *Religion in Sociological Perspective.* New York: Oxford University Press.

Wilson, Mary. 1988. *King Abdullah, Britain, and the Making of Jordan.* New York: Cambridge University Press.

Wing, Adrien Katherine, and Monica Nigh Smith. 2006. "Critical Race Feminism Lifts the Veil? Muslim Women, France, and the Headscarf Ban." *UC Davis Law Review* 39(3): 743–790.

Yakut, Esra. 2005. *Şeyhülislamlık: Yenileşme Dönemide Devlet ve Din.* Istanbul: Kitap Yayınevi.

Yannas, Prodromos. 2007. "The Human Rights Conditions of the Rum Orthodox." In *Human Rights in Turkey*, ed. Zehra F. Kabasakal Arat. Philadephia: University of Pennsylvania Press, 57–71.

Yavuz, M. Hakan. 2003. *Islamic Political Identity in Turkey.* New York: Oxford University Press.

Yildirim, A. Kadir. 2009. "Muslim Democratic Parties in Turkey, Egypt and Morocco: An Economic Explanation." *Insight Turkey* 11(4): 65–76.

Yildirim, A. Kadir. 2013. "New Democrats: Religious Actors, Social Change and Democratic Consolidation in Turkey." *Contemporary Islam* 7(3): 311–331.

Yildirim, A. Kadir. 2015. "Globalization, Political Islam, and Moderation: The Case of Muslim Democratic Parties." *Sociology of Islam* 3(1–2): 76–106.

Yildirim, A. Kadir. 2016. *Muslim Democratic Parties in the Middle East: Economy and Politics of Islamist Moderation.* Indianapolis, IN: Indiana University Press.

Yildirim, A. Kadir, and Caroline M. Lancaster. 2015. "Bending with the Wind: Revisiting Islamist Parties' Electoral Dilemma." *Politics and Religion* 8(3): 588–613.

Yıldız, Süheyla. 2015. "Asimile Olma, İçe Kapanma, Kimliklenme: Cumhuriyet'ten Bugüne Türkiye Yahudilerinin Kimlik Stratejileri." *Alternatif Politika* 7(2): 257–290.

Yinanç, Barçın. 2006. "Olli Rehn'den Abdullah Gül'e 301. Madde Mektubu." *Referans*, September 1.

Youssfi, Imane. 2017. "Mosquée de Marseille: La Justice résilie définitivement le bail." *Saphir News*, January 24, available at www.saphirnews.com/Mosquee-de-Marseille-la-justice-resilie-definitivement-le-bail_a23400.html (last accessed on November 8, 2018).

Ysmal, Pierre. 2004. "Le Voile est une régression." *L'Humanité*, January 24.

Yüksek, Fatma Sibel. 2002. "Vakıflara MGK Freni." *Radikal*, October 2.

Zielonka, Jan, and Alex Pravda, eds. 2001. *Democratic Consolidation in Eastern Europe: International and Transnational Factors.* New York: Oxford University Press.

Zúquete, José Pedro. 2008. "The European Extreme-Right and Islam: New Directions?" *Journal of Political Ideologies* 13(3): 321–344.

Zürcher, Erik Jan. 1993. *Turkey: A Modern History.* New York: I.B. Tauris.

# Index

Abdulhamid II, 3, 197
About-Picard Law, 199, 201
Adalet ve Kalkınma Partisi. *See* Justice and
    Development Party
agent-structure debate, 217
Akhdamar Island, 98, 99
Aktaş, Timotheus Samuel, 39
Algerian Civil War, 16, 110, 119, 211
Ali, Ayaan Hirsi, 115
al-Sissi, Abdel Fatah, 204
Alternative for Germany Party, 190
Anglicanism, 7, 63
anti-sect activism, 198, 199, 202
anti-Semitism, 173, 195, 204, 213
Anti-Terrorism, Crime and Security Act
    (Britain), 113
Arınç, Bülent, 144, 150
Association for Liberal Thinking, 148
Association for Republican Secularism, 153
Aum Shinrikyo, 198
authoritarianism, 17, 46, 184, 186, 196, 212
Ayrault, Jean-Marc, 165

Babacan, Ali, 55
Bakshi-Doron, Eliyahu, 187
Balıklı Greek Hospital, 48
Barroso, José Manuel, 87
Bartholomew (Patriarch), 87, 98, 141, 143,
    145, 150, 187
Bayazid II, 194
Bayrou circular, 76, 163
Bayrou, François, 75, 122, 162
Berlusconi, Silvio, 116
beur, 110
British Institute of Race Relations, 113
Brunson, Andrew, 187
Buisson, Ferdinand, 66, 80
burkini, 193

burqa, 16, 29, 72, 73, 127, 192, 210,
    211
Bush, George W., 111
Büyükada Greek Orphanage, 3, 4
Büyükada Rum Erkek ve Kız Yetimhanesi
    Vakfı, 50, 97

Caliphate, 42
Capital Tax, 6
capitulations, 6
causal inference, 33
causal mechanism, 33, 217
causal process, 33
Çelik, Hüseyin, 54, 150
*cemevi*, 56
Cercle d'étude de réformes féministes. *See*
    Feminist Reforms Study Group
*Charlie Hebdo*, 189, 193
Cherifi, Hanifa, 76
Chevènement, Jean-Pierre, 69
Chiennes de garde, 160
Children of God, 198
Chirac, Jacques, 78, 79, 122, 164, 174,
    191
CHP, 132, 135, 136, 137, 138, 139, 140,
    146, 152
Christians in Turkey
    community foundations, 47, 48, 49, 50, 51
    demographics, 7
    legal personality, 57
    place of worship, 55, 56
    political activism, 146
    religious education, 51, 52, 53, 54
    state policies after 2010, 186–188
    Treaty of Lausanne, 46
    under the Ottoman Empire, 5, 6
Çiçek, Cemil, 142, 150
civilizing mission, 109, 117

colonialism, 8, 109, 116, 117,
118
European, 108, 109, 127
French, 117, 211
Comité laïcité république. *See* Association for
Republican Secularism
Commission Islam et laïcité. *See* Commission of
Islam and Secularism
Commission of Islam and Secularism, 175
Commission parlementaire sur les sectes en
France. *See* Parliamentary Commission on
Cults in France
Committee of Union and Progress, 41
Communist Party, 178
comparative case studies, 5, 33, 34
comparative method, 33
Concordat, 63
Conseil français du culte Musulman. *See* French
Council of the Muslim Religion
conservative democracy, 46
Constitutional Court (Turkey), 44, 45, 46, 52,
54, 73, 146, 147
Coordinating Committee of Turkish Muslims
of France, 70
Coordination des associations et particuliers
pour la liberté de conscience. *See*
Coordination of Associations and
Individuals for the Freedom of Conscience
Coordination of Associations and Individuals
for the Freedom of Conscience, 201
Council of Christian Churches in France, 174
Council of Europe, 90, 106, 145
critical juncture, 15, 16, 214
Cumhuriyet Halk Partisi. *See* CHP
Cyprus, 3, 6, 7, 13, 47, 48, 90, 91, 92

Debré Commission, 78, 163
Debré Law, 13, 67, 68, 71
Debré report, 163
Debré, Jean-Louis, 78, 163
Debré, Michel, 67
Democratic Left Party, 134, 141
Democratic Party, 43, 44
Democratic Society Party, 141, 146
Demokratik Toplum Partisi. *See* Democratic
Society Party
desecularization, 14
Deyr-ül Zaferan Monastery, 52
Directorate of Religious Affairs, 42, 44, 57, 59,
104, 169, 186
Diyanet İşleri Türk İslam Birliği, 169
Doré, Joseph, 173

ECHR. *See* European Court of Human Rights
Écoles pour tous et toutes. *See* School for All
Edict of Fontainebleau, 63
Edict of Nantes, 63
English Defense League, 113
equifinality, 33
Erdoğan, Recep Tayyip, 46, 143, 144, 147,
186, 197
European Commission, 27, 35, 87, 88, 91, 93,
95, 97, 99, 100
European Convention on Human Rights,
125, 141
European Council, 8, 91, 99
European Court of Human Rights, 3, 124, 127,
145, 193
European Economic Community, 90
European People's Party, 145
European Union Harmonization Law, 49, 50,
53, 54
European Union Monitoring Centre on Racism
and Xenophobia, 109, 114
Europeanization, 15, 116,
211
Euro-skepticism, 148, 192

Fabius, Laurent, 78
Fallaci, Orianna, 116
far-right politics
in Europe, 190
in France, 121, 122, 191, 192
Fédération nationale des musulmans de France.
*See* National Federation of Muslims of
France
Felicity Party, 46
feminism, 158, 160, 161, 162
Feminist Reforms Study Group, 160
Femmes françaises et musulmanes engagées. *See*
French Muslim Women in Action
Ferry, Jules, 65, 80, 81
Ferry, Luc, 77, 165
Fillon, François, 79
First World War, 9, 195, 204, 214
FN. *See* National Front
French Code of Education, 79
French Council of the Muslim Religion, 69, 70,
71, 169, 170, 219
French Muslim Women in Action, 170
Front national. *See* National Front

Gabriel-Havez high school, 3, 4
Gambetta, Léon, 65
GDF. *See* General Directorate of Foundations

General Directorate of Foundations, 3, 41, 47, 48, 49, 51, 95, 132, 134, 135
Grande Mosquée de Marseille, 70
Grande Mosquée de Paris. *See* Great Mosque of Paris
Great Mosque of Paris, 69, 169
Greek Orthodox Patriarchate, 3, 57, 105, 137, 143
Guérin Report, 73
Gül, Abdullah, 51, 54, 144, 148, 150
Gülen movement, 132, 149, 185, 186, 187
Gülen, Fethullah, 149, 187
Guyard report, 198

habeas corpus, 111
Helsinki Summit, 91, 92
Henry IV, 63
High Council on Integration, 76
Higher Council for Minorities, 50
historical institutionalism, 14, 15
Hollande, François, 194
Holocaust, 195
Human Rights Commission of the Turkish parliament, 143
    United Nations, 101
Human Rights Watch, 105, 126

ideology (theory), 17, 18, 19
*imam-hatip liseleri*. *See* prayer-leader and preacher schools
industrialization, 13, 14
Interministerial Mission for Monitoring and Combatting Cultic Deviances, 200
Interministerial Observatory of the Sects, 199
International Convention on the Rights of the Child, 177
International Declaration of Human Rights, 141
International Helsinki Federation for Human Rights, 105, 126
Iranian revolution, 110, 117
Islahat Edict, 6
Islamic Salvation Front, 118
Islamic State of Iraq and Syria, 189
Islamism, 46, 117, 155, 159, 167, 183, 184, 186, 187
Islamophobia
    after September 11 attacks, 110
    and colonialism, 109
    definition, 108
    in Britain, 112, 113
    in Europe, 112, 189, 190
    in France, 116, 117, 118, 119, 120
    in Germany, 114
    in Italy, 115
    in the Netherlands, 115
    in the USA, 111, 112
    in the West, 109
    measurement, 109
    socioeconomic marginalization, 110

Jehovah's Witnesses, 29, 98, 199
Jews in Turkey
    anti-Semitism, 196, 197
    demographics, 195
    Treaty of Lausanne, 194
    under the Ottoman Empire, 194
John Paul II (Pope), 187
Jospin, Lionel, 74, 162
Journalists and Writers Foundation, 150, 187
Justice and Development Party, 8, 14, 21, 27, 40, 46, 92, 106, 131, 132, 141, 142, 146, 147, 148, 150, 151, 152, 183, 184, 185, 186, 196, 197, 204, 206, 212
Justice Party (Turkey), 44

Karamanlis, Kostas, 145
Kemalism, 18, 19, 43, 59, 132, 140, 214

Ladino, 195, 196
Lang, Jack, 78, 167
large-*n* quantitative studies, 33
Law on Construction, 56, 59
Law on Foreign Language Education and Teaching, 53
Law on Foundations, 47, 49, 50, 51, 98, 100, 134, 135, 136, 138, 139, 141, 142, 143, 144, 147
Law on Press, 52, 53
Le Pen, Jean-Marie, 121, 122, 191
Le Pen, Marine, 122, 188, 191
League of Education, 154, 174, 175, 176
League of Women's Law, 161
Ligue communiste révolutionnaire. *See* Revolutionary Communist League
Ligue du droit des femmes. *See* League of Women's Law
Ligue de l'enseignement. *See* League of Education
Lipietz, Alain, 178
Louis XIV, 63
Lustiger, Aaron, 173
Lycée Averroès, 71

Macron, Emmanuel, 188, 191, 194
margin of appreciation, 124
MHP, 132, 134, 135, 138, 139, 140, 146, 152
micro-level mechanism, 34
military intervention, 40, 214
  in 1960, 44
  in 1971, 90
  in 1980, 44
  in 1997, 45, 148
*millet* system, 5, 6, 40
*millet-i hakime*, 40
Milliyetçi Hareket Partisi. *See* MHP
Ministry of Religious Affairs and
  Foundations, 42
Mission interministérielle de vigilance et de lutte
  contre les dérives sectaires. *See*
  Interministerial Mission for Monitoring
  and Combatting Cultic Deviances
Mitterand, François, 67
modernization reforms, 6, 88
modernization theory, 12
Mohammed (Prophet), 110, 189
Mor Gabriel Monastery, 39, 52, 60
Morsi, Mohamed, 204
Motherland Party, 44, 142
Mouvement contre le racisme et pour l'amitié
  entre les peuples. *See* Movement against
  Racism and for Friendship among Peoples
Movement against Racism and for Friendship
  among Peoples, 171
Muslims in France
  construction of mosques, 70
  demographics, 9
  headscarf controversy, 73–81
  historical background, 9
  Islamic schools, 71, 72
  political activism, 168–173
  representation, 69
  state policies after 2010, 188
Mutafyan, Mesrob, 143, 144

Napoleon Bonaparte, 63
National Committee for Human Rights, 121
National Democratic Party of Germany, 114
National Federation of Muslims of France,
  69, 169
National Front (FN), 70, 107, 121, 122, 157,
  188, 191, 192
National Order Party, 44
national program in Turkey, 101
National Rally, 191, 192
National Salvation Party, 44

National Security Council, 45, 135
National Union of Associations for the Defense
  of Families and the Individual Victims of
  Cults, 201
National Union of Secondary Education, 159
Nationalist Action Party. *See* MHP
Necmettin Erbakan, 44, 45
Neither Whores nor Submissives, 160
Ni putes, ni soumises. *See* Neither Whores Nor
  Submissives
non-refoulement principle, 111
norm entrepreneurs, 21, 27, 212, 215
normative commitment, 24, 26, 29, 134
North League, 115

Obama, Barack, 87
Observatoire interministériel sur les sectes. *See*
  Interministerial Observatory of the Sects
Orban, Viktor, 190
Organization for Economic Cooperation and
  Development, 90, 106
Organization for Security and Cooperation in
  Europe, 90
Ottoman Empire, 3, 6, 40, 42, 88, 89, 194, 197
Özal Turgut, 44

Panagia Greek Orthodox Church, 96
Parliamentary Commission on Cults in
  France, 198
partial establishment, 14
Pasqua, Charles, 163
path dependence, 15
Patriarch Joachim III, 3
patriarchy, 107
Pelatre, Louis, 131
Pénélopes, 160
pillarization, 115
Pius VII (Pope), 63
policy agenda (definition), 31
political opportunity structure, 25
pragmatic pluralism, 14
prayer-leader and preacher schools, 43
Prevention of Terrorism Act (Britain), 113
principled pluralism, 14
process-tracing, 5, 33
progress reports of the European Commission,
  93–99
protectionism, 122
Putin, Vladimir, 17

Raelism, 198
Raffarin, Jean-Pierre, 77, 124, 164, 200

Rally for the Republic, 75
Ramadan, Tariq, 169, 172, 176
Rassemblement pour la République. *See* Rally
for the Republic
rational choice theory, 11, 19, 20,
21
Rehn, Olli, 87, 142, 145
Republican People's Party. *See* CHP
Revolutionary Communist League, 166
Ricard, Jean-Pierre, 173
Roth, Kenneth, 126
Rousseau, Jean Jacques, 64
Runnymede Trust, 108
Russian Orthodox Church, 17

Şahin, Mehmet Ali, 147
Sarkozy, Nicolas, 69, 91
School for All, 177, 178
Scientology, 198, 199
Second World War, 13, 66, 81, 90, 154,
195
sects in France, 202
secularism
assertive, 18, 45, 66
in France, 62–68
in Turkey, 40–46
passive, 18
secularization, 12, 13, 14
secularization reforms, 39
Şer'iye ve Evkaf Vekaleti. *See* Ministry of
Religious Affairs and Foundations
Sèvres Treaty, 136
şeyhülislam, 40, 41
Sezer, Ahmet Necdet, 51
Sitruk, Joseph, 173
Socialists (France), 14, 28, 35, 66, 74, 78, 160,
162, 165, 206, 211
Solar Temple Order, 198
SOS Racisme, 167
Soumela Monastery, 98, 99
Soviet Union, 20, 90, 91
Spanish Inquisition 194
spiritual security, 17
Stasi Commission, 78, 79, 124, 158, 167,
174
Stasi report, 78, 164
Stasi, Bernard, 78, 164
state of emergency
in France, 193
in Turkey, 94, 186
strategic interaction, 11, 23, 34
strict separation, 14

structuralism, 217
Syndicat nationale d'enseignement secondaire.
*See* National Union of Secondary
Education

Tanzimat
Edict, 6
reforms, 41, 89
Teachers' Union, 156
Theological School of Halki, 54, 55, 57, 87, 94,
95, 96, 97, 98, 100, 102, 104, 140, 143,
146, 150, 188
theory development, 206
Treaty of Berlin (1878), 6
Treaty of Lausanne, 6, 46, 47, 51, 52, 94, 102,
135, 136, 137, 140, 142, 194, 195,
208, 209
True Path Party, 45
Trump, Donald, 187, 190,
203
Turkification, 195
Turkish Economic and Social Studies
Foundation, 149
Türkiye Ekonomik ve Sosyal Etütler Vakfı. *See*
Turkish Economic and Social Studies
Foundation

US Commission on International Religious
Freedom, 103, 202
US Department of State, 7, 9,
126
Unification Church, 198
Union des organisations islamiques de France.
*See* Union of Islamic Organizations of
France
Union for a Popular Movement, 77, 78,
153, 177
Union nationale des associations de défense des
familles et de l'individu victimes de sectes.
*See* National Union of Associations for the
Defense of Families and the Individual
Victims of Cults
Union of Islamic Organizations of France, 69,
77, 169, 170
Union pour un mouvement populaire. *See*
Union for a Popular Movement
United Kingdom Independence Party, 190
United Nations, 88, 90, 102, 108

Vakıflar Genel Müdürlüğü. *See* General
Directorate of Foundations
*vakıfname*, 48

Valls, Manuel, 194
van Gough, Thoe, 115
Vatican, 57, 63, 65, 66, 137, 139, 144, 187
*verzuiling. See* pillarization
Vichy regime, 66, 67, 80, 81
Virtue Party, 45, 46

Wauquiez, Laurent, 192
Welfare Party, 44, 45, 46, 147, 148
Wilders, Geert, 115
within-case analysis, 33

Yazıcı, Hayati, 142, 147